I Am Family

Petra Cineálta

Published by Petra Cineálta, 2025.

I AM FAMILY

First edition. May 31, 2025.

Copyright © 2025 Petra Cineálta.

ISBN: 979-8998709517

Written by Petra Cineálta.

Table of Contents

Introduction 1

The First Years 2

A Profound Loss 4

Prajnaparadha 6

An Unusual Opportunity 9

Maundaata and the Continued Tragedy of Prajna 13

The Great Blunder 17

Asatya's First Job and the Doomed Romance.................................. 19

The Great Flood of 1995...22

Misadventures of An Uncredentialed Nomad 24

Marketing with Sama..27

Himachali Life 29

The Teaching Years 41

Chhoti Bahan..44

The Nomad Life Resumed..55

Solan..67

Family Matters 70

Bahan and Beta Come to Visit 73

2022...109

Burning Bridges and Gaining Health.. 114

Chamba 123

If At First You Fall from the Mountain, Build an Airplane Instead. 125

Pareshani 171

In Which the Poles Flip 174

Uncharted Territory.. 209

Observations of Behavior Patterns: 213

The Spiritual Journey 272

A Summary of This Condition, and the Abuse Often Associated with It 284

A Letter to Those Seeking Freedom, and Their Friends................ 332

Autonomy or Connection? 336

Closing Thoughts Before One Last Story 355

Disclaimers.. 364

Purpose 367
Suburban Vampire.. 370
Pseudonyms (aliases) for the people in this story, listed name first, then meaning of name, then origin language:....................................... 378
Web Addresses to All Links Mentioned in This Book 379

Inspired by the man who accused me of 'writing books.'
To Sama, who had my back like a real friend when all others around him re-
vealed their true colors.
To Cletus, who didn't flinch seeing me at my lowest; and who, precisely when
I lost my mooring, doubting everything and everyone, provided me with proof
that good, genuine people do exist, simply by being a real human being, him-
self.
To my parents, my husband Ian, and my kids, who don't always understand
me or my weird adventures, but who accept and respect my weirdness.
To Visounou, who never stops shining like the sun, even on the darkest days.
I thank each of you, and I never stop thanking God for each one of you.
To every person who can relate to my experiences in this book,
I see you, and I hear you.

Introduction

A few years ago, I said to my brother that he really should write his autobiography, or at least start writing his memoirs, as his life so far had played out like a drama written for the screen, and full of lessons. He declined, seemingly out of humility. He consented to let me compose the story of his life to be shared later, and so I have done, retelling it here almost word for word as he had told it to me.

Later, when I come into this story, I will shift to telling the rest of the story from my own perspective. My reason for doing so will become clear in time.

Here begins the story of Asatya Bhratra an Indian and Haryanvi by birth, a teacher by passion, a philanthropist by choice, and an enigma by fate.

You will find hyperlinks embedded in the text throughout this book. Most of these contain links to external sources, which provide supplementary or more authoritative information on the topics mentioned by the text, such as maps, songs whose lyrics were highly relevant at those times, results of medical studies, etc.

If you are reading a printed version, you will find these also listed at the back of this book with the web addresses for those specific pages, as endnotes. You could also google the footnote topics, but your search results might not take you to the specific pages that I had in mind.

If you are reading from a laptop or desktop, you can access the links by holding down the control key while clicking the footnote/link.

If you are using a smartphone or other device with a touchscreen, simply tapping the footnote/link should open the link for you; just remember that you will need an internet connection to access the links.

The First Years

Asatya Bhratra was born on October 10, 1978 near the city of Rohtak, in the Indian state of Haryana[1].

[i] His mother's name was Attri. She was one of nine children and a favorite child of her parents. Her husband, Asatya's father, would not work. However, no work means no food. Attri had left a carefree childhood with loving parents, to work hard to support her family, because her husband would not do it. Asatya remembers that she never slept in. Every day she was out of bed by four o'clock in the morning and she worked hard like a young man, raising buffalo, various fruit trees and some other things on leased land.

Asatya has a brother four years older, named Prajnaparadha (called Prajna) and a sister three years older named Maundaata, (called Mauna.)

Unfortunately, Prajna understood from a young age just how difficult life can be. Seeing how his mother was struggling to do the work of two parents, Prajna attended school only enough to pass his exams. He spent every available minute helping their mother with all her work. However, Attri insisted that the three of them must not miss school. She recognized the importance of education. Hardly any kids in that agricultural neighborhood were made to attend school, but Asatya absolutely loved school. Their house had no electricity. No problem. Prajna would sit with Asatya by the light of a kerosene lamp to teach him the times tables.

Attri was a diligent and loving mother who fed her children a good and varied diet. She taught them very well to have moral character.

Their father, however, was not home very often. When he was there, he would help Prajna with his studies. Their father liked to sing praises to God. He would bring friends home with him to feed them dinner, and he was well-known locally for helping needy people by connecting them with government programs. Yet he neglected his own family.

One day, Asatya was on duty to guard his mother's fruit trees from thieves. They had guavas, lemons, peaches, and plums. His brother came to

---

1. https://surveyofindia.gov.in/webroot/UserFiles/files/
STATE%20MAP%20OF%20HARYANA%20ENGLISH.jpg

him there and told him that a man that they called 'grandfather' had been murdered by some people in the village. This sad event was in the summer of 1984. Asatya was just five years old. This unsettling event made little Asatya worry about the future... he realized that it was mainly just his mother that cared about them. In that moment he prayed asking God to let them keep their mother all their lives. They had just finished the school year. Prajna was promoted to the sixth grade, Mauna to the fifth grade, and Asatya to the second grade. (There was no kindergarten in that time and place; Asatya had gone directly into the first grade at the age of four.)

A Profound Loss

Just a few weeks later, Asatya's mother went to Rohtak 19 kilometers away to buy new schoolbooks for her kids. Upon her return, it was discovered that they were not the right books, so she went back to exchange them. She didn't even have a bike, which meant that she made two trips by foot, 24 miles (38km) each. When she returned, she had a fever.

She continued her work as usual. She just kept on doing all her tasks like a single mother. She did not really take care of herself, and she became weak. She got some medicine from a pharmacy, but she did not improve much. Still, she continued working. Even her kids became worried. Asatya's grandmother came to take care of her daughter. It seemed that Attri knew that she was dying.

One evening, Asatya was sitting by his mother, hugging her and crying.

She said to her little son, "If I die, what would you do? Even if I die, it does not mean that I will not be around. A mother never ceases to love her kids. If I die, don't stay here in this house or in this village. Go to live with my mother. You have no one here to look after you."

Asatya was really frightened at her words, and yet he thought for sure that she would recover because he had already prayed.

The next morning, Asatya was awakened by loud cries from his brother and sister and grandmother. His mother had died in the night.

Attri's family was informed of the death. They all came at once. Attri's mouth was full of foam and her arms had gone stiff. Little Asatya still hoped that she would sit up and greet him once more. A woman that was there kept trying to lead Asatya away from his mother's body, but he kept going back to hold her stiff, cold hands - the same hands that held him and cared for him and fed him right up until the day before.

Asatya's mama jis' (mother's brothers) were all in chaos and frustration. They wanted to know why on earth no one had told them that their sister was sick? One of them refused to allow her body to be taken for the funeral. Asatya's paternal grandfather wanted to know where his daughter-in-law was being taken to.

By that same afternoon, they were already preparing to leave their home forever.

"We were preparing to leave a village full of bastards where a young, truthful woman was trying to bring up her kids and protect herself from bad and toxic people who would laugh at her poverty.

We were preparing to leave that small piece of land where our small house was built.

We were preparing to forget the memories of someone called 'mother' who would call me by the loveliest form of address, and I would be rushing out of the house in no time like a puppy...

We were preparing to leave that place for good, although the flames where my mother's body was afire had not yet calmed down.

Yes, we were preparing to leave this little world because for us, God had died. By evening, we were at our grandmother's place." - Asatya

Their father (whose name was Ram) was not there when his wife died. He came back to claim his kids after their mother's death. But his wife's family would not let him take them. His in-laws blamed him for her untimely death. After all, where was he during all her sickness? Ram was very sad, but he could do nothing. As time went on, he would visit and bring gifts, but Asatya refused to speak to him.

One time, Asatya looked up into the sky and told his mother he was sorry for not eating all his food as she had directed. He thought that maybe that was why she had left him.

Their grandmother sank into a depression and began to smoke. She was always concerned about the well-being of her grandchildren. She enrolled them all in school that year, Asatya being in the second grade. Now that he was living in his mother's native village, everyone knew him by her name. They would call him the son of Attri, which made him feel proud. He loved and missed her so much, and to be called by her name made Asatya feel as if she were close by.

The teacher in the new school expected the second grade class to learn the times tables up to 12 or 13. Asatya had already memorized all the times tables up to 70. The teacher would not believe it until Asatya demonstrated. Asatya's teacher declared him the class monitor on the spot.

5

Prajnaparadha

Asatya's brother Prajna attended school for only a few months after that. Remember I had said that he understood well (even as a young child) how difficult life can be. This little boy didn't get to have a real childhood. At the age of ten, he could see the reality of their situation. He said to Mauna and Asatya, "It was my mother who died, not yours. You must continue your studies and fulfill her dreams as she wanted us to become well-educated and officers." So that little boy dropped out of school, having only passed the fifth grade, and went to go live with and work for their mother's older brother, in order to help support his younger siblings. He reasoned that their relatives may be content at present to care for them, but over time they will begin to feel that these kids are a burden and then the three kids would be at risk of becoming destitute. In this way, Prajna did his best to ensure that all of Mauna's and Asatya's needs were met, and they could stay in school.

(I realize now that Prajna most likely had a fear of abandonment because their father was not there for them in their early years.)

Their mama ji did not live near them, so Mauna and Asatya didn't get to see their brother often, only once or twice per year.

Sometimes Mauna would teach Asatya, but he surpassed her in no time. In his first five years of school, Asatya scored 100% on every single test. Really, he was a brilliant student and his grandparents, his teacher and the principal were all very proud of him. Asatya's teacher was so impressed by his intelligence and dedication, that whenever the teacher would be out of town, he would put Asatya in charge of the class in his absence. Asatya managed it very well as if he had been the teacher all along. He was only about seven years old then.

His poor brother was having a very different experience.

"My sister and I, we both knew that our brother was living in insane conditions. Although our mother's oldest brother loved our brother, he had not much control over his family. He had three daughters and a son. My brother was given stale food. He was never given any water to bathe himself or given clean clothes. He was asked to sleep in a flour mill nearby.

I AM FAMILY

Whenever I would come to know that my brother was abused and beaten, I couldn't stop myself from crying and becoming very sad. But what could we do? My brother was by all of this, being trained to become uneducated and backward. Just imagine how old he was... he was treated like a slave by all three daughters and son, his own cousins. My aunt was a useless lady. She never loved my brother. He was living in a hell. This is the age when he should have been taught good things. He was not taught how to clean his teeth or to brush his hair. He had to work from dawn to dusk. He was growing up in dangerous circumstances. His childhood was at the mercy of God. I could witness how backward my brother was growing. Whenever I met him, the inside of me would cry in pain for his poor condition. He was never given proper food...

My mother's eldest brother had the opinion that if he taught Prajna all required skills of his trade, that Prajna could go away and find employment somewhere else. (Therefore, he did not teach him. He wanted Prajna to stay.)

My brother had no peace anywhere. He had to be at the shop for ten hours and occasionally overnight to meet the customer's demands. When he was with the family, already tired, he would be asked to run errands. Everyone in the house were masters of this poor slave. He had forgotten the definition of food. For him it was stale chapatis made of flour. No milk or yogurt, no butter, no fruits. He had forgotten that once we had a couple of cows and he could drink as much milk as he wanted. He could eat butter or yogurt, our own grown fruits... now there was no loving mother to feed him proper food. He was hardly eleven years old while he was receiving this treatment from this domineering family. My brother would be beaten if he was even five minutes late, bringing something from the market. On the other hand, their own son who was a few years older than Prajna, had every possible freedom to wear new clothes, eat whatever he wanted, attend school and slap my brother if my brother didn't get his clothes ironed well in advance. India is the most crowded country in the world, but my brother couldn't find anyone to complain to of all that was happening to him. He had already started dying from inside only to keep his tiny brother and sister alive." - Asatya

Really Prajnaparadha sacrificed himself for Asatya and their sister. What happened then was the mold that shaped the rest of Prajna's life. No doubt this harsh and extreme neglect caused some part of his brain to not develop properly. He is always generous and kind, giving of himself until nothing is left. Uneducated and backward but innocent, he has been so often exploited. Very sad, but that is his life to this day. Even now, Asatya tries to influence his brother to be careful of people, and to take good care of himself, but Prajna is not able to learn this.

An Unusual Opportunity

At the end of Asatya's fifth year of school, he was preparing to take the end-of-school-year exam, when he was presented with a special opportunity. The Central Indian Government was opening about twelve new schools specifically to nurture rural children who showed great intelligence or ability.

In each school district, there were thousands upon thousands of children, but only seventy students from each district would be selected to attend one of these schools. To be selected for this program, Asatya would have to pass a special entrance exam. Kids who gained entrance into this program would be receiving their education from the sixth to the twelfth grade free of cost. At that time in that place, there was no such thing as a free (or subsidized) education. Not even in public schools. For that reason, this program was highly appealing to Asatya, who didn't know for how many more years his grandparents would be able to take care of him. Asatya's teacher helped him prepare for the exam. Asatya stayed up late into the night every night to study. Sometimes his grandmother would wake up in the night to find her young grandson still studying. At the same time that this was happening, there was a test for which the student with the highest score would receive a prize of 1,000 rupees. Up until this point, Asatya had only ever scored perfectly on every test. No other student had done that.

It is no surprise that Asatya received the highest score and won the prize of 1,000 rupees. Additionally, he had success with the entrance exam, winning him a place at the new school. However, Asatya was already enrolled in the local secondary school.

Asatya lived in an agricultural region, and in those days, you could take grain with you to the store to buy things. A friend influenced him to steal a small amount of grain from his family, to buy sweets. His sister caught him and reminded him that it was not their house and not their grain. He never did it again. Mauna knew from listening to the gossip of the aunts that indeed their extended family was beginning to feel that she and her little brother were a burden. Altogether there were 18 people in the family. Mauna and Asatya could not afford to lose favor with these relatives.

It was then, at the beginning of the sixth grade, that Asatya began to learn English.

What about the entrance exam for the prestigious new school? There was no news, no call, and no letter. Asatya ranked sixth out of 10,000 students, so there was no question as to whether he had succeeded or not. Asatya thought that maybe he was stuck in that local school and that his dreaming was for nothing.

One day, a man appeared at his school, searching for him frantically. He said that Asatya was not supposed to be there but rather at the other school, and they were impatiently awaiting his arrival. What on earth had gone wrong? The central school administrator had sent him a welcome letter three times, but they were never received. They had made a mistake - although it was an honest one - in the address. They had addressed the letter as so: Asatya Bhratra, in care of Ram. District: Bhiwani.

Asatya was living in his mother's village, and his father was not well-known. There was no Ram in that village, but many people named Asatya, so where to deliver the letter? It was declared a dead letter and undeliverable. In Asatya's home state of Haryana, it is customary for a child to be known by their mother's name in their mother's village and known by their father's name in their father's village. Finally, this man from the school handed Asatya the long-awaited letter and his teacher urged him to stop classes and immediately prepare to go to the dream school. Asatya ran straight home to tell his grandmother who could hardly believe it. Asatya's primary school teacher was invited over to the house to be honored and thanked by his grandparents. Asatya was very excited. He had prayed for three things: to be the top student in grade five, to win the prize money, and to pass the entrance test. He had succeeded in all three.

Here was an interesting opportunity to meet kids from outside of his village, who were all different from each other, as they came from all across Haryana. Asatya was the third best singer, and he was a good soccer player, too. However, he could sometimes get into mischief as well. Sometimes he would fight with his classmates. By the end of the seventh grade, he realized his error in that and corrected it. As a child, Asatya never allowed himself to do anything wrong deliberately. Also, if he found another student deliberately doing something wrong, he would report them to his teachers.

He didn't like his math teacher, so he began to dislike math also. His other teachers were great. They loved Asatya and that great student/teacher bond helped him to excel in no time - even though all his classes were now in English! It was no problem. Asatya loved the English language, and he absorbed it like a sponge.

There was one teacher named Anita who came to know that Asatya was a motherless child. She told him "I'm your mother now," and she loved him like a son. Every second Sunday was parent's day. Parents were encouraged to come visit their student at the school, as many lived far from the school. Parents would often bring spending money or treats for their kids. Of course, Asatya's mother was deceased, his grandparents were too old to travel, and Asatya had no interest in his father coming to the school, even if his father wanted to come. Sometimes on those days, Asatya would leave school to go visit his father. Asatya was painfully aware of being left out of the goodness of parent's day.

At the school, Christmas was celebrated, even though there were no Christians in the school. Also, some Muslim holidays were observed, and all the Hindu festivals. One important Hindu holiday is Raksha Bandhan[1] [ii]. It is for celebrating the unique relationship between brothers and sisters. (And not just brothers and sisters by blood. You will often hear Indians call their friends 'bhai' (brother) or 'bahan' (sister.)) On Raksha Bandhan, two things always happen: the sister ties a simple bracelet (called a rakhi) around her brother's wrist, and her brother presents her with a gift.

In Indian society, especially in rural parts of the north, it is normal that a married woman's parents do not visit her in her married home, but she may visit her parents in their home. Her brother comes to visit her in her in-law's home, to see that they are treating her properly. Boys are raised with the expectation that they must look out for the well-being of their sisters and offer support and security whenever it may be needed.

The school that Asatya had gained entrance into was government-run. In India, public schools generally provide a better quality education than private schools. This school in particular was special in that it was one of only about a dozen schools of its kind in all of India. These schools were

---

1.   https://en.wikipedia.org/wiki/Raksha_Bandhan

planned with the purpose of elevating talented and intelligent students from rural areas. Each school was paired with a 'sister school' so to speak, from another far-off corner of the country. The idea behind this was to send 20 or so students to the other school, in an exchange program. Remember that these were kids from villages, not urbanites. Many of them had never left their home state or even their village, so this would really broaden their horizons. There were a total of 70 students in Asatya's school, and he was delighted to be one of the 20 to be chosen to migrate to the sister school. Asatya had no fear of the unknown but was enthusiastic and curious to see a new place.

Asatya's school was in Bhiwani, Haryana, not far from Rohtak. He would be going to the school in West Godavari, Andhra Pradesh[2][iii]. In May of 1991, Asatya and the other 19 kids took a 40-hour train ride to the other school, some 2,015 kilometers away.

There was a girl who had been tying the rakhi to Asatya for three years. So, she was like a sister to Asatya. Asatya would do anything to help her. Bringing her water, carrying her bags, making sure she was safe, etc. Asatya was happy that the math teacher at the new school was kind and nice. He improved a lot and passed with flying colors.

2.   https://www.mapsofindia.com/maps/andhrapradesh/

Maundaata and the Continued Tragedy of Prajna

That following summer, Asatya's grandparents began searching for a suitable man to marry Asatya's sister Mauna. In India, child marriage is now illegal. One must be at least 18 years old to marry, although it still happens sometimes. Mauna was about 17. It is still very typical that a family member or close friend will help to search for a potential husband or wife to recommend to the family. An arranged marriage[1] is still the norm for 90% of Indian couples.

It is also true that Indian households are often large, with grandparents, children and others all together. At this point in Asatya's family history, everyone in Asatya's mother's generation were already married with children. It was time to divide the grandparents' property, but Mauna was still there being raised by her grandparents.

They were ready for her to move along. At the time, dowries[2] were still very much a thing (in spite of being illegal.) So, coming up with dowry money was another concern of the grandparents. Finally, they did find a very good, kind, reasonable man for her and they were married.

After Asatya had returned back to school in Andhra Pradesh, he received a letter from his mother's youngest brother. He said that Prajnaparadha was missing. Actually, the son of the mama ji that Prajna had been living with all that time, had injured Prajna's head during a fight. It was after that that that he had gone missing. It was very, very difficult for Asatya to read that. He couldn't focus on his studies at all.

In the first year at the school in Andhra Pradesh, Asatya received a letter from one of his mother's brothers. It said that there had been a dispute between Prajna and his cousin, and that the cousin had injured Prajna's head. After that, Prajna disappeared, and at the time that the letter was written, no one knew where he was.

---

1. https://en.wikipedia.org/wiki/Arranged_marriage_in_the_Indian_subcontinent

2.   https://en.wikipedia.org/wiki/Dowry_system_in_India

Thank God, three months later he received a letter from his brother. Prajna wrote that he had left their mama jis' house and gone to Delhi to try to live there by working in a textile factory. Clothes from there were exported to the U.S. Asatya was so relieved. He had thought that he might never see his brother again.

Prajna had been raised in hell-like conditions and still his situation was not much improved. Asatya knew that the way in which Prajna had been raised was going to affect him all his life.

He had been utterly neglected. He was never taught family values... or anything at all, really. Prajna was just full of kindness, but he could never find anyone to love him. When his mother died, he had no one left except his little sister and brother who were powerless to help him.

Everyone in his school knew that he was not a happy child. He did not score well that semester, being so concerned about his brother. Also, there was a girl who would take advantage of Asatya's kind nature, and before he knew what was happening, he was doing her homework for her. He heard rumors of classmates secretly being in love. He couldn't think of anything like that. All he could think of was Prajna.

Around this time, Maundaata was finishing her 10+2 (last year of high school.) Her grandparents were under pressure to divide their estate between their grown children, which meant that she could no longer live with them. They found a kind and affluent man for her. They got married and Maundaata began a program to earn her bachelor's degree in education.

Asatya came to learn years later that many of his classmates had married each other. He was surprised. In India it is not really accepted to have a boyfriend or a girlfriend, and it is absolutely not acceptable for teenagers. There would be very severe consequences if anyone knew. Moral values are still held to a very high standard as they relate to sex and family (especially in Haryana) and it is expected that everyone is either single and celibate, or else married. A potential spouse is always searched for outside of a person's native village, (to specifically avoid anyone they know or may be related to) though they try to find someone of the same caste, same values, and similar economic level. It is very black and white. Asatya thought that it seemed as though all his class were secretly in love and only he was universal brother to all! Actually, there was a girl who liked Asatya enough that she had migrated to that school just to be close to him, but they were both shy, so Asatya didn't know her thoughts and it came to nothing.

Asatya's work that he had completed in his tenth grade science class was done so exceptionally well that his teacher put it all in frames and displayed it in the classroom to serve as inspiration to future students. Asatya came to find out about the display years later.

Now that it was the end of the school year, Asatya was desperate to see his brother. After spending a few days with his grandparents and sister, his grandmother gave him some money for the bus, and 15-year-old Asatya went alone to Delhi to find Prajna.

At Prajna's workplace, a man with a Haryanvi accent said that he would show Asatya a gurukul (a sort of Hindu religious school) where he could stay the night and have a meal, as Prajna had already gone home. Asatya followed the man to that place. It was his first encounter with a Vedic institution. Finally, the next morning he saw Prajna. Prajna had a long beard and looked prematurely aged.

Asatya wrote:

"He looked kind and truthful, innocent but sort of wild, untidy, uneducated and above all, unaware of what was happening in the outer world. He seemed very backward in his manner. I stayed with him at the workplace the whole day. In the evening, I went with him to the place where he was living. It was a dingy room in a large building where mostly tenants lived. I didn't like this place. There were no proper utensils in his room. Everything was piled up here and there, clothes, shoes, groceries, etc. It was difficult to spend the night. I had to sleep on the floor, as there was no bed. From his lifestyle it was clear that he was no longer Prajnaparadha.

I mean he was something when we had a mother. His childhood had been stolen and enslaved and he had forgotten that once he had lived so clean and hygienic. I was very much sorry for my brother's pitiable condition, but who to blame except accepting it as fate. Now his brain would work differently. He could be seen lost in unending thoughts, always. He looked like a young man with no dream, no future, no plans, nothing. I knew my brother had been turned into something bad and no hope of reform... if I tried to give him any good advice, he would really listen to it and he seemed thoughtful but he would never implement it... he gave me some money and I returned it back with sad-

ness. Actually, I knew my sadness would never come to an end. I was right to think so.”

The Great Blunder

Grade 11 began and unfortunately there was one significant flaw in the school that Asatya was attending. There was no guidance on which classes would be best for each student to take, and no one in Asatya's family would guide him either. Subjects were grouped into categories, these being: commerce, sciences and humanities. Asatya didn't understand well at that time what his own strengths and weaknesses were. Here is where Asatya made one of the biggest blunders of his life. Asatya could see that the most intelligent students were choosing the sciences, so he did too. But he was not strong in math. His personality would have been better suited to pursue a career in humanities. In choosing science, he would have to pass physics. Also, science-based careers like healthcare or engineering would require further education in a university. Asatya didn't have money for that. Really it wasn't fair to make a 15-year-old kid decide his future with no guidance. Asatya passed grade 11. In the 12th and last year, he was given more responsibilities in the school, so he had less time available to study. The chemistry teacher wasn't great but most importantly - *there was no physics teacher!* Yet physics was still a subject that Asatya would need to pass somehow. Asatya enrolled in too many courses. He really needed guidance but did not receive any. Unsurprisingly, Asatya failed physics. There was no teacher. How on earth could the school offer a course without providing a teacher?

Unfortunately, in India's school system, if you fail just one subject, you must retake the entire year of school. Remember that Asatya had gained free entrance into this school. His free years were over. Any additional education at that point would cost him. Asatya had no money and no one in his family would pay for it. He could not see how he could redo the last year in order to obtain his diploma. If he had taken the set of courses geared towards the humanities, he would have been just fine.

Now Asatya was just out of high school without having completed grade 12 on account of physics, and only 17 years old. He had to immediately find some work to support himself as an independent adult. His grandparents could not keep him with them anymore, and his sister was living with her in-laws and wasn't able to take him either. He tried living with his mother's brother, but all that family was just taking advantage of him for free labor, so he couldn't stay there.

Asatya's First Job and the Doomed Romance

One of Asatya's classmates who had also failed, invited Asatya to live with him so that they could complete grade 12 together. Of course, Asatya accepted.

One day, they saw a sign outside of a nearby school; the school was looking to hire an English teacher. Asatya walked right in to be interviewed for the position. He knew that he was capable, but the principal laughed at first, seeing that he was a kid. Nevertheless, he sent Asatya to go teach the 12th grade English class, as a test. Asatya was very nervous, but he managed. Asatya discovered that this school was where neighboring schools would send their failing or troublesome students.

His first day as a teacher was with misbehaving students at the highest level. It was a real test of his ability to bring order to chaos. That first day, the students would not let him teach a thing. He spent the whole class period punishing unruly students. Just imagine, 17-year-old Asatya beating kids his own age with a stick and drenched with sweat from the ordeal. (Back then, beating as a form of punishment was perfectly normal. Now it is illegal, just as it is in the U.S. and elsewhere.)

Asatya explained to the principal how the class had gone, thinking that he would surely be sent home, but he was given the job. The next day, the classroom was so quiet Asatya could have heard his own heartbeat, and all eyes were on him to listen and learn. He had gained their respect as a teacher.

One day, Asatya was in a rush, so he had his friend help correct test papers. His friend made a mistake. A girl that was failing received a score of 23 out of 25. Secretly she liked Asatya very much, so she really wanted him to be pleased with her. She began cheating to make it look like she really had turned a corner. At the same time, she began to make a real effort to actually improve. One day a friend of that girl gave Asatya an envelope, telling him to read the contents but to never tell anyone about it. Of course, then he was really curious as to what it could be. It read as follows:

"Dear Sir,

I am in love with you. I know you will find it really unusual. You have made me alive from a dead student. For the first time I am able to recognize myself and the potential hidden in me... I know you are not a teacher. As everyone knows that results from the grade 12 exams are still awaited which means that you are a student like me. I want to marry you and still knowing I might lose my life as I might become the victim of honor killing[1][iv] by my family. If you make it public what all I have written to you, it will mean nothing but my death. Finally, I want to marry you. Please burn or tear this letter into pieces after reading. ~ Neelam"

Of course, Asatya could not at all consider such a proposal. They were both too young and Asatya could not even support himself. Asatya liked her but he knew that it would never work. Neelam was always bringing him ice cream and other treats and just being especially kind in general. Asatya had to avoid her as he feared attracting attention from suspicious eyes. He thought that she would be perfect for him, but in addition to their age, he knew that her family might come after him. It was just not possible. Not even by waiting a year.

I should explain that in Haryana in those days, and even still sometimes today, sex outside of marriage often brings the wrath of the community, or at least the family, in the form of 'honor killing.' The offending couple are killed to remove the shame of immorality from their family. Even romance without sex can still bring the same wrath. You are only allowed to develop a romance and a sexual relationship with your spouse after the wedding. Your spouse may have been chosen for you, or possibly you may have been allowed to interview them once or twice before giving your consent to the engagement. In some cases, the arrangement is made without consideration of the bride or groom's consent.

Asatya's salary at this school had not been discussed. Other teachers were getting 3,000 rupees or more per month, so Asatya thought that he might get 1,500-2,000 because he had no formal training. He received 700 rupees. He argued with the principal, who knew that he was a homeless teenager. 700 rupees was not enough to survive on. He was being taken ad-

---

1.   https://en.wikipedia.org/wiki/Honor_killing

vantage of. The principal said to accept it or leave. He stayed. There were no other options.

Asatya was still at his friend's house with the intention to repeat the 12th grade. His friend's house was in Rohtak, about 16-24 kilometers from Asatya's hometown. Together they enrolled in a school. It was just at that time that the boy's uncle came to visit and offered the friend a job on the ship where he was an officer. The friend took the job, forgetting his deal with Asatya. Now Asatya's host was gone. It was already June and there he was in that village with no home and no hope. School was out of the question now. He would have to look for a job without graduating high school.

More trouble soon came.

The Great Flood of 1995

There in Haryana, it is semi-arid. Generally, there isn't a lot of rain, although there is a rainy season. In that summer of 1995, however, all the state of Haryana, and Punjab, and beyond received rain without stopping for *fifteen* days. Haryana is on the plains - very flat. The water would not stop accumulating.

The village where Asatya was living was on a small plateau, so the flooding was less severe there. But everything around them to the horizon was submerged completely. They were stranded. Helicopters dropped food for the people there. The landlady was understanding and did not demand the rent money from Asatya. Life came to a complete standstill for months. After that flood, the infrastructure and development of Rohtak and Delhi and the general area were set back by about ten years, the damage was so severe. It took weeks for the water to begin receding. Landlines were not working and no one had internet or cell phones at that time. Asatya was completely alone. Asatya's grandmother was very worried.

That year, many families relocated outside of Haryana. The plains looked like an ocean. About 40 days after the rain stopped, when the floodwater was still high, Asatya was shocked to find his brother Prajnaparadha there in that village! Prajna knew the name of the village where Asatya was living, and he had come to find him. Delhi and everything between there and Delhi was also flooded. Prajna had walked *74 kilometers through floodwater,* in the heat of summer, to make sure that his little brother was okay. In many places the disgusting water was neck deep. Prajna had to swim on numerous occasions. He had brought 1,000 rupees for Asatya, wrapped in plastic. The brothers were very happy to see each other. After some time, Prajna returned to Delhi, promising to send more money. Over the years, Prajna has done many great acts of kindness like this.

When the water had receded, Asatya's friend came to visit him and apologized for leaving him. If Asatya had known that his friend would leave like that, he would never have bothered to go there.

Asatya needed a full-time job to survive. The first teaching job would not be enough. He found a job in a hotel, working as a waiter and a receptionist. It was enough. But it was 70 hours per week. Sometimes he would remember his mother and be in tears. He was trying to touch the sky, but it seemed like God would not even let him reach the mountain. This would be an ongoing theme in years to come. It seemed like being honest was a great way to stay poor, but Asatya never sacrificed his integrity. When Asatya received his first paycheck, he bought some clothes for his grandmother. It was to thank her for raising him and his sister.

After working such long hours, Asatya didn't have any time or energy to improve himself by studying. He had begun his academic career extremely well, but in the end, he could not even earn his diploma because he chose the wrong courses and too many.

Asatya was not in the habit of saving money. If he had any extra money, he would always use it to help someone. This just shows what a beautiful heart he had, but he was sabotaging his own well-being. He was still barely surviving, and he should have done the 'self-centered' thing by striving to improve his situation. Being generous to the point of causing himself to suffer was a problem. His brother and sister were like that also. They never learned from it. Unfortunately, all three siblings learned that honest, kind, innocent people like themselves are easily taken advantage of, but they did not change their ways.

Misadventures of An Uncredentialed Nomad

The hotel job was enough for survival and nothing more.

A friend suggested going to Bangalore, so he went, but struggled to find a job. There, he was renting a room with a few other guys. These guys were partiers which means that they were a mismatch to Asatya. He needed to get himself established, but those guys were wasting their time, money, and dignity on booze.

One young lady asked Asatya, "What brings you to Bangalore?" She was surprised that Asatya was focused only on work, as Bangalore is the partier's capital of India with clubs and prostitutes everywhere.

Asatya left there and found another hotel job in Mumbai. It would not have been so bad except that he was expected to work 12 hours per day every day. Actually, much of that time he was working 15, 16, even 17 hours per day. It was terrible. By now, Asatya was forming the belief that he was born to suffer. However, at that hotel, Asatya befriended the bartender, a man named Virender, who was always kind and thoughtful towards him. I think this may have been the first time that Asatya had met a Christian. Whenever Asatya had a little free time, he would go into the city to search for a better job. There was nothing to be found.

His friend said to come back to Bangalore. He knew that there was no work there, but at least the house and the landlady was nice, so he returned. He did find a job in a restaurant. He knew the hotel industry was not for him. He had envisioned himself becoming a public servant such as a police officer or a teacher. His friend Virender suggested enrolling in school remotely from home to get his diploma. He did enroll, but it was useless. He was once again working long hours and had no time or energy left over. It was just work, sleep, repeat. What if all his roommates left and he had to come up with all the rent money himself? He felt that he should never have gone there.

Growing up without parents and having not graduated put Asatya at a serious disadvantage. Most jobs that didn't require a degree only paid what was really little more than slave wages. He had no choice but to accept a little help from others but most often they would give poor advice or else they would take advantage of him.

One of his roommates was a politician named Raju who was from Uttar Pradesh. He told Asatya that he could stay with him until he could find a job for Asatya. So Asatya followed him to U.P. (Uttar Pradesh.) Actually, this man invited Asatya to come with him, so that he would have a personal assistant that he had no intention to pay. Asatya was constantly running errands and doing other work for that man. Asatya was depending on him for food and shelter, and he was far from friends and family. He had no choice but to comply. This is one of many ways that needy people fall into exploitation.

Asatya followed Raju into U.P. on the promise that he would set up Asatya with a job.

What a waste of his time. Over time, Asatya developed the opinion that Uttar Pradesh has a few good people but there is more corruption and organized crime. It can be a dangerous place. But there he went with little choice. Raju gave Asatya a job as a cashier in a mining pit. It was one of many illegal sand mines along the Yamuna River.

Many years ago, Asatya's mother Attri stood by that river and prayed for another son. Later she gave birth to Asatya. Sometimes she called him 'Yamunaputra,' meaning 'son of the river.'

In fact, the Yamuna[1][v] is considered to be a sacred river, though perhaps less so than the Ganges. The Yamuna flows into the Ganges.

There he was, illegally mining right there out of the river that held such meaning for him. He cried. Everything about that business was corrupt. Al-

1.   https://www.google.com/search?sca_esv=83dfe58a007e3a22&q=Yamuna&udm=2&fbs=AB-zOT_CWdhQLP1FcmU5B0fn3xuWpA-dk4wpBWOGsoR7DG5zJBki0xbyJIUgVJn-lXKXyPv8i55c5HrZwki5zR2rxm-wqpiwkV7UvOsOAvLfBxR3fRDmYfNhGDW0kl-fuC5I7O199GQmVbOb0oenSKgw9VYkgTRWToBA5kwA48cUX4HpX1wPQ0M-Ub_EFirIdy5_mwlKxxVoHuXU-i8qtIg3aAXLxjuVhvCvw&sa=X&ved=2ahUKEwjTmKHevoe-NAxVHD1kFHbZDMQEQtKgLegQIHxAB&biw=1920&bih=901&dpr=1

so, Raju was withholding his paychecks. Asatya confronted him over the matter of withheld paychecks, right there in front of all the other employees. Then he went to work for Raju's competitor, the Giroha family.

Both of those actions were a courageous defense of dignity. I say courageous because to stand up to people like that who have power but are devoid of moral integrity.... well, it could have ended badly.

All of Asatya's coworkers were bringing in prostitutes and embezzling funds from the company a little at a time... sometimes a lot. Asatya didn't belong there. All this just added to his sadness.

The oldest Giroha brother watched Asatya's back and was always honest to him. He had a baby brother named Chhota. Chhota loved Asatya and looked up to him as if he were his uncle, and he still does. Although this family treated Asatya reasonably well, still they were a bunch of crooks without a moral compass. I have stated that this place was (and is) dangerous...

One time when Asatya was working overnight, (it was an illegal operation, after all) there was an armed robbery. Asatya was awakened suddenly when he was hit across the knees by the butt of a rifle. Asatya spoke calmly and kindly with the robbers, even calling them 'little brothers.' They demanded all the money in the till. Their supervisor had already taken the day's money so there wasn't much. They were demanding more. Asatya knew that these young men would not hesitate to kill anyone who didn't comply. He led them to where the other workers were sleeping in tents. Everyone was made to give up what money they had on them. Through all this, Asatya spoke with the robbers to keep them calm. Although they suffered a financial loss that night, Asatya's boss credited him for maintaining calm among everyone there so that no one was hurt or killed.

On another occasion, the police raided the Giroha's house while Asatya was sleeping there. They were looking for a fugitive murderer, who was in fact an acquaintance of the Giroha family. Asatya knew that he could not stay in that place. It was too dangerous.

Marketing with Sama

One time, Asatya went to go visit his friend Sama in Delhi. Sama had been a classmate to Asatya in Andhra Pradesh. His friend was a new marketing executive for a shoe manufacturer. In particular, the company made shoes for school children. They would approach schools and offer to them a large, neon street sign for the school with the caveat that they could use the space at the ends of the sign to advertise their shoes.

Sama inquired to see if they might hire Asatya. Surprisingly, they wanted him, even without a diploma. It was because they wanted to expand into the south, and for that, they needed someone who could speak Telugu. Asatya had learned Telugu while he was in the boarding school in Andhra Pradesh. Asatya would receive a set salary, and in addition, an allowance for the cost of hotel rooms and meals. (He would be traveling around the country as a representative of the company.)

Asatya figured out in no time that if he would always be given 1,300 rupees per day for a room and meals, he could find a cheap place to stay and keep the savings as income. In fact, over time he accumulated a large savings by doing this. Asatya's job was to represent the company to the schools that he would visit and obtain at least three N.O.C.'s per day. (N.O.C. means no-objection certificate - essentially an agreement form.) Asatya never got less than six per day. He discovered that he was a natural at marketing, as he can be very convincing, with good people skills such as etiquettes and humor.

One day, he found a phone directory in the hotel room. He thought, why not just look up local schools listed there, and start calling them, instead of driving all over town to visit each one? He was wildly successful and brought in more N.O.C.'s than a whole team of reps.

One time, the company sent him to Himachal Pradesh. He fell right in love with that hilly state. His sensitive sinuses loved the clean air, far from large cities and it was just gorgeous there in the Himalayan foothills. There are not many people either, which is attractive in such an over-populated country.

Not long after that, Asatya met a man that he calls Acharya ji. Acharya ji was a guru, or a teacher of the Vedas who wanted to start a gurukul (Vedic school) in Himachal. Asatya liked him very much and looked up to him as a mentor.

By 2003, Asatya had saved thousands of dollars. He hardly spent any money on himself but rather was constantly helping his mother's relatives. He paid the school fees for several cousins. He and Mauna helped another cousin to earn her master's degree. The cousin lived with Mauna and Mauna and Asatya paid the tuition fees. Asatya helped his uncle to buy a plot of land to build on. He helped another cousin to start a business.

"There is a very long list of giving away except I never took anything back. I could buy a house for myself, but I hardly did it. I know now that this was the greatest degree of foolishness on my part, when I myself was impoverished but I kept helping others." ~ Asatya

Himachali Life

Why did Asatya not stay with that amazing job? An opportunity opened up for him to live and work in Himachal Pradesh[1][vi], the place he loved so much.

He thought to grow and sell carnation flowers, as he had seen someone else doing in that area. He was told that a 500 square meter (about 500 square yards) greenhouse could yield $6,800 per year, or about 591,000 rupees. (Remember that the economy is different from that of the U.S., so a dollar has more value, more buying power there.) Asatya thought that he could save money by doing the construction himself. Actually, the cost of materials added up to more in the end. Oh well.

Prajna helped with the construction. The two brothers did most of the work themselves. They dug through the rocky soil to a depth of two feet, to prepare it for pouring concrete.

Yes... they dug 3,000 cubic feet by hand (1,000 cubic meters.)

The total investment was about $17,000 for the whole project.

Through his friend Acharya ji, Asatya met two brothers named Surajpal and Deshraj. They asked Asatya to start a peach orchard with them. Asatya thought it was a good idea, as they were good people according to Acharya ji, and Asatya would have no trouble to manage the carnations and peaches simultaneously, to increase his earnings. As a partner in the peach business, Asatya contributed 40,000 rupees for the initial expenses, which should have been sufficient.

Meanwhile after the carnations were established, Asatya received some unfortunate news.

His friend from the shoe company had come in contact with an 11,000-volt wire. Both of his hands were very badly burned. Asatya put Prajna in charge of the greenhouse, and he drove at once from Himachal down to the hospital in Hisar (250km. away.) The doctor said it would be most practical just to amputate, but with a lot of time and effort and mon-

---

1. https://www.mapsofindia.com/maps/himachalpradesh/

ey, maybe his hands could be saved. Sama's family had plenty of money, so that was no problem.

Well... Asatya could see that what that man needed was not help to pay his medical bills but rather someone who would stay there with him in his hospital room to ensure his comfort and wellbeing. Asatya made sure that guests would not stay too long or get in the way. Asatya made sure that his friend was given only the right type of food. He got him into a better room. He brushed the man's teeth and took care of every non-medical need. He kept the room spotless and germ-free. For five months, Asatya was living in a mask and sleeping on the floor in that hospital room in order to take care of his friend. At discharge, the doctor said to the patient, "I have never seen such a devoted brother as you have." He was shocked to learn that Asatya was not even related.

Upon his return, Deshraj said that the 40,000 was used up and 60,000 more was needed. Asatya knew that wasn't right.

At least the flower project was going well. It was going to be profitable. However, Asatya found that the lady that he employed was not being treated fairly or paid enough. So, he increased her wages and gave her holidays and daily breaks. Deshraj and Surajpal were putting Prajna to work on their own unrelated projects, which meant that Prajna didn't have much time for the greenhouse.

Asatya was really beginning to doubt Surajpal and Deshraj, even though he had been treating them like family. Asatya and Prajna were beginning to develop a very good reputation in that village, as they were always kind and helpful, and never caused any trouble.

Asatya's friend Sama (the shoe company executive with burned hands) had a brother who was a university student of food and technology in a university. He called Asatya to ask if Asatya could arrange an educational tour up there in H.P. (Himachal.) There were many farms and food packing and processing facilities in the general area, so Asatya began to make arrangements. Deshraj offered to help organize but only if he got 50% of the profit. What for? Asatya was the one being asked, and organizing it was a one-person job. Asatya was just trying to help his friend, and he wasn't even looking to make a profit.

At that time, Mauna's teenage daughter Agni was staying with Asatya. Asatya had helped her get into a school in Solan. He was happy to have her company. She lived with him all the years that she attended that school. After Asatya was married, he and his wife raised her during the academic year, as her parents were about nine hours away in Haryana.

Agni helped him buy supplies for all the university students that were coming, as Asatya was responsible for housing and feeding them during their short stay. It was a substantial but not enormous investment - buying or renting all the bedding, cooking supplies, food, renting space for the students, etc. Altogether 54 people came. The food was great, there was music and dancing in the evenings, and the students enjoyed visiting the area very much. Asatya didn't really want to charge his friend for all that expense, though he did accept some money which he split with Deshraj (who sure enough, was not very helpful.)

In 2006, Asatya was twenty-eight years old and not married yet. He was beginning to feel pressure from all sides to find a wife. Of course, he wanted to be married but just hadn't found the right lady yet.

Interestingly, in India, the approach to marriage is quite different than here in the U.S.

We Americans spend a lot of time and energy looking for a suitable spouse for ourselves. We spend months or years getting to know a person and developing a relationship before making a final commitment. Once married, we try to maintain the relationship, but if that become too difficult, we Americans in general are quick to divorce.

By contrast, Indians typically rely on the good judgment of someone who knows both the bride and groom well, to make that suggestion. If both the man and woman find the other to be a good match based on a few meetings, they become engaged. But really not a lot of time or research is put into it. If you trust the person who made the referral, and you like the person who has been suggested, it's enough. The matchmaker usually asks questions about one's caste, education, family, and expectations or terms of agreement. So, the bride and groom have typically only just met a couple times. They will meet with the other and their family to get to know each other a little and that's it. These are more like interviews than dates.

However, the marriage is treated with the utmost honor and respect. It is understood to love each other unselfishly and be faithful always. At least, that is what is often taught. Even when things go bad, husband and wife try to work things out. If that is too difficult, they might separate for some time, but divorce is rare.

I noticed that business trips and solitary visits to parents seem to happen often.

So you can see that Indians are quick to choose a spouse, but for them it is not a problem because they know that what preserves the health and happiness of the marriage is less about choosing exactly the perfect person with corresponding personality, and more about strength of character, just being mature and reasonable and loving. There is less focus on dating or searching for a spouse, and more focus on making and keeping the marriage strong. At least, that's the idea.

At that time, there were two different young ladies that Asatya inquired about, but neither one worked out. Both wanted someone who was from that area. Finally, Asatya was introduced to a young lady that he liked. Her name was Priya.

It's fairly normal that when a woman meets her potential husband the first time, she makes a big entrance wearing her best clothes, jewelry, etc. to make a good impression.

The first time that Asatya met Priya, she had just come in from doing the farm chores and was still dusty. Asatya didn't mind. She seemed innocent, honest, quiet, and simple.

Asatya told her that he was looking for someone who was home-oriented and uncomplicated but educated. Asatya knew that she had only a high-school diploma, but he said that if she was willing to study further, that he would be interested to marry her. Innocently, she said that she would. Asatya thought that his own sister Mauna had earned her degree after getting married, and Priya could too. Of course he would be happy to help. Although her name was Priya, Asatya liked to call her Shweta, and Shweta she became.

. Shweta said that her family didn't have much income, so they would not be able to give him a dowry. Asatya laughed a bit at this innocent disclaimer. He said that he does not believe in the dowry system but instead he believes in himself. Meaning that he was confident to be able to provide for a family and didn't want help.

At this same time, Asatya was introduced to another young lady as a potential for marriage. She was pretty, well-educated, and owned forty acres of agricultural land. Meanwhile, Shweta's father was outrageously demanding a dowry *from* Asatya, which was just backwards and shows the poor character of the would-be father-in-law. It seemed like a no-brainer to choose the girl with the forty acres over the girl with the greedy father.

Even while Asatya was in talks with Shweta's father, Asatya received a third proposal from the friends of a friend - their daughter in Delhi had just been married and she had immediately discovered that her new husband was a drug addict and a cruel man. She was married less than a week when her parents rescued her out of that marriage. They wanted to find her a good man to marry right away, and they were ready to pay a huge dowry, gifts, property... Asatya would have been set up to be really prosperous, to marry that girl.

Shweta's father was determined to extract money out of Asatya at every opportunity. However, Asatya had made a promise to Shweta, and he would not break it. He liked her a lot. Money is just a tool, but people are priceless. It was clear that Asatya would listen to his heart, and his integrity would always win.

Shweta's sweet and innocent personality was winning him over. Asatya has always been a man who understood the immeasurable importance of people as human beings, and he could not decide to marry someone based on money. He knew that Shweta's father might try to get more money out of him in the future (he was right) but he really liked Shweta.

Shweta's father had two conditions for the marriage: Asatya and Shweta would always live in that region - it was their home, they never traveled. That was fine. Asatya could do that.

The other condition was for Asatya to give Shweta's parents 100,000 rupees (about $1,300.) What a bullshit demand. Dowries are actually illegal though people still do it, and the tradition has always been to give it to the son-in-law on behalf of the daughter who is leaving home. If anything, Asatya should have received that, not given it. Asatya absolutely hated this arrangement, because it made it look as though he was buying Shweta. Shweta's father was using her as a tool to get money out of his future son-in-law.

Asatya might have considered the other girl instead, but he had promised Shweta that he would marry her if she continued her studies, and she said yes. Asatya visited their home a few more times, to get to know them better.

Asatya was making all the preparations himself. None of the relatives on either side helped. Asatya did everything and bought Shweta some very nice gold jewelry. Asatya managed all the invitations (which involved delivering a few hundred, door to door,) he bought some nice clothes for Prajna, Mauna, Shweta... he was busy shopping all day and then driving all night to return home. Shweta's father showed up at noon the next day, demanding the $1,300.

He had been questioning mutual acquaintances about Asatya. Of course, they all said good things. One acquaintance said that she could guarantee Asatya's trustworthiness and sincerity more than that of her own son. Shweta's father was completely unreasonable. In the end, Asatya paid him the bullshit dowry and continued with the wedding preparations. The wedding date was March 8, 2007. Asatya was 28 years old. All the relatives from Haryana came, vomiting along the roadway, as they were unaccustomed to the winding, bumpy mountain roads. A wedding in a rural Indian village looks like a huge festival is in progress. The village triples in population for a few days as every single acquaintance of the bride and groom comes to observe the rituals and celebrate. Asatya estimated that he was responsible for providing the main feast to roughly 3,000 people.

"The advent of Shweta into my life was a blessing. Now the house had turned into a sweet home. The walls of the house were filled with vivacity. The life seemed in dancing mode. One day when Shweta was cooking breakfast, I thought to myself that how blessed I was to have a beautiful and innocent wife. Yes, it was just true. Without a woman a house doesn't seem a home. A mother, a sister or a wife. In India women have more household responsibilities than men. She is the queen of the house no matter poor or rich. I had never imagined that I would be getting washed and ironed clothes, fresh meals and someone to share feelings or what happened on that particular day. My mother died

in 1984 and after that it was Shweta to be the woman of the house. Finally, I had her to be my soulmate and we both cared about each other." ~ *Asatya*

Asatya never forgot how his mother died, never taking time to rest while sick, but she continued to be the bread-winner and raise the children and maintain the home like a single mother, because Asatya's father was not there for them. Asatya wanted Shweta to have a comfortable life. He never asked her to find a job, only to take care of some things at home and to study. He was well aware that managing a home is a job in itself. Often, he would help with chores to give Shweta more time to study.

Now Shweta was a real country girl. She preferred quiet village life, and the company of farm animals over Bollywood gossip. She was simple, innocent, even a bit naive. She always stayed out of trouble. She was shy, not bold. She was not a leader type but rather a follower, and she preferred a slow pace of life. She was not very active, and she never drove a car, especially not after her epilepsy diagnosis.

She and Asatya developed a very strong love between them, so much so that even the neighbors would see and be jealous of them. Asatya would buy nicer, more expensive clothes for her than for himself. They wouldn't even want to enjoy something as simple as candy without the other. They were just cute.

*Trigger warning: sexual abuse mentioned in this chapter and also later in this book.

Around this time of life, Asatya began teaching more. He started doing 'tuitions' as a regular job. He would be driving all across Chandigarh and Panchkula between several homes to tutor young people. This would keep him busy all day, every day.

Sometimes there were less students and Asatya would use that free time to search for other work.

This was the case one time, when they had only been married a couple of months. Asatya was traveling around a bit looking for work. He knew he would be gone from home for a couple weeks, so he arranged for Shweta to stay at his cousin's house so she wouldn't be alone.

Women in India typically don't spend long periods of time alone. It is seen as a safety concern. The fathers, husbands and brothers are seen as protectors. Evil-minded people can make cunning reason to go to a woman's house if they know that there is a woman alone there. The patriarchal traditions that still exist, which might be seen as a negative, but the truth is that as long as rape culture exists, women won't be safe alone, even at home, and their male family members generally do look out for them.

Well, Asatya left Shweta at his cousin's house, along with a female friend of hers. Asatya should have been able to trust his own cousin, but at that time he really overestimated that cousin's integrity.

Shweta was the sort of person who could fall asleep anywhere, so easily. So it happened that she was sitting in the family room watching a movie and she fell asleep. It would have been better if she had stayed at home alone... she woke suddenly and was horrified to find Asatya's cousin on top of her. Over the next two weeks, he raped her several times. He was able to keep doing this because he threatened to kill her as well as Asatya if she ever told anyone what he did. She couldn't think of how to get away, and her friend - where was she??

No one else had any idea what had happened until a couple months later when Asatya figured out that Shweta was pregnant. Asatya is not an idiot. He could figure out that the conception occurred while he was away. Finally, he asked Shweta what had happened, and she told him.

You may remember India's obsession with sexual purity, from the story of the girl that Asatya taught at his first job... if anyone knew that Shweta got pregnant from someone other than her husband, her life would be in danger, even though she was the victim. To keep Shweta safe, Asatya and Shweta took all their money and drove down to Charkhi Dadri and begged Mauna to help... Mauna found someone who could do an abortion, although it was illegal and probably not safe for Shweta, but they spent all their money to end the pregnancy. Asatya had only been away for two weeks. He could have pretended that the child was his, and no one would know. He could not bring himself to accept as his own, the child of his cousin, the rapist. Also, he didn't know what that cousin might do when he came to find out that Shweta had a baby.

Shweta was such a lovely and innocent young woman, but she had a horrible and traumatic introduction to adulthood.

It was a dark time. Asatya continued to search for more work...

Asatya and Shweta agreed to not plan for a baby right away so that Shweta could focus on studying. Asatya thought to himself, what if anything ever happened to him? His wife should be capable of supporting herself in that case. He knew painfully well that having a good education can make all the difference in the world. What Shweta was thinking... I don't know. Perhaps she thought that her husband was earning well, and she had a comfortable life. Why study? Or maybe she couldn't focus because she had not totally recovered from the abuse. She enrolled in some courses, but it was just to make Asatya happy. She had promised that she would do it. She would study, but not much. Her heart was not in it. It became a drudgery. Asatya would keep reminding her, but she didn't really put in much effort. Asatya was frustrated that Shweta was hardly studying. Shweta was perhaps regretting her promise to study, and now Asatya was nagging her about it. Still, they loved each other very much, so it was a minor issue that they should have been able to resolve.

What went wrong... It is abundantly clear that Asatya's father-in-law never loved him. Not at all. In fact, Shweta's father, sister-in-law and most of the family were just toxic and greedy. Somehow Shweta escaped those traits. Here at this point I should explain a bit of backstory.

Sometime earlier in Asatya and Shweta's marriage, it came to pass that Shweta's brother was engaged to be married. He and his fiancée didn't really have any money for the wedding.

Asatya said to Shweta that they should sell her necklace. It was a sort of sacred item, much like a wedding ring, it had special meaning like that. But Asatya thought, a piece of gold or your brother's happiness? Of course, Shweta wanted to help her brother also, so they sold the gold necklace to pay for her brother's wedding. What Asatya had no way of possibly knowing, is that his brother-in-law was marrying a really wretched woman. She was a heartless, cruel person, and divisive, even worse than the family that she was marrying into. It was she who saw the small dispute between Asatya and Shweta and got herself involved to drive them apart. Why on earth would she do that? It was Asatya and Shweta who had paid for her wedding. Shweta's father already disliked Asatya. This new sister-in-law began to slander Asatya to Shweta's father and to plant seeds of dissension. They were toxic people to begin with. This only encouraged them more in their bad patterns.

Shweta loved her family and failed to see these people for what they were, how most of them hated her husband. She was annoyed because of the academic issue and the words against her husband were slowly starting to sink in. Remember, she was a follower type. But why on earth would her father want to break up his daughter's marriage? What kind of father would do that? The same kind that would use his daughter as a means to gain money unfairly, unwisely, and unlovingly, as was the case with the reverse dowry. Her family was poisoning her against her loving husband, and it was working.

One time in 2014, Shweta had a seizure. She was unconscious for an hour. Asatya knew that she could be dying right then and there, and he was beside himself. After the longest hour imaginable, she finally regained consciousness. It was to Asatya as if he had received her back from the dead. Incredibly, she was okay after that.

On January 23, 2015, Shweta forgot to take her epilepsy medication.

Asatya scolded her, no doubt remembering that traumatic seizure the year before. At the end of the work day, Asatya received a call from someone saying that Shweta had just left home and was not acting normally. In heavy rain, he searched everywhere imaginable. Finally, he found her at a bus stop in the neighboring city. Of course it was late at night by then, and nowhere close to home. Asatya convinced Shweta to stay in a relative's home nearby for the night.

They just sat there all night in their soaked clothes, shivering.

Shweta told Asatya that he should marry a city girl. He said that he didn't want anyone else, that he loved only her. Why would she say that? Asatya had never said, never implied, and never acted like he would prefer a city girl. This was a manifestation of the effect that the lies of her family were having on her. The idea that her husband would prefer someone other than her was an idea implanted in her mind by them. In reality, Asatya loved everything about her and... he had the chance in 2007 to marry a rich girl from Delhi, but he chose Shweta.

The next morning Shweta wanted to go to her parent's house. She said that she would return after 15 days. Her father told Asatya that they would manage the problem. Actually, they had planned to break up the marriage - or so it seemed. Those unloving people controlled everything so that Asatya could only talk to his wife through them. They continued to slander him. His only honest mistake was to insist that Shweta further her education although she had changed her mind and didn't want to.

He loved Shweta more than life. It was clear even after she left, by the reoccurring dreams that haunted him every single night without fail, even years later, ever since that separation. He would dream that he was searching for Shweta. Finally he would find her, but she would not or could not return. It was the same dream every time. Even now, every night the wound reopens like that. Asatya continued hoping to win back his wife.

Asatya being the humble man that he is, accepts the blame for his wife leaving. He said that he should have recognized that it was not in Shweta's nature or desire to be academically minded. Asatya learned a very hard lesson and well: that one should never try to force anyone down a particular path, least of all one's spouse.

Shweta never returned from her parent's house. Asatya sent money regularly for her epilepsy medication. They were still married, after all.

Asatya spent the next two years doing all he could to bring back his wife. He humbled himself and begged. He tried to talk to her kindly and reasonably. He petitioned those close to both of them to speak to her on his behalf. He left no stone unturned in this humble and sincere and faithful effort.

Two years after the separation, Shweta's brother (the only family member who was nice to Asatya) told him that their father had married Shweta off to some man who was in his fifties, who already had grown children and land and an orchard.... upon hearing this, Asatya's turmoil turned into despair. He sunk into a very deep depression. What sort of life could he have without his precious Shweta? He didn't want to live. And yet... he persisted, though he did not want to.

Asatya told me more than once, and with pain in his voice "her father never loved me. I know that." Shweta's father saw no reason for his daughter to be educated and he despised Asatya for insisting on it. That family was content with their simple lifestyle, though they were dishonest and selfish.

Asatya believes that Shweta's father got a second dowry out of the new husband.

Asatya and Shweta never divorced. How could she remarry? As it turns out, in many parts of India, people don't bother much with documentation of births or marriages. Asatya and Shweta had nothing to prove that they had ever been legally married. Photos, witnesses and all that, yes, but no documents.

After Asatya learned of the second marriage, and he knew that all hope was gone, he was determined to have something to live for, so he had an idea. He thought to form a trust to build an N.G.O. (non-profit) for young, underprivileged students there in Himachal Pradesh, in Shweta's native district, to honor Shweta's memory. In particular he wanted to help girl students. Girls and women in India are still marginalized to some degree, and the literacy rate among Himachali women is only 33%. Yes, just a third. The goal of the N.G.O. was to empower these kids and girls especially, to succeed in school, learn trades, important life skills, good character and morals, and to be really loved and nurtured and inspired to spread the good that they will absorb in this environment. Asatya had lacked much of this from his growing up experience and he suffered as a result. He wanted to help students to be well-equipped for a better life. He thought that giving back in this way might help him to heal his broken heart, and that idea helped him to continue on after Shweta's irreversible departure.

Asatya presented the idea for the N.G.O. to a few of the people closest to him. Generally, there was no support for it. Some people were not able to understand his motivation. Some people said that it would be too difficult. Asatya knew it would be difficult. He was prepared for that. For it to work, he would need support from the local people, but Asatya was not finding anyone who would support the project. Asatya gave up the idea, thinking it couldn't work, but he kept it safely tucked away in the back of his mind.

The Teaching Years

After the carnation business, when Asatya was still newlywed to Shweta, he began working around Panchkula and Chandigarh as an educator in varying capacities. At one time, he was a principal to a school of 1,500 students. He taught as a French teacher and became a member of Française Alliance Chandigarh. He developed a business as a tutor, which involved teaching math, science, and French. He earned a reputation as a gifted teacher. His students consistently thrived. He had a job doing what he loved, and a wonderful wife until he lost her...

After losing his wife, and after the N.G.O. idea got shot down, Asatya was beginning to drift, both figuratively and literally. He was going through a serious depression. He continued teaching but the light had gone out of his life.

Here I'll retell a story of one thing that happened during the teaching years. Asatya lived and taught in Panchkula/Chandigarh for about a decade. One time when Asatya didn't have much work lined up, he received a call from someone he knew in an international university. He was asked to come and teach German. Asatya replied that he did not even know any German, how could he possibly teach it?

The person on the phone answered, "Yes that is true, but I know *you*." That fellow was right to trust Asatya's ability. The first class was only five days away, but Asatya agreed to do it. Some people would call that insanity, but I call that determination. Asatya went home and spent 18 hours every day that week, studying hard, and preparing for the first lesson. His first student was not even a kid. He was a university student from Europe. This student said after his classes, that Asatya really helped him to make sense of German. The student's parents were very impressed and wrote Asatya a note to thank him. They assumed that he had been teaching German there for years. They had no idea that he didn't know even a single word of German just a week before he started teaching.

The only reason that Asatya left the Chandigarh area is that he was offered the position of administrator and English teacher with a school in Uttar Pradesh. It seemed like a step forward in his career, but this was U.P....

which unfortunately means a greater chance of running into bad people. There were students bringing guns to school... it was like being in gang territory.

It was so different from Panchkula. Asatya didn't dare take that job. Life with Shweta had been so good and now it seemed to be hell. Asatya felt alone and aimless. Asatya stayed at the home of an acquaintance while investigating that job offer and looking at other options.

That acquaintance didn't even bother to prepare a room for Asatya. He had to clean the room himself and fix the broken fan. They didn't even offer a ladder to reach the fan. Asatya had to stand on a chair on a table, which resulted in a fall and a broken arm. Also, this acquaintance 'borrowed' all $2,000 of Asatya's money.

Because of that man, Asatya was some kind of hostage. Without his money he couldn't get fuel. And with just one functional arm, he could not safely drive his motorbike. Finally after many weeks, his arm healed and he got his money back, and he left that place. He went to Gurugram, as it's a city of 1.5 million people just outside of Delhi. He thought surely in that large city, he could find a job.

In the evenings when he wasn't going for interviews, he would be reviewing language lessons or chatting in an online group to practice his French. He would always be looking to improve himself as a teacher and as a person at every opportunity.

...I wish I could say that Asatya's bad experiences were just bad luck but unfortunately, he grew up with very little family involvement or support, which meant that he was not able to further his education. In India it is very, very difficult to find a good job without a degree, unless you have some money saved to start your own business.

People in India who find themselves in need of any help are at the mercy of exploitative people. Another sad truth is that it is very normal behavior in Indian society to take advantage of needy people. There is a perceived hierarchy as evidenced by the caste system which is still very much alive and well unofficially, but in effect. The laws of central government are slowly reflecting modern times more and more, but so many traditions are still written in the hearts of the people of Bharat (India.) So, it is not strange that Asatya fell into malicious or greedy hands. The only way to escape this vicious cycle of exploitation is to achieve and maintain independence, both financially and socially, not needing any favors from anyone.

There are few people in India like rare gems, who prefer to give rather than to take. Asatya, Prajna, and Mauna are among them. What a hard world to live in as a giver, to be surrounded by takers. Asatya has learned a hard lesson to guard his heart and wallet carefully and to be wise in how, and with whom he is generous and kind. All this left Asatya with only very few real, sincere friends. Even those didn't fully understand him and were not super reliable. His own brother and sister were of the same heart in some ways, but in other ways they were polar opposites and never, ever co-operative with Asatya. Really, he had no one. But that would soon change.

Chhoti Bahan

Remember that Asatya was in an online chat group to work on his French. There was one lady in the group who was a good contributor to the group conversations. There were a few racists and spammers in that group, as well as more than a few men sending unsolicited private messages. That lady almost left the group in frustration because of them. Asatya begged her to stay, because she stood up to the racists and seemed like a pleasant, kind-hearted person.

One day in early February, Asatya posted some photos from his visit to the home of a friend who allowed him to use his large telescope. The nice woman in the WhatsApp group really appreciated the photos of Jupiter and asked a lot of related questions on astronomy. It was the beginning of a long and life-changing conversation. It was the sort of experience where you just met someone, but you get into an in-depth conversation over several hours and discover that you have much in common and the connection is just natural. They were both mesmerized at how the place that Asatya considers to be home - Himachal Pradesh[1][vii], and her home in Maine[2][viii] looked quite similar. Both are covered in hills and pine trees, and the climate is similar. Asatya said he would feel right at home in Maine, because of the nostalgia. Also, his sinuses are sensitive to pollution and the air quality in Maine is better than anywhere in India. Asatya was so impressed by this new friend. She seemed really real, not fake, and polite and kind. He had such a positive first impression that he began praising her a lot.

This was all in the first conversation. That lady didn't know what to think of him. He seemed like an intelligent, respectful, reasonable person, and always pleasant. But she questioned why he was heaping the praise onto her like this, having just met her. She confronted him about it. She reminded him that she was married and that must always be respected. Asatya reassured her that his intentions were only pure. He was further impressed

1.   https://youtube.com/shorts/AjRvozEnJ6I?si=8DCl6HvV4oK_CL1_

2.   https://youtube.com/shorts/sL9XlSypd-E?si=7plpE0F80Tna7ARu

by her insistence on moral integrity. He said, "Surely you were an Indian in a past life!" What he meant by that was that he was surprised to meet an American who had a high moral standard like himself. (Before meeting her, he had the idea that Americans have no morals.)

He thought that surely, they must have had a close relationship in a past life, or how could they have bonded so quickly and naturally? Already, he was wanting to call her 'sister.' She said, "Let's just see how this goes, okay?" He thought, fair enough. Actually, he was deliriously happy because it was to him like finding the rarest treasure: a sincere and understanding friend, possibly a dear sister.

I may as well stop writing in the third person, for this new friend was none other than myself, Petra.

One reason in particular why Asatya valued me enough to call me sister is this: Before I even got to know him, when he was still just an acquaintance - a pleasant and polite member of the chat group - I had noticed something about him. In spite of his kind demeanor and the fact that he is not very expressive in his face... they say that the eyes are the window to the soul... behind his eyes I could see deep pain. Of course I had no idea why. I saw him always being pleasant but truthful in the group discussions, but I sensed something was off, like he was hiding depression or something. I could feel a hidden sadness. I boldly mentioned this to my new friend. He was just shocked. No one else had perceived this. He knew that I could really see what he felt, and I understood. After that, Asatya never hid anything from me. He became a completely open book, because I had gained his trust. And indeed, we became family to each other.

Over the following months, that familial relationship only deepened in meaning and became further solidified. I was recognized by all in his sphere as his little sister, just as officially as Mauna or Prajna. And in my own family, my children saw him as their uncle, or Mama ji, and Asatya began talking with the others. My husband knew that he had a new brother-in-law.

Asatya was a model older brother. He protected me from shady people, he inspired and challenged me, he had encouraged me and shown his appreciation at every opportunity. My whole family has been on the receiving end of his generosity and one time when I was very frustrated with my kid's school and considered pulling them out, Asatya immediately offered to tutor them at no cost, although he knew it would be a large and daily time investment on his part. He would be honest at all costs. He was considerate to a greater degree than one would typically expect, taking care of details anyone else would have overlooked. It is clear that I was highly respected, even though I am the younger one. Often, he called me 'bahan ji' which is a Hindi title reserved for older sisters. Younger sisters are called by their first name, which Asatya didn't use with me. He considered me to be his next of kin. Knowing Asatya's family background and life experience, I could understand why he placed so much importance on me. He didn't really have anyone else.

This is how I became Little Sister = Chhoti Bahan.

Here I should give a bit of backstory about myself.

In 2017, I was feeling that my spiritual growth had stalled. That had been the trend for several years and I didn't like it. So, I asked God to do something about it. I knew that expedited spiritual growth would certainly involve a good deal of discomfort, and I could not imagine what shape that might take, but I decided that it would be worth it, and I was as ready as I ever would be.

After some months, God told me specifically, "Repair your broken relationships and build new ones." As an introverted and stoic New Englander, even just starting this would be uncomfortable, but I knew who the broken relationships were with.

I had grown up closely connected with a family that were close friends of my mother. Their older son and daughter were my best friends, and they were like family to me. The son was a great lover of nature, an adventure seeker, a lover of all kinds of animals, and he was always full of energy and shenanigans. He could never sit still.

Unfortunately, after some very traumatizing events early in his life, which included abuse from a relative when he was a kid, he became very depressed, and he turned to drugs and alcohol. At age 14, his mental and emotional health hit rock bottom. He spent a couple of years away from home to receive care. He had no friends left except for me and one other. I took his dark years very much to heart, which landed me in a depression for several months. No sooner than he finished high school, then he joined the marines, who promptly sent him to the front lines in Afghanistan. He always maintained a strong, happy veneer and liked to help other people. He never wanted to be the one receiving help. It was heartbreaking seeing him struggle just to live, and to have any joy.

Sometimes he would be clean for as long as two years, and we would think that finally he was free, and we would be so happy for him. But then something would happen, and he would get sucked back into drugs... he had tried them all. He had a wife and two small children. He tried so hard to stay clean for them, but he had so much inner pain and he couldn't really keep away from drugs and alcohol consistently...his driver's license was taken away permanently. He ended up in jail more than once. I remember that he would ride his bike more than 30 miles in one direction, so that he would not miss an opportunity to be with his kids.

I had always taken his well-being very much to heart and at some point, I couldn't stand to watch him almost be free, just to ruin his life again, and again, and again. I stopped talking to him to preserve my own sanity, though I didn't want to.

A few years had gone by without talking to him. I worried he might not answer the phone,

so I drove two hours to his house without calling first. He wasn't there. I called. He answered. I choked up and cried. I apologized for my absence, and he at once forgave me.

Over the next two years, we stayed in touch and went on a few adventures together as we both loved exploring in nature. After all these years, the drugs had taken a toll. The long-term effects of drug use were causing serious health problems.

On January 6, 2022, he had made plans with his dad, but he never showed up. He didn't answer his phone. No one could find him, even though the search went on for several weeks.

It wasn't until April 12, after the snow melted, that his body was found in the woods.

Alone in the woods... as he so often had been throughout his life, by choice. The coroner had to take a DNA sample to identify him. It was determined that the cause of death was an accidental fentanyl overdose, which likely occurred January 6th, though I am not totally sure.. Fentanyl is notorious for inconsistent potency, and he had made various plans with his family that he was looking forward to. He was just 37 years old. I am glad that I got that nudge to reconnect with him, that I could be with him in his last two years of life.

The other person to repair the broken relationship with, was a relative who could be self-centered and crass. I didn't want to talk to her, but the directive was clear.

What I found is that in less than five years, both of her beloved parents died. Also, she got into a relationship with someone who seemed very nice, and she wanted to build a life with him. They had two sons together. Her partner turned out to be a true narcissist, and he abandoned both her and their tiny sons. In fact, he was not even there when the second one was born. He left them completely and moved back to his hometown more than 1,500 miles away. While this was happening, my cousin had her first grand mal seizure. Of course she was alone at home with two babies. She found that she had no friends or anyone willing to help her. She didn't realize that likely everyone in her life gave up on her because she could be unpleasant and self-centered, or because of her narcissistic boyfriend. She was left with no one, except her kids. She was completely alone, a single mother of a baby and a toddler, with a serious case of epilepsy, which meant that she couldn't drive or get a job. It didn't matter whether I liked her or not. My cousin needed her family to step up and be there for her.

Trying to be a good mother, she brought her sons to their father's house so they could visit him. Their father's older son from a previous relationship attempted to abduct my little cousin, and beat his mother, my older cousin. The boy's father watched all this and did nothing, other than defend his son's actions. She never took her sons back there again. Her older son was about four years old at that time. He never forgot that incident.

Well, all these big shake-ups really got my cousin's attention and caused some serious introspection for her. She wasn't the awful person of her past anymore though she could still be a bit self-centered sometimes. I tried explaining to the rest of the family that she was ok to talk to now and that she seriously needed help. What if a seizure killed her and our own little cousins went into foster care? That wouldn't be right... only my mother listened. My cousin only had me and my mother, and we lived two hours away. She had two friends, but they lived outside the country. So, it was clear why God told me to reach out to her. In fact, I had an ethical responsibility, knowing her needs.

As of last year, she got her driver's license back. She is slowly growing as a person and feeling enormously encouraged to have more freedom.

I became an emergency contact for her and her sons. I went to visit when I could.

Remember that I had been instructed to build new relationships...I have always been a naturally curious person, especially concerning anthropology, psychology, culture, geography, biology, and many other topics. I am a natural explorer. All my life I wanted to travel and see other places, other lifestyles, and discover new things. Having married young and started a family right away, it was not practical or affordable to travel much in those early years. To help satisfy my desire for global connection, we became involved in a foreign exchange program, and over the years, we welcomed a total of eight young people into our home, mainly French kids. Overall, it was mostly a positive experience, and my kids profited from the exposure to kids that were a bit different from them.

One of the last kids that we hosted was a boy named Guillaume. He came from a big Catholic family in Paris. Guillaume was a quiet but very easy going kid. From the very first day, he blended into our family as if he had always been here. He looked supremely content while we had him. We all became very attached to him and wished that he could stay. Even his mother commented that I treated him just like my own child, like a true mother.

As time went on, our family and his family kept in touch, enjoying video calls between the two families.

I have since that time, learned something important about myself: I get a general sense of a person and their vibes very quickly and I usually know intuitively early on, if they are someone that I hope will remain a part of my life, or not. I realize that most people need more time than I do to arrive at such conclusions, and I have learned to patiently wait for them to sort out their opinions or feelings about me.

In the weeks following Guillaume's return to France, I cried every day feeling like I had said goodbye to my own son, having no idea when we would be together again.

At that time, I started a new job in Waldoboro, and I was grateful to be kept busy. Busyness was helpful in my sadness.

I was very careful to be respectful and considerate. I called Guillaume 'Little Brother,' because I thought that might seem less presumptuous than to call him 'Mon fils.' (My son.) I certainly didn't want to make his mother feel jealous or step on her toes in any way. In reality though, he felt like a son to me.

Meanwhile, I was noticing on calls that Guillaume's mother was struggling to follow conversation, as her English was weak. I was thinking that our families would be connected for many years, so I immediately and aggressively dove head first into learning French. I knew no French up until then. I was using an app for lessons and practicing on these French friends.

In 2019, I was blindsided by a message from Guillaume's mom: "Nous ne pouvons plus." She explained to me that they had very busy lives and they wouldn't be able to keep in touch with us. I wanted to visit them. She had reasons why that wouldn't work either. Mostly I just heard that they are too busy for us.

I loved Guillaume just as much and in the same way as my own kids. This was difficult for my kids to accept as well, as Guillaume was their friend, and they also loved him. I was in denial. I had prayed for them, I had written letters to them, I had shown all respect and consideration for them and was ready to be there for them in any way because they were my friends and also, I wanted to support Guillaume however I could. The relationship became one way. I was so deeply committed in both mind and heart that I didn't have strength to pull away... inside I was screaming in pain.

That raging pain went on for a year. It felt like at least five years. It really felt like my son had died. What made matters worse, I knew few people could understand this loss that I had experienced so I hardly told anyone, and I just lived with a fake smile all that time, which compounded my pain. One person told me, "That's not really your son, though." I knew that. I loved him just the same. The fact that we were not biologically related did not minimize my love or my pain. I cried out to God saying, "Whatever you want me to learn from this, just tell me now. I'm broken and I can't cope. Whatever you need from me so that this pain can end..."

Two weeks later, something happened.

I no longer had anyone to practice my French on, but I didn't want to lose all the progress that I had made with it, so I was looking for someone who could converse with me. I knew a couple of French teachers, but they didn't have time for that... finally I resorted to searching online and I ended up in a chat group for French learners and teachers.

On December 25, 2019, I got a direct message just as I had gotten a dozen others that I ignored as spam. This one was not spam, though. This one was polite, sensible, and practical.

It turned out to be a young man from Cotonou, Benin[3][ix] who was a college freshman studying agronomy/forestry. He suggested we alternate weeks of chatting in French and English, as he had just started learning English just four months before. It seemed ideal for practice.

His name is Visounou. He turned out to be an intelligent, wise, logical person and very considerate and respectful. I didn't know those things about him from anything that he said about himself; I could observe it. I was beginning to feel a friendship forming.

One evening as I was chopping onions to prepare dinner, I was chatting with Visounou.

I caught myself reminding him to drink water and go to sleep at a decent time. I apologized, explaining that I tend to be a bit motherly with my friends.

He said, "Thanks Mum!" just to be funny, but after a pause he then said, "I would even ask permission... to call you Mum."

---

3.   https://www.google.com/search?sca_esv=9a516f6aeda16e0b&q=coto-nou+benin&udm=2&fbs=ABzOT_CWdhQLP1FcmU5B0fn3xuWpA-dk4wpBWOG-soR7DG5zJBv10Kbgy3ptSBM6mMfaz8zDVX4b2W1tiDkb3uUgOX2bJ2QzqY7YD-tO8TAA8HVJ835OEfAs0h1UaFvNoGY0SwrCcezhAGVmh_pDTiU-uthS2Er5Qd7EoZu0_jND2l9Eouaz4DdATwllkGYsDxTp-MwVXdShrTGCzONq7uk3823XHqvN-fqM3A&sa=X&ved=2ahUKEwin04aJwoeNAxxUqEFkFHVTYHlYQtK-gLegQIFhAB&biw=1920&bih=901&dpr=1

Those onions were making me tear up, but that last message unleashed the flood. I cried. Visounou knew absolutely nothing about Guillaume, or my grief. Somehow, incredibly all at once, I was able to let go of Guillaume in my heart and I healed internally all at once that day, as if by miracle. With the outflow of tears, my grief over Guillaume left me and joy flooded in. This is how it happened that Visounou became precious to me. A year later I asked him what on earth had possessed him to ask someone he barely knew if he could call her 'Mum.'

He only said, "I don't know, but God knows." In fact, he was right.

If I had not been so committed to cultivating a relationship with Guillaume's mother, I wouldn't have bothered to learn French.

If I did not lose them, I would not have gone looking for someone else to practice with, and I would not have met Visounou, the young man who really did become my godson.

His family really does accept and appreciate me. Even his mother sometimes calls me, 'Mama Visounou.' The fact that our lives and backgrounds are so completely different does not make the relationship lopsided or awkward, because we see each other first of all as human beings, and secondly as family. It is that simple. It is all around a wonderful joy, a blessing to us and the family.

Visounou's mother, sister, and one of his brothers do not speak English. It seems as though I had learned French just to be able to communicate with these three people, and I was glad that I was able to.

I would not even have met Visounou except that there were troublesome people in that French learner's WhatsApp chat group, which frustrated me enough to want to quit the group. A man from India named Asatya sent me a direct message, begging me to stay and help make the group better... so I did, and Visounou wrote to me from that group three weeks later.

Later in February, I was leaving on a short vacation with my husband. My husband is very nervous of flying, so he had arranged for us to arrive at the airport five hours early. I was bored.

I opened the group chat...That same Indian man had posted excellent photos of Jupiter and Saturn, as he was visiting a friend who owned a telescope. Being a lover of astronomy, I got into an in-depth conversation. Well,

I was busy on vacation, but after I reached home again, I picked up the conversation again and it went on for hours...

It is true that we also met our dear friend Benny through the same group. These three didn't know each other except as vague acquaintances through the chat group, but I introduced them. Over time, we all became family to each other.

Not long after I met Asatya, I had a vision of the future. In it, Asatya was surrounded by thousands of people who were listening intently to what he had to say. He was speaking with great conviction out of his heart. Light was shining from his face and hands. He was glowing.

A couple of days later, I felt a very strong push from inside me as if being guided by the Holy Spirit. I was instructed to support Asatya in any way that I could. I understood that the purpose was to prepare him for what I saw in that vision.

I thought about where Asatya was in life, and where he was to go. In fact, I didn't know exactly what God had in mind to do with him, but it seemed clear that God would use him to influence others. Until either of us got more specific direction, I decided that I would do whatever I could to lift up, strengthen, encourage, and inspire Asatya, and support his spiritual growth for whatever purpose God had in mind. I was also ready to assist in a practical capacity to the extent that made sense to do so.

Asatya had not seen or heard these prompts from God. I figured that the reason for this must be that his mind was very much clouded by depression. He wouldn't believe good news if he did receive any. Asatya had a tendency to doubt good developments. I knew that my mission would only work if Asatya believed the vision that I had seen and would trust me enough to cooperate with my leading.

I took this assignment very seriously. The reason is that several times, I questioned it in the beginning. I thought maybe I heard the directive wrong... but every time the voice inside grew louder saying, "do it!!" I say it was a voice but in fact it was more like an iron will inside me, a burning passion that was intent on action. Not my will, I had no strong feelings about this, myself. It came from inside me but not from me. The prompts of the Holy Spirit often feel like this. I felt that I would go crazy if I did not listen to it and do as it said. Well, that push from inside was unmistakable. God didn't say specifically how to support, so I talked to Asatya to learn more about his life, why do people not listen to him? How can that change?

Sometime later, Asatya said that if it became possible for him to come to the U.S., he would like to live near me and my family, and live there in gratitude, acting like a family member, to be there for us any time we might need him.. It made sense because he wasn't really close to anyone except that my family was becoming his family. Asatya was feeling very much alone, so I agreed that it would make sense to do, if he could.

We began looking into immigration options. It proved to be a very complicated and time consuming project but we were determined. Over the next three years, we explored the various work visas, the possibility of marrying an American and immigrating by marriage (he didn't want to be alone anyway), we looked at student visas and adjustment of status, we even looked at various Canadian provincial immigration programs. I've never used Google so much in my life.

"Whether you turn to the right or to the left, your ears will hear a voice behind you, saying, 'This is the way; walk in it.'"

The Nomad Life Resumed

The Hindi word for 'brother' is 'bhai.' The word for 'sister' is 'bahan.' To give extra respect, you can add the word 'ji' after someone's name. This is typically done for business contacts, and anyone older than yourself. Perhaps the best English equivalent to 'ji' is either 'sir' or 'ma'am.'

I had tremendous respect for Asatya, so I never called him by his first name, but always chose to address him as Bhai ji. It's true that I'm American, so I didn't have to do that, but it was my choice.

From this point onward, I will sometimes refer to Asatya Bhratra as 'Bhai ji,' and sometimes as 'Asatya Bhai,' or just 'Asatya.' Sometimes Hindi speakers will just say, 'bhaiya,' which is equivalent to the English, 'bro.' I also use that word occasionally.

Bhai ji spent a few months in Gurugram, job searching. He received two very nice job offers, but neither would hire him in the end.

Recently, India made a new law that school teachers, regardless of the subject they teach or whether they are full time or part time, must have a bachelor's degree or greater. Bhai ji could not work and pursue a degree simultaneously. His hands were tied.

By March, the COVID pandemic was in full swing. Being in the city, Bhai ji left the house as little as possible. He was renting a room from a nice family. The wife made enough food to feed Bhai ji also, knowing that he still wasn't employed yet. He was using only his savings.

How could he find any work now? Nearly all businesses were closed due to the pandemic. Bhai ji made use of this boring time by helping the landlord to repaint the house and working on his French.

Meanwhile, little was known or understood about the coronavirus as yet, and it was spreading around the city. At one point, several people on Bhai ji's street tested positive, but still the landlady was welcoming in neighbors daily. Bha ji is very hygienic, and he would try to remind the others to be careful, but they didn't really listen. He had to share the bathroom and the kitchen with these careless people, which made him ill at ease. That family was nice but careless.

The landlady made the food so spicy that Bhai ji developed blisters inside his mouth. Bhai ji can't have gluten but of course chapatis (basically the same as tortillas) were always there at every meal and the pollution was making his sinuses act up a lot. Bhai ji didn't see the sense in staying there, especially when he was running out of money and couldn't make rent payments. He went to visit a friend of the family in Charkhi Dadri (near Mauna) to inquire about what opportunities might be there. He had a nice visit but only for a couple days.

Prime Minister Modi announced a nationwide lockdown to begin the next day. Bhai ji quickly packed up and rushed back to his old room in Gurugram which was still vacant. There he remained for a few more months.

In late spring, Bhai ji's friend Acharya ji invited him to stay with him at his gurukul[1][x] in Himachal. Himachal Pradesh is mountainous and quiet and serene. The air is much cleaner there, which for Bhai ji means some relief from irritated sinuses. Bhai ji wasn't going to be able to find a job during lockdown anyway, and a pleasant, COVID-free locale was really appealing.

However, the borders between states were closed, and patrolled by police. I condoned the move even though it was illegal, on the condition that it could be planned carefully and done wisely to avoid legal trouble and cross-contamination. Bhai ji was offered assistance by an acquaintance for the border crossing. I thought that there would be a few days of planning and preparing. I asked those close to me to pray for protection and guidance for Bhai ji. I awoke the next morning to find photos on my phone taken from somewhere in Himachal. When that man makes up his mind to do something, he wastes not one second. He has no ability to procrastinate. Everything must be done yesterday.

Trying to find the home of the helpful acquaintance was difficult. It was becoming dark as he drew near to the place. All of Himachal Pradesh, including along its border with Haryana, is just an endless labyrinth of narrow, zig-zagging roads often without any signs.

1.   https://youtu.be/VRDsfv56_B4?si=8bW-YELtMsxpwlS5

Bhai ji had never been to that particular neighborhood. There were five or six different intersections at which Bhai ji had no idea where to turn. Incredibly, at each one of these places, there was someone there already, as if waiting for him to show up, to direct him down the correct road. The fact that there was someone there, after dark at each place was uncanny, but what's more, Himachalis are not known for helping strangers. They may be friendly and pleasant but never lift a finger to help anyone (according to Asatya bhai.) When we asked God to guide Asatya bhai.... he did it literally. Bhai ji knows that God showed up that day. Bhai ji drove the remaining three hours on his motorbike bearing a Haryana license plate but was never stopped except by a little rain.

Bhai ji 's few weeks that he spent there were pleasant. Being a Vedic school, there was a prescribed routine that everyone there had to follow... including Bhai ji. This involved waking up before dawn to go for a run, meditation, yoga, teaching a few students in academics, a little free time (hardly) and helping Acharya ji with his large garden. There were peaches growing there, which made Bhai ji happy. He ate many.

Asatya bhai was a helpful guest, but still just a guest. He knew he could not stay there forever. He would have to resume the job search the moment the lockdown was lifted.

Towards the end of July, Bhai ji received a call from a school in Uttar Pradesh. They were interested to hire him as their principal, possibly. Bhai ji wanted to go for it, but he knew he could not say yes without seeing the facility and meeting the staff. Asatya bhai knew that if he didn't take that job, that he would have to find *something*. Finding employment was becoming more and more urgent. Bhai ji went there and toured the school and met with the staff. Bhai ji could see that there wasn't a professional person among them, and he knew it would be an uphill battle to cultivate a "we are all in this together" mentality. He also worried that there would be a high number of misbehaving students. Asatya bhai was ready to take on the challenge. However, with further talks, Bhai ji was beginning to see that the person doing the hiring wanted to get him to start working without a paycheck, seeing as there was prep to be done before the lockdown would be lifted and the students would return. They would not pay him until school would be in session again, the next April. Also, it was a sad little salary, and they wanted him to contract for ten years. They had no idea about how to negotiate such things. It was their way or the highway, so Bhai ji hit the highway.

Meanwhile, Asatya bhai had found some local students to tutor. Even that was a waste of time. Of the twelve students that he was tutoring, only two paid him. Bhai ji wasn't going to work for free, so he stopped.

At the home of his friend Tamo, where he was staying during the school meetings and tutoring, things weren't going well, either. In fact, that man was not a friend at all but the very same acquaintance that Bhai ji had stayed with the summer before. The same place where he had broken his arm, and his money was stolen. Things weren't much better this time. Twice during his one month stay, police were called to break up fights among the family members of that household. It was a rough and careless crowd and there was never a shortage of stress under that roof. Tamo would talk to Bhai ji needlessly for hours about all kinds of rubbish, which drove him crazy. Asatya bhai is a friendly type who likes conversation, but Tamo had nothing useful or nice to say, ever. The only nice thing about the time spent there was the acquaintance's grandfather who lived there. The old man was grieved to see how his grandchildren were living. He was very glad for Asatya's company and likewise Asatya bhai liked to spend time with him.

That very stressful and disappointing experience further solidified in Bhai ji's mind the decision that he never wanted to go back to Uttar Pradesh - not to live there, not for work, not for any reason. Every person that he met there and every experience that he had there was riddled with trouble. It is true that he has only been to one region of U.P., and possibly the rest of the state is much different, we don't know. Bhai ji packed up his bike and set out for Charkhi Dadri. There, he went to the home of an old friend, a classmate from the Andhra Pradesh school: Pareshani.

Pareshani looks like a timid and quiet fellow most of the time. He's not very ambitious. He has a particular talent for drawing portraits. In fact, I myself possess one of his sketches.

When Bhai ji arrived there, Pareshani was helping his sister with the construction of her home. Bhai ji helped them over that weekend. Bhai ji knew he couldn't stay there with his friend a long time and yet he had no job prospects. There was no one hiring in Charkhi Dadri except for hiring laborers. Why not just take a job as a laborer until something better could be found? Asatya bhai said that this is his sister's hometown and there are many people there that know him. He could not be seen working as a laborer. But why not? At first glance, this looked like a matter of ego.

This is where I must explain another significant difference between American culture and Indian culture. In the U.S., laborers can earn anywhere from $12-20 per hour (at the time of this writing), which is not really enough to accumulate much if any savings, but it's enough to pay all the bills for one frugal person, generally. A few people have the attitude that this is some kind of lesser career choice, but there is no shame in it, and you can find laborers, doctors and people of all different professions socializing together during happy hour in many places, though a little societal segregation can still be found in some locales. It is just a job and people don't care as much what you do. People only care that you support yourself to the best of your ability through honest work, whatever sort of work that may be. The only thing preventing a laborer from enjoying the same things as a wealthy person is the matter of affordability. There are far fewer artificially imposed barriers, because discrimination is illegal. If you can afford it, you can have it. If you can prove your income, you can rent or buy what you wish.

In India, life is very different for the laborer. A laborer is paid barely enough for four walls and basic food, essentially slave wages. Employers very often ignore worker's rights. Police and municipal officials often take bribes, so standing up for your own rights can easily get you fired, with no severance pay. Laborers are expected to do strenuous work for 10-12 hours, seven days per week, and there is only time afterwards to cook and eat, wash up, and sleep. A laborer has no life besides sleeping and working. With no time and certainly no extra money, a laborer has no hope of ever improving his/her life. What is worse than this, is that Indian laborers are routinely stripped of their dignity. Poverty is considered shameful in Indian culture, very much so. A laborer is by default of the wage, poor. No one would even dream of associating with laborers for fear of tarnishing their reputation. Some people will walk by construction sites just to mock the workers. Remember I had said that it is very common for people to exploit the poor. Many people will think nothing of slandering, insulting, cheating, even stealing from a laborer. Above all, poor people are avoided like the plague. The caste system encourages this as well. Laborers and those in 'lower' castes are artificially held back from being successful by institutionalized oppression in every corner of society. The only exception to this that I know of, is through the few charities that can be found here and there. For example, ashrams are known for taking in vagabonds and travelers for a few nights. People sometimes like to donate to ashrams, temples, and non-profits, which sometimes help the poor. I have seen several Indians make such donations, who wouldn't be caught dead associating with a low wage earner. Not all Indians are like this, but this attitude is still very common.

So, Bhai ji was right. If he took a job as a laborer, there in Charkhi Dadri where all his acquaintances could see him working like that, his reputation as a respectable man would be gone forever. He would have no time to search for a better job. He would not be able to save any money. His hope and dignity would be taken from him. Also, he had a problem with a vertebral disk so he couldn't be too hard on his back. However, there was nothing else available and he was coming to the end of his savings.

Bhai ji heard of a construction project on the other side of Haryana, near the Rajasthan border. At least nobody knew him there, so if he worked as a laborer for a little while, no one would know, so it would be okay. Asatya took Pareshani and Prajnaparadha with him. Asatya bhai was still feeling stressed and tense from the experience in Uttar Pradesh. The daytime temperatures were around 100F (38C). The job was carrying and laying bricks. That first day, Asatya was violently ill. He became dehydrated and weak. The three guys persisted for a week. Pareshani didn't like being far from home and wanted to go back. There was a young man who was harassing Bhai ji to the point of abuse. They were the only guys from Haryana in addition to being new to that work team, and the other workers were content in their own Rajasthani clique. They seemed eager to drive these new guys away. In the end, Asatya bhai put his foot down and appealed to the supervisor on account of the abusive young punk. The man just laughed. Bhai ji refused to be walked over like a doormat. The young dude came at him again and Asatya punched him. An uproar ensued with the Rajasthani guys coming to the young man's rescue, and so Asatya left with Prajna and Pareshani in a rush.

Now what? He had tried his one last option. Bhai ji was already stressed, and now this. That was the worst day. Pareshani didn't bring Asatya back to his house. Pareshani was mad at him for dragging him down to Rajasthan and then getting into a fight, and Asatya was mad at Pareshani for never lifting a finger to help with preparing meals or anything else and then ditching him once they returned to Charkhi Dadri.

After Asatya blew up Maundaata's phone with constant calls, she finally made arrangements for Bhai ji, for a place to stay for a few nights.

After that, Bhai ji stayed with a man who seemed honest and kind. He was with that man for a week or so, while he contemplated what to do next. It was suggested that he could work from home making pencils for a supply company. His host thought of getting a food truck.

In those weeks, Asatya bhai hardly had 700 rupees left, enough for three or four meals. I questioned him to know how he was eating? He said that he was eating just one meal per day to make his money last until he could find work. I was crying. I told him that this was intolerable, and I begged him to accept a little money from me to get him through that time. He absolutely refused. He said that he would lose all self-respect if he accepted any money from his little sister. He insisted over and over that he is the giver and never a taker or borrower. I was sad but my hands were tied; I could not help him.

At that time, Bhai ji got a call from Chhota. Remember Chhota was the little Giroha boy who loved Asatya. Chhota invited him to come stay with him. He was at an ashram in Haridwar. An ashram is something similar to a gurukul, and they are designed with hospitality in mind. Haridwar is in the Indian state of Uttarakhand, beside the Ganges River. Bhai ji took the offer and went there. He figured he could search that city also for work. There were plenty of schools and ashrams there. Chhota came into contact with a well-known guru who was looking for an assistant in his ashram. Bhai ji went to investigate. The man seemed interested in him even though Asatya ji explained that he's spiritual but not religious. It was presented like a real job offer but actually it was more like a live-in servant type of arrangement. Asatya bhai had no interest in that.

It was at this time that Bhai ji mentioned to me his dream of forming a trust to set up an N.G.O. I was shocked that he had never mentioned it before. I asked him why on earth he had never said anything about it. He explained that at first, everyone had said that it couldn't work.

He was afraid to mention it to me, thinking that I would shoot down the idea, too. But something interesting happened then. Just as when I had first met Asatya and I saw deep pain behind his eyes, at this time when he was telling me about the N.G.O., I saw a fire in his eyes that I had never seen before. He seemed to suddenly come alive. I said to him, "Many people go through life just working at a mundane job that means nothing more to them than a means to pay the bills. They wonder if their lives counted for anything... but you have a fire in you. It is a gift that few people possess. It should not be wasted."

Asatya is more than just a passionate or motivated person. It is clear from all his traits that he is a revolutionary. He had once said that he kept trying to fly but it seemed that he couldn't even climb the mountain. He has struggled and persisted through everything. He has never sacrificed his integrity. He is sensible and logical and yet also emotional. Even under a deep depression he continued forward as if driven by a motor. I understood his reason for wanting to form the N.G.O., and I knew that if anyone could do it, he could. How could I say no?

Even as we were discussing this, a politician of Himachal Pradesh, known to Asatya bhai, called him saying that her son has an apartment in Solan, but he's not in it at present. She said that Asatya would be welcome to use it. She said maybe he could stay there and look for a teaching job in Solan. Actually, Bhai ji had other plans for her. To set up an N.G.O. would require local support, and a land grant or at least a lease. The only people that Bhai ji knew in H.P. were his ex-wife's family (who mostly all hated him) and this one politician named Pāsana. Because she was the only person that Bhai ji knew in that area, that he had an amicable relationship with, and because she was a well-known community figure, he thought to approach her with the N.G.O. idea.

He went first to the Solan apartment, then took a bus into the Sirmaur district (near her house.) I didn't understand at the time why he left his bike behind. The bus ride was a mistake for two reasons: It has become clear that Asatya bhai is susceptible to motion sickness. Also, once he ran out of money he would be stranded in that remote village or you can say, at the mercy of his hosts whether they would give him bus fare to return from there. Asatya reasoned that if anything happened to his bike, he would have zero money to get it fixed. Anyway, Bhai ji thought to stay and visit her and her family there, to build up a better relationship so that he could gain her support for the N.G.O.

It was difficult to begin any conversation. It was a busy household and there was a lot of activity related to an upcoming election.

While Bhai ji was there working on that, there were two other things going on. A year or so before, the administrator of a brand new school in Solan had interviewed Asatya ji for the position of French teacher. Asatya bhai hadn't heard from them again until December 2020, probably because of school not being in session during the pandemic. They were interested in a second interview and a class demo. Bhai ji said to me that there was no point in going for it, because once they discovered that he didn't have the required teaching degree, they would toss out his application.

I said, "Bhai, why would you decide for them? Probably they will say no, but if you don't respond, then the answer is definitely no. So go for it." So, he did another interview via zoom.

After a few weeks, they added him to the staff and had him compile the required documents, even though he had no degree, and they knew it. We thought at last, the endless job searching was finally over, and Bhai ji could relax a little. Salary was discussed. What they wanted to pay was a fraction of even a part-time salary. It would hardly cover basic living expenses. It could only work if Asatya bhai had another supplementary income, which he did not. Why such an insultingly low salary? They told Bhai ji that even though they were well aware of his experience and proven skill, they could get away with offering this small salary because he didn't have the formal qualification. They knew that he could not make a formal complaint, because then it would be found that he also was in violation of the law.

The other thing that was going on... over the passing months, it came to my attention that Asatya would be an excellent match in every way for a certain single friend of mine. They both had the same important values as far as marriage is concerned. They both wanted the same things in life. They were both uniquely equipped to meet each other's needs perfectly. Everything about it looked so right. After much careful consideration, I presented this idea to both of them separately. The friend seemed interested but hesitant. Bhai ji thought about everything that I had told him about her. I told all that I knew, out of genuine loving concern for both of them. You know that arranged marriages are still a thing in India. Bhai ji had no problem to trust my judgment in this matter. He was just delighted that I, as his dear sister would try to help him find a life partner. Also, he liked the description that I gave of my friend very much. He hated to leave Shweta behind, but she was never going to come back. Finally, he was ready to move forward, and he did not want to live the rest of his life alone. He wanted a wife to share life with. To take care of each other when they would grow old. He wanted to start a family, if his wife agreed. As he had said, 'A house doesn't seem to be a home without a woman there.' More importantly, he wanted someone to share life with, someone to love who would love him back. Bhai ji expressed his sincere interest in pursuing the relationship.

My friend said it could be possible but demanded one impossible condition: to come to the U.S. independently, without a fiancé visa. In a way it made sense, to prove that he was interested in her for her, not to use her for immigration. Bhai ji would have moved heaven and earth and done everything possible to come. He was not eligible for immigration at that time, except by marriage. He could not even get a visitor visa... Visitor visas were not being issued at all at that time due to the tremendous backlog from the visa center being closed during the pandemic. It was impossible to meet this demand, no matter how much Asatya bhai wanted to do it, and he wanted to come to the U.S. more than anything, to be near his dear chhoti bahan and her family... who also were becoming his family. Still, she insisted. To Bhai ji, this was nothing less than heart-breaking. It seemed hopeless. Still aiming for the sky, still falling from the mountain. What now? Once when Asatya bhai was feeling frustrated on the endless job search, he told me that if he received a job offer from Mars, he would go there. I can verify that indeed he would do it. He is highly motivated and has no fear of new things.

I thought that it seemed weird that Bhaiya had been in Pāṣana's home for a few months without explaining why he was there, neither had they asked him why he came. Very strange behavior on both sides. Bhai ji tried to explain to me that he needed to make himself valuable to them so that they would be inclined to support him, but that just didn't seem right to me.

Pāśana would be sometimes selfish, but she had developed a benevolent attitude towards Asatya ji. He had been there in their house for a few months, and she could see what kind of man he was. Her husband on the other hand, did not have a warm heart. He seemed to pride himself on gaining unfair advantages, and he would sometimes brag about this while they sat by the fire. So, Bhai ji knew that he had to be very careful of him.

Over the four months that Asatya bhai lived at that house, I (Petra) witnessed every single family member in that house use my Bhai ji however they could. Being a politician, Pāśana knew how to be nice at just the right time to get people to act the way that she wanted. I saw Asatya bhai being put to work 13-15 hours per day, hauling and spreading manure around the gardens. Also, Pāśana forced him to help forage fiddleheads from the hillside to sell illegally. It absolutely broke my heart to see these useless people stripping my brother of his dignity, who had no intention of reciprocating anything good to him. I asked Bhai ji, "Why don't you stand up for yourself? Just because they say, 'do this,' doesn't mean that you must do it."

Bhai ji scolded me saying that he didn't want to risk losing favor with them because the whole purpose of his presence there was to gain their support for the N.G.O. I still thought it was crazy that he was letting them drive him crazy, but he wouldn't listen, so I kept quiet about it after that.

While Bhai ji was there, a mason came by bus with his wife and small kids. The mason was just a poor guy from a different state who was desperate for any work. He had spent the last of his money to travel by bus several hours to that remote village with his family. Bhai ji watched Pāśana's family exploit those people too, like indentured servants. But they were stuck there without money to leave.

Without any local support, the N.G.O. idea was once again dead.

The Solan job was still months away.

Without job offers, starting up a new business seemed to Asatya bhai like the best (and perhaps only) path forward, which would give Asatya independence also. Without money to start a business, that didn't seem possible either.

Pāśana had suggested to start a small dairy operation. She wanted us all to contribute to the initial expense and Asatya bhai would manage care of the cows. I felt surprised that Bhai ji could mention this suggestion to me. It seemed like an obvious risk to invest in anything where Pāśana would be involved, especially if she would be making the larger investment, making her the majority owner. Asatya bhai asked me to invest, saying that we three would jointly own the business and subsequent profits. He would need about $1,500. I said no, and I explained why. Asatya bhai was angry. He reminded me that he had never asked for money up until this time. Couldn't I see the importance? Was I not his family? He said that even stubborn, egocentric Mauna would not even ask for details, but would sell anything just to come up with some money to help her brother... I stood my ground.

Asatya bhai was aware that Pāśana knew Shweta and her family, as Shweta's parents lived on the mountain just across the valley from her.

Pāśana called Shweta 'just to say hi,' but Asatya was there listening. He hadn't spoken to her directly for a few years, since finding out that she remarried. Actually, he asked Pāśana to call her to get a sense of how she was doing, if she was happy there... he was thinking, what if she was not happy? What if she could be persuaded to come back? In fact, they never divorced... they had a common law marriage. They had the ceremonies but not the legal paper. Shweta's sweet but shy voice could be heard saying yes she's fine...yes her parents are fine... but she hadn't gone to visit them in several months as she had a newborn baby, and didn't want to travel for hours over the bumpy and winding roads through the mountains of Himachal.

So, there it was. Not only was she remarried, but now she had a tiny son. Just imagine that a woman who felt too timid to travel with a baby, would absolutely be too timid to leave her new family there to go back to her first husband... Asatya knew that he would never see her again.

Solan

Asatya ji remembered that Pāśana's son had an apartment in Solan, but because the son was in a different city for his studies, his apartment was vacant. Pāśana thought that Bhai ji could use it. He took the opportunity to escape from that household. It was a day that marked a step toward freedom.

Reunited with his motorbike, Asatya bhai felt encouraged.

After some days went by, it became apparent that Pāśana had merely stationed Bhai ji at the apartment in Solan because it was a strategic location for sending and receiving her packages, as well as a stopover point for her guests or workers who would be coming to her from afar.

It was a small, studio style apartment, but she really expected him to pick up people from the bus stop at any time of the day or night, cook their meals, and send them on their way, whether it was one person or six, as was the case one time. One time, Pāśana's daughter came to the apartment and took away the LP gas canister for her own use. It was a mean act, as it left Asatya bhai with no means to cook food for himself.

Finally, around this time, Bhai ji was called back by the school and officially appointed as their French teacher.

After collecting his first month's salary, he left that apartment to get his own, closer to the school.

He had finally broken free from Pāśana.

It was a newly built school. It was a beautiful property overlooking the valley. The other teachers seemed nice.

The managing director (MD), however, was a real piece of work. Things started out reasonably, teaching 3-4 grade levels in French as expected. Pretty soon Bhai ji was asked to also teach English, after the English teacher quit. He was not given any pay increase to reflect the additional work.

Sometime after that, MD asked Bhai ji to help design their website. Bhai ji knows absolutely nothing about coding. He did his best. He was made to compose a newsletter every week, which is not unusual, but the workload was.

For the rest of the academic year, MD kept giving him odd assignments that involved writing essays, giving reports and other things of that nature that looked suspiciously like assignments that one would expect from a college level French course. Interestingly, MD was enrolled in a French course at that time and demanding free tutoring in French from Asatya ji on the side.

Bhai ji would have gladly quit except that he had no other job prospects (these were pandemic times) and also, he hated the idea of abandoning his post mid-contract.

Later in 2021, Asatya bhai reconnected with the mother of one of his old students from his days of tutoring in Chandigarh. He found out that her husband was an immigration consultant. It seemed worth keeping in touch with her...

She seemed like a nice and caring lady.

When she learned that Bhai ji wanted to remarry, she (Samaji) and her friend Sakhi arranged for him to meet two single ladies. Asatya bhai did meet them but neither seemed suitable to him.

At the school, Bhai ji became the favorite of every teacher, as he was always helpful to them and would make more efforts than others to not just teach well, but he always tried to maintain good discipline and teach his students good values. Some of these coworkers became friends. The music teacher is still in touch. Also, when Bhai ji is not stressed, he likes to be a comedian. It does not happen often, but the other staff appreciated it, as they also were stressed by the MD.

After the chaotic year that was 2020, it was a relief to just be living in one place, at least for the duration of the academic year. Bhai ji never had the pleasure of having any pets, although not many Indians do have pets. However, Indians are generally kind towards animals and will often feed the wandering cows, monkeys, and feral dogs. Near Bhai ji's room, a dog had a litter of puppies that would wander up the hill by his place. Bhai ji loved dogs. Those puppies were thin and mangey but so cute and innocent looking. Every day at breakfast, Asatya bhai would cook extra chapatis to feed the puppies. Every morning, they came to his door expectantly. He called them 'his puppies.'

The man that Asatya had stayed with in the past (Tamo, the man in whose home he had broken his arm) was talking about possibly trying to do some business in Himachal as a real estate agent or something of that nature. Bhai ji was the only person that he knew in the area. He was talking to Bhai ji hoping to recruit his help by using Asatya bhai's apartment as a place from which he could work while getting started. Asatya was polite but really not interested. Trouble seemed to always follow Tamo, as he was volatile and prone to fights. Tamo was sensing some pushback, which he resented. Also, Asatya ji never accompanied him when he went out partying or looking for prostitutes. Whatever Tamo was thinking, he began to resent and hate Bhai ji, to the point where he threatened to kill him.

Tamo lived near the Yamuna River in Uttar Pradesh, the same area in which the infamous Giroha family resided, and Tamo was known to them. One day, Chhota Giroha heard about this threat from Tamo. Soon after, Chhota appeared without warning at Tamo's house along with more than one dozen other men. The Giroha family is powerful, and in some ways above the law. It is very unwise to upset them. Chhota and his men put the full weight of intimidation on Tamo that day. Asatya bhai never heard from Tamo again after that.

We were feeling very grateful to Chhota for ensuring Asatya bhai's safety. At the same time, Asatya bhai was deciding to slowly and carefully pull himself away from the Giroha family. It is true that Chhota loved him, but it is also true that the Girohas are volatile. If you are good for them, they are good for you. If they perceive that you may be bad for them, you could end up dead. Bhai ji did not feel it would be wise to remain connected to them. Bhai ji thanked Chhota, but he did not intend to talk to any of them again.

Family Matters

After the eighth grade, Asatya's bhai never returned to live in his native village. Staying away was completely justified.

You may remember that Bhai ji's 'mama ji' had exploited Prajna when he was growing up... unfortunately that was not the only case of exploitation. It seems quite surprising that such extremely generous people come from the same family as extremely toxic people that selfishly use others, but in this family both exist. It's such an unfortunate dynamic because those that are loving give without hesitation or expectation because they love to be loving. At the same time, the users are living like wolves in the rabbit's hole - they have easy prey.

Years ago, Asatya bhai completely funded on his own, the construction of another uncle's house. The uncle never paid him back and never thanked him. That uncle (mama ji) was the father of Shweta's rapist. It seems crazy to think that both of these people exist - in the same family, no less. Bhai ji fully funded the startup of another uncle's business. He paid all the tuition fees for his cousin's master's degree. That cousin lived with Mauna at the time to be near her university. Remember also that Mauna's daughter Agni was raised by Asatya bhai and Shweta through her teen years. In the winter, Asatya bhai would buy sweaters for all his cousins.

Although it's true that at many times, Bhai ji struggled to maintain adequate employment, still he worked like a draft horse. He would have had a reasonably comfortable life except that he had a very big heart and would give, give, give...

There were two known abusers and all the others that would gladly receive but were never there for Bhai ji or ever gave anything in return. There were hardly any kind-hearted relatives. A couple of aunts seemed reasonable but not much interested to keep in touch, much less invest in Asatya bhai's well-being.

Asatya bhai was always concerned about his younger relatives (especially since he himself didn't have any kids) and he always wanted to try to

teach good values to them and inspire them to build their lives, and honestly. Even with Mauna and Prajna over the years, Asatya bhai would from
time to time reach out to them to encourage them to be wise and take better care of themselves. He would suggest to Prajna how he could build himself up stronger by learning a trade, such as tailoring. Prajna never ever tried
anything suggested by his brother. He only ever worked as a laborer and
then he would give away the lion's share of his wages to beggars. He himself
was always in some stage of suffering because he never kept enough money
for his needs. Asatya bhai would scold him, but Prajna was like a brick wall.
Mauna always did the same, but at least she had the security of a marriage
and a home. Agni was beginning to look like the toxic relatives, which was
very concerning, in addition to following the example of her mother's stubbornness.

In May of 2021, RK (Mauna's husband) contracted the Delta variant
of Covid. Two years prior, he had lung cancer which he recovered from,
but the family was concerned that his weakened lungs might not be able to
fight the Covid. At that time, Rohtak and the surrounding cities were hit
hard by the Delta variant. BBC, NBC and other international news out-
lets were talking about it. The hospitals were overflowing, with sick people
lined up in queues, patient's make-shift beds crowding the rooms and lin-
ing the hallways. Every day, people died because doctors couldn't treat them
fast enough. RK was in a hospital room with seven or eight other sick men.
Every day, Mauna was there with him. She saw other patients die there. She
called me on facetime from the hospital and I could see the fear in her eyes.

If RK died, she would be alone with her nine-year-old daughter
Vidushi. Life for widows in India is just twice as hard as for a widow in a
developed nation where widows carry no stigma.

Asatya put me on facetime with the doctor who explained RK's health
status. Maybe he thought my concern would help further motivate the doctor to be diligent, I'm not sure. I, Petra asked my friend (who was an in-
ternist) about RK's prognosis, explaining his health history, vital signs and
other relevant info. My friend, who is ever the realist, said that he had a 50/
50 chance of survival. Every single person known to us prayed for RK. His
oxygen level was less than 70% *with* oxygen.

The next day, he was given the 'ok' to return home. Within a couple days, he didn't need the oxygen anymore. He recovered completely and quickly, shocking his doctors. Everyone thanked God.

All that time, Bhai ji was there. He took a few days off teaching to help Mauna, not knowing if RK would survive. He got to spend some time with his niece Vidushi and realized that Vidushi is almost like a little Asatya... when I asked her what was her favorite thing to do, she answered, "study." We would worry about her, surrounded by the villager mindset and toxic relatives. We knew she would have a bright future if she was simply nurtured and encouraged. Asatya bhai talked with Mauna seriously, saying that she really needed to think carefully what will be her plan for someday when she would become a widow... as RK is much older than her. She needed to think ahead to the future. As usual, Mauna tried to find fault with Asatya bhai rather than talk proactively about her own well-being, just like Prajna-paradha always did. It devolved into a fight. Finally, Bhai ji was forced to leave in anger. It wouldn't be the first or last time that series of events played out like that.

Bahan and Beta Come to Visit

I, Petra had been contemplating when might be an opportune time to visit my brother in India. Considering his family dynamics, Asatya bhai suggested that possibly I could be a catalyst for some positive or healing interaction. I wasn't sure if my presence would make any difference, but it seemed to be worth a shot. Covid made international travel impossible until the very end of 2020, and after that it was a matter of watching statistics to see when the number of cases/deaths would be falling. Elevated numbers would mean that incoming travelers would have to go immediately into quarantine for several days. Finally in November 2021, Petra purchased airline tickets round trip from New York-Delhi. Thank God... after a big spike, the number of cases fell dramatically just before the scheduled trip.

Predictably, Bhai ji was a bit mad at me (Petra) for spending so much money on him (for the visit). I didn't care. I had been waiting two long years to see my brother for the first time, and he was going through a period of sadness. I wanted to be there for him. In fact, He was super happy that I was coming; he just wanted to express humility.

Asatya bhai asked who was coming with me. I had forgotten because of my typical American independent mindset that Asian families are usually very tight-knit and so naturally he was thinking that I might bring my family along as well. Everyone from his side encouraged that... well I had bought my tickets with only a month advance planning. I didn't have money saved up for others to come also. My husband would have too many responsibilities to leave behind. Also, he was still recovering from shoulder surgery which meant that one of our kids would have to help him with household chores and cooking. The oldest child had just moved out to live with my younger brother and his wife. Our son was struggling in a couple of subjects, so he really needed the time in the classroom. My parents and siblings were only beginning to get to know Asatya and maybe didn't feel comfortable going to India quite yet. My mom is afraid of flying.

PETRA CINEÁLTA

So, our younger daughter Ausmerrone came with me, by special permission from her school principal. She was eleven years old then.

Asatya would sometimes call her 'Beta,' which means, 'son.' Many Hindi speakers will call a child 'beta' as a term of endearment even if the child is neither related to them, nor a boy. Personally, I never liked that tradition as it looks sexist, but there didn't seem to be much point in arguing over it.

Some people might question my judgement in going across the planet to meet someone I met online, with my daughter, no less. The truth is that I was on video calls every week with Asatya for the past two years, and we would write every day without fail, even if it was only "good morning, dear sister." He would hardly even make tea without me knowing about it, because he would tell me all his thoughts and everything he did. Also, at that point I had already met almost everyone in his life via video call and I was keeping in touch regularly with a few of them independently, such as Samaji and Mauna and a few others. If anybody might dispassionately give me the real story about Asatya, it seemed logical that his siblings would. Prajna didn't have a smart phone and only spoke Hindi, so I only talked to him when Asatya bhai was there to translate. Mauna never spoke to me against Bhai ji but only offered the opinion that "he is not like us," (herself and Prajna.) What she said was both true and false.

On February 19, 2022, my daughter Ausmerrone and I drove to Providence, Rhode Island where we spent the night in the home of my husband's best friend. In the morning, I left my car at his house, and he brought Ausmerrone and I to the train station. From there, we took the train into Penn Station on Manhattan Island.

Penn Station is the busiest mass-transit station in the western hemisphere with approximately 500,000 passengers travelling through it every day. Luckily, it was not very complicated to navigate, except that the metro line I wanted was under construction. We went upstairs to Moynihan Train Hall to ask the guy at the counter for Long Island Railroad which would be the best route to JFK airport. He got me a good deal on a train that would be leaving about 20 minutes later. Perfect. So, we took LIRR to Jamaica Station. From there we took the airport metro line directly into the airport. Everything went fine except that the burrito in my backpack set off the sensors at the security checkpoint. Funny.

I AM FAMILY

Ausmerrone had never set foot in an airplane in her life. I did not know how she would react. It was a 16 hour flight. I brought a bag of things to entertain her and lots of snacks. As it turned out, Ausmerrone was a wonderful travel partner and enjoyed all the new experiences. It's true that she loves to keep busy and be social. It was disorienting flying across 9 time zones, and the meals on the plane didn't make sense. Is this breakfast? Dinner? What time is it? We sure didn't know. It was interesting flying over and seeing places that I had only heard of in the news, such as Kabul, or Ukraine. The crisis in Ukraine was just beginning to unfold as we were returning home.

When we arrived in Delhi, an airport official pulled me aside right out of the gate to do a random Covid test. It didn't feel random... Ausmerrone and I were two out of only five white people on an aircraft carrying 300+ people. Eh, whatever. I found it amusing that I was required to pay a fee for the test in rupees. They had taken me directly from the gate, and it's illegal to bring in local currency from outside the country. I used my debit card.

The line through immigration was long, and my joints were fatigued as I had only slept one hour in the plane, but that went smoothly. Prior to travel, I was advised to have my husband sign a waiver that indicated that he was aware and consenting that his daughter would leave the country with me (anti-kidnapping law), but they didn't ask to see that paper. The real trick was figuring out at which exit to find my brother Asatya. I didn't have cellular data, so finally after a little searching, I located free Wi-Fi in the baggage claim area and called him.

Outside the exit, front and center of a small crowd of others waiting to pick up arrivals, was my very, very happy brother. It looked like the best day of his life. With him were Mauna, RK, and their daughter Vidushi. Another couple were there that were friends of Samaji. Vidushi said goodbye to her parents and came to travel with us for about ten days.

We hired a car and driver to share with the friends of Samaji, as they were traveling to the same city: Mohali. Mohali is sort of a twin city of Chandigarh. By then it was almost midnight. After traveling over thirty hours since Providence, I had hoped to go to sleep, but instead we went straight from there to Samaji's house in Mohali, five hours away. (It's true that Asatya himself always travels like he's on a mission, sleep be damned!)

We stopped at a Haveli for dinner at 2am. Haveli is a restaurant chain that tends to be on main highways and open 24/7. Yes, it sounds like a cheap diner, but actually it is a spacious, clean place with good food. When the food was served, the others looked at us to start eating first, except that we had no idea what was the correct way to eat chapatis. See, every time Bhai ji had to eat while on video call with me, he would just hang up and call back after, because he needed his hands, so I had never witnessed it. Bhai ji thought it was amusing that we didn't know what to do with the chapatis. They are part of most meals in northern India. In fact, most North Indians will tell you there is no food if they don't see chapatis. Asatya did show us how, but regardless, Ausmerrone just piled her food into it and ate it like a taco, which the others at the table found amusing.

Samaji's house was the largest and nicest that we stayed in. We had our own bathroom. There was a hired household driver and a maid. But no clothes dryer or dishwasher ... in fact, most Indians have very few appliances. I only saw two refrigerators among the nine homes that we visited.

Samaji bent over backwards to make us feel very welcome.

Unfortunately however, it took no time for Bhai ji to notice a clear-cut trend of her and her husband giving preferential treatment to me and Ausmerrone, but not to Asatya, and they straight up ignored Vidushi. (Vidushi had come with us to spend time with us while we were in Himachal and the area around Chandigarh.) Bhai ji wasn't bothered much to be a bit left out, but he was deeply bothered by the fact that his niece was treated as 'less than'. I very much disliked this as well. I knew that the reason for this behavior was simply that many people in this part of the world including Samaji, see a relationship to an American as an asset to invest in. Bhai ji didn't have anything to offer other than just being an excellent human being, which apparently does not interest many people, and Vidushi was in the same boat.

While staying at Samaji's house in Mohali, we visited Sukhna Lake, the Rock Garden, the Rose Garden, and Pinjaur Garden. Pinjaur Garden is a serene little place just at the base of the Himalayan foothills that is full of coconut trees, mango trees, fountains, and hundreds of parrots. The sun was setting, and the place was full of birdsong. Beautiful.

The next day we went to the office of Samaji's husband. He had us assemble a lot of papers related to a visa application for my brother to possibly be able to visit my family in the U.S. He wanted to advise us about immigration matters.

He seemed to think that it would be quicker and easier for Asatya bhai to obtain a visitor visa, which I found surprising. He reasoned that Asatya could come visit anytime and meanwhile, work on the actual immigration process. I didn't see how that made any sense... A U.S. tourism visa for most foreigners including Indians, entails showing ample ability to pay for the trip, and ample assurance of the intention to return to one's home country. Samaji's husband promised to guide us through how we could fulfill that criteria. He also said that government officials often check a person's online presence to get a sense of their intentions and connections. Asatya bhai told me that Samaji's husband had said that having a U.S. host will be good, so sharing photos on social media that demonstrate our connection will help. This didn't make sense to me... wasn't Asatya supposed to show his connection to his home country, not motivations to want to stay in the U.S.? Well I was not the expert, so if that's what professional counsel said, then alright... everywhere we went, we made FB posts with a total of about 1,000 photos altogether.

Afterwards, we went shopping in the big, outdoor bazaar.

Some friends of Samaji came to the house for the evening. We all sat together, but they spoke in Hindi the entire evening and made zero effort to include me in conversation. Finally, I felt tired of being blatantly ignored and I just got up and went to my room without even saying goodnight. I realized then that I wasn't so much a human being to Samaji as I was a trophy to show off to her friends. I was a couch decoration.

Later Bhai ji confirmed... obviously he could understand what they were saying. He told me that there was racism peppered throughout that conversation... staying in Samaji's house did help us understand better what sort of person she actually was, which was disappointing, but at least the truth came out.

In fact, my visit to Asatya bhai helped to sift several people who couldn't hide their true colors while I was there, as they would act differently while I was around. The intentions of these people became less mysterious and more black and white. I was glad of that for Asatya's sake because it meant that he could make better informed decisions. Apparently, Samaji was thinking to have me in some marketing for husband's business as having an American face would be an attractive pull to the Indian public. All her gifts to me and excessive efforts of hospitality were not kindness. She was trying to motivate me to do something for her...she was shmoozing me. As the months went by after that, Bhai ji and I both slowly distanced ourselves from her.

Samaji's friend Sakhi and Sakhi's husband picked us up, and all together we went on a little adventure into the mountains... The foothills in the state of Himachal Pradesh are a bit like the rolling hills of Maine, my home state. I say this mainly on account of the plentiful pine trees, many of the same herbs and weeds are present, and the rural nature of the landscape and general attitude of local people is the same. Himachal is very gravelly, which means that it is prone to erosion. The horizon cannot be seen anywhere except from high peaks. Also, the roads are narrow, and they zigzag dramatically to reach anywhere. There are frequent landslides because of tectonic movement and the loose soil, but mostly in the wet season. The wall-like mountainsides come right to the edge of the road surface and there are often a few scattered rocks across that side of the road. There are pine trees, cactuses, ferns, rhododendron trees (yes, they are over forty feet tall there), apple orchards in the valleys, feral dogs and monkeys, but no palm trees. The palms stop where the mountains begin. We stopped once or twice on the side of the road so that Sakhi could feed the feral cows and monkeys. Sakhi especially loves to do this. She came prepared with over-ripe bananas and bread.

It is an amazing and unforgettable place for a road trip. We encountered a large road construction project[1],[xi] so the road surface was not great at the time. They were excavating tunnels for a more direct route through the mountains to Manali. Bhai ji said to my daughter, "The road is bumpy, the car is jumpy, and we are getting grumpy."

---

1.   https://youtube.com/shorts/AMtg0gkkF34?si=r-9BHJOEUmHuown9

In fact, we were having a great time and joking all the way. Knowing that my brother had spent most of his life in survival mode, it made me so glad to see him having such a good time.

The temperature dropped rapidly as we went deeper into the mountains, from 70 Fahrenheit in Chandigarh to only 30 in Manali, less than 100 miles away.

We made a little detour into the village known as Kasauli. There we found hot springs and a religious site that I didn't understand. It's interesting that ordinarily any personal item left unattended would likely be stolen, but at such places, everyone removes their shoes. We walked a couple of blocks through that place, and all the shoes and socks were still there when we returned. It seems that even thieves wouldn't dare steal shoes from a holy site... Beside the shrine there was a hot spring that had large pots sitting in the water. The simmering spring cooked the rice. Most of the village could only be accessed on foot by crossing a single-lane suspension bridge over a rushing stream. It seemed like a sort of magical place.

Finally, late in the evening we reached the little valley town of Kullu. By then, the rain had changed to snow. We stayed the night in a hotel that looked out across the valley. The two men took one room, and the two women plus my daughter took the next room. Vidushi preferred to stay with her Mama ji (mother's brother.) Probably she was a bit shy. In the morning, the surrounding mountains were snow-capped.

From there, we continued to Manali. Manali is the last small town in Himachal on that main road, before the road continues up through Rohtang Pass, into the heart of the Himalayas and then into the remote side of China beyond. We would have explored Rohtang Pass, but unfortunately the road was closed. At that time of year, no one cleared the snow from the road and drifts would make it impassible.

Snow came down in fat flakes in Manali. Tall pines lined every slope. It felt very much reminiscent of Maine, U.S.A., the pine tree state. In fact, Himachal Pradesh is also known as the pine tree state. For Vidushi, it was the first time seeing snow. Again, we spent another night at Kullu. Then Sakhi's husband drove us by a way known to him to continue back to Mohali. It was a scenic route (all routes in Himachal are scenic) up over a mountain pass[2][xii] by a single-lane dirt road. It was still quite snowy there. We stopped at the top for a half hour or so.

My daughter befriended a well-behaved feral dog and made plans to bring him home. Later she spotted monkeys and wanted to make friends with them, but we held her back. Bhai ji spent the rest of our visit in India, teasing Ausmerrone about the monkey.

He said, "That poor monkey went to collect his documents and has been waiting for you at the train station all this time. You promised to take him to America, but you left him behind and now he is heartbroken. That poor monkey!!"

Ausmerrone laughed hysterically anytime that Bhai ji brought up the monkey.

At one roadside public bathroom, I stood outside while my daughter went in, to keep a watch for monkeys, as there was a large family of monkeys just next to the bathroom, eating wild berries.

Eventually the slushy, serpentine road led back onto the Shimla-Chandigarh highway (a paved two-lane road.)

Back at Samaji's house, she attempted to recreate the tabbouleh that I had made on a previous night there. She remembered that it is supposed to include a whole grain... well we were served oatmeal-based tabbouleh for breakfast. It was absolutely *not* the same, but we choked it down politely. Imitation is the greatest compliment, right?

A few days before, when we were visiting the Rock Garden in Chandigarh, the MD from the Solan school called Bhai ji. She was saying something like, "I know that you requested time off from teaching for today, but I really need you now." Asatya bhai reminded her that it was his first time ever requesting a day off (which she had already granted), and that his sister had just traveled from the other side of the planet to visit him. Also, his sister was there with him at that moment, three hours away from the school. It would not even be possible to go to the school that day.

When the MD found out that I was there, she told Asatya to come to the school at once and bring me with him. That woman had a habit of using every possible opportunity to market her school. (She needed more enroll-

---

2.   https://www.youtube.com/shorts/dQAEVxeKR-Q

ments.) It seemed obvious that she wanted to have me photographed in her school to fabricate a story to use for publicity... and also that she did not view Asatya ji as a human being, but rather as a drone worker to exploit.

Actually, I was curious to visit the school, but certainly not under pressure like that. I could hear Bhai ji's voice slowly going from calm and amicable to more and more agitated. Finally I heard him yell, "You stupid woman!" as he reminded her in forceful tone, of all the many, many things that he had done for her in the past school year, that didn't remotely resemble his job description, all while being paid the minimum salary of 10,000 rupees per month ($125,) and never complaining or taking any days off. At last, he hung up on her while we could still hear her robotic voice mid-sentence of a tone-deaf response.

The little girls looked a bit concerned, having heard the yelling. However, they understood that their Mama ji had stood up for himself against a heartless woman. At last, that demeaning job was over. I expressed my respect and pride in Asatya for his boldness in defending his sanity and well-being.

At the same time though... he was jobless, and only three days into our one-month visit.

At this point, I thought that now he would be more available to spend time with us, but that the time would mostly be spent searching for a new job. I was surprised to see him insisting that our plans not change, but rather continue, and he would be free to be with us every minute. He said he would pursue the job search in earnest the second we were delivered to the airport. I didn't approve of this, but at the same time I was also glad to have that time with him.

I felt that I really should not let him pay for any of my needs at that point, but he wouldn't take my money... hardly... just for some bus fare or other small thing. It seemed like an obvious indicator that my comfort was more important to Bhai ji than his own well-being. Selfless as usual.

Next on our agenda was to go up to Solan where Prajna was living in Asatya's room. He was out of work for a few weeks as he had broken his leg and was waiting for it to be reset. I saw the x-rays.

We took a bus from Chandigarh. About half-way through the two-hour drive, the bus pulled into a parking area on the side of a hill and stopped. The driver got out. There was a little diner type of restaurant there, so we thought he may have gone in to grab some quick finger food. He didn't come back until more than an hour later. It appears that he had enjoyed an entire sit-down meal. Perhaps if he had explained to his passengers, then we all might have gotten out to feed ourselves as well!

I was grateful to arrive in Solan. It is a beautiful small city sprawling over the valley and small mountains, and Bhai ji's small apartment was on the hillside overlooking the valley, by the road to Rajgarh.

We found Prajna there, smoking on the balcony, and I greeted him with respect and feeling grateful to meet him.

Prajna is a hopelessly unwise person who always puts himself into unsafe, unhealthy situations that invariably result in his own suffering, but he has zero desire to improve himself. I believe that he is stuck in a very bad depression which makes him punish himself. However, this also means that he is the most selfless person on the planet. As much as he doesn't care about himself, he cares very much about everyone else. He always treats everyone as more important than himself, no matter who they are - young, old, rich, poor, politician, foreigner, male, female - it makes no difference. While much of India tries to shmooze their way into better positions and avoid 'lowly' people, Prajna easily talks to beggars like equals. He is the opposite of a social climber. Prajna also is not comfortable with others giving him any kindness or support to improve his life.

When I arrived there, I attempted to touch Prajna's feet. Touching feet is the standard way of greeting an elder relative respectfully. Prajna immediately stopped me and raised my elbows to make me stand. There is nothing wrong with that either. Stopping someone from touching your feet is a way of showing modesty or humility, and that you want to be treated like an equal.

Asatya bhai's apartment was a single room with a closet-sized kitchen attached, and an equally small bathroom. His motorbike was parked in the empty space below the apartment building, as it is built into the side of a hill, like most buildings in that mountainous state. The only appliances were a fan and the LP gas burners. No hot water heater or heat at all, in spite of being in a cold-weather region. In fact, very few Indian homes have heat, though there is usually a hot water heater for just the shower. South

India has no need of any heat except in the small mountain range there. Overnight winter temperatures in Solan are frequently in the low forties and once or twice per year there may be a bit of snow.

Normally Bhai ji would be living there alone, though recently Prajna had come to live there, so there were just two thin mattresses only, but with our arrival there were two men, one woman, and two little girls... luckily I had brought my backpacking air mattress which I let Prajna use. The girls and I shared the other two mattresses. It seemed so very basic, but it was perfectly comfortable and functional to us. Most importantly, I was in my brother's home. Where family is, that is home, and so I had come home, and it absolutely felt that way. What a feeling of serenity. Not a single pretentious soul in that home to contend with. Just genuine love.

India has myriad holidays and festivals, but my favorite is Raksha Bandhan.

Raksha Bandhan comes in August. Well, I had no idea when I might ever be in India in August, so I decided to surprise Asatya and Prajna by bringing Raksha Bandhan that February. Traditionally, a sister will buy or make a simple bracelet of braided embroidery threads and beads called a rakhi and tie it to her brother's wrist. She will make sweets to share. Her brother brings her gifts. It's a whole thing. Conveniently, Bhai ji had gone downtown for an errand. I cooked Prajna's favorite sweet dish - a sort of rice pudding with spices added to it. I thought, I have both the best AND the most underappreciated brothers on the planet, so I was determined to make the very best bracelets/rakhis. I learned two fancy macrame patterns and added genuine mother-of-pearl beads to Prajna's. Asatya's had two birds - one in flight and one perched. The birds were to represent us. Imagine if you can, why one was flying but the other was not. Bhai ji was so extremely pleased, proud, AND surprised. My daughter took a video of the whole affair.

The only problem, according to Asatya was that, "Sister, this is not fair! You did not warn us, so we have no gifts for you." It seemed to me that the hospitality they gave was gift enough...

In the morning, we left from there to go an hour or so away to pay a visit to Asatya bhai's friend from school, another teacher. That lady lived with her son at her parent's homestead in the middle of nowhere, beside a stream. It was a lovely property, really. There were lots of vegetable gardens with tiny onions just coming up. They were all nice. It was a traditional home where the elderly parents lived. The friend's brother lived there with his family on the upper level, and the teacher friend had her own room. They had an old-fashioned kitchen with a fireplace against the far wall, a hearth where dishes of food sat to stay warm, and more food cooking over the fire. It was cozy. Everyone came in to sit on the floor near the fire and pass the dishes of food around.

I found out later from Bhai ji that this lady had wanted to serve me wine. He adamantly told her to absolutely not do it. It's not that I don't drink alcohol, but that there is still a stigma attached to alcohol consumption in India, and especially for women drinking it. Quite often, the only Indians drinking alcohol have questionable morals in other ways or are addicted. A few affluent, well-traveled Indians drink alcohol without the stigma. As a general rule, it looks like those who have had more education, more culture, travel, exposure, etc. are less superstitious and more open-minded. Asatya bhai knew his friend well enough to figure out that she would take photos with me to put on Instagram and make a mini scandal about the alcohol-drinking American sister of Asatya Bhratra. He was right to tell her no.

The next day, the friend's brother gave us a ride into Shimla. Shimla is the next small city north of Solan. The entire city is situated along a ridge, where there are gorgeous views from every point, in every direction. The frequent fog just adds to the mystique.

As we came into the city, we found several streets packed shoulder to shoulder with protesters. It was some kind of local farmer's coalition, or something similar. Shimla is the government center of Himachal Pradesh, so it makes sense that political demonstrations or gatherings would be found there. We did our best to avoid the crowd though at some point we had to get through it. We made a human chain with white knuckles clenching each other's hands and pushed slowly through with the two girls between us.

Shimla is one of many places in India marked by the historic presence of the British. The Indian Institute of Advanced Study with its' striking architecture was host to many meetings between Nehru, Lord Mountbatten, and a host of others. It was fun to just wander around and explore. Towards the end of the day, we were thinking to find a bus to take back to Solan. With the sun sinking low in the clouds, those thousands of protestors and other visitors were all thinking the same thing...

At first it wasn't clear which bus station we needed, so we had to walk around a bit more. Even after finding the correct bus station, it took an hour or so to find a bus for Solan. Bhai ji knew that the bus service in this quiet corner of India would shut down for the night, and if we were stuck there overnight, there might not even be any rooms available, with so many out-of-towners there. Time was short and every minute counted to get on a bus going south... finally Asatya bhai asked me to stand in one particular place with the girls on the side of the road, while he ran here and there, inquiring with every bus driver and local. I knew that Bhai ji always had our safety in mind, but still it was uncomfortable, standing on the roadside in a completely unfamiliar city as dusk fell, as a foreign white woman with two children... it looked insecure. One side of my mind knew to trust my brother, and the other side of my mind was having a knee-jerk reaction of feeling insecure. When Bhai ji returned, I mentioned to him that I felt uncomfortable and why. I can never forget how his face fell, even from behind a mask. His eyes showed a pain like that of a stab wound.

He only said, "You don't trust me?" Immediately I knew that I had made a mistake. Bhai ji had no one else left on earth to love except me, and these kids. Only over his dead body could anything bad happen to us.

He then said, "You think you have two eyes? I have ten! Everywhere we go, I am watching everything and everyone around you. You could not see me from here, but where I was looking for a bus, I was looking back at you constantly. If the trust is missing from a relationship, what is left? Trust is the foundation. If you can't trust me, it means that our brother-sister relationship is nothing."

I wanted that Asatya understand why I had felt unsettled, though I trusted him, but he seemed to only see the matter in black and white.

It was a painful interaction between us, and yet it was the reassurance that I needed to quiet the reactive side of my brain. From that day forward, I felt a profound feeling of safety and peace to be anywhere with Asatya.

While it's true that to trust was my choice, that feeling of serenity was not contrived; it was a gift. Not once did I ever doubt again, not even days later when we sat on a different bus waiting for Asatya to come back from getting snacks, and the bus driver came and started the engine. Asatya jumped through the door of the moving bus as it was pulling out, as many Indian men often do. They always know the precise moment that it's leaving, somehow. It's just true that despite a few less-than-ideal situations, no harm ever came to us, mainly because my brother was there. I hardly knew what I was doing, but he knew what he was doing.

We did find a bus that was going to the Solan side of Shimla. We took it. From there another bus was bound for Solan. We took that one also, although it was crammed full, and the traffic was backed up and very slow.

Late in the evening, the bus stopped in Solan at the end of a dirt road where Asatya's friend (from school) was waiting to walk with us down the hill to his house. There, his family and one more school friend were waiting to greet us with a delicious dinner and music. Asatya's friend teaches music. He played an interesting contraption that looked like an accordion (Asatya knows the name of it.) His song choices included 'Jiye To Jiye Kaise Bin Aapke[3].' It is a very popular Hindi song that has been around for a few decades. I was quite struck by it, as everyone in the house joined in singing. It looks sort of like a love song, but everyone in India loves this song and will sing it for anyone with no need to be asked twice. Sort of like in the American context when we would hear "Sweet Caroline," and no one can resist to sing along.

Later I found it online to memorize the lyrics and I sang it for Asatya bhai on the occasion of the next Raksha Bandhan.[xiii]

The next day, we had lunch with another lady from school, though it felt sort of like an obligation. It felt like an obligation only because she wasn't really a close friend of Bhai ji, but she specifically wanted to meet me. Sure enough, I turned up in her Instagram and FB posts before we even parted ways with her. Yup. She had met up with us to score bragging rights. Haha. Americans are sort of like celebrities in the eyes of many Indians. It was a bit annoying, but harmless.

---

3.   https://youtu.be/b0LpFrr85_Y?si=yROZT3A9gXcAm2XF

During my four-week stay in India, I was approached by no less than five *dozen* strangers, mostly in urban or 'touristy' areas, with requests for selfies. The last time that it happened, after the photo was taken, I said to the young selfie-taking couple, "100 rupees please." They looked almost panicked and speechless, not knowing how to answer me. Maybe it never occurred to them that the foreign tourist might be the one to do the money grabbing. Maybe it never occurred to them that I am a person and not a tourist attraction. They really thought I was serious about the 100 rupees. Everyone present had a good laugh after I reassured them. I joked to Asatya that I should have charged 100 rupees every time, and the selfie fees would have paid the bus fares for all of us. Asatya laughed but said, "For real, you should have; that would absolutely work."

We were to take the train from Solan to Kalka. The Solan train station is at the top of a large hill, so we had to hike up at maximum walking speed to reach it well in time. It was a fun and quaint little station. It had a sort of old-timey look. I knew that it had been built by and for short people, because I accidentally struck my head on an eave at the edge of the waiting area. I am just average height for an American, but in the Indian context, I'm quite tall. The train ride was such fun, to watch the sun setting[4][xiv] on the surrounding mountains as we went along. Partway through the journey, we encountered a pine tree fallen across the tracks. After less than an hour, some local guy known to someone on the train came there with a chainsaw to clean up the tree off of the tracks. At Kalka, we took a bus to Chandigarh just half hour away. Later at Samaji's house, Samaji was annoyed that we were late, in spite of the fact that the tree was 100% out of our control.

It was time to head south into Haryana to go visit Mauna, RK, possibly Agni, and return Vidushi home again.

A month or so earlier, Asatya bhai had talked much with me about Agni. He thought I could initiate contact with her and befriend her, to help mend her broken relationships with her mother, and with Asatya and Prajna, her mama jis. He thought I could be a good influence to her. Bhai ji said that I should do everything I possibly could to make a good first impression, like bringing a gift, touching the feet of her mother-in-law, father-in-

---

4.   https://youtube.com/shorts/zoupeE1hFRI?si=9QZ9oW0Ep6dKWhsX

law, etc. In fact, he was adamant that I should bring a gift. He suggested a new smart phone. I tried to explain to him that I was already breaking the bank by just bringing myself and my daughter to India for a month, but he kept insisting that this was of the greatest importance. I didn't have money for that before leaving home, but I did not tell Asatya because he was so nerved up about it. I thought I could wait until a couple more paychecks went through and just buy one from Chandigarh or even Charkhi Dadri. Well, upon arrival in India, I was so extremely exhausted and disoriented that I forgot. The constant busyness kept me distracted, so I didn't remember about the gift until we were again in Chandigarh preparing to go to Mauna's house.

Actually, while on our road trip through Himachal, Asatya bhai had one or two phone calls with his sister Mauna. Mauna told him that finally, just a couple of days prior, she had talked to Agni about my arrival in India, as Agni didn't even know that I existed before that phone call. Agni was in a rage. She was furious at her mother for allowing her little sister Vidushi to go off with her mama ji Asatya (whom she absolutely hated) and a foreign woman that she had never even heard of before. Well, we all agreed that it seemed very unlikely that Agni would tolerate a visit from me, but we would cross that bridge when we came to it. Meanwhile, I remembered about the gift for Agni, but I thought I should wait and see if a visit to Agni would even be possible, so I would just get the gift from Charkhi Dadri.

It was apparent from these phone calls that Mauna herself was in a hostile mood towards Asatya, and didn't seem willing to cooperate. He kept asking her, "What is the plan?" as we intended to visit her, but she wouldn't say. So, we had no idea what to expect upon arrival in Charkhi Dadri. Would she even receive us? We had no idea.

We took a bus from Chandigarh to Rohtak. From Rohtak we took another bus to Kalanaur. The bus going from Rohtak to Kalanaur was packed like a sardine can, with three men per seat, two more sitting on the back of the seat, and two more standing in the aisle. It was the same for every seat, and more on the roof. I only saw two other women on that overloaded bus, near the front. Perhaps if we had planned ahead better, we would have avoided the Friday rush hour. It occurred to me in that moment how glad I was to not be a lone female traveler... on a bus packed full of 99% men, after dark, in a place I did not know. We sat in the last seat at the back - my daughter on the inside, myself in the middle, and Asatya bhai blocking off the end of the seat. Apparently one or two dudes in a nearby seat said something inappropriate about me, as I heard Asatya snap back at him in Hindi and the other guy quickly shut up. A brother is a great blessing in many ways...

At Kalanaur, we stood by the road waiting and watching many buses go by destined for Bhiwani, but none for Charkhi Dadri. While we stood there, a few guys walking by stopped to talk to Asatya. Although Asatya had not lived in that area since childhood, still they recognized him. Finally after an hour, a bus came for Charkhi Dadri, and we were on our way to Mauna's house.

I had been forewarned about Agni... that she can be a bit of a tyrant or unreasonable. Agni is the older, married daughter of Mauna and RK. Asatya bhai reminded me of the plan, that possibly Agni could have me as a good influence in her life. As it was, she would be like an impervious brick wall to older relatives, unwilling to cooperate. It meant that Agni had hardly any relationship with her other relatives or anyone in the family, except her father and younger sister.

So, they were looking at me as the last ditch effort to reach out to her. In fact, we were concerned that we might have to drop off Vidushi with her parents and then find somewhere Asatya, my daughter, and myself could stay overnight which would not be easy in Haryana... no place anywhere would give a room to an unmarried man and woman and a child... if it came to that, we would have to pretend to be married.

Surprise, surprise, Mauna *was* ready for us. She even invited her friends to greet us, with garlands of carnations and treats to share. Thank God, that went well. Mauna's house is a very typical home that is a bit narrow but has three levels and a flat roof with walls, so that one can go on the roof to escape the heat on hot nights. There is a standard Asian toilet and shower located on the corner of the balcony. There is no hot water heater. To heat water, one must fill a five-gallon bucket, then clamp a heating coil to the side of the bucket so the coil heats the water. One time, I was still a bit sleepy and also unaccustomed to this way of heating water, and I put my hand in the bucket to see if the water was hot yet. Mauna was amazed that I did not electrocute myself. I felt pretty stupid. Asatya bhai was upset at me for making such a dumb and dangerous mistake. Poor Asatya had many things weighing on his mind. Being jobless but still not searching for a new job yet, what would happen at Agni's house if we went, and tension with his sister and older brother. Around this time, Prajnaparadha had left Asatya's apartment, and we didn't know yet where he went. Unfortunately, this was typical of him.

Remember that I was supposed to bring a gift for Agni, and that I still did not have it yet. I thought it wasn't too late that Charkhi Dadri is a city of over a million people and we could surely find something there that would be suitable. When I told Bhai ji about my shopping need, he was very much taken aback. He thought that surely I had arrived there already prepared. Also I had truly underestimated how problematic the relationship with Agni was, and how critical was every detail of diplomacy, though what I knew shouldn't have made a difference...the important thing was that I had promised to bring a gift and there I was not having it with me yet, the day before we would go there.

Mauna had been afraid to tell Agni about me right up until my arrival in Delhi, so I had not even been introduced over the phone. I was a stranger to her (though not to Vidushi who had met me on video calls.) Also, Agni was raised by Asatya and Shweta, who had to be very strict with her as she was rebellious as a teenager. Agni hated Asatya. Bhai ji felt that the family was relying on me as a last resort, that I had made a promise to do my part, and I blew it. Bhai ji's trust in me was shattered. He said that without trust, what is left?? I said that we could go into the city to shop (we had an evening and morning free before going to Agni's house), but it was like he couldn't hear me; he said there was no time. Also, he seemed to forget with the population explosion that it was not a little town anymore.

He was very angry and said that he would put me and my daughter on a bus for Delhi in the morning. He meant to send me home. He felt betrayed and he didn't want to talk to me - possibly ever again. He found it hard to believe that I had neglected this thing by mistake.

His eyes had a fierceness that I had never seen in anyone. It seemed like they had gone black, and he could cut through me with those eyes. It was truly terrifying.

It is absolutely true that all his life, Asatya had been accustomed to disappointment, to mean and irresponsible acts done by others. Bhai ji trusted me, but this incident brought all his doubts and fears to the surface. Two years prior to this, the voice of God in my heart pushed me very hard and told me that I must do my all to support and lift up Asatya, by whatever means. I didn't know what exactly God had in mind to do with Asatya, but it was obviously extremely important. That day that Asatya spoke so harshly to me, saying he would send me home, I felt that I would fail in the task that God gave, if I lost Asatya, and I believed that this task was one of the most important of my life...

That day and night was the most stressful and painful of my life up to that point. I knew absolutely everything would change if I went home early. Bhai ji would once again be alone in the world, and he would be dead on the inside.

No one in my life would believe me again but would forever question my judgement of people. I didn't feel safe. I was in a foreign country with my young daughter, in a small town where few people spoke English. It was three hours by different buses to get back to Delhi. I would have to buy new plane tickets. If Asatya could just ship me off like that, I worried what else he would do if I ever disappointed him again. There was so much at stake. I could not eat or sleep, and the internal pain grew into a physical pain in my chest. What could I do?? I knew that Asatya bhai was too angry to receive an apology or to listen to me. Trying to explain myself had backfired in the past, so I knew that would not work. And yet, if we didn't talk about it, then it was over. Every minute felt like an hour. I was praying for calm, trying not to panic. Asatya had never taken action against me like this before, so I was totally blindsided.

Ausmerrone was there in the house, trying to entertain herself and work on a writing task for school while waiting for Vidushi to return from her school. I felt like I was in shock and trying to look normal for my daughter's sake. I had no idea how I would explain to her that we had to go home right away. I was physically ill.

Finally, Bhai ji calmed himself enough to think a bit more clearly. I had originally planned to give Agni a new phone. Since I didn't have that yet, and Asatya was not taking me into town to shop, I was prepared to substitute my own phone. I was ready to upload and backup all my photos and other things to iCloud and to take out the SIM card. Asatya refused to let me give that. He said it would be mean to take that from me. Maybe he realized that he still cared about my well-being in that moment. Maybe he saw my willingness to do anything to fix my mistake. I don't know what he was thinking. I only know that finally by mid-day the next day, as I was sitting on the dirty floor of the roof with my head down, Bhai ji asked, "Should I give you another chance?" I said that for a second chance to happen, he must be willing to let me prove my trustworthiness. I would have to regain his trust through my own effort, but he would have to be willing to let me, and in the end, trust doesn't just happen on its own; it is a conscious choice.

We did not go to Delhi. We did not even tell Mauna or RK what had happened, just that I brought money thinking that we don't know Agni's needs and she could use the money as she thought best.

In this, I learned that great damage can be done even when the intentions of the heart are right.

Actually, Asatya bhai said that the end result is more important than the intention. I thought that didn't sound right, although I could understand that it's true that one must live with the result, whether it be good or bad, so results do matter. However, shouldn't what is in a person's heart matter? Maybe it is just that Bhai ji was thinking that actions speak louder than words. It is true that he had difficulty trusting people, even me.

Bhai ji warned me, reminding me of Agni's last interaction with her parents.

He said, "She might slap you, or she might love you." At least I was going knowing that ahead of time. I was told that I could back out. However, that did not seem like a viable choice to me, considering that last conversation with Asatya. Bhai ji didn't want to force me, knowing the visit might not go well for me. I decided to take a huge leap out of my comfort zone and just do it. I felt that I had to prove my good intentions to my brother.

I have to say, the general area and Agni's neighborhood in particular feels very patriarchal and restrictive. Even Asatya bhai once called Haryana the 'Taliban of India.' The customs around marriage, gender roles, women's freedoms (or lack thereof) and traditions around food and drink, do look sort of 'taliban-ish,' to people like me from the outside. Even Agni would keep her head covered in her own home although the only guests were family. The head covering is called 'purdah[5].'[xv]

Agni's village, like most villages in India, was a tight labyrinth of narrow streets and alleyways in between concrete homes and shops. Outside the village, fields are broken into family plots lined with trees and dirt roads. Mustard, wheat, sugarcane, and cotton can be found growing there in abundance. At Agni's house, first only the two little girls and I went into the house. We agreed that we would have RK and Asatya come upstairs later, only if it seemed okay to do so. We greeted Agni's father-in-law and mother-in-law with the standard foot-touching ritual. It is very normal in India that sons stay in their parent's home all their lives; they simply just move upstairs or build an addition onto their parent's house. Daughters go to live with their husband at their in-law's house. You can see how sons in practical terms are sort of assets, while daughters are a sort of liability, because it is the sons and their wives that care for the parents in their old age. That and getting a daughter married is expensive - the cost of the wedding itself, plus a dowry to send with her. Dowries are very often still given although they are illegal. Most families try to not show sexism, but this system favors boys.

I climbed the stairs to the second floor apartment with much apprehension. Knowing the prickly mood of Agni, and the tension of hopeful expectation of those who brought me there, I had never been further away from my comfort zone in my life.

I am an introvert that much prefers to mind my own business, and I avoid conflict like the plague. Yet there I was, a typically reclusive New Englander acting as a mediator for a feisty Haryanvi family. Only love of these people could motivate me like this...also I was determined that Bhai ji regain his faith in me.

Agni was there, with her four-year-old daughter and her husband. She greeted me with a straight face. I gave a simple and diplomatic introduction. She invited me to sit in her bedroom (which meant private conversation.) I don't remember all that was said, but Agni politely declined to accept any gift or money from me. She was pleasant but not exuberant. I tried

5.   https://en.wikipedia.org/wiki/Purdah

to introduce myself as her 'mausi,' (mother's sister) but she said, "No, I'm beti!" Which meant that she wanted me to think of her as my daughter, not just a niece.

I told Vidushi to go downstairs to bring up the gifts from the rest of the family. She misinterpreted and brought up not just the things but also RK *and* Asatya. Agni hardly spoke to Asatya (her Mama ji), but she did not yell him out of the house, and that was a *very* significant development.

Agni made dinner for everyone, and it was good. She even sent the left-overs home with us. By the end of the evening, everyone was smiling, and we had some photos together as well. What a great relief.

While staying at Mauna's house in Charkhi Dadri, RK took us by bus to Pilani, Rajasthan to visit a small religious site there. It was a tower paint-ed red, with a bell. It was situated at the top of the only hill, which required climbing barefoot over about two hundred steps to reach the top. RK went slowly, but I was impressed that he reached the top, after lung cancer, and the covid several months before. I remember eating lunch at a dirty-looking little diner in Pilani. The food was very cheap but very good, and there was a boy bringing chapatis who was most attentive.

In Charkhi Dadri, Mauna took us shopping for clothes. Bhai ji got matching track suits (sweats) for the girls. Mauna insisted that I should have no less than three new suits. She wanted the bragging Samaji to shut up about being the best hostess. We picked out some fabric for me and brought it to a tailor to drop it off and measure me. A suit is a woman's complete outfit, composed of pants (leggings, Patiala, palazzo, or other style,) a long tunic with side slits called a kurti, and a dupatta, which is a decorative scarf used for styling or head covering in some places.

On our last day in Charkhi Dadri, Mauna's friend and her daughter came, and our driver, Bhai ji, three women and three girls all piled into that little car to visit a couple places known to Mauna - an ashram and a tem-ple nearby. The temple reminded me a bit of a Catholic Church, as it had many murals, incense or candles everywhere, and small figurines or idols. As someone that is neither Catholic nor Hindu, I was struck by the sim-ilarities, and still am. The chants, songs, and traditions are all different in detail, but it's like they follow the same format.

I AM FAMILY

We had a picnic at the ashram. To our surprise, Mauna's friend had brought some of her grandmother's traditional Haryanvi clothes that she wanted me and my daughter to try on so they could photograph us - just for fun. I hate lipstick and I also hate red, but I found myself wearing both. I also hate to pose for cameras or have people staring at me, so it was a little uncomfortable. However, these other women and Bhai ji also, were so much amused by it, I was glad to make them happy.

I could not stop myself from laughing in photos... I felt ridiculous to be forced out of character.

Asatya bhai, my daughter, and I took the bus back into Delhi, crossed the city by metro, and went to the home of RK's nephew. He seemed alright. His wife looked cold and aloof but at least she fed us.

I asked Bhai ji about this later. He said there may be some gossip about him from RK's side of the family, as he is not very close to RK and his sister Mauna tends to fight with him, so she likely hadn't said anything nice about her brother.

The next day, we traversed Delhi to come to Vyapari's house. Vyapari is not a very close friend, but he is a lifelong friend of Asatya ji going back to the sixth grade. At that time, Vyapari, his wife, and two teenage sons lived in a comfortable but small apartment building on the west side of Delhi. Vyapari designs, makes, and sells tiles for flooring and home decor. He took us to see his showroom and manufacturing facility. Vyapari and his wife took us to see a historic site in Delhi known as Qutab Minar, and also to Taj Mahal in Agra, Uttar Pradesh. Vyapari and his family have a relaxed, sort of Americanesque vibe, though they are still thoroughly Indian. We had a lovely visit with them.

Vyapari seemed like someone with more exposure or perspective. I thought I could talk to him about my job, but it didn't work. I was cleaning for work at the time. Cleaning is considered to be one of the lowliest jobs in India. He got the impression that I was very poor which doesn't make sense... I had just spent a lot of money to bring myself and my daughter to India. The truth is that my husband and I own multiple properties and have multiple sources of income. The cleaning was just to have extra for travel and savings. I believe that was a good example of how hard it can be to escape the prejudices, worldviews, or superstitions that one has been raised in and surrounded by throughout life. An open mind can happen only by a very conscious act of the will.

After visiting Vyapari and his family, we were supposed to meet up with a friend of Asatya (also named Asatya Bhratra) who is from the same area of Uttar Pradesh as Tamo. Asatya Bhratra runs an academic institution that targets mainly college students that just want additional instruction so they may perform well in exams. My brother Asatya had first met him a few years prior when Asatya Bhratra had hired him as an instructor.

Interestingly, my brother Asatya never succeeded to finish high school, much less did he ever acquire any teaching degree, but nevertheless, he taught a teacher's final exam prep course. His students were destined to have the bachelor's degree in education weeks after completing his course. Asatya ji always encouraged honest study and never tolerated any cheating ever. Incredibly, every student of his passed their final exams. Bhai ji has zero credentials and yet he had the knowledge and skill to bring every student of his up to the required level set by the central government.

As we were preparing to go there, Asatya Bhratra wasn't answering his phone. Maybe he was busy, I don't know. We didn't have a plan B; we were just supposed to go to his house that night. Well, we had to land somewhere for the night... In fact, I was not quite aware of the issue. I wasn't sure what was next, but I had become so very comfortable and felt so safe to be with Bhai ji, to the point that just being in Asatya's presence would cause such a great feeling of peace to wash over me, so I was content to just blindly follow Asatya wherever like a small child. I knew that no matter what, no one could touch us as long as he was there with us. It wasn't until we had already been on the bus for 45 minutes, that I asked Asatya bhai out of curiosity, "Where are we going?" Bhai ji had contacted a distant relative living in Rohtak, who was better known to Mauna.

Mauna was supposed to meet us at a landmark in Rohtak, to escort us to that house, as it was not easy to find. We didn't see Mauna. Apparently, there was another place in Rohtak with exactly the same name and she was there. Then she said to meet her somewhere else near there. It ended up being an hour-long wild goose chase.

While looking for Mauna, we were walking along roadsides that did not all have street lights. Ausmerrone and I almost walked right into live wires that were hanging randomly from an electrical pole. I saw it at the last second. I never let go of my daughter's hand any time that we walked on the streets.

When we finally caught up with Mauna, Asatya was angry. He argued loudly with her there on that quiet street. Finally, he slapped her, then horrified me by telling me to also slap her. After his blow-up at me the week before, I couldn't correct him, that would make him angry at me again, and I had no idea what he might do in that case. At least I did not slap Mauna. I could understand Asatya's frustration, but he was overreacting and abusing his sister, right there in front of me, my daughter, and their relatives. Asatya told Mauna to go home. She went, and I don't blame her for not wanting to stay.

Our host was a widow with her three young adult children living together. They welcomed us into their house for the night. That lady must have been skeptical of us, I feel sure. It is a part of India that is very conservative and old-fashioned in human relationships. In particular, interactions between men and women who are not biologically related are very minimal. Even married women hardly address their own father-in-law. Well, there we were, a brother and sister unrelated by blood, plus an 11-year-old girl. My daughter lightened the mood with her usual humor and silly antics. The widow's two daughters walked my daughter down the street to meet a litter of feral puppies. I think the puppies' mother was accustomed to attention... some feral dogs are friendly and approachable and others, one must shoo away.

At last, we had made a plan with Asatya Bhratra. His wife was very excited to meet an American lady, although she hardly knew five sentences of English. She was a cute young woman who was a perfect hostess and even woke up at four o'clock to make an amazing breakfast for everyone. She wanted to hand-feed me for a photo which was something that I had never encountered before, but I have seen other Indians doing this, mostly at special occasions. It's a gesture of affection.

Around 4:30am, Asatya Bhratra took us (Asatya bhai, my daughter, and I) on a road trip to Jaipur, Rajasthan. Jaipur was eight or more hours away, by taking main routes. It was a hot day, about 100 degrees Fahrenheit, but a bit dry and breezy.

That day was the first time for either me or my daughter to see both an elephant and a camel in their native environment. Really, we saw so much wildlife in India including the obvious feral dogs, wandering buffalo, families of monkeys, peacocks, squirrels, crows (they look different,) parrots, geckos, and teenagers.

Jaipur looks exactly like something out of a medieval novel. It hardly seems real. Although it is situated on the plains, at that place there are several small mountains jutting up out of the two-dimensional landscape. They are some of the oldest mountains on earth, so I was told.

The city is nestled between these mountains with a small lake beside it. The city is walled in with gates at the main roads leading into it. There is another wall surrounding the city that goes along the ridges of the hills and there are two or three forts on the wall, at the peaks.

We visited two forts. At one fort, my daughter's hat blew away in a gust of wind, to an area below us where some wandering goats were grazing. As other tourists looked on curiously, I ran down around the bend in the road and climbed over the low wall to where the goats were. I rescued the hat just before the curious goats reached it. We did not spend very much time in the actual city. Mostly, we spent the day wandering around exploring the forts and taking photos which was fun and interesting.

At one point, we stopped to use a public bathroom. I set down a water bottle in there as I did not want to get it germy, but I forgot it and left it in there. I remembered ten minutes later, but it had been stolen already.

At the same bathroom, I waited at the other side of a courtyard for Bhai ji to come back from the toilets, but I could see him lingering there and scolding a man. I asked about it after he returned. He told us that the bathroom was filthy, and the sink did not even work, so why should he pay to use the toilet? He asked the bathroom attendant what on earth he was doing with his time if not maintaining the bathroom. He had one job! Should he pay him to do nothing?

This is an interesting point about Asatya bhai. Being Haryanvi, he does not shy away from conflict. It is true that he is right most of the time, and he has a highly developed sense of right and wrong, and of justice. He is willing to take the time to address issues that most people either sweep under the rug, or else they are annoyed about a thing but not willing to do anything to change it. This makes some people around him uncomfortable, but many others I've witnessed, have a sense of relief that someone has enough backbone to speak out.

That hot day, we all had at least three kulfis. Kulfi is a dessert made of milk and jaggery (unprocessed dried sugarcane juice) that has been reduced in a pot, then pistachios, coconut or other things might be added to it. Then it is frozen in the form of a popsicle and sold on the street.

We left Jaipur after sunset. It was a very long but memorable day. My brother Asatya and the other Asatya took turns driving, but I knew they would need me at some point, so I took a nap in the car. At 3:30am, I was awakened by a request for relief from the driver's seat.

It was my first time driving with a manual transmission in over 10 years, and my first time ever driving on the *left* side of the road. At this point, we were approaching the outer Delhi arterial. At this time of night, traffic was reasonable. I discovered at that time, why everyone in India uses their horns liberally. All the large trucks have no side mirrors. If you want the truck drivers to be aware of your presence, you simply have to make a lot of noise and sometimes flash your high beams. To me as an American, that felt rude to do, although it was necessary. I didn't notice this at first. I dutifully switched on my turn signal out of habit, which hardly anyone in India ever does. Unfortunately, the windshield wipers were situated exactly where the turn signal would ordinarily be in my own car, so I turned on the wipers several times without meaning to.

All of this was a bit disorienting and required greater focus. In spite of all that, my driving skills had made a significant impression on Asatya Bhratra, and he was even more impressed to know that I had been driving since the age of 17. Of course, where I am from, 17 is a bit late to start driving, but in India that is very young to be driving, and many women don't even drive at all. I can understand why not; it's a hot mess out there. Meanwhile, Bhai ji Asatya was doing the most expert backseat driving of his life. He refused to let me surpass even 40kph in the slow lane, even though we were on the highway. Of course, I could drive much faster, but I think my lack of understanding around how to pass other vehicles the Indian way was making him nervous.

Finally, we reached Asatya Bhratra's house around 4am. His wife was just getting up to start making tea and breakfast. Naturally, we all went to sleep immediately.

Around 9am, I was awakened by Asatya Bhratra's wife when she came into the room to say "Up! You eat!" I didn't want to be rude, but I wanted so much to sleep. She wasn't having that. So, I went out of my room to eat... it looked like only the women and kids were home. Asatya Bhratra appeared to not be there. I wanted to ask his wife where the men were, but she seemed to have trouble understanding even Google translate. Asatya Bhai's door was shut. Maybe he had followed Asatya Bhratra to work or maybe he was still in there... it turned out that Asatya was still sleeping. It felt unfair that he got to sleep more while I was awakened so soon. Well, I could understand her not going into the bedroom of a male guest, but she didn't even knock on the door. Asatya Bhratra returned from his teaching duties around midday.

There was a lady known to Bhai ji who lived in the same village, who had her heart set on meeting us, so we went to meet her at her school. There we were greeted with flowers and treats, like Mauna had done. She brought out a few small gifts as well. We ate lunch there and many teachers and students came in to gawk or sneak into group photos. I remember this lady seemed a little over the top. She dressed all in red, with perfect makeup and red lipstick.

She literally squealed when she saw me. More than once. It looked like Taylor Swift had come to town. As a modest introvert, it was uncomfortable, but I politely let this woman do what made her happy.

To tell the truth, her attitude was not at all unusual. You remember all the street selfies.

We also walked down the street to meet the parents of Asatya Bhratra, which meant more foot-touching and greetings of "Namste ji. Sab log kaise hain?" ("Hello Sir/Ma'am. How is everyone?") Another home visited, another gift to find space for in our crowded bags. They sent us home with a vibrant, thick, soft blanket. It is still on my daughter's bed to this day.

When we stayed at Bhai ji's apartment in Solan, the overnight temperatures were in the forties. Indians in the northern states are accustomed to wearing thermals and sweaters every day in winter, possibly even hats and outer coats, even indoors as no one has heat. However, the blankets are thicker than any I've ever seen. They could put a carpet to shame. If you were to use two, you would be warm even if the temps fell below freezing. We were quite comfortable. From my perspective, the only real discomfort of winter in India is taking a bath or shower in an unheated bathroom.

Asatya Bhratra drove us to a busy intersection on route 44. Route 44 runs north/south between Delhi and Chandigarh, so it should have taken seconds to find the bus we needed to go north on that route. We stood there at the edge of the road on that very busy intersection for over an hour. Motorbikes cut corners... we were on the corner. The sun was setting and this time it wasn't me who felt insecure in that place; this was not the lovely, innocent Shimla. This was on the Haryana/Uttar Pradesh border which just isn't the same. At that point, it seemed safer to take any ride than to continue standing there. Strangely, there didn't seem to be any buses destined for Yamunanagar, which was where we needed to go. Asatya bhai was approaching taxis and Ubers.

He couldn't find any ride for Yamunanagar except from one man who happened to be going that way. I heard the drop-off location and the mutually agreed on amount to be paid on arrival. Everything was fine until about halfway through the trip. The man was mostly speaking Hindi but also some Telugu, which Asatya knows well, but never English.

The fact that he never spoke a word of English mattered not at all. I found that in general, I could understand more of conversation than people realized, because of their intonations, hand gestures, and use of a few common words that I did know.

So then, I could understand exactly what happened next. The man smiled and said something to Bhai ji. I could see Bhai ji open his calculator to confirm the math for the kilometers traveled multiplied by the agreed rupees per kilometer. Asatya bhai said something to the man to which the man replied "Nahin," (no) but he still smiled. It continued back and forth like this for several minutes. The driver was beginning to look cocky and had a sort of mocking look as he laughed. Bhai ji's voice was beginning to sound stern. Asatya bhai opened his phone to show his math to the driver. The driver was disagreeing, saying something different and laughing.

When the driver realized that Bhai ji would not back down, he pulled off to the side of the road. We were miles away from anything, and anyone that we knew. At this point, I knew that there was a real chance that the evening could end very badly for Asatya ji, but I never questioned that my daughter and I would be fine. Whatever was going to happen at that point, I knew that Asatya was going to bear the brunt of it. It was a reassuring thought, and yet I never ever wanted my brother in harm's way.

I thought the driver might try to force us out of the vehicle, there on the highway in the middle of nowhere.

The man had gotten out of the car and maybe was calling someone... Bhai ji got out. (We didn't want to drive off and be accused of theft; Asatya bhai would certainly have gone to jail for a few years.) He tried to wrestle the man back into the car. After several minutes, he finally forced that cunning man back into the car.

We succeeded in reaching the next city which was Karnal, before the man pulled over again. This time he would not get back in, and we could see him talking on the phone. What for? For a friend to bring back up? Now that we had reached Karnal, it was possible that we might find another bus, maybe. Not yet. Bhai ji wanted to teach that man a lesson.

All this time, I had seriously instructed my daughter to keep quiet and do not get out of the car under any circumstances. We kept the back doors locked, just in case the driver might try to force us out. She cooperated and stayed calm, perhaps not fully understanding that the circumstances were sketchy at best. I took a photo of the man from where I was sitting in the backseat, just in case.

We called the police and just waited. Police came. They talked to Asatya. They talked to the driver. They took us all to the police station to further sort out the matter. Bhai ji explained to me what had happened in the car, which was precisely what I thought had happened based on what I had observed:

Part way through our journey, the driver tried to gaslight Asatya bhai into thinking he had misunderstood the deal, and that he actually owed more. In fact, that pompous prick was demanding several times more than the original amount. Maybe he thought we were sort of hostages and that he could force us to comply. Remember the driver had stopped randomly on the highway, perhaps to show that he wouldn't drive unless we paid, but Asatya bhai forced him to keep his word, which only got us as far as Karnal.

At first the police were listening to Bhai ji, but after some time they began siding with the driver. They said to Asatya ji that no one forced him to get in that car, that it was his choice, but they ignored the fact that an agreement had been broken. I had witnessed Asatya bhai slap that driver on the side of the highway, and I worried the driver might cry victim, but the police agreed with Asatya that the man had deserved it. (Remember, this was in Haryana.)

After a couple hours of standing around talking, nothing was resolved. It clearly was a slow night at the station, with four or five police officers standing around debating a shady impromptu Uber driver. While they talked, I took a piece of paper and started writing a report of the incident to formally submit. I dated and signed it.

The police were not cooperating. I told them all seriously that as an American guest in their country, I had the right to complain to the U.S. embassy. I had found myself in an insecure situation, and that the local police did nothing to help when I reached out to them, and I could report them at a much higher level. All of them suddenly changed their tune and wanted to be helpful.

That night, we were intending to meet up again with Samaji and her family, as they still had some of our bags at their house. We were going to celebrate Holi with them. Bhai ji called Samaji's husband to let him know why we were so late and still had not reached them. Bhai ji told me that Samaji's husband was furious. He and Samajj had it in their minds that word might get around that a guest of theirs had an unfortunate encounter where the police had become involved, and they thought this might reflect poorly on them. They never expressed a single word of concern for our well-being. Samaji's husband was ready to disown us if we made any formal complaint with the police, even though the incident had absolutely nothing to do with him. He threatened Asatya bhai that he would toss our belongings out onto the street (which does mean our things would all be stolen, including the copies of our visas and other documents.) At that point, it was clear to Asatya and I that those people had no love for us. They were only shmoozing until we proved to be useful. The second we looked like a potential liability (however small), the niceness was over. After Samaji's husband yelled at Bhai ji on the phone, Bhai ji had to request me that I not submit that police report... mostly we just wanted to be diplomatic enough that our things would still be there when we returned. Also, Samaji's husband was still working on Asatya's visa project.

Later after I was at home again in Maine, Asatya bhai and I reflected on my visit and we both came to the conclusion that most of the trouble that we encountered during my stay could have been avoided by choosing to hire a personal chauffeur for our travel needs. The buses were ok but sometimes not dependable, asking friends for rides meant that we were captive to their schedules and whims. Renting cars isn't done much in India and the cost is close to the cost of simply hiring a driver/chauffeur. Hiring our own driver and car would not be the cheapest but would eliminate some potential problems and allow more freedom. Ordinarily Asatya ji travels alone and his motorbike is adequate, but with a sister, niece, and others at times, a car would be best.

Grudgingly, I tore up the police report. Samaji's brother-in-law came to pick us up from the station at Karnal.

We joined them at their father's house in Yamunanagar, which is a small city near to the place where the state borders of Haryana, Uttar Pradesh, and Himachal converge, on the Yamuna River.

Everyone at the house greeted us as if nothing had ever happened. It was so obviously fake, but at least no one was fighting. The elderly father was pleasant and peaceful, as most grandparents are. He lived there with his other son and granddaughter. The granddaughter took my daughter for a ride around town on her scooter, which was my daughter's first time on any motorized two-wheeler. I had just got my first saree which I wanted to wear for the occasion of Holi. It was a deep, vibrant blue, which had an ombré fading into green. It had tie-dye dots all over, and a golden embroidered edge, which is called zari. Samaji, who loved any excuse for shopping, overheard me mention the saree. She said that I of course must do it properly and even though it was a holiday, she inquired with a few tailors to see who she could pressure into making the blouse for the saree right then on the spot. I didn't want to bother any tailors on a holiday, but Samaji was on a mission. One tailor agreed and a few hours later, I had a sleeveless silk crop top in the same material as the saree. Samaji got a matching slip, and I was ready to suit up. A saree gets pinned to the slip, then wrapped around the waist, and 4-5 pleats or folds are made at the waist and pinned again to the slip. The remaining fabric is wrapped around the back, under the opposite arm and up over the shoulder, usually with more folds.

Samaji was not done. My daughter and I were whisked away to a neighbor's mehandi parlor. Most westerners know mehandi by the name 'henna.' My daughter and I then spent an hour sitting doing absolutely nothing while waiting for our mehandi tattoos to dry. As a busy mother of teens, it felt weird to sit doing nothing. Well, next thing I knew, the other two women in the house were bringing out makeup and hair things... I was beginning to feel like a doll that was just there for these ladies to play dress up with, but I admit that we looked nice.

My daughter wore a very busy looking but lovely lehengi (skirt) with a matching tie-back blouse.

The morning was a delightful blur of snacking on fruits and sweets, and the most epic water battle in the street. Some people could be seen working coconut oil into their hair which I didn't understand until later when I tried to clean bright colored stains out of my clothes... the coconut oil was meant to prevent colors from soaking into the hair and scalp. My daughter had a few pink spots on her scalp for the next two weeks or so.

We filled a large tub full of water balloons. Water guns were brought out. Pouches of chalky, neon colors were lying about everywhere. The adults could be seen sweetly and gently painting small amounts of the chalky colors onto each other's faces and taking selfies together. Ah, so polite and innocent.

However, my daughter, who had no concept of Holi traditions, saw the water balloons and water guns, and she absolutely did know what those were for. The morning of playing in the street slowly escalated into an all-out color war, and there was quite a lot of chasing and screaming and laughing and drenching! There was not a person in dry clothes anywhere within blocks. Every person, every tree, every wall and all the streets were awash with blue, pink, yellow, and green.

That night, we got our dinner from Burger King. Apparently, it was the tradition of this particular family to get take-out on holidays. I was surprised to see that the Burger King had a drive-through as I had assumed that drive-throughs are just an American thing. Unsurprisingly, the menu was strictly vegetarian, which meant veggie burgers.

There never was another word breathed about the driver/police incident. Samaji and her husband reverted back to their vague attempts at shmoozing. All Bhai ji and I wanted was to inconspicuously sneak out the back door of that relationship.

That night, we were back at the house in Mohali, gathering our remaining things. When we had arrived in India, I had purposefully left one bag half empty, knowing that I might buy a couple items or that there might be gifts. We had been given at least seven new outfits, plus several other items including that blanket from Asatya Bhratra's parents. No matter how I packed, it was not possible to fit everything. Samaji sent us home with one of her backpacks and she chuckled, saying that she knew she was partly to blame for us returning home with so much stuff.

The next day, we had a private driver pick us up from the house to take us to the airport in Delhi.

Mohali/Chandigarh to Delhi is a five hour journey on a good day. Driving in a straight line almost without stopping, on a cloudless day, the horizon could be seen closing in a bit and becoming more hazy. The area around Delhi has notoriously bad air quality. In contrast, the air in the hill state of Himachal Pradesh nearby is nearly as clean as that of my home state, Maine.

For an entire month, we had lived out of backpacks and stayed in no less than nine homes plus a hotel. All that time, we hardly carried our own bags. Every time, Bhai ji would be taking our bags even if all he had free was just his little finger. This was just one of many small examples of someone who didn't have good qualities and behaviors modeled to him, as he had practically raised himself without parents and living at his school, and somehow he knew deep in his soul the way that things really should be in an ideal world. Maybe it is that when a person experiences the lack of something, they become very much aware of the need for it. Asatya's mother was an innocent young lady who was highly responsible and worked like a single mother to give her kids a good life. Bhai ji loved her more than anyone, and he never saw anyone offer her any support or kindness, not even to help carry her things...Asatya bhai has always known the irreplaceable nature of a mother and he has always shown extra respect for mothers in general.

At the airport, Bhai ji stayed with me and my daughter until it was time for us to find our gate. I knew it would be at least a year or more before we would be in the same place together again. My daughter and I wanted more than anything to bring him with us. It is just true that I had spent three years looking for a way for him to come and live near us or at least be free and eligible to visit any time. Only God really knows just how many hundreds of hours I have spent to research and inquire about every possible immigration route, and the efforts made towards that end; just everything imaginable. I had even made a plan for him to possibly immigrate to New Brunswick and had met with an immigration lawyer from there. Immigrating to the U.S. seemed too hard, but Canada has favorable immigration laws and New Brunswick isn't far from where I live with my family.

Finally, we were in line to enter the airport and pass by the first round of security. My daughter and I touched Bhai ji's feet and hugged him. Giving only the very best of both Indian and American goodbyes seemed appropriate in the moment though Asatya ji has always been too modest to feel comfortable having his feet touched.

At the gate, I had only 300 rupees left in cash. The nearby snack shops only took cash. We ate a little something outside with Asatya bhai, but we were hungry again. I just got my daughter some kulfi, and then my rupees were gone. I had hoped to keep at least one bill as a souvenir, but oh well. Two years later I was cleaning my room and found a five-rupee coin.

Our plane arrived at JFK airport at 7am just as the sun was rising. Our entire 16-hour flight had been in the dark. We took the metro back to Penn station, then walked north for several blocks to the bus station, passing the Empire State Building on the way. My daughter was chipper and energetic this whole time, until around lunchtime when she finally fell into a dead sleep on the bus.

With the chaos in Ukraine, and other world events, the price of fuel had gone up sharply and people in the area were preferring trains over driving... I couldn't find any available train seats for under $300. Wild. Even the bus was a bit more pricey than usual, it was reasonable. We got off the bus in Providence and drove home the remaining four hours. Just two hours from home, I pulled over to take a brief car nap. The total journey coming home without sleep (except one nap in the plane) was nearly 40 hours. We arrived home safely around 10pm.

2022

No sooner had we parted ways at the airport, then Asatya ji went straight from there to spend the night with a nearby relative, then attended a job interview near Gurugram. He stayed there and worked at that school for about one month. He couldn't stay any longer than that because of several factors, one being abysmal management. Teachers were never allowed to sit. Not good for Bhai's bad disc. Monkeys lingered on the roof of Asatya's room, where they could pounce on him any time he walked through the doorway. There were problems all around and it was over all, a poor fit for him.

Asatya bhai had another interview for a place in Nahan, which is in Himachal, a bit to the east side of the state. He felt skeptical of it as he only saw an office and no classrooms, so he couldn't see how many students there were, or how the school was managed. The salary that was offered seemed reasonable, though it did entail being a hostel warden in addition to teaching.

A hostel warden is like a live-in parent for the boarding students. He would be responsible for overseeing the safety and good behavior of the students in his dorm, both while they were present in the dorm/hostel, as well as accompanying them around school grounds or on outings. Also, he was responsible for receiving guests and deliveries, and for overseeing maintenance of the hostel.

Well, Bhai ji was single and didn't have kids, so he agreed to this, as it meant earning a bit more, and saving money on food and rent.

While teaching at Nahan, Bhai ji befriended an older gentleman named Charles. Charles was from a Catholic family and was himself a Christian. Charles was not close like family, but he remained a friend and would often inquire about Asatya ji's well-being.

The school in Nahan didn't maintain good discipline with students, and sometimes this put Asatya bhai in the circumstance of needing to discipline his students or hostel residents to avoid escalating situations that put him or other students at risk. It happened one time that Asatya bhai was talking very seriously to one problematic and provocative student and he slapped that kid.

There is an unfortunate mismatch in India right now, between the way that Bhai ji and all his generation were raised (misbehaving children were beaten, whether by teachers or parents) and today it is illegal for teachers to issue any form of physical punishment. Old habits die hard, and many teachers and parents still slap kids that are out of line. In Asatya's case, there is more to unlearn, as anger and some mild violence are culturally a bit more accepted in Haryana than in other parts of the world. Bhai ji knows that this is wrong and toxic and conscientiously chooses to be as diplomatic as possible, but still the student slapping has happened more than once, mostly because the principal or MD left him unsupported in a bad situation. It even happened once that there was a boy known to prey on unsuspecting female students and the administrators did nothing about it. The other students needed to be protected somehow. Ethical dilemmas are not fun or fair to anyone.

Well, this one student in Nahan was well aware of the 'no-touch' law and complained to his parents, who complained to the school owner.

Meanwhile, Bhai ji had contracted covid from a student in his hostel. He became so sick that his fever made him delirious, and his head was screaming in pain. His throat was in such pain, and swollen so badly that he could not swallow at all, nor could he talk. I recognized this as a real emergency. He was becoming dangerously dehydrated but unable to ask for help and too weak to take himself to a hospital. Also, at what point would his inflamed throat cause breathing to become difficult or reach a life-threatening state?

We had agreed long before this that it would be wise that we both have a phone number of someone who lives nearby to the other, in case of emergency. In this case, I believe it saved Asatya's life.

I contacted Mr. Charles and explained the situation. Mr. Charles came to collect Asatya from his bed. The people at the hospital neglected Asatya bhai. All he really needed was an IV drip. An anti-inflammatory medicine would have been useful too. It was just a small hospital in a small town - there were not a lot of English speakers that I could talk to, to advocate for my brother. I had Mr. Charles speak up for Asatya ji's needs and finally he got the IV drip, and five or six medicines prescribed. Interestingly, one of the medicines was actually a substance that is primarily used by surgeons to sterilize surfaces. Asatya bhai was instructed to gargle with it. His throat was swollen. Gargling seemed laughable. If only he could laugh...

My dear brother would never miss a day of work, even if he had to teach through nausea or a migraine, but this sickness took him out of the classroom for about ten days. During this time, the parents of the slapped student had put a lot of pressure on the school owner. In the end, the owner had to fire Asatya to save face - and to not lose the tuition fees from that student.

Mr. Charles like a true friend, tried hard to advocate for Bhai ji - both in that school and with professional acquaintances in other schools. He arranged for Asatya bhai to visit and interview with a school in the Chamba district - a high-ranking school beside the border with Jammu, and not far from Pakistan. It is built right into the mountainside. Asatya doubted that they would really consider him, as he had no teaching degree, and it seemed like a really excellent school with highly professional and qualified staff. The location was breath-taking. It is in a somewhat remote area. Chamba is famous for mountain sides like walls, and scary-looking narrow roads snaking along cliffs and meandering through tunnels. It is a region rich with history and culture. There, as is the case throughout Himachal, you can find signs of pride in Tibetan heritage. Indians never forget who they are and where they are from.

Chamba gets several inches of snow in mid-winter, making it even less accessible, which is perhaps why the academic year runs from March-November. The school grounds seem equally lovely with a sprawling campus and spacious outdoor areas. The indoor spaces are more modest but still ok.

The interviewer said that they would call him back later in February to confirm the position. How to take that? Should Asatya have kept searching for another job? They didn't give a hard no or yes. Surely, they would find a better candidate in the meantime...

As Asatya bhai was driving back from Chamba, he felt desperate to find some work. He didn't know if he would receive a call back from the Chamba school, and the start of their academic year was still months away. He inquired about teaching positions along the route as he made his way south-east through Punjab[1][xvi]. He talked with two different guys in the small city of Mukerian. He took a job as an instructor for an IELTS prep school. Most of his students were young adults looking to attend a university overseas, as receiving a reasonably high score in the IELTS exam is a requirement for admission of foreign students in English-speaking countries.

Bhai ji found a room to rent near the school that was not too expensive. Unfortunately, the room had no secure place to park his bike. The landlord was not helpful. One of the neighbors agreed to let him park his bike in their courtyard. Unfortunately, walking to the neighbor's place for his bike required him to pass by another neighbor who had an aggressive dog, and the lady who owned the dog was also aggressive. Asatya ji had been bitten by a dog just a couple of weeks prior while recovering from covid, and he was still taking medicine to combat infection in the wound on his leg. The dog made him nervous, but the woman was the real problem. The woman tried to imply that Asatya bhai made her feel insecure or that he had threatened her somehow. Actually, he was just walking past her house to get his bike which would get the dog's attention, making him bark. That's it. The woman escalated and finally threatened him, saying that she would see him at the police station.

The other neighbors told Asatya bhai to be careful as that woman was the village busy-body, and she had succeeded in getting her husband thrown in jail. In recent years, Indian government has tried to crack down on rape, and courts have been harsher in punishing perpetrators as well as inadvertently punishing innocents. Women are realizing that if they have some hatred or grudge against a man, she can simply claim that he assaulted her, and many courts would accept her testimony as enough to put the man in jail (so I have heard.) So many men are justifiably afraid of angering any woman.

Well, Asatya knew that if he failed to show up, that would not look good. He recruited his boss to come so at least he would have someone there in his defense, being very far from any of his friends in northwest Punjab. They stood around at the station all morning and the woman never

---

1.   https://www.mapsofindia.com/maps/punjab/

showed up. Thank God. Bhai ji moved out of that room the same day and found a different room across town.

Near that place, something interesting occurred many years ago. When Asatya was about eighteen years old, he was traveling by bus far from home, through Punjab. He had somehow lost the little bit of money he had brought, and so he only had his receipt for the bus fare. As he sat on the bus feeling bored, he developed the most maddening itch deep inside his ear. Being a sort of typical youngster and not thinking what might go wrong, he rolled up his receipt into a tight spiral to insert into his ear to reach the itch. He succeeded, but there was another problem: That tiny receipt was now hopelessly lodged in his ear, and he could not retrieve it. What made matters worse was that he had stepped off the bus at a bus stop to use the toilet or some such thing, and he couldn't get back on without the receipt. He was a few hundred kilometers from home without any means of communication. Without money for bus fare, he was desperate. He implored several people for help, but they refused, thinking he was a runaway.

At last, he asked a cobbler to help him get the receipt out of his ear. The man wasn't much help in that regard, but he did pay the bus fare. Also, he took Asatya home to feed him and dry his wet clothes over the fire. (Apparently it was a rainy day.) Asatya hated to take money from anyone, much less a poor old man, but he had to get back home somehow.

Fast-forward to the present, Asatya was back in the same town in northwest Punjab. He had never forgotten that man's help. He had always been curious to know if that man was still living and still in that town. He went back to the exact place where he had found that man twenty-six years before. The man was in the same place, doing cobbler's work near the street, just as he was all those years ago.

Asatya's eyes welled up with tears, content to find him. He told the story to the man of how he had helped him many years ago when he was just a teen and asked if he remembered... the man had to think about it, but he *did* remember! Asatya thanked him for the second time and finally paid him back for his help.

Burning Bridges and Gaining Health

All this while, RK became sick again. The cancer from a few years prior had returned and was in multiple systems. Maundaata was taking loans from friends and relatives and accumulating an unmanageable amount of debt to pay RK's medical bills. RK seemed to be holding steady but still not great.

One Sunday night, Asatya received an unexpected call from his sister, who was distraught. Asatya immediately dropped everything and took buses through the night all the way from Mukerian to Charkhi Dadri. RK had died the night before.

The next day at noon, RK was cremated. That is standard procedure in Hindu society. They don't use funeral homes. Instead, they do a cremation within 24 hours of the death, before decomposition can occur.

Asatya was there. Everyone known to them came. Everyone. It is typical in India society that for weddings and funerals, every single person known to you comes, so the whole affair goes on for a few days, and many people may come and go. And no one really needs to say they're coming... it's just assumed.

Maundaata received a call from their mama ji saying that he was coming and bringing his household. It is the same mama that Asatya had helped years before with thousands of dollars, that never so much as thanked him. The same mama whose son had assaulted Shweta many times. Maundaata did not tell them to stay away. She told Asatya to hide on the roof while they were in the house. Asatya was livid. His sister really was going to welcome his wife's rapist into the house but make him hide as if he were the criminal. Asatya questioned her, wanting to know if she had been in contact with them, as he had cautioned her to always avoid them... she couldn't give any acceptable reply. No apology, just excuses.

She said something like, "But they are family too..." as if rape and exploitation can be easily swept under the rug and forgotten. Had Maundaata really forgotten that it was she that was there for Shweta to help her with her physical needs in the traumatic aftermath of her assaults?

They did in fact show up. Asatya sat on the roof for a couple of hours. Beside the question of loyalties, there was the question of safety. How can anyone just allow a sexual predator into their home, and around their daughters? It was also understood that if Asatya crossed paths with him, there could be violence. If there is any force on earth that could rival the formidability of a 'mama bear' protecting her kids, it is the husband of a victimized wife when he encounters the assailant.

After those men left, Asatya spoke very seriously with his sister to grow a backbone and don't let them back into the house. Agni could hear his stern voice and came into the room. She put herself between her mother and Asatya (her mama ji.) Agni was inches away, screaming at him with the most blood-curdling verbal abuses. As an American living in a casual culture, I have had the unfortunate experience of being exposed to all sorts of filthy language, but nothing I've heard in my native context rivaled what was coming out of this young woman's mouth, that I will spare you from by not printing it here. All that weekend she had been composed except for understandable tears at her father's passing. Now that the crowd had dwindled to a few guests, she was letting out all of the ugly. Poor Prajna who had kept a low profile as usual, was also included in her verbal assault.

Later that night as we tried to make sense of what just happened, I said to Asatya that it's true that sometimes some people express grief as anger, and it's true that Agni never liked you...but her tirade just seemed extreme. Asatya, having been raised in a sub-culture that doesn't shy away from yelling or slapping, did not react, and did not touch her. I am proud of him for that.

I was on a video call with Asatya when he and the others left the house. I could see Agni and her mother by the door, as everyone else was walking away from there, down the street. Even Agni's husband looked like he wanted to get away. Having been sort of run out of the house by a young and provoking tyrant, Prajna and Asatya had nowhere to sleep. They found a cheap hotel in town.

The next day, Prajna and Asatya went to their native village to meet with a potential buyer. They took with them an acquaintance to serve as a witness and for additional security, as they would be transporting a fairly large amount of money. The small plot on which they had all lived with their mother in their first years of life, was sold. Prajna and Asatya and their acquaintance drove back to Charkhi Dadri, as they had agreed to use the money from the sale of their land, to pay off most of Maundaata's medical debts. If they had not done that, Maundaata would have been in debt for the rest of her life, as she only earned a minimum salary as a kindergarten teacher. Being a widow and in debt also would have made her more susceptible to exploitation, and the brothers knew that she did not possess the wisdom or restraint to avoid insecure situations. The amount was equal to about five years of Maundaata's salary. Maundaata wasn't even earning enough to pay current bills. As much as Maundaata needed that help, Prajna and Asatya were not under any obligation to do that - but they cared about their sister's well-being.

Once back at the house, they went straight to Mauna to present her with the money - every single rupee. It was a challenge to count it out; Agni was still there. Once again, she got into their faces to rip them into pieces with her words. Wasn't it abundantly clear what kind of people were her mamas Prajna and Asatya? They had just made an immense sacrifice to support her mother. This act of Agni made it clear that no matter how much any of us sacrificed or made any Herculean effort to connect with her on a meaningful level, Agni had made up her mind with a will of steel - she didn't want us.

It was also clear that she viewed me as simply an extension of her mama ji Asatya, which meant that she didn't want to talk to me either. It was then that I realized that Agni had never even called me 'mausi ji' which would have been expected, and a bare minimum gesture. At the same time, she wanted that I call her 'beti,' or daughter. It just shows that she wanted a title of honor or greater intimacy without even giving me basic respect. She never even called Prajna or Asatya 'mama ji' as she should have.

All the time that I had known Asatya, he would always paint a picture of his siblings being good people with good hearts and no doubt his love for them highlighted their good points, but to observe their actions in reality... they are both kind and generous to a fault, but the ego and stubbornness are immense. It's true that they didn't grow up in the same environment as Asatya.

116

Asatya was in a boarding school in Andhra Pradesh, Prajna was exploited and neglected by their mama, and Mauna was mostly with the grandparents. Prajna and Maundaata were completely uncultured, lacking etiquette, and had absorbed the superstitions of their village, all while never learning discretion. How they were raised was not their fault, but they could at least try to grow and improve their lives. Asatya would often try to talk to them kindly to encourage their personal growth and wisdom, but they were absolutely uninterested. It was a source of deep and lifelong pain for Asatya to see his siblings in self-destructive patterns, but they refused to change.

Maundaata never even thanked her brothers for their sacrifice of love.

Over the following weeks, we worried because Agni had moved in with her mother and that now she would try to control her mother and everything in the household. It's true she was a tyrant. But after a couple of months, she moved with her husband to Jhajjar, the next city to the east, to try to find work for herself and some independence, as she never had any freedom living in her in-law's house, with no bike or car. Mauna was living alone with Vidushi. We worried about Vidushi in particular.

At this time, Samaji and her husband were looking to add to their business by opening an IELTS center, like the one where Asatya was working. She was trying to entice Asatya to work for them. I discouraged this, knowing that they would pay a meager salary, but the Chamba school would pay at least twice as much. I also knew that Samaji would hire him based on a certain expectation, but that it would snowball to include so many responsibilities outside of the original job description, much like the MD in Solan had done.

After RK's passing, Asatya went back to Mukerian to teach while waiting to be called by the Chamba school. In fact, the owner of the IELTS place in Mukerian wasn't any better than the Solan MD. When Asatya originally took the job, he was feeling insecure in terms of having adequate employment, so he was very eager to please.

At that time, I offered to do a once weekly zoom call with Asatya's IELTS students, for their English conversation practice. In that environment, a native speaker to converse with is a valuable asset that is not easy to find. A few students joined the call regularly. It was just 20-30 minutes of my week, so I didn't mind.

The IELTS guy asked Asatya to teach two classes in the afternoons at his K-12 school. There was no increase in salary. Unfortunately, the students were all village locals whose parents didn't bother to teach them any good values, and some classes seemed like a chaotic free-for-all. Of course, teachers are not really allowed to punish students, and the owner/principal would just turn a blind eye, no matter how inappropriate or disruptive kids might be. Asatya's blood pressure and stress levels continued to rise in that place.

While Asatya was in Mukerian, he found out that a friend of the school owner had a business procuring bachelor's and master's degrees for a price. Asatya wanted to buy a degree from that guy for his niece Agni, as one last attempt to reach out in peace to Agni.

I was surprised that Asatya could suggest this. Wasn't he a man of impeccable moral character? He asked me to contribute funds for this. Actually, I had agreed to help at first because I thought he was saying that he wanted us to pay the tuition fees for Agni to enroll somewhere.

He clarified that this is an illegal business from which a person can literally buy a degree. He explained that the man has connections with a few universities, or should I say, a few people who work in the records department of those universities. Those people were being paid quietly to forge documents.

I asked Asatya how he could even consider this. He justified it by saying that Agni is smart and already has some skills, and she needs help to get ahead. He said that maybe she will accept us after receiving practical help. He said that it's almost impossible in India to make any progress in life without a little corruption and it is very normal.

I knew this was not ethical and I was not swayed at all. Still, I was pressured to help because of my earlier commitment to be a peacemaker in the family. Well, I sort of got off the hook because the man was stalling and kept asking for more time. Asatya accused him of scamming. In the end, even Asatya's employer refused to talk to Asatya, even though he still owed payroll. I was made to attempt diplomacy with Asatya's boss so that at least he would get paid. I was not happy about being shoved into the drama, and yet I believed in solidarity and loyalty. Asatya was my brother, even if he was wrong in this case.

In mid-January, something happened. Asatya bhai had a dispute with his siblings. They said in their own words, and not for the first time, that 'You are not our brother. How can you be? You are not like us. Also, we don't want you.' That wasn't precisely what they said, but they had said similar things many times. This time, things were worse.

Ordinarily, Bhai ji is able to compartmentalize private versus professional things, and he always is focused on doing quality work when he is at work. Asatya's siblings are the people closest to his heart, and how they are doing always reflects in his mood.

Despite his commendable and expected effort to not let his personal affairs affect his job performance, it happened the next day after the vein-bursting interaction with his siblings, that a certain student of his, who had been provoking him for weeks, was in particular poor form and causing problems in Asatya ji's classroom. Asatya bhai finally snapped and slapped that kid. The kid complained to his parents. The parents complained to Asatya's boss.

Unfortunately, the student and his parents were well-connected in the community and word got around. I think they figured out that Asatya bhai was a transplant from out of state and he didn't know anyone local to that place, which meant he was alone. Those people were stirring each other up and there was talk of making an example out of Asatya. Bhai ji was ready to offer an apology and probably stop teaching in that school, but his boss told him to not even come to the IELTS center, and that he needed to get out of town until the blood boiling simmered down.

It just so happened that Asatya bhai's friend (the PE instructor from Solan) was planning a short trip to Jammu with a few friends. Asatya joined them. They went into the mountain state of Jammu to climb a mountain that has a well-known religious site at the top. I worried about Asatya bhai doing a mountain climb with a bunch of young guys, while he was having sporadic chest pains over many weeks. On his return to Mukerian, Asatya offered a sincere apology to the student in the presence of the boy's family and other witnesses. His boss fired him. The boy's family had put pressure on him... Asatya wrote to me:

"You see, I grew up in times when even a one-year-old child would be punished for their innocent and natural mistakes...

I have seen this cruelty so, so much and being a Haryanavi even very much...

Also, it depends...

For example, some others are hardly punished or disciplined but rather are sort of neglected.

You can't expect anything from an agriculturist village parent...

They are sort of animals by themselves...

They work in fields just like animals and behave like mad animals...

No education or internal thought process... (though humanity is reflected in them, in their rude behaviour even...)

And I mostly grew up in such circumstances...

And that's why it's very, very normal to physically punish for a Haryanavi, except only in recent years, school rules have changed for punishment and it's still so common in rural schools to punish kids of any grade...

But not in big cities like Delhi or Mumbai and still it depends if the school is located in slums..."

"That's why despite being such a hardworking and nice teacher, I end up punishing trouble-creating students sometimes and then hold back myself realizing I should not have done it in any circumstances...

I MUST IMPROVE THIS BEING A HARYANAVI..."

Bhai ji was always such a wonderfully nice person except for his anger, the one remnant of his upbringing that he was still working hard to shake off.

Now that Asatya was not working and wouldn't be for another month or so, he thought to take the time and the small amount of money that he had saved, to go to PGI (a university hospital in Chandigarh) to have general health checks, which he had completely neglected all his life. The year prior, he had his eyes checked because he felt the need for prescription lenses. The eye doctor said that he had cataracts in both eyes. At PGI, he inquired about cataract surgery. In fact, he was told that his eyesight problem was not from cataracts... most of Asatya's health checks and blood tests looked fairly normal. However, his blood pressure was at 250/140. These numbers fall within the range of life-threatening and causing long-term damage. The poor eyesight was a direct result of high blood pressure. Bhai ji's frequent, multi-day, incapacitating migraines were mostly from the high blood pressure. A few times, those migraines were so horrendous that he had to be hospitalized. They would totally incapacitate him. In that moment, we stopped and thanked God that Asatya was still living, and that he had the time to prioritize his health exactly when it had become critical. I wrote this note to Asatya:

"Brother,

I am thanking God that you are still living and walking.

Oh my God 😣

I am remembering the chest pain... with blood pressure at 250/140 you should have had organ failure... look at you going for a walk like everything is normal...

Doesn't it seem weird or amazing to you that in just the past two years, you've had a number of things happen that could have ended you, but they didn't.

Like Tamo wanted to kill you, but Chhota shut him up.

Or having Covid and you couldn't swallow at all, and the doctors neglected you mostly, but you lived and even your voice was not permanently damaged.

Or that woman in Mukerian who threatened to put you in jail, or the kid's dad who could have put you in jail...

You could absolutely have had a heart attack climbing that mountain or at any time really.

Anything I missed or forgot?

I have sometimes thought that it looks like a sinister force wants to end you, but God has not allowed it.

Didn't I tell you that you will not die before you do something very important? I don't know exactly what God has in mind to do with you but believe me, you haven't seen anything yet. Hardly.

There is a reason that you are still here, alive.

Today marks one year since the first day that I saw my precious brother in the flesh.

I never stop thanking God for your life and for connecting me to you.

Now I hope you are getting that prescription..."

After that dispute on January 15, 2023, Asatya didn't talk to either his older brother or older sister again, for a long time. He did not mean to, ever.

I could see over time that all Asatya bhai's efforts for them came to nothing, and that every interaction with them just amplified his stress and misery. I knew that he needed to break ties with them, but I always felt that it was not my place to advise him to do that... finally Bhai ji knew that it was well past time to burn that bridge. We cried together, and then we turned our attention to the future.

Over the following year, Asatya bhai's blood pressure came down to normal levels and after several months, he hardly needed BP meds anymore. His eyesight improved. His migraines almost went away completely (I had noticed a direct correlation between stress and his migraines.) It really looked like stress from his family had pushed his health to a life-threatening point.

It was a lesson to consider, that doing the hard thing and breaking away from toxic people does more than just preserve mental health - in some cases it can save someone's life.

Chamba

February came and the school gave Bhai ji a formal job offer and subsequent teaching contract. It would be another case of teaching French to several grade levels and holding the position of hostel warden.

As I write this, I have three teenage kids. Asatya bhai has never been a father, but he has spent years in full classrooms and hostels of teenagers, not just teaching academically, but encouraging the development of life skills and teaching good values to so many kids. I think he has more experience with parenting teenagers than I do...

The Chamba school looks absolutely stellar from the outside. On the inside, the lack of discipline that seems endemic throughout most schools was no different there. This school in particular had it worse, because the tuition rates were high, the administration wanted to retain and attract more students at all costs. Parents of students very rarely viewed their own children as problematic, instead they saw the school only as a service they paid for, and if their kid wasn't happy, they would threaten to just put their kid in a different school. Of course, none of this is actually good for the development of the young person in question...Aside from removing their kid, the parents could also put pressure on the school to fire a teacher. Bhai ji was teaching illegally, not having a teaching degree. He was there only on the superior recommendation of his good friend Mr. Charles, and merit of his own conduct in the school.

At some point, Bhai ji was feeling very discouraged that he had no support from administration regarding misbehaving students. He tried to discipline one or two students by asking for push-ups or some other benign method like that. The student was a real prick and threatened to get him fired by telling stories to his parents. Bhai ji was despairing and wanting to quit. I reminded him that this was his best job since marketing, and he should not let it go. He didn't like it, but he knew I was right, and he did stay.

The truth is that everyone in that school loved Bhai ji, as he would always go above and beyond to improve his classroom and the work culture, and he would always inspire and motivate coworkers and students, all with a sense of humor. The only thing that others would complain about is that he didn't let the students bring chaos to his classes, or other bad behavior. He did his best to correct students kindly and gently, but not all would respond well to that. In fact, a lot of the other staff secretly liked that he tried to maintain discipline, but they could not openly support that because it wasn't good for business. One or two teachers didn't like Asatya bhai, but that was only because he would work in circles around them, which made them look bad. Ha!

If At First You Fall from the Mountain, Build an Airplane Instead

It remains to be seen what on earth God has in mind to do with Asatya... All I know is that shortly after I met him, I saw a vision in which Asatya was glowing from inside and thousands of people were gathered around him to listen to him. After seeing this, a voice in my head told me to support or help Asatya by whatever means possible. A few times I questioned it, wondering if I had imagined it, but then that push from inside would become ten times stronger. It was clear that God had in mind to do something important with Asatya, and that I was to support him in whatever way that I could. I didn't know for how many months or years I was supposed to do that, but I was willing, and it became my mission. I was determined.

The saying, "you might not be able to change the whole world, but you can change the world for one person" had made a strong impact on my approach to life, so investing so much blood, sweat, and tears in one person made sense to me.

When Asatya was young, he had a recurring dream of climbing in the mountains and then falling from the side of the mountain. Funny, at that time in his life, he had never even seen a mountain. It is true that later he had started married life with a young lady in the mountains and in the end, he lost her... but in a broader sense, Asatya had been working hard and honestly his entire life only to get nowhere. Climbing and falling, climbing and falling. Part of the problem was staying connected to problematic relatives or 'friends.' Part of it was being so overly generous that he could never accumulate savings. Part of it was the corruption and prejudice that are so rife. People would default to passing over him because of his caste. He had to lie several times about his marital status, just to rent somewhere to live. Landlords prefer to stay away from single men. Many times, Asatya was ignored by people whose job it was to help him, simply because he didn't offer them a bribe. Asatya needed to update his permanent residence for official records which was required for some documents that he needed. The only way to obtain those records was by asking his old landlord. The land-lord refused to cooperate. Asatya was unable to acquire that important doc-ument. And so it is that other people are able exert power over others and artificially hold them back. I wondered how Asatya or any kind-hearted and honest person could possibly 'climb the mountain' successfully in an environment that was rigged to function on corruption and 'who-knows-who.'

The India that I have seen is a place where most people treat life and especially interpersonal relationships strategically like a chess game. As an innocent person, Bhai ji is not a chess player, nor did he ever want to be... he is an authentic human being if I ever saw one. I cannot in good conscience encourage him to be any different.

I had promised myself that I would do whatever I could to empower Asatya. The main thing that really knocked down his spirit was that he had no relationship with his biological family, and just a small handful of friends that were not even very close. Really, he *was* alone and that made him feel dead inside - except that he had one little sister, not by blood but by choice, and her family was his family. I thought that probably the best way to lift up Asatya would be to find a way for him to come and live near us in my home state of Maine. I thought then he will be near family, and he can work doing whatever to build a life for himself, and no one could take that away from him - unlike in India.

Also, for my own sake, I needed him to develop more positive connec-tions, because it was not sustainable for me to be everything to him or to anyone. Being Asatya's entire support system on my own was quite drain-ing.

Over three years, hardly a day went by that I was not researching im-migration or carefully working over a potential plan. I tried setting him up on two separate occasions with two people known to me, to consider dat-ing and possibly marrying eventually. (Bhai ji really wanted to settle down and start a family anyway.) I set up profiles on dating websites for him. Re-member, Indians are accustomed to arranged marriages - my involvement was appropriate from that side. We thoroughly explored and started work-ing on a work visa. We found that most work visas for Indian nationals have a 10+ year backlog, according to the visa bulletin[1][xvii](the official government webpage that shows updates on visa processing.) I even met with an attorney from New Brunswick to discuss the possibility of Asatya moving there, even though it's a different country, it's not terribly far. We worked over so many possibilities that all seemed... not impossible, but extremely challenging.

I thought that the best chance of success would mean to rely on other people as little as possible and maintain control of the future ourselves as far as we could. But how?

That winter, our mutual friend Benny from Togo, was talking to me about his mother making and selling coconut cookies. He wanted to explore the idea of exporting them. Benny is another friend that I like to encourage and support, so I helped to research more about exports. The cost of producing cookies would be too expensive to allow any profit, but it seemed like he could get into exports another way. Looking into what exporting entails, I stumbled across information for foreigners in the U.S. on business, and I was surprised to discover that foreign entrepreneurs even of small companies can be eligible to come to the U.S. on business for a period of 1-7 years. I was looking at the EB-1[2][xviii]visa and L-1[3][xix]visa. In the past, I had not given thought to the EB-1, as it appears to be for top executives, which didn't seem applicable. The L-1 was for transferees, and Asatya wasn't in any company that would consider transplanting him to the U.S.

What I did not know when researching these things earlier was that the company transferring an employee does not need to be huge; it just needs to be multi-national. What if *I* was the owner of the company? To be eligible for an L1 and possibly a subsequent EB-1, (a type of green card) the transferee would have to work in a foreign company for at least one year in an executive or managerial position or a position that contained specialized

---

1.   https://travel.state.gov/content/travel/en/legal/visa-law0/visa-bulletin/2025/visa-bulletin-for-may-2025.html

2.   https://www.uscis.gov/working-in-the-united-states/permanent-workers/employment-based-immigration-first-preference-eb-1

3.   https://www.uscis.gov/working-in-the-united-states/temporary-workers/l-1a-intracompany-transferee-executive-or-manager

knowledge (L2). The foreign company would have to have a close relationship to the company that would receive him in the U.S., such as an affiliate or subsidiary. I liked the fact that this possibility didn't rely on the hope that some random, unknown potential employer would be willing to sponsor a work visa and go through the paperwork and waiting. If I owned the company, I could at minimum, offer a job that would be secure and guaranteed, and not in a hellish work environment, which is more than Bhai ji had ever had. Depending on the business model, and the eventual size of the company, possibly I could offer the same thing to our friend Benny, and to my godson in Benin, who by then had a bachelor's degree, but after months of searching for a job, was still unemployed.

After RK's passing, Prajna, Maundaata, Agni, and Vidushi were all estranged from Asatya, and were hardly even speaking to each other. The idea of starting a business and working for chhoti bahan (little sister) was very appealing, as was the idea of leaving India behind and starting afresh.

Asatya had spent all his life in survival mode, and he was burnt out from drifting almost like a nomad from one location and job to another. He was very tired of 'starting fresh,' and just wanted to land somewhere. What he needed and craved more than anything in the world was to put down roots. To build a home and start a family. To have a life partner, and permanency.

Well, we discussed a few business ideas. Somehow, we hoped to figure out something that would allow remote work from different continents, or else one or more of the three guys (Benny, Visounou, and Asatya) would need a work visa so they could work together in the same place. Feasible, viable, desirable... what could work?

Just a few months before this, Bhai ji was trying to convince me that any time anyone in my family needed clothes or shoes, that I should just have Asatya buy them and send them to us, as the cost of living, including the cost of clothes, is much less there in India. I estimate that general costs are about one eighth that of costs in the U.S. I could have a complete, tailored outfit for $30, minus the cost of shipping. He sent my measurements to a tailor who had me choose colors and styles, and she made a couple of winter weight suits for me. Asatya bhai also bought sweaters, hats, and merino wool socks for my entire family. The box was close to 40lbs. (18 kilograms.)

My husband, three kids, myself and my parents all had new things. It was a good confirmation to my family of Asatya's practical and kind nature which I had always told them about.

Later as I contemplated business ideas, I remembered the box of clothes. I loved that tailors in India are just everywhere and reasonably affordable to the middle class. I could have them make whatever I wanted, and it would fit perfectly. I thought, instead of saving money on clothes by buying them in India, and having them sent here, we could do the same but sell them for profit. It's true that the #1 clothing industry problem in the U.S. in terms of user experience, is poor fit, or inaccurate sizing. It is also true that tailoring services affordable to the middle class are almost non-existent here. I had received more compliments on my Indian clothes than I've ever received on any of my other clothes and so I thought there could be significant interest in some Indian styles... I did a lot of market research over months and everything I found indicated that I was not only on the right track, but that I may have exactly the right idea at exactly the right time to ride the wave of impending changes in the garment or fashion industry... If done right, we had the potential of developing into not just a successful company but a household name.

I would oversee sales, marketing and design from home. The other three (in Benin and India, respectively) would collaborate with me for product development, design, manage sourcing and oversee order fulfillment.

I knew that I could teach myself using online and local resources about entrepreneurship, e-commerce, and all that, to fill in my gaps of knowledge. But the fact remained that we would be doing business across international borders, and we knew that meant taking care to follow the advice of at least one attorney. We knew to start small, and yet it was a somewhat complex thing that we wanted to do. The entire operation would be owned by me, and all of it would be in our control - with only a little outsourcing. I learned before too long that step one of a start-up is to learn and learn we sure did.

We knew that Asatya wouldn't have any time whatsoever to focus on business things if he continued teaching and functioning as a hostel warden. Unfortunately, they only wanted him as a teacher if he also was hostel warden; it was all or nothing. Asatya decided that he would not return there at the start of the new academic year in March, so he would be available for our things. Still, it was a sort of leap of faith to decide that, not knowing how quickly we could begin sales. We felt anxious but hopeful. Our friend Benny had done the same, but he really couldn't wait for me to offer a job, and so he took on a teaching job to see him through until at least July.

Asatya thought to recruit his old friend Pareshani (from the Andhra Pradesh school), as Pareshani needed consistent work, and he already had some tailoring skills. Pareshani began doing apprentice work with local tailors to increase his skills and quality of work. Pareshani lives in the same town as Maundaata, surrounded by cotton fields and textile mills...Asatya got free from school in the first week of December. He went from there to Charkhi Dadri, to Pareshani's house. He figured that it would be conducive to guiding Pareshani in the direction we want to go and working on business things together. Asatya ji added Pareshani to our business project chat group and included him in our efforts without consulting me first. I didn't know why he did that; it looked impulsive. I chose to trust his judgement, though I was skeptical.

I told the guys to not tell anyone what we were doing, except when necessary for business purposes. Unfortunately, it was a known fact that there were a few jealous people around who might attempt sabotage, or else try to weasel their way in, if they knew that we were building a business.

I'll just call Pareshani 'Shani' for simplicity. Shani was living in a house that was not complete. Asatya bhai felt a strong desire to help finish the construction, perhaps because he was living there. In fact, he helped Shani with a lot of his personal things.

Asatya made a deal with Shani that Asatya would give him 10,000 per month (enough for basic living expenses) if Shani did not go work elsewhere but rather make himself available to us and contribute all relevant knowledge or skill. I felt skeptical of that, as Shani was selfish and lazy in our last interactions with him. Shani claimed to have skills as a tailor. I thought, "why is he not already doing that for a living, if he knows how?" but I trusted Asatya, so I didn't question it.

As time went on, Shani made small efforts at improving his skills, but he didn't seem serious about it. I asked him to stitch up a few sample items for me, but Asatya insisted that Shani hardly had any skill that he could see since going to his house... he said let's find a local professional tailor to do the samples and Shani should watch and learn. Shani showed me a few things that he had made. The quality looked fine to me in photos and videos, but Asatya insisted that it was not acceptable quality, so they talked to a couple of tailors. The tailors wanted to take the measurements in person which was ridiculous, because the people who were to wear the aforementioned samples are all in the U.S. I was also told that the fabric I had bought was not enough for the shirt that I wanted them to make. I knew that it was enough. The tailors only spoke Hindi, so I was getting all this information through Asatya and Shani.

Asatya and Shani didn't pursue the matter more as they were busy building an addition in Shani's house. In addition to the 10K rupees per month, Bhai ji was also funding that.

I was trying to be patient. There should not have been a gap in working and earning for Asatya, especially after all the worrying he had done about how soon he could start earning again. He left the teaching position to work for and with me, but he prioritized putting his time and money into his friend's house. He never asked me if it would be okay to delay our project a bit. He just did it.

Also, he had said that he would reserve some of his funds to help launch the business project. I planned that into the budget.

Meanwhile, I discovered that Benin has many things going for it. There is a trade agreement that allows most of West Africa to import to the U.S. without paying customs duties. In particular, garment imports. Benin grows more cotton than any other country in Africa. Myriad vibrant and interesting fabric patterns are available there. And many types of fabric unknown to many people outside of Africa... I knew we could create unique, interesting, comfortable garments. Also, setting up (the legal aspects of) a business in Benin is almost 100% online. I already knew French (the national language) and I had local people there to guide me.

In early January, Asatya bhai developed a respiratory infection. It was not diagnosed but it took away his sense of taste and made him numb all over, weak, lethargic, and unable to concentrate, even after the sickness passed.

Asatya ji is an expert driver, but I was grateful that he had taken a bus when he had gone north to attend the wedding of a friend's sister. Navigating Indian roads requires significant concentration and the ability to react quickly. On his way back to Shani's house, he went to the hospital in Rohtak to find answers to his neurological symptoms.

I had been looking for the opportune time to visit Benin. I was trying to conserve funds, but I could see that I could make better progress if I spent some time there in person. I had arrived at the conclusion that rather than be rigid in my designs and be ever searching for the holy grail of fabrics, it would be much more practical (and culturally relevant) to simply see exactly what materials *are* available there, then nail down the design details once I have a solid comprehension of what we have to work with. This approach made it difficult to tell Visounou what to look for... fabric shopping (especially where design or creativity is involved) is often a case of knowing the right material only when you see it or touch it. Also, photos can't show everything, such as texture, for example. Anyway, most shop owners would not allow Visounou to take photos or sample pieces. None of the suppliers had an online presence. Beninese people have been slow to trust online shopping, therefore most shops do not have an online shop. This reason among others motivated me to make a visit. I thought to buy a few hundred fabric swatches to catalog by merchant and fiber/fabric type, label them, and leave a second set exactly the same with Visounou, for future reference.

After four years, I would finally be seeing my godson face to face. I was so much looking forward to just spending time with the family, aside from work.

The trip had been delayed somewhat. I thought to go in January, but things were moving slowly, and I knew that when summer came it would be difficult to go. As I searched for a good deal on airline tickets, I noticed that adding India to the itinerary would only add another $200-300 more. Considering that I would need to travel to India probably by the end of the year as a separate trip, which would cost around $1,000 by itself... $200 to add to this trip looked like a great deal. It's true that we planned to open an order fulfillment center in India at some point as well. All my reasons for going to Benin were equally applicable for going to India.

That same week I had a root canal done. The dentist insisted that I should get a crown for that tooth. The two-part procedure for the crown was quoted for $1,500-1,800, depending on the fit of the crown.

Unfortunately, during the root canal procedure, not all the pathogens came out... I felt perfectly fine for more than a week. Then, under the dead nerve, an abscess formed and grew larger and larger over a day or two. I was in immense pain from the building pressure. Overnight, I woke up in overwhelming pain as the 800mg. of ibuprofen wore off. Suddenly, I felt something burst inside my face, on the topside of my gums facing my cheek. Within minutes, that whole side of my face was swollen, and my nose was running. The pain behind the tooth lessened a bit, but my face was hurting and puffy. By sunrise, I had a fever of 104 Fahrenheit. I begged a pharmacist to help; I knew I was in serious trouble. That morning, I started taking penicillin. The pathogens had multiplied rapidly in the abscess under my tooth to the point where there was just an enormous amount of germs that suddenly invaded my body all at once like it was D-Day (or a ruptured appendix.) My poor immune system was absolutely overwhelmed as the infection spread through my whole body unchecked.

I know I could have died if not for the penicillin. The infection had a very unfair head start on my immune response. Thank God, the infection had completely ended a few days before my scheduled departure to Africa.

All of a sudden, squeezing in a visit to India was looking even more attractive. Crowns typically cost about $150 there. It is true that I knew from Bhai ji's experience where all the best facilities and doctors were. Asatya bhai pointed out that his own friend in Panchkula (next to Chandigarh) was himself a dentist. So, it was settled in my mind. I would get the needed crown in India, possibly from Asatya's friend.

I felt like a crazy person booking tickets for destinations in two continents, to travel to all within five weeks. I knew that when I reached home, I would need that beautiful and homey grounding experience of getting my hands and feet into the soil... by then it would be mid-April and time to plant. Yes, lots of gardening, and so much sleep...then I would be going right back to work, finishing up the construction of my website and all the many last pieces of infrastructure to be ready to accept orders.

As I was preparing to leave for Benin, Bhai ji was buying bricks and recruiting the help of Shani, Prajna, and some friendly neighbors to construct a simple home for Prajna in their native village. That's right. He went straight from Shani's building project to yet another building project. What about business progress and earning?? I knew that Asatya wanted to build a small home for Prajna eventually, but I thought he would wait until he was earning again instead of draining his savings. I had instructed Asatya to inquire with various suppliers about certain types of materials and designs. Shani sent me a list of wholesalers with phone numbers, and Asatya didn't really do anything. After all his enthusiasm and determination earlier, I was baffled and frustrated by this behavior. Asatya would have to stop messing around and work seriously if our business efforts in India were ever going to work.

Prajna could never be persuaded to leave his native village. He was a villager, for better or for worse. Although Bhai ji knew there was no future of maintaining any relationship with Maundaata or Prajna, still he had been wanting for years to do this one last thing for his brother. Asatya told me that he would feel that he had tried everything, and his conscience would be clear if he helped his brother this way before disowning him. Prajna was always drifting around or couch surfing like a homeless person. Now he would have his own home, which was becoming even more important as he had aged prematurely, and his health was not good. At least he had a roof and walls.

Asatya felt that he could finally separate from his siblings with a clean conscience, after doing such things for them. I believe it was a noble thing to do. Prajna didn't treat him like a brother, but Bhai ji took care of him as a brother should. I just didn't understand why he was doing it then, when I had already been waiting for him since December, which was when he had agreed to join the business project. Really, I had been waiting for him since the summer before, when we originally agreed to the plan.

On my way to Africa, Asatya bhai asked me if I was absolutely sure that I could trust Visounou, as I was sort of putting my life in his hands to go there. I reminded him that I had to ask myself the same question about him before I left for India the first time, with my daughter. I did not tell him that, at that point in time, my faith in his decision making was faltering, but Visounou had up to that point, always and consistently been a person of admirable character and unusual wisdom for his age.

This is what I found in Benin[4][xx]:

Some businesses will 'punish' you for shopping around by raising their rates.

Otherwise, business contacts were straightforward, helpful, and professional.

Visounou had the required skills of negotiation, and he handled negotiations like a boss.

The Chamber of Commerce is a great place to start to learn about local resources and important considerations.

As a whole, the local people carry themselves with dignity and confidence, but they have a casual nature that seems to indicate humility.

I noticed that the local people have unusually good situational awareness, and adjust to conditions seemingly instinctively and immediately, even the small children.

These people adore children, and happy, playful children can be found everywhere, especially on side streets playing soccer.

These people love to have lots of color and structure in their clothes, and their best clothes are head-to-foot busy prints.

There are two volume settings for speech: a light whisper, and the booming thunder.

I ran into almost zero people problems while I was there. This may be partly because Visounou didn't tell anyone about me, except for a friend whose car he wanted to borrow for my use, once or twice. As a part of the

---

4.   https://www.google.com/search?sca_esv=9a516f6aeda16e0b&q=benin&udm=2&fbs=AB-zOT_CWdhQLP1FcmU5B0fn3xuWpA-dk4wpBWOGsoR7DG5zJBjnSuuKZNj-6zieDk_gkn6CyymgG_tEVFNWvBwycIom9R04i0ngVt1ZZ8CP5TcyhCAGT7r0wNU-tIMw6hI7tWBYzy4gFCH9QDL3Fxg6XZ38sRVVZJFAucKDmfgi7H7dmLxBHwC19LFVvgrfok-cOySD46Rn9CztvxYQxLf930C8xfF7-3eiQ&sa=X&ved=2ahUKEwj-27-KyoeNAxW-cFVkFHY24LUcQtKgLegQIDxAB&biw=1920&bih=901&dpr=1

world that is infamous for scams, I worried I would find people problems, but that simply was not the case.

This was my first experience riding a motorbike, which I did almost daily. Most of the traffic there is motorbikes. I found it easy to adjust to this different normal.

I reminded Visounou that I was in a completely new environment, which meant the possibility of dangers unknown to me. I told him to protect me like a child. He took those words seriously and literally... He wouldn't let me cross any busy street without holding someone's hand. That made me chuckle, but at least he understood the assignment.

Visounou's mother and siblings took such good care of me in their own home and made me feel truly loved. They put me in the new apartment next to them with my own personal bathroom, and refused to let me know the whereabouts of the outhouse. They spent a lot of money keeping me supplied with bottled water. They made me breakfast every morning without being asked, even though they themselves are never in the habit of eating breakfast.

The wife of Visounou's pastor (who was also like a godmother to the household) asked me if Visounou and his siblings were taking good care of me. I told her that they had done the very best. She said that she had told them strictly that they must be very good to me.

I think they would have anyway, as their love is evident, but I think the pastor's wife wanted me to go home with a good first impression of Africa.

While people were less problematic to me, the local ecosystem seems designed to repel fragile white people. Fortunately, I did take a prophylactic anti-malarial drug, as my body became the new favorite restaurant of every mosquito in town, in spite of bug repellant and mosquito nets. Also, I absentmindedly brushed my teeth with the well water, bringing on bacteria-induced gas and diarrhea. The family couldn't understand why my appetite was so small... Of course, I got a bit sunburned as well, being just seven degrees north of the equator. Daily temperatures were in the low 90's (33C) with truly incredible humidity. I am not accustomed to running on concrete. I got a few massive blisters.

A walk to the corner pharmacy resulted in four new prescriptions, that I had in hand after just ten minutes. So quick. So painless. So inexpensive. I was feeling back to normal in a few days.

Meanwhile, I observed my family there, and their friends:

They never got sunburned.

The tap water bothered them not at all.

They could easily run 12km after work and probably would have ran more if I did not protest.

I watched them eat entire crabs, shell and all.

They all looked like the absolute picture of health.

I was beginning to think I was among superhumans. It was then that I saw the movie, 'The Woman King[5][xxi],' which is about the legendary Amazon warriors native to that area. Hearing the characters in the movie speak my godson's native language, I realized that the Amazons were probably his ancestors, as only a limited number of people speak that regional language.

Well, business progress aside, it was a truly unforgettable visit, and I found the people I loved there to be exactly as expected, and I found that I loved that place there by the ocean, which looks very much like south Florida, but is full of Africans.

From there, my journey had me layover in Istanbul. While sitting at my gate resting and waiting, I opened my messages and saw some photos of Asatya and Shani and a couple other friends, sitting outside the airport in Delhi, waiting expectantly. Those were posted hours before. I realized at once that Asatya must be panicking wondering why I had not yet emerged... I called him and told him that he had mixed up the dates. I would be there the next morning, not that morning. I thought it seemed sweet that he was so psyched to receive me that he confused the dates and came too soon.

Well, I arrived the next morning and funny, I called Bhai ji to let him know that I had connected to the airport Wi-Fi, and I was headed for the door. He was barely even out of bed... so I sat by the door waiting for about an hour.

Finally, he came to the door.

5.   https://g.co/kgs/GZcyiyA

Vyapari pulled up in his car to pick us up and deliver us to Sama's house.

Remember both Vyapari and Sama were Asatya's classmates from 6-12th grade in their school days. Sama was the one who had lost a hand to extreme burns years ago. They both are successful businessmen living with their families in Delhi. It was my first time meeting Sama. His wife is a typically sweet and hospitable Indian housewife, although she also works in a bank. They have a young son that is sweet, friendly, very smart and a bit of an energetic monkey.

Sama was aware of my tooth issue. As it turned out, his nephew is a dentist. Sama said that he could do it right away. Once I arrived at Sama's house from the airport, I had a shower, breakfast, a nap, and then he drove us across Delhi to his nephew, the dentist. My brief experiences have shown me that most Indian medical establishments are quite acceptable. Up-to-date tools and equipment, correct sterilization and sanitation, well-staffed, knowledgeable, and efficient. The economic difference means paying about one tenth of the typical cost for the same procedures in the American setting. It was also pointed out to me that Indian doctors and dentists are accustomed to treating a high volume of patients and therefore accumulate career experience quickly. One surprising benefit of overpopulation...

While in Delhi, Asatya took me to visit the Lotus Temple. The Lotus Temple was built by Bahá'í devotees, for use by anyone. It is designed to be a house of prayer for anyone regardless of their religion or lack thereof, regardless of gender, race, nationality, etc. Volunteers on site guided in one group of visitors at a time to minimize chaos, as just a brief glance around indicated that there were thousands of people on the grounds at any given time. This place unlike others, employed a person to guard guest's shoes outside the door. Inside the temple, one or two people got up to recite scripture or sing, but otherwise it was totally silent. It seemed almost mythical to find any place in Delhi that was absolutely quiet. I took advantage of that moment to pray silently. It was definitely restful.

I was praying, knowing that Sama and Vyapari both cared about Asatya's well-being and didn't want to see him getting involved with any lost cause. I would need to be articulate and confident to explain to them why I believed that our business was likely to be successful. Asatya was nervous to know their opinion about our business plan. Once back at the house, Sama asked questions wanting to better understand the business plan. I could see the wheels in his head turning... he said he wasn't sure but maybe it would prove useful to talk to somebody from an export house. Neither me nor Asatya had heard of an export house... I thought maybe they were a business who prepared large shipments, so I wasn't sure that would really be relevant to our needs. Nevertheless, Asatya, Shani, and I took the metro the next morning to Nehru Place as Sama had directed. Nehru Place is a large 'market.'

A market in the Indian context is just a neighborhood of the city devoted to shops, boutiques, vendors and other merchants. There were several blocks with a few hundred businesses in each. The commercial buildings were all at least six to eight stories tall. Nehru Place has many businesses in the garment and fabric industry, and especially those selling fabrics that are certified as 'export quality,' although the primary focus at Nehru Place is info-tech.

We visited several fabric merchants, taking samples and business cards. We visited a few export houses. Some of these sold fabrics in addition to offering stitching of designs from clients. We talked for a while with one that was also in touch with a fabric dyer, as they only had black and a wall of white bolts of undyed fabric. We had the dyer dye our fabric a lovely peacock blue. (I had a number of friends at home who were interested in purchasing a sample pair of pants, so we were going to have these made to order while I was in India.) The export house could manage our international shipments also. It seemed ideal to start producing our designs through one of these export houses (or a few of them) until later after we grow, when we might operate our own facility with all operations under our own roof.

All we would have to do is buy materials and communicate designs to the export house's head tailor.

Going back to Sama's house for the night, naturally he wanted to know if we were able to make any progress.

I told him all that we discovered. He looked very thoughtful and encouraged.

Asatya later said to me, "I was doubting whether this business idea would work, but hearing Sama's response, I feel encouraged and confident that we can do this."

I didn't like this comment. It meant that all my months of market research on resources and feasibility, my consultations with my business attorney, business friends, and positive responses from potential customers all meant very little to Asatya. Because Sama was an established businessman and Asatya heard the positive response from his own lips, only then he felt assured. It made me wonder how much he trusted me.

Sama urged us both to make use of every hour, to optimize this short business trip. We both agreed, as it was understood by us three that it was a short visit of just two weeks, so business matters were the top priority, and I would need most of those days just for that. I said that of course, it is my intent to be very efficient and productive with my business trip.

I had warned Asatya to not tell anyone that I am coming to India, except for one or two people that would need to know, as we might stay at their house on the way to somewhere... I was there for a business trip that would take me through at least three states, and I had only two weeks. I emphasized efficiency of time. I knew that I very much wanted to go to Jaipur, because my research indicated that this city is a major hub in the fabric and garment industry. Jaipur and the surrounding area are famous for many styles and designs originating there, some of which go back hundreds of years. In particular, I was interested to find authentic Sanganeri block prints[6].[xxii] Sanganer is a town very close to Jaipur.

I was open to suggestions of other places to visit also, like Sama had mentioned Nehru Place in New Delhi. Asatya suggested Surat, Gujarat, as it is a hotspot for synthetic materials. However, we agreed that Gujarat was quite far and that didn't fit with using time wisely. Sama said he knew a guy in Surat, and we could talk to him on the phone... alright then.

I had it firmly planted in my mind that I absolutely wanted to at least spend a few days scoping out Jaipur in person, and I communicated this to Asatya bhai.

It seems as though we should have only visited people to the extent it would be required to not be rude. Asatya did tell people that I was coming. Maybe he couldn't contain his excitement, but I thought, he's a grown man, he needs to be self-controlled.

---

6.   https://youtu.be/pw3qs-DdKYo?si=be7IjabLQKk8qU4A

After we had explored Nehru Place and one other market in Delhi, we went north into Uttar Pradesh (known to locals as UP) to see Nakali Madhur, a friend of Asatya. In fact, there were two other people in that area hoping to see us. At least Asatya was able to arrange that they come to Nakali's house for lunch so we could consolidate stops rather than running around between even more houses.

I didn't quite understand why we were there. Less than a month prior, Asatya was saying that he was thinking to end the friendship with that lady, so why was she now important enough to give her my precious time? Asatya told me that she had proposed to take him as a business partner in opening a new school. Why even discuss it? We were already setting up our own business. One cannot start two businesses simultaneously. This friend was not helping us with our business things. It made no sense to be there from my perspective... I guess Asatya thought, why not visit? As she is just one hour from New Delhi, except we stayed there overnight. It's true that Asatya often seemed to have difficulty telling people 'No.' He can be a serious people pleaser.

Nakali was having her awards day at her school, as it was the end of the academic year. She was excessively excited about our arrival and made us her guests of honor in this school function.

What that meant is that we were the center of attention to 100+ people all morning. I hate being the center of attention, which Asatya already knew. Asatya seemed unbothered by it. Asatya just said, "Let her do her thing, it makes her happy, and there's no harm done." There was a massive vinyl banner at the front of the room with my name and photo featured on it, along with Asatya and Pareshani. To me, the attention on us felt contrived, weird, uncomfortable, and we were not at all relevant to this school.

Shani could not sit for the awards ceremony as he was becoming very sick. He laid down somewhere at the back. Asatya and I were escorted to the front. We were given marigold garlands. There was a large table completely covered in awards. I wondered how there could be so many awards for a small school... actually, this was for stroking the ego of the student's parents in an attempt to retain more student enrollments for the next academic year.

To my surprise, it was not the principal to issue awards and pose with students for photos - I was made to do it. I had hardly set foot in that school... this just goes to show the level of celeb craze among many Indians. My credentials or level of involvement was not important. What was important in their eyes was that I was a white American. To me that felt like racism in reverse, and it felt wrong - the prejudice skewed heavily in my favor for no other reason than my skin color and nationality. Bhai ji also gave out some awards though it was mostly me. We both were expected to give speeches which we did. We had an interpreter. I chose to talk about engaging with people of other cultures and learning from each other. I talked about American values like personal responsibility and viewing all others as equals, denouncing prejudice in all its forms. I'm not sure how many people were still listening. All the students got photos with me and their awards. No one told me about that ahead of time, either.

Our host took us to her house to feed us lunch. Asatya Bhratra and Chhota Giroha were there. Chhota was one more person that Asatya bhai wanted to slowly remove from his life. Asatya did not need to tell Chhota that I was coming to India. I ate and then excused myself for a nap as I was sleepy. I did have a bit of jet lag but mostly it was exhaustion from the non-stop and intense social pressure that day. I'm an introvert with an autistic neurotype. I pushed myself out of my comfort zone to go to the most densely populated country on earth because I was doing something out of kindness to my brother, and then I got pushed even further out of my comfort zone. I told Asatya this. He already knew it. I thought, why don't they force me to do a spacewalk while we are at it?? They were causing so much unnecessary anxiety.

We had more photos with these friends. There must have been a couple hundred photos taken that day. There was a very casual and friendly vibe in the house. I noticed the way that all these people were interacting. I mean Asatya, Asatya Bhratra, Nakali, and Chhota. I knew that Asatya Bhratra and Nakali had met each other once before, but Chhota didn't know either of these people. In that case, there most definitely should have been some level of formality or reservation in their demeanor, but they acted like they had always known each other, like they were old friends. I thought, maybe it was nothing, but it seemed weird to me.

Our host walked us around the corner to see her mother in her mother's house. Her best friend had come to see me out of curiosity. She was so excited to meet an American lady that she invited us to her place the next day, despite her not knowing a word of English... We were only supposed to be in that village for the morning and through lunch. We ended up not leaving until the next day around noon, although the host's friend was very nice. To me, she seemed nicer and possibly more sincere than Nakali. She had a reserved and modest, but pleasant demeanor.

That night, we slept at Vyapari's house. I always liked this family. They seem down to earth. They were in a new apartment in a 'society' - a homeowner's association, really. It was a gated community of some 12,000 people all in four very small blocks. The apartments went up eight floors. Sama's home was very similar and in the same district.

Over those last three or four days since my arrival in India, Shani was not well and had a fever. Asatya bhai speculated that it was malaria. I reminded him that malaria is life-threatening. If it was that, Shani would need to be treated for it ASAP. I did not understand why Bhai ji appeared unconcerned about his friend's health. Asatya kept saying yes, we will do it when it's convenient, as we were busy with the school function and traveling... I insisted that it could not be neglected for another hour, and finally Shani had blood tests. On the way to Vyapari's house, we got the results back. Asatya bhai told me in a sad tone that it was typhoid. Finally, Shani was escorted to the metro where he would take a bus home from outside the city.

Thinking of the metro reminds me that while we were in the Delhi area, we used the metro a lot. It happened once that a turnstile malfunctioned and shut after only a half second. I was trapped behind it and had to request the clerk at the counter for help. Asatya scolded me. I explained what had happened, but that did not stop him from 'teaching' me like a child at every single turnstile we encountered after that.

I thought to myself, now is the time that Asatya should be feeling happy and hopeful, but he seemed more stressed and crankier during that visit.

After that, we prepared to leave Delhi to go to Rajgarh (near Solan in Himachal Pradesh) for a job interview for Bhai ji.

He was thinking that he should not stop earning while waiting for our business to become profitable. He thought this teaching job would be more low-key than the one in Chamba, allowing him some time to also work on business things. His old friend, the music teacher from Solan, had shifted to that school and had recommended Asatya to them. Asatya had already done an interview with them, and this would be a second interview.

In the past, we had a few frustrating experiences with buses, so we hopped off the bus outside Delhi, to hire a private driver. There were several in that spot, all haggling with other potential passengers. All the talking was in Hindi, but there was one man who clearly had the biggest ego, who seemed to be loudly throwing his weight around. He seemed entitled and wanting to be the one to drive me...I never spoke a word to that guy, but he was talking like he owned me... Bhai ji got sucked into an argument. There was chest shoving. I told Asatya bhai to come away. I said, "You will never teach anything to an egoist on the street, just let it go." He agreed that I was right. Finally, we did get a reasonable driver, so we had a comfortable trip for the most part.

At one point, the driver tried to talk Asatya into paying more and it brought back memories to me of that night at the Karnal police station two years before. I cannot hide the fact that I am a foreigner, being very white. I knew he was only asking for more money because like so many others, he surely thought I'm made of money or that I don't know what appropriate local pricing should be. After that day, Asatya would always have me wait at a distance or hide behind a tree while he negotiated prices.

From the Chandigarh bus stand, we took a bus to Solan, where Asatya's old friend, the music teacher welcomed us. I always liked him and his family. They seemed like just normal people. Not pretentious or fake, and happy to receive us. It was night when we reached there. Above us was a sky full of stars. Below us, in front, to the left and right, and even above us, were the lights of the small city of Solan. Most of Solan is situated in a valley between small mountains (2,400 meters above sea level), with the main routes snaking along the mountainsides and many random homes can be seen up and down these mountains. It seemed weird and surprising to see in the dark of night, the light of a home high above us where the sky should be, but the hills and mountains are tall... The music teacher's home is on the hillside looking across the valley. Standing on the flat roof, a gorgeous panorama can be seen.

Regardless of whether or not the interview would be successful, one simply couldn't help but drink in the clean fresh air, the gorgeous weather and stunning views that can be seen from nearly any random spot in Himachal. I always love riding those roads, although seeing rocks sitting in the road were a reminder that these rapidly growing mountains of gravel were prone to erosion and landslides. The fact that there were far less people meant almost no crowds and relative peace.

My bed was in the main room by myself. The family crowded into one bedroom to give me privacy, and I don't even know where Asatya bhai slept - the roof perhaps? I knew that these people were not irritated to be inconvenienced. They were so glad to have me for a repeat visit.

The next morning, we packed up all our things (as we didn't plan to return there that night) and took a bus to the village of Rajgarh in the Sirmaur district. Rajgarh is the near to where Shweta grew up. Asatya's blood pressure was a bit high, so we stopped at the small pharmacy, but they didn't have any BP meds.

We were at Rajgarh because Asatya was to have a second interview with the school where his music teacher friend was then teaching. They were expecting him. They wanted a class demonstration and a speech - a speech from Asatya ji *and* a speech from me, as they knew that their French teacher candidate was bringing his sister along.

I recorded Asatya's class demo which I thought was good. He did it for both the middle schoolers as well as the high schoolers. We presented our speeches. Naturally, they wanted a few group photos with us and the students, though the sun was very bright, and it was difficult not to sneeze from the sun in the photos.

Asatya searched for the principal to talk to him. The principal asked for introductions and talked with us for hardly one full minute.

He *had* talked to Asatya bhai before... that behavior seemed very weird and rude. It was like he didn't know us or expect us. All that traveling just for a cold shoulder.

After that disappointing experience, we went to Music Man's room (he rented a room in Rajgarh to be near his work but went home on weekends.)

We were just going to wait for him to return there after he was finished teaching, so we had about an hour or two to kill, waiting there. Since it was just Asatya bhai and myself there, I thought we would just sit outside by the lane in the sunshine to wait, but Asatya wanted to sit in the room on the floor to discuss plans. I remembered then that just a month or so before, Asatya was telling me that his brother had gone to a widow's home to visit her alone, which is never accepted in Indian culture. Even though everyone understood our brother-sister relationship, we were not biological relatives. Therefore, the rules of propriety applied to some degree. So then, it seemed odd to me that Asatya seemed perfectly comfortable to sit there alone with me for an hour or two. Music Man's mother stopped by, and I thought, 'this can't look good,' though Asatya bhai had no reaction. That minor incident did not bother me at all, I just thought it odd.

Asatya bhai realized that we were just seven kilometers away from his friend and guru, Acharya ji. He had the spontaneous idea to go there.

I thought that he was thinking of just going there for the evening, as he was inquiring to know when the last bus of the day leaves Rajgarh. But he meant the bus going east, not the bus going west towards Solan. He looked annoyed at my confusion, saying that of course we would stay overnight. I don't know the bus schedules of Himachal. How could I know that?

We hired a car from Rajgarh. Bhai ji pointed out the hillside where his greenhouse had been many years ago. The car paused at the top of a tiny lane that appeared to be just a rough ATV trail going very steeply downward. I thought we would walk from there. I was wrong. The little car when straight down the side of the hill past pine trees and tall grass and at least one landslide.

Acharya ji runs a small gurukul. It is a sort of boarding school where kids learn not just academics, but also life skills like etiquette, accountability, gardening, cooking, housework, moral values and character building. There is a heavy emphasis on learning and even memorizing the Vedas. The Vedas are books of ancient wisdom for life, held in high regard by many Hindus and others.

I wasn't quite sure what to think of Acharya ji. He seemed to have a kind manner. He doesn't know any English, only his native Hindi and much Sanskrit. He would always be completely covered with long sleeves and pants and head wrapped. All his clothes are white. He is very particular about hygiene, sanitation, and daily routine. He has some interesting philosophies, some of which are logical and science based, but I don't agree with all of it.

For example, he thinks it is more sanitary to never touch animals or other people. Personally, I feel like I would cease to be human if I never patted a dog or cat, or never gave anyone a hug, a handshake, or any kind of touch. I could dismantle the pathogen argument as well, but to each their own.

Acharya always ensured that dinner was served before sunset. Bedtime is 9pm (unheard of to most Indians) and he awakens at 3:30am every day. He would start with meditation, running, havan, yoga, breakfast, chores, school subjects, gardening, and so on the day would go. Overall, I like the general concept of the immersive and holistic learning set-up, as I myself was home-schooled. Personally, I felt that maybe not every tradition was logical... Havan supposedly cleanses the air. But doing it outdoors didn't make sense to me. Also, I thought that if there is any real benefit to wearing all white, wouldn't the students also wear white? But they did not. Perhaps it is only a formality, which seemed somewhat out of place on a humble man. Bhai ji always insisted that the Vedas and subsequently Acharya ji's teachings were highly beneficial and scientific. Asatya had once said that he only believes what can be proven by logic or science.

Well, he believes in reincarnation which doesn't seem to be strictly scientific... I noticed that Acharya ji never had any girl students. Maybe it is that he needs a full-time female staff person, or maybe he wants a completely segregated learning environment, I don't know. I will admit that I am just an outsider trying to understand some things that are foreign to me. Most of what I saw there looked so much better than anything that could be found in a typical school setting.

There was a sweet lady who came every day to help with the cooking. She was nice to me.

Something happened then that I didn't know what to think of at the time.

I had remembered that Asatya said a while back, 'People in Himachal are more laid back, and women are not restricted to wearing Indian clothes only; many of them wear shirts and pants like a 'westerner' and scarves/dupatta are less essential.' I had noticed that, myself.

I only brought a white kurti and salwar, and running pants and a T-shirt.

I had arrived there wearing the white. Bhai ji said, "Acharya ji wears all white, always. It doesn't look good that you are also wearing all white. Go change." I needed a shower anyway, so I showered and put on the pants and t-shirt.

I went to rejoin the others but Asatya bhai saw me first and immediately he said, "Go back and change *immediately*. Those clothes are totally unacceptable here." He had never explained whether a gurukul has any sort of dress code, and he knew very, very well that as an American, these things must be explained to me, like he always explained other things. I told Asatya that my only other clothes were the white Indian suit that he said not to wear, which was dirty anyway.

He said, "I never told you not to wear that." I responded, "You definitely did. You said I shouldn't be matching Acharya ji." He insisted that he did not say that.

I just said, "You must not remember that conversation." Asatya forced me to change my clothes again, which I did, and then I wrapped myself in a blanket. I really wondered whether Asatya had actually forgotten what he said. Normally his memory is great. I had just caught Asatya gaslighting me and I could hardly believe it.

As we had arrived there after dinner, we brought some fruits and vegetables from the market as a gift. We made our own dinner in the kitchen, and Acharya ji came to join us and chat. Asatya bhai translated for us.

He told me that Acharya ji was surprised that I arrived there wearing Indian clothes and not pants and shirt, which he thought was just great. I thought it interesting that he assumed that I would show up in American clothes, after the great fuss that Asatya bhai had made over it.

Bhai ji said that Acharya ji was appreciating me as a kind and good sister, mother, and human being. I could figure out that Acharya ji likes Asatya and has a fair amount of respect for him, but Asatya does not have frequent communications with him, and this was Asatya's first time visiting there in over a year.

Asatya had told me that after losing Shweta, he had donated his car to Acharya ji. I asked what happened to the car as I didn't see one. He said that recently the car had been stolen. Acharya ji was also originally from Haryana.

I had my own separate bedroom with a deadbolt. The heavy blanket was just enough. The nighttime temps are definitely much cooler in the valleys of the mountains than down in the plains.

In the morning my presence was requested for havan. I reminded Bhai ji that I don't feel comfortable doing things that I don't understand, and I know very little about it. Asatya tried to assure me that it is perfectly harmless and actually helpful. Ok... that may be, but I want to know more about it, or else sit out. This was as we were walking down the hill to the place where they do havan. In the brief five minutes in which we sat there waiting for the others, Asatya googled havan to have me skim over the info.

That was helpful but not really enough time to absorb and consider. Havan involves throwing spices and herbs into a fire. Supposedly this purifies the air. There is also some sort of spiritual significance, but it is sort of general, like expressing gratitude and care for our natural environment, etc. There were chants in Sanskrit, but these were not interpreted for me. I couldn't find anything about it that was very clearly objectionable to my faith, but I also felt that I didn't quite understand it well enough to be comfortable with this either, especially not knowing what was being chanted in Sanskrit. I was not allowed to simply observe; they seemed to feel that they were honoring me by insisting on my participation. Having my concerns dismissed did not make me feel honored.

We had a few photos together. I never did get Acharya ji's phone number, though he doesn't speak English. I can at least say that he seems like a kind and attentive man, and more humble than he appears.

I had left my stainless steel water bottle behind at Music Man's house in Solan by mistake. Naturally, Bhai ji scolded me. He was right, although it seems near impossible to remember everything every time, when shifting from place to place so frequently. Like one of my suits got left at Nakali's house, even though I was very careful checking my room. Someone at her house must have grabbed that set of clothes to wash when I wasn't looking. I didn't like Asatya's scolding. He made it sound like I took no care in packing, but I always do. He said I was wrong to scan the room, and I should only be noticing what goes into my bag. I told him that I would definitely leave more things behind by his method, as I don't remember what I had brought for this excursion. I explained that I didn't have a packing list for the backpack, only for the big suitcase. He still insisted.

As it turned out, Bhai ji had left his jacket at Music Man's house as well. When Asatya bhai got the call about his jacket, he then decided that it would be worth it to go back (although we had to go straight past the house on our way back, anyway.) Music Man's daughter promptly met us on the roadside near her house to transfer the items. Sweet girl.

While there in Solan, we took our lunch with a young friend of Asatya who had been a kind neighbor when Bhai ji was living in Solan a couple years before. The lunch place was in an indoor market. I made the mistake of paying the bathroom attendant before going in, instead of after. It was filthy, there was no working lock, and no working water faucets (these are especially critical when you remember that much of the world including India, does not offer toilet paper.) Some people have no concept of hygiene, and some others clean obsessively. Households that have at least one adult at home full-time, or who can afford a cleaner, generally have cleaner homes than those that are poor and busy. No surprise, right?

Always, always keep hand sanitizer while traveling around India. Public bathrooms there are always a wild card. I ordered food for lunch that required a fork so I wouldn't have to touch my food.

From Solan we took a bus south towards Chandigarh. Asatya had been invited to visit the home of one of his students from Chamba. The parents of the student are quite wealthy. The father is a landowner and developer, which is a big deal in India, as real estate is very expensive. Asatya bhai had been thinking that it was unknown how many months he would have to wait before he would start collecting a paycheck from our business, and that meanwhile he needed to keep earning to support himself. Also, he still needed more money to finish the house project. He thought to talk to the student's father and find out if he had any employment position available, or if he might connect him in such a way. Asatya said that he doesn't like connecting with people for the sole purpose of looking for benefits, but he felt that he needed to, especially after the failed interview. The student's family lived in Amritsar a few hundred miles away, very near the Pakistan border. Well, there we were, eating lunch in Solan... the day was already half gone, and we had to reach Amritsar by that evening. It didn't seem possible to me.

In Chandigarh, we hoped to avoid buses, saving drive time, so Bhai ji was trying a ride app. He booked a ride, but the driver said we had to come to him. We paid for a moto rickshaw to reach the place. The driver wasn't there and ignored Asatya's calls. No doubt he found a higher paying customer and just didn't say anything. After all our experiences, it's hard to say what was the best or worst mode of travel. The metro was always fine for moving around the city, though it was extremely crowded at times, and we still needed to take a moto rickshaw to go the last kilometer or three. Rickshaws were fine if I kept out of sight so Bhai ji could negotiate a reasonable fare.

We ended up in buses to reach Amritsar. It was ok. It was after 11pm by the time we reached there. Once at the house, I thought we might have a quick bite to eat and then sleep, but the father, mother, and son were all clearly excited to have us (by us, I mean me ... I'm sure you can figure out why at this point.) The table was full of excellent food choices, plus more than one dessert. The son was only in his third year of learning English, but he knew more than his parents by a long shot. The mom gave me a new blouse as a gift. This is a very typical procedure for receiving an important guest in India - prepare them your best food, give them clothes, and let them use the best bed in the house. That marble and glass house was very large with about seven bedrooms, although they are a family of four.

Even in this wealthy household, there were less appliances and no good cleaning tools like Americans are accustomed to. Mopping means passing a rag over the floor on hands and knees. Most Indian households do not have a refrigerator, and it's hit or miss whether there is a clothes washer. In many cases, the only appliance is the gas burner for cooking. Housewives like this student's mother would have their days consumed by cooking three meals a day, cleaning all the house, and whatever little time they had before their kids came home from school, they would visit their mothers or friends, or go shopping. It's not surprising that many of them hardly give any focus to self-improvements like learning another language such as English, or anything about the world outside of their city... they have little free time. If they live on a farm, there is no free time... and yet, some people push hard to accomplish the seemingly unattainable.

The next day, the father drove us around his housing development, which he seemed very proud of. Being married to a contractor, I could understand much of the operation. Then we drove to the Pakistan border. There is an arena situated directly on the border, blocking the road that continues on to Lahore. This place is commonly known as 'Wagah Border.' There, the Pakistani and Indian border officials have what I can just describe as a patriotic pep rally. There is a parade and some songs, and they stir up the crowd to see if the Pakistanis or the Indians will make more noise. I only saw a few dozen Pakistanis, but on our side, there were about 3-4,000. The Indian flag behind the arena was tall enough that I first noticed it nearly ten miles (16km) away. The roads are very straight there, as Punjab is a continuation of the plains.

Once back in Amritsar that evening, they took us to see The Golden Temple. That temple is the number one holy site in the world for Sikhs[7] [xxiii]. Sikhs being followers of Guru Nanak. Within the outer walls of the temple, there was a large and beautiful market wrapping around the temple. Marble monuments and fountains were there, food carts selling snacks, many retailers, and kids playing with toys and in fountains. It brought to mind the story of Jesus entering the temple in Jerusalem, seeing the market there, and exclaiming, "The scripture says that my house will be a house of prayer, but you have made it a den of robbers!" Then he flipped the tables

---

7.   https://en.wikipedia.org/wiki/
Sikhism#_853ae90f0351324bd73ea615e6487517__4c761f170e016836ff84498202b99827__853ae9
0f0351324bd73ea615e6487517_text_43ec3e5dee6e706af7766ff-
fea512721_The_0bcef9c45bd8a48eda1b26eb0c61c869_20ba-
sis_0bcef9c45bd8a48eda1b26eb0c61c869_20of_0bcef9c45bd8a48eda1b26eb0c61c869_20Sikhism_
0bcef9c45bd8a48eda1b26eb0c61c869_20lies_c0cb5f0fcf239ab3d9c1fcd31fff1efc_high-
er_0bcef9c45bd8a48eda1b26eb0c61c869_20still_0bcef9c45bd8a48eda1b26eb0c61c869_20is_0bcef
9c45bd8a48eda1b26eb0c61c869_20truthful_0bcef9c45bd8a48eda1b26eb0c61c869_20liv-
ing._0bcef9c45bd8a48eda1b26eb0c61c869_22

and chased out the sellers. Well, this is Sikhism, so perhaps it's not fair to make any correlation.

To enter the middle part of the temple (which is still quite large) one must cover their head with a scarf, turban, or borrow a bandana, then remove shoes and walk through a shallow pool to wash feet before entering.

The inner courtyard had very high walls and five small towers at the corners and gates. The walls were painted beautifully, and the tower spires were encased in gold. A very large pool was in the middle. Supposedly, there is something holy about the water to have additional cleansing benefit in similar fashion to the Ganges River. Many guys could be seen stripping off shirts and jeans to go in. I find it interesting that in northwest India, the rape culture still persists to some degree, while at the same time they have a purity culture that to my American eyes, looks extreme. There at that immense pool in the temple, I saw a small building in one corner of the pool. I saw the sign by the entrance. It was for any ladies who wished to bathe in the pool. A woman could go in there to enter the water without any men seeing her. Some might argue of the differences between men and women, but to me it doesn't make sense that women must be hidden but men could just strip down publicly. The concepts of modesty are just different. Come to think of it, I never saw any women's legs while in India. You might find women of any age or background wearing a cropped blouse with their sari, showing off their midsection, but you will never see their legs, and throughout parts of Haryana and Rajasthan, you might not even see their faces. Well about that pool... honestly the water looked murky. I did see a few koi fish which caught my interest.

A causeway spans the pool. In the middle of the causeway is a building about 60 feet (18 meters) long and 40 feet wide, and three stories tall. The entire building is encased in gold leaf. The light bounces off the gold walls, leaving a beautifully rich golden glow across the entire pool and inner courtyard. Near the entrance to the gate are some very old Sikh manuscripts under glass. Nearby I could see a man in a turban holding a large, old book and another man with him appeared to be studying it. I think it was what is called the Guru Granth Sahib. Aside from these two guys, none of the tens of thousands of people there that night seemed to be doing anything truly spiritual with one exception...

Every night, hundreds of volunteers would come to the temple to pre-pare a simple meal[8] [xxiv]to serve to the thousands of temple visitors. It means that several hundred people showed up to donate time and food without expecting anything in return. No thanks or recognition was given, except a simple 'dhanyawad' (thank you) from one or two grateful visitors. Really the hospitality of this place was something of epic proportions. A few homeless people appeared to be living right there in the temple, which I can understand.

We walked through several cavernous rooms where the meal prepara-tion was done. One large room was full of carts and racks of dishes to be washed. In another room, we could see several people working over enor-mous mounds of dough to be cut off, handed off to several groups of people working in teams to roll chapatis, before handing them off to those tending fires where the chapatis were cooked. The room next to this had cooking vessels the size of a hot tub where two or three types of dal were cooked. Another room housed dozens of pallets of cabbages, potatoes, tomatoes, chili peppers, onions, and other vegetables. I was told that on weekends, they would feed up to 200,000[9][xxv]people per night. Having seen all this with my own eyes, I can easily believe that number.

Upon leaving that place, our host asked if we wanted ice cream. They had already given us sweets at least five times that day. We politely declined. We found ourselves holding bowls of ice cream anyway. I ate some. We had just had dinner less than an hour before so I couldn't finish it. The father coaxed me at least three times to finish it, but I did not. I thought in that moment that I need to create personal boundaries somewhere... incredibly there was dessert again upon reaching the house.

In Africa, I had found myself spending three weeks in a household that consumes almost no sugar. It had helped me to finally break my lifelong sugar addiction, and it is hard to express the joy and relief that I had about that. Being force-fed so many sweets was extremely frustrating to me, but I knew that my hosts could never understand that. Sometime before that, I

8.   https://youtube.com/shorts/UVg8eOBZssc?si=xtHjCacK2e0LS_Xs

9.   https://youtube.com/shorts/effxEYUjuug?si=LiUd1IfAWTHuIS6J

had expressed my happiness to Bhai ji about breaking out of the sugar addiction.

I brought it up again that night and he just chuckled and said, "No one is forcing you. It is ok to leave food on the plate." It was an interesting comment from someone who would typically coach me how to interact with other Indians and would remind me to use only the best etiquettes to make a good impression. Also, hardly any host I ever had while in India would accept food left on my plate. They would take it as an insult, or else worry that I was sick.

The next morning, Asatya bhai was contemplating when to speak to his student's father about work-related things. The mother moved painfully slowly to prepare breakfast. I offered to help but of course she declined. The father did not make an appearance until after 11am. They both knew that we had to catch a train and that we had to travel far before dark. They knew that we absolutely had to leave no later than 9am. They were not doing anything besides house chores and sleeping in. It's like they deliberately made us late.

Later, I said to Asatya, "To travel in India, you have two choices of currency to pay.

Option #1: You take public transportation and stay in hotels, paid in money.

Option #2: You stay as a guest in someone's home, possibly getting a ride from them. With this choice, you pay with an unforeseen quantity of your time, and the obligation to offer reciprocation."

The reason for coming to India would indicate which choice would be more conducive. In my case, I had barely two weeks in which to pursue our business interests, so paying in time didn't make the most sense. However, Asatya bhai got carried away and mentioned my visit to several people. Many people would take it as an afront if you only come once every two years, but you don't at least spend a night and a morning with them... that's why I wanted to keep the trip quiet...

When the student's dad finally appeared, we socialized a bit to not be rude. Actually, he was our ride to the bus station, so we couldn't go until he made a move. Our bags were packed and sitting by the door for a couple of hours before he even showed up. We stayed up until after midnight but got up by 7am to be sure to make good time. If we had known that our host wouldn't be moving towards the car until noon, we could have slept in, too.

At the bus station, we searched for a government subsidized bus (always cleaner and better) that would go directly to Hisar. There were none. We searched for any bus with a direct route. We searched for a private driver... weirdly, there was zero public transportation going directly from Amritsar to Hisar, even though they are both relatively large cities. Maybe if we had gotten to the station in the morning, we might have found something.

Well, we boarded a bus destined for Jalandhar which is more or less on the way to Hisar. We looked for any good bus available from Jalandhar to Hisar. Again nothing. However, there was a bus from Jalandhar to Ludhiana. Once again, we boarded another bus to Ludhiana and conducted the same search again. There were no decent buses, but there was a train available that went as far as Dhuri (still in Punjab), and we would have to switch trains there.

By the time we reached Dhuri, the sun had set. We tried to make sense of our tickets. They didn't say which platform our train would be on, and the station signage was not helpful. Finally, a local person seemed to know which platform to find. By then, we were running upstairs and across a skywalk to reach the correct platform in time. The train was a few minutes late, so it was fine.

Asatya poked his head into several train cars, looking for the best one for me to ride in. Asatya explained that this train would mostly be full of local poor and lower middle class people who are not much educated or exposed to the outside world. Indians tend to get involved in other's business, for better or for worse. When you add a layer of ignorance or superstition as can so often be found among the villagers, they can cause issues. Of course, being white, I am very conspicuous there. Asatya found a train car where there were a couple other women. He explained that it would be safer for me to be in proximity to other women. He also said that I should keep myself well covered, using a dupatta (scarf.) I found this to be supremely annoying, but I did it.

The ride seemed reasonable until the women got off at a stop along the way. Then there were only men left in that car. Unfortunately, those cars didn't have doors between them, so I had to stay in place. I noticed stares from a couple of men seated across from us. I covered my head completely with the dupatta because they made me feel uncomfortable and I was trying to deflect their attention. I would have covered my feet even, if I could have. It was close to three hours from Dhuri to Hisar. It felt like 30. For at least two solid hours, I could see one man in particular staring at me and sometimes at Bhai ji for several seconds, once every couple of minutes. That man really stared at me for two hours or more. I felt every single passing second. Time slowed down. Whatever intrusive thoughts that man had, I wondered how long it would be before he acted on them. I didn't dare move, although my hip was starting to hurt. I didn't want to attract any more attention. I pretended to be asleep, but my eyes remained open under that dupatta, keeping an eye on those sinister looking men.

I knew why that man was staring at Asatya bhai also. Unfortunately, I know how many Haryanvi villagers think. He saw a brown man and a white woman traveling together and thought that probably we are engaged in an immoral and illegal relationship. People who do that in Haryana are at risk of violence, even death. Or, if the onlooker themselves is a 'loose' person, they might think I am also, and they may feel entitled to try something with me. Rape culture is still there. I felt completely unsafe, and I knew that this problem would not exist if I was brown. In that moment, I very much wished that I was brown.

It is also true that if we had been able to leave Amritsar at 9am as planned, we would not have encountered this insecure scenario. I thought to myself, the family in Amritsar are wealthy and never use public transportation. I know it never passed through their minds that they had put their guest in an unsafe situation by having a lazy morning and ignoring our time constraints. Maybe they just didn't want to say goodbye.

Finally, we arrived in Hisar. We disembarked but felt confused about where to wait for our ride, as the main street closest to the train had been completely excavated down to the sewer level for some sort of infrastructure upgrade, and there was nowhere to walk. We found a dry area in between, and Bhai ji's cousin found us there.

We had come to Hisar to have a brief visit with Asatya's bua jis (father's sisters.) Asatya bhai had been out of touch with his father's sisters since the age of five when his mother died, and he left his father's native village. Only two years ago, he had reconnected with them both. Really it was like getting to know them for the first time. He had visited only one other time, but he had been keeping in touch over the phone here and there over the last two years. As it has become very clear from past experiences, Bhai ji's siblings, niece, and all the relatives that he had been in touch with, were all of them opportunists, toxic, or else impossible to get along with. Asatya bhai and I were both under the impression that he did not have any good relatives, until meeting these aunts... Asatya found them to be wise, level-headed, and kind. He felt very hopeful about them and hoped to find their kids and grandkids to be the same. It is true that they barely knew him, and as yet they didn't know that his wife had left him. He wanted to make sure that they felt confident of him as a person. He knew that bringing me there might raise questions but also settle questions.

In fact, it was a strategic visit to bolster family connections. I had predicted that the aunts would be genuinely happy to meet me, but that the others would only accept me superficially because the matriarchs put them under pressure. That appeared to not be the case. These two aunts lived next door to each other. Perhaps they had married brothers, I don't know. But they both had a few sons and just one daughter between them. Their grown children lived with them or on the same street, along with all the grandchildren. It was one big extended family all living on the same street with about 15-20 grandkids roaming about at all times, most of them teenagers.

The kids were very much fascinated with me if not a little obsessed. It's true that white foreigners can hardly be found even in Delhi, but out in the villages, foreigners are almost never seen. Therefore, I was an oddity. A curiosity. A circus attraction. The two or three kids who had fairly good English comprehension were the primary leaders of the pack of children who followed me every second like I was the pied piper. They took me for a walk around the farm roads to their favorite spot - a fruiting mulberry bush on the far side of a field beside the house. They ate all the berries within reach. They had me pose and do selfies and videos with them. I taught them swing dance. I taught them 'Somewhere Over the Rainbow' by Louis Armstrong, and 'Jiye To Jiye Kaise Hain,' which is a well-loved Hindi song - the only Hindi song that I know. Their mother heard me sing it and looked very pleased, enjoying a moment of nostalgia. I called my husband Ian and had him introduce himself and our son to the aunts and others around. My husband hates video calls but consented as it was important.

It was important because perhaps these people would not believe Asatya and I, that we were family, and not a couple. Meeting my husband and kids was to show what I am - a genuine lady with a loving family and husband of many years. No doubt this added to Asatya's credibility.

The kid's mothers became curious and wanted to be with me... I think they were happy to have a guest with whom they could uncover their faces. Remember that throughout much of Haryana, women cover their faces when non-related men are nearby. They all looked super happy though a bit shy. None of them knew any English.... Out of two dozen or more family members there, just three kids knew English. It's a farming village after all; they had no need for English.

We had just come from an enormous and beautiful house full of all comforts. The aunt's homes are very basic. Most floors were only dirt, there was no running water and no appliances except for a ceiling fan and gas burner for cooking. Nevertheless, I was quite comfortable. I was a guest of honor and if I even wanted to just wash my hands, two of the granddaughters would run for soap, a pitcher of water, and a towel. I didn't even have to search or ask.

I noticed that bua's daughter and youngest son had the same face as Prajna and Maundaata. Naturally, that shouldn't have been surprising as they are first cousins, but I was struck by the similarity. Though I had made a conscious choice to not talk to Prajna or Maundaata anymore, seeing the cousin's faces, I missed them, and I could feel tears welling up. Seeing the innocent joyfulness of all these kids, and the manner in which this family so readily accepted me, I was moved to tears. In the simple mentality of Indian villagers, it is not easy to understand the sort of crazy idea of having a sister by choice not blood, come to see them from across the planet. No doubt it was a lot for them to wrap their minds around, but they accepted me after a visit of just one Sunday. I was very happy because it really did seem like after all, Bhai ji did in fact have some good relatives. I think for him it was sort of life changing.

Briefly in the afternoon, Bhai ji and I borrowed his cousin's motorbike to go to the other side of Hisar to visit Asatya bhai's English teacher from his days as a middle school student. He was one of two or three teachers that kept in touch. Asatya warned me that he could be nice but also a bit cunning. It is true that some months before, that man had offered Asatya a job from his relative, in Spain. We figured out before long that it was a sort of scam.

We were just there for a couple of hours. He knew that I wanted to go to Jaipur. He said that his daughter has a good friend that works as a clothing designer in Jaipur. He gave us the girl's phone number.

When our visit with the aunts and cousins concluded, they dropped us off at the train station. Late that evening we boarded a 'sleeper train.' I thought that meant private compartments, but it simply meant that cot sized loft beds hung from the wall much the same as the loft beds on the older style military naval vessels. No privacy, just the ability to lie down. The 'beds' were assigned so we could not choose. Bhai ji got a bottom bunk, and I got the middle bunk above his. Supposedly this was a better train than the one from the other night. In fact, the 'toilet' and the sink were both non-functional. One simply had to do their business over the hole that refused to drain and use a bit of bottled water to wash their hands before drying them on their not-very-clean clothes. I slept a few hours but not well. I woke up around three or four o'clock with a horrendous muscle cramp in the bottom of my foot. I could not eradicate the cramp from my bunk. I had to climb down and try to walk it off. Finally, after half an hour it seemed to calm down. An hour later the cramp was back, and I repeated the walking routine.

Soon the sun was rising and outside the window, I could see Rajasthan[10][xxvi] going by. Flat, dry looking farm lands, with a few striking hills in the backdrop. It is a very typical scene in Rajasthan. Except for the hills, it looked the same as I imagined Texas to be - hot, dry, flat, and with lots of ranches and farms. I looked down and to the sides. At the last couple of stops, we had apparently picked up a lot more passengers. Asatya bhai was still asleep on the bottom bunk but I almost couldn't see him as more than half a dozen people were now sitting on his bunk in front of him and standing around.

---

10.   https://youtube.com/shorts/mL7n2o23AW8?si=m7qxVlfCKONbegUB

I AM FAMILY

The train station in Jaipur was fairly large. We were feeling very groggy and lethargic and a bit hungry. I wished for a shower. Surprisingly, there were almost no restaurants or food carts near the station. We walked randomly down a road until we came to a diner. The food was quite reasonable and cheap.

We were in Jaipur strictly for business, but we looked sort of like a pair of vagabonds, wearing large backpacks, and not exactly being fresh from the shower. Well, we figured a way to sneak in a sort of improvised 'shower.' At a public bathroom across from the train station, I took a bar of soap with me to the toilet. Most toilets in India have a small faucet in the wall near the toilet, along with a pitcher. I used the little pitcher and soap to bathe at the toilet. (Every toilet stall has a drain in the floor.) I dried my hair with the pants that I had just taken off. I got dressed still damp. Oh! I felt like a new person… but the bathroom attendant knocked loudly and barked at me to wrap it up.

We didn't have a lot of direction for where to search in this city, although we could see from google maps and road signs where the bazaars, markets and other things were located. I think we just asked our moto-rickshaw driver to take us to where we could find export houses, which he did. I probably would have done some google searches before arriving there except that I only had internet when near Wi-Fi or a hotspot which was not often, and even when I did have those things, I was forced to socialize.

Bhai ji had been given the name of a couple of places. The temperature reached 95 degrees Fahrenheit, closing in on 100. Although we had washed up in the morning, we still looked a bit haggard, and carrying large, dusty backpacks, we must have looked either homeless or like world travelers. Funny that, we were in fact both of those things, respectively.

Well, you know Google maps doesn't always lead you to the precise place, like it might show you where the office is, but not the warehouse, for example. We walked down the street, and a local man told us to follow a side street. I don't know what that guy was talking about. Nothing was there. Asatya bhai said that he had new information, and it was on the next street. Ok then. So, we followed that street for a while without seeing it. Bhai ji wanted to turn back as we had walked a few blocks already, but I said that we should continue to the end of the street.

Near the far end, we found the place with a large, bold sign out front, and granite steps. They had lots and lots of cotton cambric block prints, another back room with sample bins full of many other fabric types undyed and unprinted, all of them well labeled. A young lady of about 25 or 30 years appeared to be the manager and we talked with her. It was an export house that also supplies fabrics, as previously mentioned. Some do sell fabrics, and some don't. I think most of them do, but they don't all have the same type of fabrics or other materials. I bought cambric for a kurta (ladies tunic) and one or two sample pieces.

The next establishment that we went to, turned us away the second we approached them. The man there told Asatya, "We don't have any fabric here." As he was speaking, I turned my head as if in slow motion, to observe at that moment, a large cart being wheeled down the hallway loaded with bolts of fabric. I turned my head back, making eye contact with that man. I raised an eyebrow at that man, then turned around to leave. We both knew that his reaction was because of our appearance. So apparently, we must book a hotel room for our belongings if we want businesspeople to take us seriously. This was my very first experience ever, of encountering blatant snobbery in the business world.

Fine. Anyone with that attitude, I don't want to do business with, anyway. We went back to the door and put our shoes back on and left.

Another place that we visited had a lot of cool-looking materials and items hand-crafted on site. I got my hopes up, but they said that they would only accept measurements done in person by one of their tailors. I tried to show the man my AI-powered tech for acquiring measurements remotely from customers. He wasn't really into it. Bhai ji was keen on these people because their rates were fairly low. I tried to explain to him that low rates are meaningless if they can't accept measurements sent to them electronically. Accepting measurements taken from my tech tool was the paramount number one criteria, as our customer base would be in the U.S. and these guys are in India. I'm not sure that the importance of it had completely penetrated to Bhai ji's mind. Well, Bhai ji insisted that we evaluate these people by leaving some fabric and getting them started making a dress for me. Asatya bhai would have to ship it to me later, as there wasn't enough time to complete it before I would return home.

We stopped in at one or two other places. We found several tons of cotton block prints, in the showrooms alone. Also, there was a lot of white and cream colored cotton eyelet fabric. It was a bit pricier, but so pretty, and there are myriad varieties. The day was getting on and I didn't even get to look at any silk, which I definitely wanted.

There was one more place to check out, though it was a bit far from the exports neighborhood. We arrived on a street corner on what looked like the edge of town and there was no sign out front. It was close to 6pm and I thought they might not be open, if it was even the correct place. We stood there checking the street number and looking around a bit confused. A man saw us, who appeared to be leaving to go home from work. He said that the place was up on the third floor. We followed him. Sure enough, we stepped out of the elevator onto a gorgeous granite floor and walked a short ways to an equally gorgeous showroom.

Two men there said that the owner was out of town, but they were authorized to answer questions as far as they were able. They seated us and gave us water, and they did not request shoe removal as others had done. I briefly explained my business concept and what services I was looking for, as I had done with the other establishments. I asked every relevant question I could think of, that would indicate their ability or inability to fulfill our needs, and what was their general attitude or level of willingness to cooperate. They said yes to everything. Whether they really could, or if they just said that to make a great first impression, I don't know, but I was sitting in a large room full of examples of their work hanging on clothes hangers all around me.

I looked over many of these sample pieces. The quality was not at a top designer level but definitely not cheap or weak either. They looked quite acceptable and there were a wide variety of styles and techniques employed. Overall, this place seemed great. The only downside was that they didn't sell fabric; we would have to source our materials elsewhere and have them delivered there. Well, that's certainly manageable and worth it, everything considered. Asatya bhai saved a business card.

The young woman that Bhai ji's English teacher had referred us to was expecting us on the other side of Jaipur at a coffee house to meet and talk business. Naturally traffic was bad at that time, and we were running 20-30 minutes late. She gave up and went home. We felt frustrated thinking that we had traveled to the far side of Jaipur in an overcharging moto rickshaw, for nothing. She wrote and said maybe we could come to her house but then she changed her mind. No doubt her parents said no (she was a fresh graduate and unmarried.) Then she said... 'Meet me at this other place... and my mom and brother are joining us too.'

I suspect that when she mentioned to her family that she wanted to invite some business people and that one of them was American, they became suddenly curious, or else her mom wanted to chaperone her to meet this unknown foreigner.

However it was, we did meet them at a very nice sort of 4-star restaurant with fountains and a garden, and very good, traditional Indian food choices. I felt that I should use discretion to understand how much I should actually tell this girl. She's a designer of women's clothes for a domestic retailer so she is not quite a competitor, but still I felt some caution was warranted. I didn't need to deal with that sort of challenge... it looked like she knew many vendors, wholesalers and others that would be useful and necessary. I felt that really, I just needed a list of reputable, cooperative, and professional companies that fit my needs, along with their phone numbers. It turns out that almost all reputable businesspeople in India have a reasonable level of English, which means I myself could call them directly if needed.

This girl's brother disappeared from the table for some time, and it became apparent why: She had sent him off to obtain a gift for me. As a business contact, this was totally unnecessary but for whatever reason, she wanted to make a good impression. It was a forest green silk blend saree.

We expressed our concern to her that we were having trouble coordinating transportation, like between Amritsar to Hisar had been such a headache with no good quality transport making a direct route. We needed overnight transportation which meant that 'upper class' travel was needed to avoid entanglements with riffraff. (I know, that sounds horribly snobbish, but after the terrifying train ride from Dhuri to Hisar, the reasoning made sense.) I felt sure that this young lady, being a native of Jaipur, could make a reasonable recommendation. She said that there are sleeper buses that are ok. I would be on an airplane leaving Delhi in less than 48 hours, so it was important to travel overnight. She got the ticket purchase set up for Asatya bhai.

Later at the bus stop, we waited there at the designated time, but we spent half an hour wandering between the buses that were pulling in and out, reading the license plate numbers to find ours. Finally, it arrived. I was surprised to find that our accommodation was not two bunks, but one, about 4 feet wide (1.2 meters). This seemed like a mistake... Asatya and I were not traveling with others, and sharing a bunk to sleep did not seem right, especially in the Indian context. Had the business lady thought that we were a married couple? Or was it Bhai ji that had bought the ticket himself? I don't know. Well, I was with my vigilant brother, so I felt safe. My conscience was clean, but I worried that other passengers could cause trouble, like the Dudes from Dhuri had done. Asatya bhai lined up the backpacks between us and let me sleep against the outer wall so I would feel more at ease. With the backpacks between us, there was no space to even roll over. Amazingly, I actually slept 5-6 hours. In the middle of the night, the bus stopped for a toilet break. It was at the same Haveli or similar roadside restaurant where we had stopped with Asatya Bhratra two years ago. The exact same one.

Later in the night, I woke up randomly for a minute because I got elbowed in the face by mistake. I sleepily thought that if he was going to elbow me in the face, that elbow is my pillow now. Fair is fair, and he couldn't do it again if his elbow was pinned down. He had not woken up and seemed comfortable. I was comfortable and went back to sleep on my new pillow. There was never any question, not even a doubt about the nature of our relationship as brother and sister and this one small incident is evidence that I still had complete trust in Asatya's moral character and benevolent intentions toward me. However, it is true that if he had reserved two bunks, my eye socket would not have been struck by an elbow.

Once in Delhi, we got off at the metro. The line that we needed didn't open until 6:30am so we had to wait half an hour. There was nowhere to sit, and I felt like a zombie. From there, we went to Sama's house to have showers, breakfast, nap, and launder clothes before I returned to the dentist. It was my last day in India.

I don't know why we didn't take the metro to the dentist. The road was in poor condition, and it was one hour by bike, just beyond the border of Delhi. Riding around by bike with Asatya bhai made it clear how bad his eyesight was becoming from the cataracts. In bright sunlight he was unable to see bumps in the road, so I would watch the road ahead to warn him ahead of time so we wouldn't hit the potholes too hard. Nevertheless, we hit a few bumps hard enough to rearrange my internal organs a bit. This reminds me of something... Bhai ji had been diagnosed with cataracts, but when he had gone to PGI the year before, they said that his bad vision was actually because of hypertension. Bhai ji needing my eyes to help him avoid bumps in the road led me to ask about his eyes. He denied ever saying that the vision problem was hypertension and insisted that it had always been because of the cataracts. Well, then I started questioning my memory, what had he actually said?

At the dentist, the hygienist tried to set the new crown. It would not go. In two weeks' time, the neighboring teeth had moved closer together. I was told that the dentist was on his way back from Chennai, so he could do it.

Chennai is on the opposite side of the country. I wondered how long it would be before the dentist arrived. As it turned out, he was just disembarking from the plane when they called him. He walked in the door over an hour later. He really had flown straight from Chennai to Delhi, driven to his practice, walked right in, and set my crown. I was feeling grateful for the good timing. The crown even came with a warranty. He would ordinarily charge $100 for a crown, but Sama managed the cost, and they would not accept payment from me.

At Sama's house, the washing machine with my laundry in it, flooded across the house suddenly. The drain was clogged. I then saw the benefit of all the marble flooring (and the fall hazard that wet marble creates.) Nothing was damaged. Bhai ji helped contain the water.

I had a nap. When I woke up, Vyapari was in the other room with his son and Sama. I had hoped to sleep most of the night, but that was not in the cards. My flight was scheduled for 6:30am, which meant arriving at the airport no later than 3:30. The airport was an hour away. It seemed like to reach anywhere from within Delhi, it was always an hour plus. Of course,

Sama didn't want to wake up to take me there at 2:30am. I think the metro does shut down overnight. Sama dropped off Bhai ji and I at the airport around midnight. Asatya bhai would take the first metro back to the house in the morning, so he stayed with me until about 3am when I said goodbye and went inside to check my bags. Sitting on a bench and waiting outside with Bhai ji, I felt it important to do something that I had never done - pray *with* Asatya while I was there in person. I was thinking about our business plans, and the frustration with Pareshani, his house project, possibly Asatya would be moving to Jaipur, etc. He didn't add anything, but he thanked me for the prayers.

Overall, I felt that the trip was productive.

As I was traveling back home, I wrote back and forth with Asatya bhai, urging him to go to Jaipur right away, telling him that we were less than a month away from opening our webstore, and that I just needed him to do two to three weeks' worth of tasks in Jaipur, and then I could finally start paying him routinely as my associate. (I would have to subcontract him at first.) I even offered him some cash to float him until then.

Asatya said that he really needed to at least get a roof on Prajna's house, and locks. I thought that seemed reasonable, except that he had no money for this, and I offered my opinion that he should finish that when he started earning. He sounded nervous about going to Jaipur. His attitude didn't make sense. Asatya was perfectly capable of acting boldly and quickly, as I had seen him do many times before. Early on he had said, it would be a dream to work for his caring little sister. So, what was the problem?

Over the past few months, Asatya was becoming less and less cooperative, insisting on doing things his way on his time. He seemed the same as ever, not malicious, but he was really becoming frustrating to me, and I could hardly reason with him. I had serious doubts at this point, about working with him. I didn't know what to do with that, other than just keep moving forward, hoping that the way things should be, would become more black and white.

At the same time, the discovery of export houses made me wonder if I could even give Asatya enough work from day one to constitute a full-time job (which would be important later for visa purposes.) Still, I would need a local contact as a coordinator.

Business progress had come to a halt while Asatya was building in his native village. I had done everything that I could do without his help at that point, and I absolutely needed him in Jaipur immediately. I had a Shopify subscription and a couple of other recurring expenses, so it was important to open for sales as soon as we could be ready for it.

Flying from New Delhi to Istanbul was uneventful. The layover in Istanbul lasted several hours. It wasn't quite a long enough layover to have any meaningful city adventure in Istanbul, so I occupied myself inside the airport by becoming more familiar with it. It is about two miles from one end of the massive terminal to the other. It is good for flyers who may layover there to be aware of, as it often happens that the gate numbers are not announced until 40 minutes before departure.

While flying from there to Boston, I napped as much as I could. I had an unusual and unexpected dream.

In this dream, one thing happened repeatedly as if over the course of my whole life, with such regularity over time that it was maddening. Anywhere I went, no matter who I talked to, no one ever listened to me.

You can imagine the consequences of this...

Sometimes I could see trouble coming and I wanted to warn someone, but because they didn't hear me, they walked straight into a disaster. Or I would simply want to share a joke or happy news, but I had no one to share it with because no one listened... Or I would need something, but I would be ignored... No matter the context, no one listened to me. It was extremely frustrating, and my voice was becoming hoarse. I would try to speak louder, but I was slowly losing my voice. Peter was misbehaving but he himself was so loud, and our environment was so loud, that even though I screamed with all my might, he could not hear me.

I lost my voice completely.

I felt powerless, invisible, and alone.

After that, I was in Evan's office. A lady was there to talk to him. I think she was a client of his. I just wanted to briefly mention something, but every time I tried to speak, one of them would be talking over me. It happened over and over and finally everything I was feeling about not being heard, came out.

My extreme frustration, my loneliness because I couldn't connect with anyone, feeling that no one valued my thoughts, needs, dreams, or my care for them... I didn't just cry, I was wailing. I just sat by Evan's feet with my arms wrapped around his knees...

I woke up in the airplane to find a flood of tears soaking my face, neck, and blanket. Interestingly, no one asked what was wrong, because I didn't make a sound, just as in the dream.

Well, it is true that it often happens that people talk over me or don't hear me, which is one of the reasons that I am generally quiet. I don't like to fight for airspace.

But this problem of being disregarded has never been to the degree of it totally ruining my life, as it felt in the dream... Right?

After thinking about the dream for several minutes, it occurred to me that maybe what I saw in the dream was actually Asatya's life. He was always trying to make people understand him, but people don't listen.

Four years ago, when I met Asatya, God showed him to me in a vision, that he would be glowing or emitting light somehow with thousands of people listening to him enraptured...

It is true that all this time, I've felt absolutely certain that at some unknown time, Asatya's life is going to flip around 180 degrees and the life that he will be living will bear no resemblance to the life that he had been living...

Well, time will tell what exactly God has in mind for him and though we make our efforts, in the end nothing good comes except by the power and love of God...

We will see.

Interesting that this dream came hours after I had prayed with Bhai ji and asked God for wisdom or insight for myself, too....

At home, I developed a cold that I felt sure I contracted from somebody sneezing on our bus in India. I spent much of the next two weeks planting my vegetable gardens and resting.

Around this time, Asatya bhai reapplied the pressure for me to help him find a wife.

Many times I had tried to explain to Asatya about how dating works in the U.S., that very few people are open to long-distance relationships with foreigners, and also that people find their own spouse - they don't often accept connections through friends or match-makers. I had told him I would try to look but the chances are small. I told him he should wait until he arrives here and then start making his own connections and start dating.

Nevertheless, Asatya bhai was adamant that I persistently keep searching for a potential bride... he was talking like he was losing faith in me, thinking that I was just playing with his emotions rather than truly helping. He was beginning to talk like he could give up on me. This was not the first time. Asatya was no longer talking like a normal or reasonable person. The only way he could be satisfied was if I would actually procure a genuinely interested lady in a very short time frame. Dating in today's world as a forty-something-year-old is a whole job in itself, even at a slow pace. The level of demand was insane. It could only happen if I recruited all my friends and family to help search. I actually considered offering a reward for anyone who produced solid leads. My friend Cletus is a witness to this; he knows how large of a reward I was willing to give, because I had made that proposition to him.

At this point, I was beginning to realize that my choices were to either strain all my close relationships for Asatya's sake, or potentially just lose Asatya. I could feel in my heart that I was now doing this only because of coercive control and no longer out of love. My heart knew, but it's like I had a mental block or hypnosis.

At the time, I was preoccupied with household things after having been gone for five weeks and working on business things like the actual legal formation. Well, I didn't want this fragile brother of mine to give up, so I facetimed my dear friend Cletus J. Beauregard III.

I knew that town where Cletus lived had a fair number of hippies and other people who think outside the box... Surprise, surprise, he was really listening and encouraged me that many people there indeed had married foreigners, some of them simply to help the other person to immigrate. He said he knew a few people that might consider it. I felt grateful for my open-minded friend.

I later apologized to Cletus for asking him to help this crazy person.

Pareshani

On April 23rd, I received a message from Bhai ji that something bad had happened.

He told me that after I had gone home, he went straightaway back to Shani's house to be useful, as Shani was still sick with typhoid. On April 23rd, Shani told him to leave the house. Asatya bhai was taken aback.

He asked Shani, "Where am I supposed to go??"

Shani replied, "I don't care. Just anywhere away from my village."

Altogether Asatya bhai had given Shani about $3,600 or 300,000 rupees, Bhai ji's entire savings that he had accumulated with such frugality while teaching in Chamba. It was a year's salary from one of the best jobs that he had ever had.

Asatya told Shani that because he did not honor the deal to help us in our business, he owed back to Asatya all the money that Asatya had given him.

Asatya bhai told me, "It is because Shani knows that I am running out of money and then I won't be any use to him anymore. He won't even let me stay and feed me." Where was Asatya supposed to go without a job and running out of money? I wanted to remind Asatya about going to Jaipur, but I knew better than to call him out or put pressure on him when he was already agitated. That never went over well with him. Everyone tried to talk sense into Shani.

He wouldn't have it. The situation escalated. Shani began using intimidation tactics, having the police request Asatya bhai to come to the station but didn't say why... Shani accused Asatya of trying to take over his household. He told others that Asatya had taken him to Delhi in order to sell his kidney.

It used to be that rape and molestation victims would be blamed or dismissed often, but the Indian government was at that moment working hard to crack down on rampant rape. Remember that woman in Mukerian that had put such fear into Asatya on that occasion. Now, some Indian police

171

more often will throw someone in jail based on just an accusation without requiring proof. It is true that Asatya had been living in that small house with Shani's family for a few months, but he always left the house every time that Shani went out, just in case someday one of them might turn on him to craft a story about him.

Shani said that if Asatya tried to force him to pay back the money, that he would make an official counter claim of molestation. Asatya didn't have a family, a home, a job... he had just his reputation. Everyone that knows him regards him as a super nice guy, if not a saint or guru. If Asatya lost his reputation, he would be really left with nothing at all. This is why I would talk him up to others at every opportunity.

Nobody in that village knew Asatya bhai except as a recent acquaintance. His sister Maundaata lived in a different village of the same city. Asatya bhai didn't ask her for any help in this. I don't know why. Asatya was so infuriated by Shani taking all his money, doing nothing to reciprocate, then trying to frame him and throw him in jail for no reason. He wanted justice. He wanted his money back. Asatya spent every second on the phone looking for help. It was a group effort with his cousins, his teacher friend from Hisar, a few local acquaintances, Sama, a politician and a number of Shani's neighbors all involved to strategize and make a case for Asatya. I myself called Sama and wrote to Vyapari. Vyapari stayed out of the mess.

Sama just told me, "I only need to make one phone call, and that will shut up Shani. Don't worry."

In the end, there was an army of supporters. (Ironically, Shani's own neighbors and friends were against him.)

Pareshani had bribed the investigating officer to be favorable towards him, which did not work. He also bribed a few elderly local men to testify falsely against Asatya. I worried how the police might respond, as Asatya was a new guy in that area and not really known to them. That worry was unfounded. This was not the police's first run-in with Shani. They listened to both sides and they were laughing at Shani's claims. Naturally, the laughter made him even more flustered and irate, which didn't help his case. In the end, Shani was forced to shut up concerning his wife, and the village headman drafted a document showing that he must pay back 90,000 rupees to Asatya within one year's time. Asatya had to give the headman his bank statements to have the document made.

Asatya returned to Shani's house to retrieve his personal effects with an entourage of 20 men. Shani's neighbors were cheering and wishing Asatya well. Some people had begun calling him 'Masterji' - a great display of respect very surprising to see from neighbors that had only met him a few months ago.

However, Asatya had to go somewhere... he ended up back at his aunt's place for a few days.

All this transpired two weeks after I had returned home to the U.S. This is how Asatya had narrated the story to me. The only other person involved in this fiasco that I spoke to was Sama.

Asatya expressed the most tremendous satisfaction to me that so many people had come to support him, and he was clearly feeling vindicated. At the same time, he told me that he was really questioning himself, why did he always sacrifice for others when it just ends up ruining him? He said he was so depressed and feeling like he had a life full of mistakes, feeling like he had no hope.

I was confused because I thought he was finally free. Shani was behind him. Finally, Asatya was free to work for me and he didn't have to stress about looking for work, probably not ever again.

So much regret behind, but so much hope on the road ahead. The future looked so bright. Everyone was scolding Asatya, saying, 'When will he ever stop wasting his money on toxic and untrustworthy people?' He used the word 'suicide' again.

In Which the Poles Flip

Many times in the past, Asatya and I had talked about God and spiritual things, as he claimed to be spiritual, and he knew that I was not just a Jesus-follower, but that this fact played a central role in how I live my life. Asatya had always shown himself to be a humble man who claimed to be serious about self-improvement, so spiritual topics were a comfortable and natural part of our conversations, from time to time.

I explained to Asatya that the reason why I don't worry about the future and my baseline is inner calm and joy, *because* of my faith in Jesus. I poured out my heart intuitively, sincerely, out of understanding and compassion. I explained a bit more and took photos of some key scriptures[1] [xxvii] and sent those too. I did this with every fiber of gentleness and kindness in my being, making sure that the message of salvation was clearly understandable. That was clearly the missing piece; all my efforts these past four years was with that vision in mind - that God was going to transform Asatya and make him a beacon of light and life. I reminded Asatya of that, too. Asatya was seriously floundering, and I knew that he needed God's help.

I wrote to him realizing that problems will continue to follow Asatya until he reconciles to God in his spirit and begins to heal and transform from the inside out, which is a work done and directed by God. He looked like a ship on the sea without a compass or rudder, and he desperately needed the guidance of the Holy Spirit, which meant that he had to face Jesus. Asatya had admitted one or two weaknesses but seemed powerless or possibly unwilling to change them, and he clearly had never healed from childhood trauma.

Change from inside, and your life changes. This is a piece of wisdom understood across continents, religions, and eras in time. I admonished Asatya to think on the messages and scriptures I sent, and to not respond for a couple of days. I took the time to be comprehensive in my message,

---

1.   https://www.biblegateway.com/

remembering that Asatya would often think in black and white, or misinterpret. I had to be clear and specific.

These are the scriptures that I sent:

"Blessed are the poor in spirit, for theirs is the kingdom of heaven." Matthew 5:3

'All of us, like sheep, have gone astray, each of us has turned to his own way; 'But the Lord has caused the wrongdoing of us all to fall on Him.' Isaiah 53:6

'Jesus said to him, "I am the way, and the truth, and the life; no one comes to the Father except through me."' John 14:6

'Jesus said to him, "Have I been with you for so long a time, and yet you have not come to know me, Philip? The one who has seen me has seen the Father; how can you say, 'Show us the Father'? Do you not believe that I am in the Father, and the Father is in me? The words that I say to you I do not speak on my own, but the Father, as he remains in me, does his works. Believe me that I am in the Father and the Father is in me; otherwise believe because of the works themselves."' John 14:9-11

'We did not follow cleverly invented stories when we told you about the power and coming of our Lord Jesus Christ, but we were eyewitnesses of his majesty. For he received honor and glory from God the Father when the voice came to him from the Majestic Glory, saying, "This is my Son, whom I love; with him I am well pleased." We ourselves heard this voice that came from heaven when we were with him on the sacred mountain.' 2 Peter 1:16-18

'For all have sinned and fall short of the glory of God, and are justified freely by his grace through the redemption that came by Christ Jesus.' Romans 3:23

'What then shall we say that Abraham, our forefather according to the flesh, has found? For if Abraham was justified by works, he has something to boast about; but not before God. For what does the Scripture say? "Abraham believed God, and it was credited to him as righteousness."' Romans 4:1-3

'In hope against hope he believed, so that he might become a father of many nations according to that which had been spoken, "So shall your descendants be." Without becoming weak in faith he contemplated his own body, now as good as dead since he was about a hundred years old, and the deadness of Sarah's womb; yet, with respect to the promise of God, he did not waver in

unbelief but grew strong in faith, giving glory to God, and being fully assured that what God had promised, He was able also to perform.

Therefore it was also credited to him as righteousness. Now not for his sake only was it written that it was credited to him, but for our sake also, to whom it will be credited, to us who believe in Him who raised Jesus our Lord from the dead, he who was delivered over because of our wrongdoings, and was raised because of our justification.

Therefore, having been justified by faith, we have peace with God through our Lord Jesus Christ, through whom we also have obtained our introduction by faith into this grace in which we stand; and we celebrate in hope of the glory of God. And not only this, but we also celebrate in our tribulations, knowing that tribulation brings about perseverance; and perseverance, proven character; and proven character, hope; and hope does not disappoint, because the love of God has been poured out within our hearts through the Holy Spirit who was given to us.

For while we were still helpless, at the right time Christ died for the ungodly. For one will hardly die for a righteous person; though perhaps for the good person someone would even dare to die. But God demonstrates His own love toward us, in that while we were still sinners, Christ died for us. Much more then, having now been justified by His blood, we shall be saved from the wrath of God through Him. For if while we were enemies we were reconciled to God through the death of His Son, much more, having been reconciled, we shall be saved by His life. And not only this, but we also celebrate in God through our Lord Jesus Christ, through whom we have now received the reconciliation.' Romans 4:18-5:11

'For the wages of sin is death, but the free gift of God is eternal life in Christ Jesus our Lord.' Romans 6:23

'Therefore there is now no condemnation at all for those who are in Christ Jesus. For the law of the Spirit of life in Christ Jesus has set you free from the law of sin and of death.' Romans 8:1-2

'For in this hope we were saved. But hope that is seen is no hope at all. Who hopes for what they already have? But if we hope for what we do not yet have, we wait for it patiently.' Romans 8:24-25

'Now faith is the certainty of things hoped for, a proof of things not seen. For by it the people of old gained approval. By faith we understand that the world

has been created by the word of God so that what is seen has not been made out of things that are visible.' Hebrews 11:1-3

'As the body without the spirit is dead, so faith without deeds is dead.' James 2:26

'Therefore if anyone is in Christ, he is a new creation; the old has gone, the new has come!' 2 Corinthians 5:17

'His divine power has given us everything we need for life and godliness through our knowledge of him who called us by his own glory and goodness. Through these he has given us his very great and precious promises, so that through them you may participate in the divine nature and escape the corruption in the world caused by evil desires.' 2 Peter 1:3-4

'Dear friends, do not believe every spirit, but test the spirits to see whether they are from God, because many false prophets have gone out into the world.' 1 John 4:1

'And I will ask the Father, and he will give you another advocate to help you and be with you forever- the Spirit of truth. The world cannot accept him, because it neither sees him nor knows him. But you know him, for he lives with you and will be in you. I will not leave you as orphans; I will come to you. Before long, the world will not see me anymore, but you will see me. Because I live, you also will live. On that day you will realize that I am in my Father, and you are in me, and I am in you. Whoever has my commands and keeps them is the one who loves me. The one who loves me will be loved by my Father, and I too will love them and show myself to them. Then Judas (not Judas Iscariot) said, "But, Lord, why do you intend to show yourself to us and not to the world?"

Jesus replied, "Anyone who loves me will obey my teaching. My Father will love them, and we will come to them and make our home with them. Anyone who does not love me will not obey my teaching. These words you hear are not my own; they belong to the Father who sent me. All this I have spoken while still with you. But the Advocate, the Holy Spirit, whom the Father will send in my name, will teach you all things and will remind you of everything I have said to you. Peace I leave with you; my peace I give you. I do not give to you as the world gives. Do not let your hearts be troubled and do not be afraid." John 14:16-27

All of that I sent on April 25th. I know for most people, that would be a lot of messages to receive all at once. However, it was normal for both of us to send long-winded messages from time to time, when there were important matters to discuss, if facetime wasn't practical in the moment, so that was not unusual. Asatya especially did it often.

I never saw the train that hit me...

Asatya didn't wait even hours to respond. He didn't even sit and think about what I wrote for five minutes. Just that fact alone showed that he was not the same as the persona that he had always shown in public, or to me earlier in the relationship. He used to always listen to understand and would read every word thoughtfully. He used to also thank me for my thoughtful words.

You will at this point, and here and there later in this book, read some long-winded messages that were sent back and forth between me and Asatya. I do not make it my habit to share private messages. I do not believe in prolonging or regurgitating drama, as a general rule. Yes, I could write my memoirs for myself only, as a sort of therapy. Sure, it's been a bit helpful to me to put in writing what happened to me. That is not my main reason to write this book.

I publish this true story because it is totally normal and typical for anyone to learn about the basic concept of a particular mental illness without really having a deep grasp of all the under-pinnings: the abuse that sometimes comes with it, the dysfunctions, the comorbidities, the vast range of every-day manifestations of such disorders (a casual observer really should be careful of comparing one case to another) and the impacts on society when a large number of people have the same condition.

I am talking about the overall picture and what it looks like in everyday life, not just a clinical description in a medical journal, or an oversimplification or misrepresentation on Tik-Tok. My experience in becoming entangled with someone suffering from a specific mental condition is just one story, though the patterns of what I encountered are very much consistent with the experiences of others who have encountered someone with this same condition.

I am saying that this particular condition is highly predictable in terms of patterns, though often well camouflaged. I've heard many survivors say that their (narcissist) abuser talked and acted just like an ordinary loving person for several years before morphing into a nightmare.

Personally, I feel that if they can pretend to be good for years, why stop acting good? (Of course we know the answer has to do with what they are getting out of it.)

Everyone has very different experiences. A narcissist, a psychopath, or other disturbed person can be a mother, grown child, friend, life partner, politician, student, pastor, doctor, serial killer, therapist, *or a president of an entire country.* They can come in any form. Some look homeless and some look highly professional, gregarious, and nice. Patterns of behavior are where you will find the truth.

As I have said, there is quite a lot of misinformation floating around the internet these days, and far too many people casually call others things like, 'bipolar, psychopath, autistic, OCD, narcissist,' etc. who have no such condition, only one or two of those traits. What that does is breed even more misconceptions, fearmongering, and lack of empathy. Narcissistic abuse in particular is extremely complex. Considering that it typically takes the victims months or even years to try to untangle and understand what happened to them (let alone heal from it), it is not surprising that almost everyone else who has never become shackled to a narcissist, finds it very difficult to understand and to empathize with the victims.

So, I am here giving my first-hand account, and I am not skipping over the nasty drama in order to make you comfortable. I will share just a small portion of the dialogue and then try to summarize some of the patterns of experience that I had and then spend some time clarifying important aspects of the disorder. This is for learning and awareness and sometimes the truth is very uncomfortable. We don't want to hear about other people's drama, but if we do not learn from other people's bad experiences, understanding the entire story, we ourselves may fall prey to similar traps. Thinking "That would never happen to me, I'm smarter and stronger than that," is not a wise attitude to have. This can and does happen to all sorts of people. It is better to be open to receive a greater level of understanding.

Authenticity is important for telling stories accurately. You will notice that some of Asatya's messages have typos and grammar mistakes. I have noticed that every time Asatya would become agitated and reactive, his writing would become sloppy and at times would even look like word salad. In these dialogues, I have simply copied and pasted directly from our chat history without making any edits. (I can't include every single chat; if I were to include all of them, this book would have to be published in five volumes, and no one would have the patience to read it.)

In my case, Asatya almost never confronted me face to face; he preferred to do it in writing. This worked out in my favor, when I later went back, combing through past conversations to try to identify where the problems were, which I didn't think to do until late May...

Here is what Asatya actually wrote in response to my pleas for introspection on this day in late April:

"Remember
You can't teach spirituality to an empty stomach..
Didn't you know what all help I had been doing to Pareshani?
I don't need more preaching.
I want to marry and get settled and this is the only way to move ahead in my life and nothing else..
I am very much stuck in my life and even more since I met you..
Do you think I am less spiritual than you are?
Do you think I am less spiritual than Acharya ji?
Wow..
I have given my blood to drink to this world and the world did it shamelessly and cunningly..
I knew world used me but I kept quit.... Don't teach me Bible...
A follower of Bible would do just the same that I have done all my life....
I am giver...
I am a giver at the age of 45 plus..
When I realised that I was born as a human being, I had also realised that I was born just penniless but I took nothing but started giving to society..
Now I am tired
If I have to survive I must think of myself..
Just myself..

And yet hurting or harming anyone..
You are a US citizen..
Can you help me come to US..
Yes or No
Either is fine..
And you are still my sister..
But I don't want to force myself into fake, unreal and virtual American dream...
This fake hope has left me a dead man than I was before..
It's very much clear that you enjoy giving me lessons on value and spirituality which I don't want..
I already practice it a lot..
Do you think I am a thief or a demon?
Do you think I have problem related to immorality?
Who am I?
Have you forgotten that I worked from 5 am to 10:30 pm while at Chamba?..
I took just one day leave to get my MRI done at Chandigarh..
I even did prep duties of other teachers and round the year I did with so much pain...
Can anyone dare to give me more lessons..
A human being in me who is innocent, full of values, humanity, loyalty is dying slowly..
And almost dead
One year your childhood friend on mind..
Disgusting
Later in years I got a job at Chamba which could elevate my living standard..
I left it for cloth business
What...
I must kill myself..
Now I have no money to buy food..
Disgusting...
And now you want to teach me Bible..
What do you want from me?

Stop it before I die..

Do you want to see me dying?"

Dumbfounded and confused, and seeing how unreasonable he was, I knew that no fruitful discussion would take place that evening so I simply replied, *"I can't talk to you like this. After a couple days I will answer you."*

Asatya didn't slow down.

He said, *"And no more preaching plz..*

After this incident took place I knew that you would write / speak to me like this which would serve no purpose..

Do I respect and love you or not?

But did I like all you wrote..

*Your will never never understand that you are dragging me in a direction where **death is waiting for me** and that is nothing but excessive preaching to a person who is already a good man..*

Does it make any sense..?

I know you will stay stubborn and express your frustation in whatever way..

I will not accept it

Do you still want me?

Of course no..

Ok then..

Leave me in peace..

The good news is that you think you are right and I am wrong..

So what is the problem ◇

It's me who is wrong

Ok..

Not you..

Listen

So many people in India know you through me and this is my greatest mistake that I have introduced you to every single person I know here..

I give you the freedom to carry on your friendship with them except I am not interested in any one including Vyapari, Sama or just anyone..

If I would manage to be alive I would rather like to give life a new start than life at present..."

My heart fell into my stomach - what the hell was this? The immediate, angry, and shockingly self-righteous rejection of everything that I had stayed up late into the night praying over, gathering scriptures and thoughtfully composing... The whole message was dripping with ego and emotional manipulation, which was blatantly obvious.

All those years, I had purposefully not been 'preachy,' and never put any pressure on him until this day when it became critical. Rather, I had just shared my own experience of faith and tried to set the best example.

I wanted to make a video call, as it had been a couple weeks since the last call and I felt that talking face to face might be calming, as Asatya only ever made his confrontations towards me in writing. I wanted my husband and son to greet him also. Asatya said that he was busy on a call with some students, and that he didn't want to bother my husband Ian with his troubles. The truth is that I rarely disturbed Ian with my frustrations or stress concerning Asatya.

The next morning, I discovered that Asatya had left our family chat group. He left our business chat as well as another mutual group. I knew that to Asatya, leaving the business chat was nothing less than abandoning our business endeavor.

I had always had a bit of an empathic connection to Asatya in that I could often sense what he was feeling, though I did not know his thoughts. He didn't have to express what he felt, I knew it. If he was very stressed, I was too. That was the only mood that always crossed over to me. If he was especially upset at me, I would feel sick with a headache and nausea and low energy. This time was different. At the time that he left the business, he made no mention of this action of his whatsoever, only that he was still going on complaining that he had no job.

I could feel in my heart that Asatya was gleeful or pleased with himself for leaving the business. I was very much surprised to sense that. He had never hurt me intentionally, to my knowledge. I thought my intuition must have been broken... Asatya would not be happy about a thing like that.... right?

Just a couple days later, I somehow thought to myself that Asatya's choice to abandon the business and also distance himself from Benny and Visounou must be accepted. I didn't understand why he did it and it was crushing, but I accepted it and weirdly, I felt peace about Asatya not being involved with the business. That was another feeling that surprised me and I really did not understand it. In the past, these sort of actions from Asatya would have caused me over-the-top anxiety, but somehow even in my shock, I found it easy to accept that Asatya would not be involved in our project. It didn't seem to make sense to feel that way. I was doing the business for Asatya, and I needed his help to do it.

I thought I should at least do what I could to mend the relationship. It seemed as though it always fell to me to do what I could to smooth things over, although it was always on Asatya's terms...he would just move forward without resolving anything, unless the 'resolution' was that I conform to his thinking.

In 2020 when I had only known Asatya just a few months, I told him that I would not rest until I made him laugh until his cheeks hurt. That promise had been very uplifting to Asatya at the time. I couldn't accept his depression. At this point, I realized that no amount of love would ease the depression and he probably needed to be medicated.

This same day that Asatya blasted me out, I and my husband and kids all came down with the same illness, simultaneously and having exactly all the same symptoms. We never got a diagnosis, but it seemed to be either Covid or the flu. I could hardly smell or taste anything. I found myself mostly in bed, trying to regain my health, while taking care of everyone else also.

In fact, since the infection under the root canal in February, I had one sickness after another in almost endless succession. Just the illnesses by themselves were driving me crazy, but on top of that, one of the people that I had loved and trusted most was cutting up my heart. I tried to tune out to numb it, but the verbal assault from Asatya never ceased.

I found Asatya's behavior to be increasingly confusing. I couldn't make sense of it. Sometimes he would say things about himself that actually seemed more applicable to me or someone else. Sometimes he would say things about me or another that seemed more applicable to himself. He would speak of me or himself, the precise opposite of the truth... it was beginning to look like dyslexia of the soul.

I know it is not that we didn't communicate well enough. We talked and rehashed and talked more, I always clarified and paraphrased to ensure understanding. Also, Asatya tended to repeat himself and write at length.

Asatya never stopped writing:

"Now you know me for a long time... Do I need to tell you who am I... I think you know me more than anyone on the planet... more than my own siblings..

I can't be telling every now and then to prove who am I and if I still have to do it proves that my relationship and understanding is nothing...

with you..

I have lost Shweta which made me the saddest human being...

I found you..

And I may lose you which means It will be another shocking incident making me literally dead from inside....

But the real question is that my own people either from my blood line or not...

No one is proving to be helpful at times when I am completely traumatised...

Infact my life is not my life anymore..

People would say anything and I blindly start following them out of stupidity or innocence..

No idea..

And it has resulted into nothing but ruining me by all means..

No progress except I have aged even more every year..

No one wants to take a serious note of it including you..

I have seen it..

And I have no hopes from you..

You wrote that you have spread the word of finding a spouse for me and also you reinstituted some matrimonial site..

This is ridiculous..

People play dirty jokes with me...

You are no exception..

What were you doing all these years.

It was your second visit to India and you didn't or hardly work on this issue..

I have been asking you to take it seriously but you never never did it...
Every time I asked you of this I felt as if I was begging like a lazy begger..
Imagine..
If I would have not met you I would have married and would have reasonable life..
An American dream which would never be accomplished..
never
I know that how it is in US and India..
I am not that blind....
Maundaata, Prajnaparadha, you or more people all are my well wisher but I am slowly dying at your hands..
I must think of myself..
Or I will be forced to consume poison after 5-10 years...
As of now I may earn to supoort myself..
Who will feed me once I stop earning..
Only suicide will set me free..
I don't want anyone's sympathy..
This is clear...
Also
I am sorry to say that I can't believe your words...
I am tired of people around me..
I have hardly anytime to fix my problems...
IF YOU FEEL BLASTED OFF OR CRITICIZED..
I MUST apologize.. EXCEPT IT SHOULD STOP...
Trust me I have no intention to trouble you or criticize you..
I know I am wrong..
I start expecting from people
I know I am just alone in my life..No friend, no comrade, no family, no job, no money.
It looks I am a perfect example to commit suicide..
But I wont...
Yet I have zero chances of any growth..
I should thank God if I would be able to manage for two times meal for me..
But I don't care..

I was not born into any royal family..
I was born to a poor lady who died while trying hard to bring up us...
I have lived my life..
Who knows what future holds..
Now I have to settle scores with many bastards...
And need of the hour says
I must stop believing in God..
I must believe in myself.
You say that you are my sister and you love me..
Ok I agree but I don't want any discussion on me..
Better we talk in general......
like how is the weather etc.."

The way that Asatya was writing brought endless questions to my mind. Why did he feel the need to keep explaining himself over and over and over again? I had assured him many times that I understood. He had claimed me as sister *because* of my understanding. Asatya clearly knew that he could not blindly trust anyone and yet he always seemed to be in a vulnerable position to be victimized. Asatya had acknowledged this to me more than once before. This was not a new revelation. The situation with Shani looked like Asatya set himself up on purpose to be victimized. In fact, Vyapari accused him of this, which is perhaps why Vyapari was silent and did not involve himself in bailing Asatya out of the mess with Shani.

I was totally confused at the accusation of me playing dirty tricks on him and offering false hope. Asatya had been included in the conversation from the beginning concerning his immigration. He knew about every single effort of mine, why we agreed not to pursue one avenue or another, and how we came to agree to start a business as the solution. Altogether, it had been more than 1,000 hours of focused and organized work on my end, and Asatya had the screenshots of my dozens and dozens of pages of notes on the topic.

Simultaneous to the wild ride of drama going on with Asatya through April and May, while I was sick, and also starting back at my other seasonal job, I was interacting with my first customers who were all thrilled with their new items of clothing. No complaints about sizing, pricing, or any complaints at all. Just lots of smiles and thanks.

On April 29th, the same weekend as this fallout, the business registration was submitted to the state, and the official business formation was recognized and documented a few days later, complete with tax I.D. number and a registered agent.

All that remained to open our online store to the public was for Asatya to go back to Jaipur to confirm with a couple of export houses what our specs would be with them, source a couple of materials, and for me to get serious about marketing.

Asatya never explained why he refused to go to Jaipur, other than his claim that I was 'playing' him. He knew the plan. It was plenty clear enough and he knew we were days away from producing income. I could have gotten him started on a contract, and I would have been paying him routinely within a few weeks. I told him that. He was talking like this enterprise was destined to fail in spite of his earlier optimism and commitment to the project, and the very satisfactory evidence that we found on my recent trip, that we had everything necessary to succeed.

After the incident with Shani, Asatya had committed yet another great act of self-sabotage concerning our business project. It looked like he had convinced himself that I was leading him on, deceiving him with false hope, and he wanted to get revenge by withdrawing his help and support. I guess? His actions were making no sense, and he had gone out of touch with reality.

It really looked like Asatya was trying hard to provoke me. He had sabotaged me and was raging against me. Even gentle replies were met with more rage. Yes, it did make me angry knowing that over the last four years I was devoting anywhere from 15-20 hours per week on talking to Asatya and working on his things, as well as going far outside my comfort zone for some of these things, helping with money from time to time, and he had the gall to say that I had done nothing.

Interesting point there... in 2020, Asatya had been jobless and eventually ran out of savings and was going hungry. He refused to accept any help from me.

He had said that 'It is for brothers to take care of their sisters, not the reverse.' But months later after that he relented and even requested monetary help for his sister, niece, and a couple other things.

He then was saying, 'Because we're family. After all, I would sacrifice anything for you...'

Fast forward to May 2024. Then he was talking like I was not doing a thing. It made no sense, and I was super frustrated. I knew that Asatya was too upset to accept even the gentlest correction from me, but he was becoming delusional in paranoia. Actually, it had been a long while since Asatya had last responded well to any sort of correction.

He said that he should not blast me out - in all capitals, which is the same as shouting. What the hell was that? A mockery? Every single thing he said was twisted if not completely upside down and backwards.

He started talking about suicide again but then said that he didn't want sympathy. Right. Yup, ok. Sure dude, whatever you say. It was very clear that he wanted as much sympathy as possible.

I was taught to always take every mention of suicide seriously (and I had explained this to Asatya about two years before this) but I was beginning to feel unsure. Still, his suicide threats produced so much anxiety for me.

"The need of the hour says I must stop believing in God," Asatya had said. In the past, I had seen him make significant personal sacrifices because he stayed true to his values and morals. The way that he was talking didn't even sound like Asatya anymore. And what was that line about- "You say you love me. I agree but..." But what? How was there even a 'but?'

It was now looking as if he had never believed in God or in anyone, including himself. I recalled what Vyapari had said to me a few weeks prior- "Asatya does not believe in any god or God." At the time I couldn't imagine why he said that.

My birthday came. I was in bed, sick. Asatya was very much aware of both of these things, still he was verbally attacking me. In the past, he would write such beautiful messages and posted them publicly on my birthday. He would do the same for our family members. Asatya loved to point out to everyone the good qualities in a particular person, especially when introducing them. He could be so uplifting and encouraging like that. Here I was sick on my birthday, and he was actually being cruel. I had seen Asatya handle conflict poorly on many occasions, and I knew that he had unresolved trauma and trust issues, but his intention always seemed benevolent. This meanness really took me aback and I knew I had to get to the bottom of this strange behavior. I couldn't accept this from him.

That same day, Asatya was beginning to tell me that Shani had some further plot to attack him.

I said, *"I'll never understand how anyone could be so malicious towards such a kind person."* Obviously, I meant to express sadness and compassion, but Asatya misinterpreted this.

Asatya replied, *"You have to understand the motive behind this. He wants to scare me and distract everyone from the actual matter..*

And that is huge amount of money that he doesn't want to pay. Why can't you understand. I have given you every single update of him since beginning. And you know I was not happy with his cunning and stupid moves...

Sometimes, you must understand few things even without mentioning. Were you not there when I was writing to him while on buses / trains..."

I simply said, *"I saw what was unfolding. Understanding the thoughts behind actions is another thing."*

Asatya continued, *"I can't explain everything to you. You create more problems for me. You are not a child..*

Don't you know who that Bastard is after all.."

I did not appreciate Asatya trying to make me feel stupid. In fact, I could feel anger rising up - a new thing for me. Asatya had sometimes caused me extreme anxiety by saying similar things but this time I wasn't afraid - I was angry.

I answered, *"I'm not a chess player and there are hardly any chess players around me. It takes more effort for me to see through these people and know the motives. I don't mean to disturb you, I just wanted to know how are you and everyone there...I think you've misunderstood. Of course it's not surprising what he is doing now, I just couldn't imagine what was the purpose behind his accusations. I should rest."*

Asatya clearly didn't like this answer.

He said, *"I don't want to start a war with you. I am in pain* ☹

I AM FAMILY

And sometime you must understand without telling.. Don't pretend like a scientist.. I have no time to write a book on him for you...I am already about to commit suicide and then you start with different topics...How should I tell you why he is doing it...Ask him..Do you want me to block you...What do you want to say..

Will you stop or I should jump from the wall?

Get lost

Ok😣😣😣😣 "

I had just tried to express my feeling of what a horrible thing Shani was doing, and somehow the conversation had come to this place. It seemed that I could not say anything right, and that Asatya was conjuring up the war that he supposedly did not want from out of thin air.

I only said to Asatya, *"I can't say anything. You won't let me. I don't want to argue either. I will give you space.... ◇😣*

I hated that Asatya wanted my emotional support, but he was controlling and twisting every word of mine. I couldn't say anything right in his eyes. What was the point of answering? I was at a loss how to handle this. Asatya was super riled up yet again. Again!

He said, *"I will block you if you dare to write anything now.. I told get lost..You are troubling me a lot..I wanted to say something but you start your stupidity.. I am not able to discuss anything with you.. You make me lost..If you don't listen to me.*

YOU WILL LOSE ME..

REMEMBER..

YOU ARE GIVING ME MORE TROUBLE THAN ANYONE ELSE RIGHT NOW...I AM IN EXTREME PAIN AND YOU ARE PREACHING ME...YOU ARE NOT A CHESS PLAYER..

WHAT nonsense IS THIS?

WHAT DO YOU WANT TO SAY BY THIS???

AM I A Chess player? You write anything.. Just anything.. What is your problem???

This is how you are helping me in my bad times??? Behave yourself or you will certainly lose me and forever..

DON'T TRY TO PROVE YOURSELF..

I NEED HELP..😣😣◇♀😣😣

*I am boiling with anger.. It's me who is in great pain..Not you. Can you
listen to me* 😫😫😫😫😫😫

Don't give me unnecessary explanation..

Ok"

I replied, *"I want to cooperate with you. Truly. I'll keep quiet. No writing
from me."*

Actually, I absolutely did *not* want to cooperate with this mean and unhinged person. At this point, it was impossible to have any rational discussion with him, so I was trying to calm him down by seeming to agree. Even
that was not working. I believed that if he could pull himself together, our
relationship was salvageable and eventually we could have more mutual understanding if he would see the value or need for a therapist...

It had never once entered my mind that Asatya himself might be a chess
player (nepotist/opportunist/social climber/manipulator), but his blow-
up over this imagined accusation opened a whole new can of worms that I
had not considered. It was a very unnerving thought.

I had always believed in us as a team, as family, and my trust was unwavering. It never crossed my mind that Asatya was not just being highly
strategic with his other relationships, but with me also.

I thought about his highly defensive response where he sarcastically
asked, "Am *I* a chess player??" Why was he assuming that I was accusing
him when I was not even talking about him? Why was he over-the-top defensive? He was reacting like someone who was secretly guilty. After all of
Asatya's confusing and frustrating behaviors over the past few months, this
last spew of words from Asatya definitely looked suspicious. I made a mental note of that as I pondered what to do.

It seemed as if Asatya didn't even notice my answers, like he was totally
stuck on some narrative in his mind and he couldn't hear me. He didn't
calm down or slow down at all. I hated that I was allowing him to crumple
me into a tiny ball. I had never, ever allowed anyone to do that to me in my
life. I had never knowingly tolerated bullshit before. I had never even taken
a job as a waitress, because I knew that I would be too blunt with guests,
and I might even refuse to serve the worst of them.

The confrontational interactions with Asatya were the first time in my
life that standing up for myself felt not just uncomfortable, but unsafe. Re-

member in 2022 when I didn't have the gift ready for Agni, and Asatya almost sent me and my daughter away. I already felt traumatized, as it was. I just wanted him to calm down so we could talk normally and sort things out. Nothing I said was working.

I know that most people under these circumstances would cut off such a toxic person. It is important to remember that I had taken this man as my brother and sincerely. Also, I had made it my mission to raise up this person out of the mud, to the extent of my ability. I am a loyal person by choice, and to me it feels like a betrayal to myself and my values to give up on a person close to me without first trying everything to improve or save the relationship. There was another factor at work to keep me tied to him, that I did not yet realize at the time. We will come to that later.

Asatya still wasn't done.

He went on: *"You are writing me books.. You useless.. Do I have time even to read your unnecessary messeges.. Maundaata is proving far better as of now.. She sent me 50 K...*

knowing that in times of distress it's money that will help me keep alive..

She knows I need money at every step. I don't need preaching..

Stop it..Stop making fun of me.. Remember. You have lost me..You are a fake and so called sister..

How can you understand my pain..Whenever you will have chance to write to me..

You will start proving you and I will not allow you.. I am done with you.. Get lost.. Remember

I can only and only allow you further if you stop fucking around and just listen to me..

Or be prepared to chat with me for the last time.. Yes or No.. Decision is yours...

Remember. If you truly think that we are still brother-sister..

Learn to listen to me or be prepared to lose me.. I won't listen to you now..

Enough is enough..If Acharya ji would come to know about my present situation. He would just try to understand my situation and act accordingly which would be in best interest of mine but never giving me lessons on Vedas.. never..

I am struggling hard with Shani and you have time to prove yourself..Re-membere

If I lose you

I will be one hundred percent dead from inside...

I love you more than I love myself..

I would sacrifice my life just for a small thing for you..

My morning starts by looking into your messege and everyday I write you

" Good morning dear sister" with my eyes half shut which means I do it with so much happiness..

I cherish you more than anyone..

But I don't want to keep writing this over and again and millions of times..

I have got more things to do..

I would never think of coming to US except I found you there.. You did nothing all these years except I am forced to fall in the trap of more and more suffering.. I know you will never admit it except making excuses saying that you are not God... But at least leave me in peace.. Now I have no expectations from you.. But don't play with me.. I am a poor guy and I can't afford it..I have ruined myself even more ever since I met you.. Sooooooo much talking and zero practical progress... I am totally done with you.."

I said to Asatya that if he would be willing to talk about practical things, I would like to do that, but he just laughed at me saying what a joke that is- me and practical things. So, I thought to myself, communication has become impossible. Trying to do anything practical with Asatya also seemed impossible as he wouldn't even talk about our plans even though he expected me to be practical...

It felt like he had cut off my hands and feet and wouldn't let me do or say anything, while simultaneously calling me useless. It was immensely unfair and confusing. All this writing took place on my birthday.

Asatya was still livid over the fiasco with Shani. In the past, when Asatya had been wronged, I had noticed that he would keep a low profile to minimize the damage to himself. Rather than seek revenge, he would just distance himself from the person at fault. This time he seemed to want to make an example of Shani... Asatya said to me that Shani wanted to falsely accuse him of molesting his wife, humiliate him, destroy his reputation forever, and throw him in jail.

Asatya thought it would be just perfect to turn the tables and do the same to Shani. He asked me if I would be willing to make a police report accusing Shani of molesting me.

Shani had never touched me, but that wasn't the point. I had to ask myself if putting Shani in jail was really justice, or if it was overreaching revenge. I thought about it, only because I was trying to make amends.

I researched some Indian laws as they related to the topic. I thought about those three to four days when Shani was traveling with us, and which other people had seen us together. What possible ramifications could come from my legal involvement? While researching both Indian as well as international laws[2][xxviii] regarding sexual assault, I made a startling discovery which further compounded the trauma that I was experiencing. When I was just three years old, something unexpectedly happened to me that at the time felt very wrong, but I had no idea what had just happened, nor did I have any understanding of it. I certainly didn't realize how serious it was. Only many years later as an adult, did I come to understand that what happened to me was sexual abuse. I knew that only because an acquaintance was telling her story of abuse which was very much like mine, and the outside perspective helped me to see it for what it was. Thirty-eight years after that incident, reading legal definitions of different types of sexual abuse seemed to indicate that what had happened was by definition, rape.

I will not write here the details of that story, except for one thing: the older child who did that to me had said that he wanted to try something that he had seen on TV. At that time, not only did I have no concept of porn, I didn't have any idea of sex, either. I was hardly more than a baby.

Looking back years later, it is apparent that that child had somehow become exposed to pornography. I want to strongly caution anyone and everyone to keep porn absolutely inaccessible to children. Think of all the precautions necessary to keep guns out of kid's reach. Please treat porn the same way. I was not the only child who had that unfortunate experience that day. I can't help but wonder how often it happens that kids are sexually

---

2.   https://www.un.org/sexualviolenceinconflict/wp-content/uploads/2019/06/report/rape-and-
sexual-violence-human-rights-law-and-standards-in-the-international-criminal-court/
ior530012011en.pdf

abused by older children who found some porn and thought it would be cool to try the things that they saw. Please do your part to keep the children around you safe.

The revelation itself of what happened to me was a bit traumatizing, but at least I was finally coming to terms with it. All my life I had hardly told a single soul about that incident; I never wanted to recall that memory. It is one of my earliest memories, yet it has not faded even a little over time. But... I realized that trauma of that event seemed to lose its grip just a little bit after talking about it. I decided that choosing to speak of the abuse was an act of rejection of any shame or embarrassment that may have still been attached to it. Maybe, just maybe talking about it would somehow make that memory less traumatizing over time.

I want to take this opportunity to say that the sexual abuse did affect me, though the effects seem to have been fairly minimal. I still have some very strong aversions (strong enough to trigger a panic) of a few things that remind me of that incident, and recalling the details of the event makes me want to scream or throw something. Otherwise, nothing serious came in the aftermath of it... Although, I really don't know how that experience may have changed my psychology or affected me indirectly, as that happened so early in my development. I had experienced what many people consider to be the worst form of abuse that there is, but I'm telling you that the effect of that sexual abuse was minimal compared to the fallout from the psychological abuse that I have just come out of. This is my personal experience, and I speak for no one else.

Not all abuse is the same, and everyone reacts to it differently. Some people are more sensitive than others. Some people already have baggage. Some people have a support network and others don't. Everyone has vulnerabilities different from others. It makes no sense to compare one person's abuse to another's, but it does make a lot of sense to acknowledge that all forms of abuse in any circumstances, is abuse, and never tolerable.

You will notice that often in this book, I refer to the receivers of abuse as victims. I know many people do not like that, but I do this for a reason. Very often, abuse takes place under a heavy fog of grooming, brain-washing, shaming, or gaslighting. In such cases, the victim is conditioned to believe that somehow, they are at fault. Sometimes the abuser will even 'flip the script,' claiming that they are the one who is suffering, and accusing their victim of being the perpetrator. In order for an abuse victim to survive or even thrive, they must first acknowledge that they absolutely never deserved the abuse and acknowledge who are the true offender and victim. Healing becomes possible when you proclaim to yourself the truth of your experience. Freedom and survival begin when the victim identifies and rejects the lies of their abuser, and decides to choose freedom, and to rebuild their life.

If you have been abused, you deserve to have people around you who don't judge you or try to imagine how you may have put yourself in that position or how you may have deserved it.

You deserve to have people around you who don't tell you that you're being over-dramatic or overreacting.

You deserve to be validated.

You deserve to have your experience validated.

You deserve understanding and not pity.

You deserve reassurance and support.

You deserve to be healed and empowered.

If you find the courage to speak of the abuse, you deserve that the people who claim to care about you, take a moment to grieve with you - without rushing through it, without trying to minimize what happened, without making the story about them.

Well, I explained to Asatya that I understood the seriousness of the matter. That I wouldn't need to fake distress or upset over talking about molestation (if I needed to testify verbally,) because indeed such a thing had happened to me many, many years ago as a small child. After thirty-eight years, I remember the precise setting, who was there, the time of day, what was said and done and by whom. As much as I have wished to erase that from my memory, I cannot. It is very difficult for me to talk about but nevertheless, here I am choosing to.

I'm not sure why I told him except that in my mind, he was still my brother. Maybe I hoped to remind him that I'm a human being too, and he needed to cut me some slack.

Asatya's response surprised me and made me regret telling him. At this point, I was still believing that Asatya cared about me as his sister, and it was just that he was angry and confused and dysfunctional.

He said simply, *"This is sad. It is possible that when I was small, it may have happened to me also but I don't remember. A generation ago, women could not come home from the fields without getting raped by the landlords. Such actions were ignored or glossed over in years past."*

I don't know what he meant by that, but what I heard was, 'Rape and molestation happen every day; you're not special.'

This man of many words directed only three words of sympathy towards me before making the conversation no longer about my experience, which was in fact the topic.

This man of such strong emotions and very big heart barely acknowledged this most horrifying event in my life. It felt very cold, and I was gutted by the complete lack of empathy.

All his warnings and careful guidance about how to travel around India and interact with tricky Indians safely (because my safety was his paramount concern) naturally led me to believe that he spoke the truth when he told me how important my well-being was to him... his three words, "This is sad," did not make sense.

Asatya was doing a fine job of making me feel unsafe to even talk to him. I felt very 'iffy' about the ethical question of a false accusation against his old friend, but on top of that, I didn't feel it would be safe for me to become legally involved in a revenge plan. I did not feel that Asatya would have my back. The second he stopped trusting me (again) I would be in such hot water and for what?

Asatya had always talked about keeping me safe, as if he would take a bullet for me. He always articulated in various ways that he loved me more than he loved himself. It was clear by the way that he spoke that he understood what sacrificial love is *supposed* to look like. It occurred to me that to accuse Shani would put me in a risky legal position, but Asatya would remain safe - just so that Asatya could have revenge. He was asking me to do something unsafe and unethical for him that was not even necessary, all while stirring up traumatic memories.

I decided that the revenge plan was a horrible idea. Really, I had only entertained the idea briefly because I thought at least I could save my relationship with the man that I called 'dear brother,' by taking this bold action. It is true that Shani wasn't exactly an innocent, upstanding citizen, but that still didn't make it right.

I didn't even get a chance to tell Asatya that I would not do it, as we were still embroiled in some kind of war.

I said to Asatya that I had only needed him to do a few tasks in Jaipur before we could officially open and start selling, which would also mean I could start paying him in a regular job. He was to be the local affiliate or manager, but he was refusing. My visit to Benin yielded some results business-wise but not a lot. Mostly it was invaluable for the purpose of meeting my precious godson in person and forming memories there to be treasured forever. The two weeks in India were surprisingly and very encouragingly successful in terms of business development, in spite of the fact that we only spent three days on business things. I had entrusted Asatya with making my travel arrangements, but Asatya had taken most of my time for his unrelated personal things.

We were once a team of one mind with one goal, and Asatya had led me to believe that he was enthusiastically going to cooperate, which of course makes so much sense as he was to benefit considerably from this endeavor, over time.

I felt bewildered how to proceed, as I was on a roll with good prospects, but Asatya seemed to be showing a different face than before. Not only was he not trusting me, but he was turning the tables claiming that I was the number one person to be ruining his life. I knew that I was not perfect and had surely let him down here or there unintentionally, as is only human, and in spite of my very best efforts. I *never* wanted to let down that very insecure man, because that would torment him, and also he would vomit all that insecurity back onto me in one way or another...

Asatya wrote to me:

"I was forced to leave Chamba job because you gave hopes from business..
Can I ask you how much business is done so far
Any progress in any way..
Nothing..

Why I was planning to come to Benin?
What real purpose it was going to serve..
And what was your purpose visiting Benin or India..
Ridiculous.. The result is that poor me is starving..
I am jobless
No money
Can't move on..
You have ruined me..."

Asatya went on to assure me that he is not mean; he would give some assistance for my business and also send me that dress that I had ordered from the Jaipuri tailors, that had not been finished in time before I had to return home.

A couple days later he took back these statements for no apparent reason, saying that I was terribly mean to ask him to send that package for me (a simple matter of mailing that one dress of mine, which he had no right to withhold from me) while he was 'in pain and ruined with no future.' Interestingly, it was the very same dress that he had insisted be made for me at the export house the he was interested in but I said 'no' to.

Asatya continued:

"Before I say anything on anything..
I want to say one thing finally..
You have no right to play with people..
Yes this is true that you are playing with people and not ready to accept it..
Today I am finding you guilty, tomorrow Visounou, Benny will be in the same train and they will be in tears if they won't resist you like I do, because my face is hundred percent reflection of what is going on in my mind or heart..
You have no right to be excessively emotional with people and yet you never accept it that you are unnecessary and extremely emotional that you end up adopting a black son in Benin, making brother in India and do nothing..
Can you understand that in any any relationship in this world there are some responsibilities and obligations to do..
You can't make a drama out of it..
Why Visounou, his family are or Benny are so obsessed with you..
Just for one reason that you are a US white lady..

Imagine if Visounou would have found a lady to call her mother from neighboring African countries, I am pretty sure he would not /hardly would consider her a mother because she would be an American or European..

But when an white person comes to your house in Benin, Togo or even Indian middle classes they find it big event because they can show off to people that they have white guests from US or Europe..

From India I can give you two example

Nakali from U.P.

Samaji from Punjab.

We both witnessed that these two ladies wanted an American face to visit there house and not Petra Cineálta which means if they find more people from US / Europe they will not even feel the need of inviting you there next time which mrans there requirement was just finding any white face to show off..

Nakali or Samaji would never be so obsessed with Visounou, Benny and their families to invite them to their house..

Nakali would never like to invite Visounou even if becomes the president of Benin..."

In fact, every single word of what Asatya had written there was 100% false, except for those Indian ladies that he mentioned; I could see that he was probably right about both of them.

I never told Visounou or Benny this ugly motive that Asatya had accused them of, but they both proved him wrong in several ways, regardless.

I didn't question them or retract my trust in them, but I felt relieved to see them proving themselves to be genuine, especially after these events going on with Asatya, that they were aware of. I think they saw how much trust I had put in Asatya, whom I had met in the same forum as them, and they saw how my trust was cruelly betrayed. Possibly they were rightly concerned that I might question them, too. Anyone in my shoes might feel like the ground was coming out from under them, and they could start questioning everyone.

In the beginning, Asatya used to be kind and gentle and humble in the way that he would occasionally correct me. It is because of this that I finally came to a point in life that I felt truly comfortable with being corrected. Asatya had always maintained a narrative of deep familial devotion and great benevolence towards me, and for a long time, he didn't give me any reason to think that such words were not authentic. Therefore, I trusted his feedback about me. As time went on, the corrections began to make less sense, and to be laced with shaming. These last words of accusation stung and felt false, but I did a lot of introspection to see where he may have been right, just in case. I knew clearly that my intentions towards Asatya were sincere and good, and that I had made my best efforts to follow through on the things I had said I wanted to do for him. The only thing lacking was that results were late in coming, though Asatya knew the reasons for the delays and that they were not my fault.

I remembered then that during the first visit, in which we went to see Agni, Asatya had aggressively drilled into my head that thoughts, prayers, intentions, and even efforts all meant nothing, that only results mattered. I felt conflicted about that. It seemed to me that both intentions and results mattered... looking back, I now believe that results are what matter most in the context of business and some other contexts. Intention and effort are more important than results in the context of personal relationships. Think about it. If you can clearly see that somebody is making real, sincere efforts in their relationship with you, but they screw up a bit occasionally, will you hold that against them? Not one person among the human race is perfect. It is enough that the person truly is trying, because it means that you have their heart.

I suddenly remembered a brief conversation that I had with Asatya in the spring of 2020, not long after the conversation about U.S. immigration had begun...

I had said,

"From your side, I've worried that you want to come here and get married, but how long would that take, to reach here? A year? Five years?

I was thinking what if, in choosing to come here, you end up never getting married... or too late to have any kids... then you might be bitter towards me for suggesting that you immigrate..."

Asatya replied with no hesitation, *"I would never be bitter against you* ☺

It makes no sense..

It would be my destiny..."

I AM FAMILY

I was always careful to be realistic of what Asatya could expect to the best of my knowledge and to keep him abreast of every development. Surely he realized that my efforts to start up a business that could support his immigration, and my help to find him a spouse, mediate and support his relationship with his relatives, and other things I was doing to lift him up, was taking 20 or so hours of my week every week. Never in my life had I sacrificed so much of my time, money, energy, and mental health (on account of Asatya's deep insecurities and erratic emotions) for anyone outside of my immediate family.

I had taken Asatya as my brother in all seriousness and with fierce devotion and loyalty, as he had declared the same. I gave my all as far as I possibly could without reducing my availability and presence with my husband and children. I did it like the work of God, and I took it very seriously with so much prayer and determination not to fail. I knew I was not perfect, but my conscience was clear.

Asatya was well aware of all I had done for him and yet here he was berating me.

One thing that he said stood out to me like a flashing neon sign:

"You have no right to be excessively emotional with people and yet you never accept it that you are unnecessary and extremely emotional..."

All my life, people have called me "Spock," (a fictitious character known for displaying zero emotion and operating purely on logic.)

I've been called robotic. I've never been called emotional. In Asatya's case especially, I was always extremely careful to maintain composure at all times even when traumatized, because Asatya's own emotions were so volatile, I often felt unsafe to express myself and I thought he needed my calmness to help him stay calm.

Meanwhile, I had always observed Asatya to be an emotional creature, though I never held that against him. I was confused why Asatya would accuse me of something that was clearly not true of me, but fit him to a T. It was pure and blatant projection.

All those weeks from the end of April through late May, Asatya was in a rage. I kept trying to just give him a couple days to calm down and then try again to communicate productively and with an enormous amount of tact, gentleness and diplomacy, thinking I could talk him down from his frenzied, panicky state.

I acknowledged our frustrating circumstances and expressed my sadness over his current state:

"Whether you want it (my sympathy) or not, of course it is upsetting seeing you go through this.

Also, I lost my business partner.

You were going to help me, and you were to earn from it.

Now I am forced to make major adjustments.

This is the reality..."

The truth is that I had just witnessed Asatya victimize himself by throwing himself and his money at Pareshani, and then abandoning our business project, but blaming me for his jobless state.

At times I had seen Asatya be extremely proactive and hardworking, ready to put in the hard, honest work of bettering his life. So, I believed that his many experiences of exploitation and suffering were truly out of his hands. Seeing him sabotage himself with my own eyes, I suddenly began to wonder how many times he had done this before but later retold those stories from a different angle. Pāṣana of Himachal came to mind.

My gentle but truthful comments incensed Asatya even more, unfortunately. These brief words were the only words that I wrote or spoke in these weeks of Asatya's rage, to speak up for myself in defense. I was trying to minimize the risk of more rage or retaliation, but I had to insert the truth somewhere into this madness. All my brief, gentle, humble replies made zero difference.

This man who once held me in the highest regard and would speak of me and to me with a level of respect befitting a queen, proceeded to shred me to pieces:

"You are the ugliest face I have seen. Shall I use the ultimate word to describe who you are? A few days ago you were thinking of your fabric to be sent to you while I am dying here..

Wow..

How can you do it you useless ugly...

And now you are more worried about your business..

You ugly..

This is who you are...

Maundaata hardly knows what all circumstances I am going through and she sent me 50 K even without talking to me...

She could say too

" It's extremely frustrating to me also "

You just said...

You useless so called sister...

My own sister didn't do that..

She tried to become part of my problem's solution when I am completely lost...

Maundaata is richer than you???? You are thinking of your business??? This is your real face.

YOU HAVE LOST ME..

THOUGH I KNOW YOU WERE USING ME CUNNINGLY..

SO

ITS OVER

GOOD BYE

Because of you I lost my job.

Do you know that you fucker..

Do you at least realise I am slowly dying..

I am extremely stressed because of you..

When you came to India I was trying to build a small house for my brother or for me..

But then I had to be with you leaving all priorities behind..

And you are thinking of your business developement thing..

You are uglier than bastard Shani... This is clear..."

Asatya continued on and on in this manner and mentioned more people who he claimed were doing more than me, or whom he had supposedly lost favor with because of me.

Just a couple weeks later, I was judiciously talking to these same people, to understand who my real friends were and what were they actually thinking. What Asatya had claimed that these others were saying was 100% fabricated by Asatya. Those people were just fine, though they were concerned by Asatya's agitated mental state.

Asatya posed an ultimatum:

"LISTEN HERE ◇◇◇◇◇◇

I CAN GIVE YOU JUST LAST CHANCE TO PROVE YOUR-SELF..

OKKKK?

YES OR NO?

OR

YOU ARE NO MORE GOING TO BE CONNECTED WITH ME IN ANY MANNER..

THAT'S IT.."

These words felt hugely unfair and like a trap. With the stakes so high, he should have at least clarified what his expectation was. Instead, it was very vague. What was I to prove? Not knowing what precisely was expected of me seemed like a setup for failure. I was getting really sick of Asatya's rage fest.

I wrote a note to address some of the points that seemed to be on his radar, and because he had the gall to compare me to his sister, I sent him $600 from my credit card (because I was in fact broke at that moment, something Asatya could never understand or believe.) What else could I have done to 'prove myself' right then on the spot? Anything else would have taken time *and* cooperation from him, two things that I did not have.

In fact, I was feeling that I had exhausted all methods of diplomacy or attempts at relationship healing and this was *his* last chance with me, as it seemed no longer possible to even talk to him. I thought I would see how he reacts to the note and the money, and if he would accept that and calm the fuck down, maybe, just *maybe* our brother-sister relationship might be salvageable. If he responded negatively, then that's it. It wouldn't be possible to proceed at that point and I would cut ties with him.

I wrote:

"You asked for proof.

Will you accept said proof, or will you need more...

When you see my effort to prove myself by my actions, you need to stop cycling around through so many negative thoughts that are leading you nowhere good.

In addition to the 50K (rupees) that has been added to your account, it is also true that a few weeks ago I had a long video call with Cletus who was very understanding. He agreed to start asking among his knowns for someone who would be willing to help by marrying for immigration. I asked a relative of mine. She is considering it.

A relationship dies when there is no longer at least some trust, and when mutual listening with intent to understand does not take place.

It's unfortunate that you would believe people that have never looked to see what U.S. immigration entails, over your own sister who you know has dedicated 1,200+ hours to carefully investigating every minute detail for any possible route, to find the most likely way to succeed, and then a year of putting the foundation in place for that pathway.

Does Vyapari know about e-commerce in the U.S. market? No.

Does he or Sakhi actually know me? Not even 1%.

What is happening with them is super unfortunate, but it is not too late to prove their negative views to be wrong.

Just understand that it does require teamwork between you and me.

You're right that you and Visounou are in the same boat. Feel free to ask him his thoughts about his future. You might be surprised...

Seeing that our attempts to communicate are leading to no good effect, and that we both have much to do, I believe it would be wise for me to quietly focus on my things, and for you to quietly focus on your things.

I'll maintain my typical greetings with our mutual knowns but just greetings.

I will be out of contact with you for some time, not out of meanness or anything like that, but because we aren't able to communicate in a good and healthy manner. ...just see that my attempts to write to you have backfired consistently since the end of April. This Cold War with occasional skirmishes is not good for either of us.

Even yesterday I asked you, 'How are you?' and it ended poorly. Our connection should be a net positive and right now it is just negative.

I believe we will both be better off to have no contact for several weeks at least.

Who knows what might transpire for me or you in coming weeks.... I hope after some time to receive, and to give some good news. And what personal changes we might undergo as well...

We both need peace.

If there is any emergency, one of our mutual knowns can contact me/you.

I want to wish you well and speak kindly but I know you won't accept that... just

Take care." ◈

I had thought to wait for a response before blocking as I said that I would do, but I was so traumatized and thoroughly disgusted, that I had reached a tipping point. My anxiety was through the roof, but instead of cowering as I had done before (a self-protective trauma response) my anger was finally emerging. I had consistently been gracious towards Asatya even when he clearly did not deserve it. He had trampled all my kindness and trust under foot, which was killing my desire to reconnect with him at all, even after these years of love and unwavering loyalty.

I did not even wait to block him. Yes, sending the money was to test Asatya to see his reaction, but I was over it.

I found a peaceful place to sit, and I sat there hardly having the strength to even hold my head up, as I was extremely emotionally drained to the point of having no physical energy or strength. My finger hovered over the block button.

I wondered after a few weeks of radio silence, would Asatya realize any of his mistakes? Until May 18, 2024, I had never failed to greet Asatya twice per day, knowing that these greetings always buoyed him up. Would he scream at me for blocking him? Would he abuse me even worse than before? Would he stalk me or try to get revenge through some additional form of sabotage? Or would he have remorse and a changed heart...

Not knowing what repercussions would come as a result, I blocked Asatya.

The series of events that would unfold next, I never saw coming.

Uncharted Territory

Day #1 no contact:

A feeling of dread came over me as I waited for Asatya to find some way around the blockage to attack me. Would it be a public character assassination on social media? He had access to my bags while traveling. Maybe he had my debit card info or other sensitive info that he might exploit. It is true that every single time that we had shifted anywhere, Asatya would remind me multiple times to check my bag for my money and documents (which made me feel infantilized.) Maybe he would scream at me more. Maybe he would call up my Indian business contacts to destroy my business connections. I had seen his wishy-washy ethics, and the recent delusions, and I knew those were a dangerous combination. I had no idea at this point, how far his rage might take him.

Twenty-four hours went by. Nothing. I was afraid to let my guard down.

Asatya's atrocious behavior was beginning to look in my eyes like that of a real narcissist, what little I knew of them. It was shocking... Asatya, the man of impeccable morals and character, the self-sacrificing saint, a narcissist?? It seemed paradoxical.

I was so confused and had such a chaotic jumble of questions that no sooner had I blocked Asatya than I immediately began to feverishly search for answers to explain what the hell had happened.

My dear boy Visounou had some basic idea of what I was going through with Asatya, but he had refrained from giving any opinions.

He told me to "Search your chat history. God's gonna put a light on that. You can't imagine how long I have prayed for you..."

He claimed that he had a bad feeling in the early days and had tried to warn me. I had no memory of that. I realized then that for four years, Visounou had watched me become entangled with someone that he believed to be treacherous, and he had felt powerless to stop it. My heart broke a bit, realizing the pain and worry that I had caused inadvertently. It is true that I have witnessed Visounou show unusual wisdom for his age, so I believe what he said.

So, I did just as he said. I couldn't imagine what I might find that I didn't already know.

It did seem like there was a sort of pattern of topics that could trigger Asatya to become agitated, so I went into our chat and typed keys words of those topics into the search bar. I was looking for patterns of behavior, good or bad, any patterns.

I spent the entire day systematically searching and composing a list of behavior patterns.

By the end of the day, I had a long, comprehensive list.

In spite of Asatya making little twists in his stories, it really was true that I knew Asatya better than anyone on the planet. It would appear that he hid nothing from me. His whole life story. I knew all his friends and relatives and had their contact info. He would let me borrow his phone without asking. He seemed like an open book towards me. I could also perceive his un-expressed emotions. Heh. Speaking of that, that day that he removed himself from all our mutual chat groups, including our business planning chat group, I sensed that he was gleeful or laughing. I did not expect him to do that or to feel that way at all. Sensing that emotion shocked me, but it was unmistakable. I never told Asatya that I knew he was laughing.

I generally knew what he was feeling without him showing it, but this same intuition did not apply to his thoughts. I only knew what he was thinking by what he told me. Sometimes those sensed feelings and his words did not match, which I had always found quite puzzling. If he was depressed or anxious, of course I assumed that it was for the reasons that he said.

Well, back to that list of behavior patterns...

I knew from day one that Asatya had a lot of unhealed trauma including trust issues. I knew that he came from a toxic local area (which he always stayed away from until the house building) and of course there were differences of culture that we factored in. Knowing all this, I always gave Asatya a lot of patience and grace. He treated me very well in the beginning, and the way that he talked made it clear that he understood very well about good values and what it should look like to have a good heart that embraces personal growth and maturity. He would talk about things like true authenticity and the real meaning of family; he would denounce ego and prejudice often. He could give really informative and inspiring TED talks or a podcast if he wanted to and probably would be successful. So, my trust in him grew strong and deep. It was easy to overlook little misunderstandings or slights. He changed so slowly over time as to be imperceptible. His manipulations never looked like manipulations, until near the end. It wasn't until late April that Asatya slipped off his mask and his hidden pathological nature became obvious. Once I saw it, I could not unsee it.

Looking at my list of behavior patterns, I can't find the words to describe how I felt, seeing there in front of me just how much toxic behavior I had endured or tolerated, and how much I had misinterpreted or didn't notice.

Actually, I can. It felt like waking up from a drugged sleep to discover that I was being choked and molested.

I do not say that for dramatic effect. I am doing my best to testify accurately to what happened to me, as clearly and precisely as I can, using familiar vocabulary, as this was a new experience for me, for which I had no frame of reference. However, the feeling itself was unfortunately familiar to me, and super creepy. I felt completely violated and deceived and gagged into silence. The fact that I was sick at the time, and my throat was so swollen that I could barely swallow water, really added to that feeling of being strangled or choked.

The waking up made sense, because I was suddenly becoming very aware.

The feeling of being molested made sense, because I had been exploited, my boundaries demolished, and my personal agency or autonomy had been taken from me. I had been used and not loved.

The choking feeling made sense, because over time, Asatya shut me down more and more. If I did not express my agreement with him, he would make problems for me. There were always some fear-inducing ramifications of speaking my mind, so I learned that it was safer to just let Asatya do the talking. Any time that Asatya was agitated or feeling defensive, anything and everything that I said in those times got twisted by him to shame, accuse, intimidate, threaten, or attack me. It would cause stress intense enough to induce nausea for me. Even if I knew he was wrong, I just let him be wrong and kept quiet. I adapted by staying quiet and agreeable until Asatya calmed down, usually two or three days later. However, there was hardly ever any real conflict resolution, because if I tried to address issues when he was calm, he would often turn it into an argument, so I had to just move forward without resolving anything. Remember I had dreamed that I lost my voice. I did lose my voice...speaking up wasn't safe, so I felt forced to keep quiet. It was like he just wanted me to be an extension of his voice.

He didn't seem to view me as an autonomous person. I was unable to see that until after I got free.

You may recall the movie called The Truman Show[1][xxix]. In the movie, the main character is the subject of a popular sitcom, but he knew nothing about it. His entire life from birth to middle age was purely for the TV show. His 'wife,' his 'friends,' and his 'boss' were all actors. His own role was the only one left unscripted, so he was the only person being his authentic self. He was being filmed every day and had no idea. One day, something weird happened, and he tried to find out why. He was confused and felt something was wrong. In his quest for truth, he tried to leave town. Everyone tried to distract him or create roadblocks. This is how he discovered the outer limits of the TV filming set in which he lived. He discovered that even the weather was fake. His marriage was fake, his job, his social circle, everything was fake. He had been living as an authentic individual in a world designed just for him that was absolutely and completely fake. His life was being used for profit and entertainment without his knowledge. It was an extreme shock.

I do feel that I can understand how he must have felt at that realization... Being in a close relationship with a covert narcissist is just like that, but with more complex dynamics.

Below, you will find my original note of observations of Asatya's behavior patterns that I made that day, copied and pasted without edits. This was done before doing any research about NPD/narcissism, and only the observations that I made on that day. I realized much, much more over the following weeks that's not reflected here.

---

1.   https://g.co/kgs/aAzcqqD

Observations of Behavior Patterns:

In no particular order:

- 1. Trust:
- Claimed to be too trusting in the beginning of relationships, only to regret it later.
- Claimed me as family after the first conversation (which lasted several hours.)
- Trusted no one completely, and expressed doubts in almost everyone, *including* me.
- Always expected 100% and total trust in him or else he became very sad, angry, and questions the relationship.
- 2. Communication:
- Misunderstood me or twisted my words, then refused to listen to my clarification saying that he understood me perfectly and won't listen to my defense because (according to him) the defense shows my ego. This in particular happened a lot.
- He preferred me to talk less and listen a *lot*. Accused me of 'writing books' if I had a lot to say once or twice, while he himself wrote pages and pages, quite often.
- Wanted thoughtful replies, but expected them to be prompt, like same day, even if it's a huge question.
- Remembered to ask about my family's well-being.
- Expected me to understand him always and starts questioning the relationship and is very sad/angry if he thinks I didn't get something. He would *often* think I didn't understand him when I actually did.
- He would over-explain or repeat things and get mad at me if he thought I didn't understand the first time. He even expected me to read his enemy's mind.
- Thought in black and white, only understood me if I was literal, but expected me to untangle his cryptic or word salad messages.
- Never apologized.
- Talked more about people and navigating relationships (admittedly complicated in his context) and less about actual plans.

•Worried or complained about a problem that didn't exist, and he had plenty of reassurance for. Later after I failed to address the 'ghost' problem, he would surprise attack me.

Surprise attack looked like: Gentle correction in one paragraph followed by a 'why do you never listen,' lament, then accusations, then vicious attacks on my character laced with profanities, removal of familial status ('you're not my sister,' or 'you so-called sister,') then threaten suicide. The very last step - extend to me a 'second chance,' which required that I prove myself according to his demands. Typically, over 2-3 days and always via text, not face to face.

•Frequently reinforced several ideas towards me:

That he is poor, humble, hard-worker, surrounded by toxic people and opportunists, that he is dead inside and feels he has no future, that he is unusually kind and generous to anyone without discrimination, that he has a very high level of character and is himself never an opportunist/nepotist, that he loves me unconditionally, I'm his everything and he would do *anything* for me, even laying down his life, that I must remember his bad situation and bring results on marriage/visa thing. That he is aging rapidly and nearly out of time to settle down. That I need to listen to him. This last point was extremely important to him.

•3. Shows himself to friends/acquaintances as:

A lifelong victim (gave many, many stories of struggle, suffering, exploitation,) spiritual (generous, kind, moral, honest, family values, responsible,) doesn't value material things but rather people, just an ordinary guy.

•Introduces everyone by highlighting all their best qualities.

•Many times, I saw him meet someone new and feel that they were potentially nice people worth keeping. So, he would build the relationship and possibly extend kindness or monetary help. After some time, he would almost *invariably* find reasons to doubt them or find faults. Then he would either confront the person, or in cases where he sensed that the other person had more power, he would discreetly slink out of that relationship.

To summarize: meet, build, doubt, confront, leave.

•4. Outward habits:

•Keeps nose clean - single and celibate, no alcohol, smoking, or even meat.

- Claims to be interested in personal growth. Encourages the same in others. I have seen no evidence of personal maturation after four years...
- Excellent hygiene, housekeeping and healthy cooking.
- Uses excellent etiquette among acquaintances and strangers.
- With me and other siblings he is very generous, thinks carefully of our safety and well-being, bossy, critical, enjoys teaching me and others (which is ok most of the time), lots of doing and practicality, but zero conflict resolution skills or desire to improve them.
- Out of control anger on occasion. (He showed remorse and desire to change that, but months later broke his brother's rib during an argument, which indicates that his anger was still out of control.)
- 5. Accountability:
- Claimed to appreciate correction, being humble.
- Was always the first person to start correcting others.
- Over time, accepted correction less and less to the point of becoming aggressively angry at even an *imagined* question of his character.
- Minimized my concerns or simply didn't acknowledge them.
- When very gently confronted, flipped it around to make me look like the bad guy. This became routine towards the end.
- 6. Other:

Said he never wanted to pressure me, but expected me to prioritize him above all others, with clear cut 'homework' for me to do on his behalf that totals up to equal a 20-hr./week job, including our communications. (He knew I'm raising three teenagers and working a part-time job while also starting a business.)

- Followed laws, ethics and honesty until there was urgent need and then 'ends justify the means.'
- Called my plans immature, without hope, or childish - the same plans he had previously agreed to.
- Openly expressed all his feelings to me, expected me to coddle, but never considered my feelings.
- Said that my status as U.S. citizen was not important to him, but when acquaintances that he didn't care about asked for me, he gladly took me to them for group photo shoots, speeches, parties... was that for them or him? He also seemed to think that being a citizen gives me more clout or pow-

215

er to advocate for his visa approval- a common misconception, and simply untrue.

- Sought out sympathy, validation, or other specific response, but only accepted those things from me when he was in a good mood. If he was in a bad mood, he would say I'm insincere.

- Had denied saying something that I distinctly remember him saying. (Usually, his memory is good, but everyone forgets sometimes...)

- Said we should put our all into something but instead looked for progress updates from me while he procrastinated getting involved, himself.

- Forgave selectively, but in my case remembered every mistake (or perceived mistake) and brought up all of them during every new conflict.

- Needed a lot of reassurance which often did nothing to ease his worries anyway.

- Often indecisive, which made it difficult for me to plan precisely.

- Liked to get things done immediately.

- Worries a lot.

- Chronically depressed but hid it well most of the time.

- Weaponized or leveraged his own or his sibling's extreme generosity by making statements such as, "I could donate both my kidneys for you, but you can't be bothered to do the smallest thing??" ('Smallest thing' actually being something very big.) So basically, questioned my love because I wouldn't sacrifice absolutely everything.

- Is often generous to an extreme and thrives on the reputation of being known as a 'great human being.'

His generosity is his most well-known trait.

- Busy bee building relationships, and afterward, introducing me to everyone he knows, and often coaches me how to interact with them - which makes sense to some degree in a different culture- but why introduce me to just everyone?)

- By contrast, he hardly ever reached out to my family and friends.

- Took very seriously his responsibility to keep me safe, which I could witness while traveling *except* that he knew I brought funds for hotel/private car, but he preferred to be frugal and save my money which meant less secure travel.

•Many, maybe all his accusations, doubts etc. about me were actually his own - projection. Some of the accusations were very obviously projection. For example, he blamed me for the fact that he had no job when he purposefully abandoned our joint project which would have supplied him with a regular income, and starting within weeks.

•Tried to recruit me to falsely accuse his enemy to have him thrown in jail but told me to work on it from my side, implying it would be just me to make the legal case, without him.

•Explosive conflicts/accusations (resulting in extreme behavior and silent treatment) would happen every four months on average, starting from the beginning, but increased in frequency, especially in the last year.

In between, we got along ok, but there was a lack of mutual understanding, sort of a lopsided relationship in his favor. I tend to be peaceful and go with the flow, aiming to be supportive.

Conflicts/accusations always came without any hint or warning. It felt like surprise attacks.

I often felt confused as to what he was even talking about

Looking at my list of behavior patterns, I felt like surely there was a mistake somewhere... because it looked like the diagnostic criteria for a narcissist. When I first met Asatya, he looked like the opposite of a narcissist: humble, very unselfish, and innocent. That is the perception that I had all those four years, but as time went on, his actions that I myself witnessed, demonstrated something else. Looking at the list, I thought maybe it's not narcissism, maybe it's not what it looks like. I googled psychological conditions that are commonly misdiagnosed as narcissism. I googled the currently accepted medical definition of narcissistic personality disorder, and the precise diagnostic criteria for it. There are nine common traits of NPD. To qualify for that diagnosis, at least five of the nine traits must be present. Asatya had at least seven, no question, though I could see traces of the other two traits also.

I still could hardly believe this... I lived on Google for weeks. The only other condition that Asatya's traits came close to matching was ASPD (antisocial personality disorder,) commonly known as psychopathy or sociopathy, which is very similar to NPD in some ways.

I learned that narcissistic personality disorder is rarely diagnosed not because it is rare, but because the people who have it almost never seek a diagnosis or treatment. The reason for that is that one of the defining features of narcissism is an inability or total unwillingness to introspect and admit that either they have done something wrong, or that something is wrong with them. A narcissist lives in an extensive web of lies of their making, which is purely for their selfish benefit. Their entire life is dependent on these lies, which makes them more resistant to therapy. In fact, many therapists who are not trained to handle NPD have also been manipulated by narcissists. Many narcissists have extraordinary skill at mind games.

So I understood then, that essentially, this person whom I had adopted as family and that I loved with my whole heart, had a miserable and incurable condition, and that it is natural for someone with this condition to be abusive. They are so self-centered and with minimal if any empathy, that it would be strange if they were not. I felt like I had just learned that my best friend had terminal cancer. He would never be healthy or normal. I cried inside, knowing that Asatya was not capable of ever being happy. I remembered what Asatya had said at age 15- *"I knew that my sadness would never end. I was right to think so."* Only a supernatural act of God could alter his future and change him. I knew that I could not stick around for Asatya to destroy, while waiting for a divine intervention that may or may not come. At first, I felt survivor's guilt. I could escape the misery by cutting Asatya out of my life. I could leave him behind and be free. Asatya would never be free. He would always live in a sort of hell, with no hope of escape. I left him alone in that.

Even after his sadistic emotional manipulations, it was difficult to accept that I needed to abandon this tortured soul. I could not stay with him, and he could not escape with me.

The week that I blocked Asatya and then came to understand that he is a narcissistic abuser, was a very weird week.

The sudden revelation that my dearest friend, my precious brother whom I had once looked up to and felt inspired by, was and always had been a chameleon, a charlatan and a vampire, was beyond what I had the capacity to cope with or to mentally process.

218

After a couple of days, it appeared the blockage had really worked, because Asatya was not sneaking through anywhere to berate, attack, shame or threaten me. I knew that he would be super angry that I blocked him. He has no patience or self-control to hold back any words, so I was cringing, not knowing in what form the retribution would come.

After a few days of silence from Asatya's end, I finally began to realize that I was safe from his tirades. I was free.

Even in the midst of all the confusing and nauseating emotions of that week, there was a serenity of knowing that he could not reach me. I could rest now. All the pressure was off. The threat had passed.

I suddenly felt extremely tired.

I had been a happy, confident, healthy woman who had fallen for the extensive trickery of an actor- an actor more skilled than the greatest Academy Award winners.

I've always been an independent thinker, stubborn, and content to never follow the crowd, and yet Asatya had brought me down into coercive control. We had agreed that God had sent me to lead him on a quest to really live. By the end, this quest had been utterly warped and turned on its head. Instead of following, Asatya like a tyrant, only accepted any action or word of mine that parroted his narrative. I had to perform at an impossible, super-human level.

My experiences of being close to Asatya taught me to overcome procrastination, to be comfortable receiving correction, and it taught me patience to wait. I learned many, many life lessons. I also learned paranoia of even the smallest red flags, and to constantly second guess myself. I learned a whole collection of insecurities that had never been on my radar before Asatya. I learned people-pleasing and walking on eggshells. He had me trained, and in chains.

Not anymore.

Those who have always been free cannot appreciate at the same level as someone once enslaved, how sweet, precious, and serene freedom really is.

I wore the clothes that I wanted. I did my things on my own time. I did things my way. I talked to the people I wanted to; I avoided those I didn't want. So many times, I would pause and notice that no one was pressuring me to hurry up or shaming me for my clothing choices. My phone was no longer blowing up with notifications from a clingy and insecure man who would freak out if I did not respond satisfactorily within the hour. I no longer had social obligations to a dozen people that I really had no interest in.

My time was mine again. My money was fully my own again. My future was my own again. I was slowly reclaiming my own mind from the web of lies. I was reclaiming myself.

No one was breathing down my neck to analyze and judge every decision. I was just living my life without being nit-picked, coerced, infantilized, or attacked. I could feel the lack of those things. It felt weirdly quiet... it felt weird to have a normal level of autonomy once more. It was like standing alone on a boat on the sea, wide open in every direction. The absence of The Talker and his abuse left such a void. I could move in any direction, do anything, and nobody would pounce on me to criticize. At that time, no one really knew what I was going through. It seemed lonely and quiet out on that sea...

It is also like after a tornado. The air is calm, and you know the tornado will not return, but the terror is slow to leave. You just look around the quiet neighborhood at the wreckage, feeling stunned and overwhelmed at the mess that you must clean up and rebuild. But you are safe. The threat is gone.

First there is terror, then serenity comes, then later comes the anxiety... from any rattle of a window, any screech of wind, any siren.

That is how it was for me in the aftermath.

Within hours of blocking Asatya, I could feel a great fog lifting away from me. I had never noticed any fog up until that point, so it was surprising. I was baffled how I could have been living under such a thick fog without even being aware of it. It is true that many things that Asatya had done confused me and just didn't seem to make sense. Now it was not just making sense; the true full picture was materializing and becoming crystal clear. The clearer things became, the more questions arose for me.

Over the next few days, my thoughts became more and more chaotic and loud. My mind was in an absolute frenzy. Imagine enjoying the freedom of the open ocean, but not seeing land, having no instruments, not knowing which direction to go, while your mind is in chaos. I felt totally disoriented and disillusioned, and yet extremely glad to be free. I worried I might do something crazy.

Meanwhile, something else happened that I've never experienced before:

My emotions completely shut down.

The only feeling I had was anger at realizing that Asatya knew that he had caused me so much distress and for sure, at least some of it he did deliberately. I also had anxiety wondering what Asatya might do next. Otherwise, I had zero emotions, no feeling at all.

Around this time, I stumbled across the song entitled 'Numb,'[xxx] by Linkin Park. The lyrics and the sentiment spoke of my precise experience at that time. I started listening to Linkin Park almost daily.

It occurred to me suddenly that I had been traveling with Asatya, which meant that he had access to my wallet. What if he wrote down my debit card information? He could find ways of getting revenge for blocking him... he was not acting sane. He could do just about anything at this point. It is true that he would remind me every time we went anywhere, to double check my wallet and travel documents. I thought, what if he was really thinking of himself? What if he knew that he was the real threat? I replaced all my cards.

Aside from the anger and anxiety, I could not feel any emotion at all for the next eight weeks or so. I had no opinions, no reactions.

That week and for a while after, I tried to force myself to go about my normal routines, getting kids off to school, going to work, making dinner and all that. I was putting all my effort into simply focusing on the task in front of me, but I just could not concentrate for even one or two minutes on anything. What would normally take five minutes to do took me one hour. Mindless work was easier, but still slow due to my low energy. The mayhem of shock and hundreds of questions in my mind kept me living inside my head for months.

Those first few days and weeks, one of my kids would talk to me like normal, but it was like I was not even there. I would think, does Maundaata know? Is this why she never wanted to talk to Asatya, or even to me, being

---

1.   https://youtu.be/kXYiU_JCYtU?si=DAN81p3HMZQURcuE

connected to Asatya? Was this a long-con?? Was he jealous of Visounou? Did he think that disrupting my business would cause havoc in my relationships with Benny and Visounou? Maybe that is what he meant when he said that later they would also find fault with me... I wonder if every single person I know in India will take Asatya's side? Will anyone believe me or understand? Will Ian understand? How long will it take for Asatya to stop trying to contact me? I couldn't even hear my kids trying to talk to me...

"Mom."

Oh God. What if, in trying to cope with this guy, I've developed some dysfunctions or become toxic?

"Mom."

What if *I* become the next monster??

"MOM!"

"Oh. Sorry. What?"

"Are your ears still working? It's like you're deaf. You keep doing this."

This scenario would play out numerous times in a day. I really did try to be attentive, but it seemed impossible. My husband and kids started to worry about me.

I was so lost inside my own head that I was not living in the present at all. I missed hundreds of moments, all the conversations, every movie we watched, and even at work I was trying with every fiber of my being to stay focused during team meetings and to remember whatever we had agreed on. Notes and alarms set in my phone helped me to have at least some functionality. I worried somebody would realize that I was totally out to lunch and tell me to take a mental health day. I didn't want to explain to my boss or coworkers that one mental health day would absolutely not be enough. I knew I would not be back to normal again for a long time. Meanwhile, I needed to work. I worked alone as much as possible so that nobody would notice that I was just going through the motions in a zombie-like stupor, and a bit slower than usual. I didn't want my coworkers to ask me what was wrong.

My energy level and motivation plummeted almost over-night.

At some point, I realized that every time I sat down, including in my car, my head would slump over or fall back. My energy level (both physical and emotional) was so low that I didn't want to talk or even hold up my own head.

I had never felt so extremely drained in my life, physically, emotionally and mentally. Not even as a new mother. What was causing that? My theory is that I had been giving so much of my time, money, emotional and mental labor to one person out of love and compassion, only to suddenly realize that I had been *conditioned* by the recipient to feel more compassionate and subsequently give, give, give. I had no idea how much had been taken out of me until I finally stopped and was able to rest.

I started out doing everything out of compassion, but by the end, I was a slave under coercive control. Nothing I did was ever enough. There was always another need, another request, another demand. I had been drained of all the love I had to give by an energy vampire who disguised himself like a chameleon. I felt almost dried up and lifeless. I wanted to be there for my kids, though it was a massive struggle just to engage in basic conversation with them that summer of 2024. It was like Asatya was still taking joy and life away from me even after going no contact.

My business development had come to a screeching halt as I pondered these personal developments. Asatya was out of the picture, so that eliminated one of my motivations for forming the business.

The two other people who would have benefited from it were now actively pursuing their own developments in ways that looked hopeful.

I myself felt that I was not in a good mental state to be able to really focus on the work.

At the same time, my daughter's health appeared to be deteriorating in ways that I didn't understand, and I knew she would need a lot of my time and attention, probably for the next few years. If I was going to be there for her, the business would have to be shelved until sometime later, probably for a few years.

My husband was struggling to understand what was happening to me. My life had been upended. I was angry. In fact, in those weeks, the only emotions that I could feel were anger and anxiety.

I had just discovered that a large part of my life over the past four years had been based completely on deceit and manipulation. I had poured my heart and soul into that person, and I had no idea what to do next. I felt totally unmotivated, except for one thing: Survival.

Having neglected myself more or less, to help someone who turned out to be using me, I then became determined to take control of my future and my life, and it started at the most basic level- my health. I became especially devoted to physical fitness.

In the winter of 2024, I had an abscess in my mouth grow out of control then rupture, sparking off a sudden and very serious full body infection which required immediate and very strong antibiotics to keep me alive. Later, I got a water-borne gastrointestinal upset while traveling. A cold, a flu, and some other virus came to plague me. I had precious few healthy days between January to June. In late May when I had just broken free from Asatya, I was still sick.

I had been sick for so long, and mentally and emotionally totally depleted. I began to take care of my health as if my life depended on it. It really did feel like a matter of survival. I could have sunk deep into a depression, and I was afraid of that. Depression is just another kind of captor... I refused. I did not want to become a lifeless ghost or shadow of my old self. I was determined to live. I was living in a sort of survival mode. This survival mode was based in fierce determination whereas the survival mode that I had been in while under the abuse, was based in fear. In fact, I had so many vague fears and lies in my mind from Asatya that I still needed to untangle and be freed from.

Survival mode is obviously draining and unpleasant, but I found that there is a benefit in it that does not exist in comfort. In survival mode that is based on the will to live, that will to live intensifies. Motivation to make one's life better becomes very strong. Because one is already far from their comfort zone, making necessary changes seem easier. The crisis that caused the survival mode uprooted me like a tree, and roots became legs to walk straight out of there. I could go in any direction and become a whole new person. It is like when you get a surge of adrenaline, and you suddenly feel stronger for a few moments. I realized that while I was living in survival mode, I had almost superhuman strength to make significant changes in myself to ensure my safety and well-being. While my physical body struggled to summon energy, internally, my determination to really live intensified like a fire. To quote my favorite movie, "From the ashes a fire shall be woken, a light from the shadows shall spring..."

I still felt half dead and traumatized, but my resolve was like titanium.

It was weird, to be both strong and weak at the same time, in different ways.

I found it easy to say no to most things as people had become a bit scary to me. I began to walk and run and hike most days. Eventually, I started swimming laps at the pool and lifting weights. God knows I needed those endorphins. All this physical activity made me feel my anger getting channeled into a fierce determination, a passion. I felt half dead, but I had to push through. This was my physical act of rebellion and resistance against the depression that threatened to take hold of me.

You may wonder how I was able to be so physically active if my energy level was low. Truly, the motivation is what pushed me to move. I felt that I just had to do it no matter what. My energy came back eventually, slowly.

About three to four weeks after blocking Asatya, it would appear that he finally began to panic, thinking that I might have given up on him. Over the next several weeks, I received messages (which I could clearly identify as his writing style) from our mutual contacts, most of these pressuring me to get in touch with Asatya. They said that he had lost his mind, that he was lost in his head, just repeating my name over and over. That he was deeply distraught with grief. All this accomplished was to help me identify what more people I needed to block.

It was frustrating trying sort out the mayhem in my head, and the perpetual anxiety which just continued to build, while Asatya was relentlessly trying to shame me, appeal to my compassionate nature and loyalty, or else make it sound like he would die without me.

It started with passive aggressive posts on social media.

One day, Asatya had posted:

"In a relationship like this, you end up feeling like a worn out puppet - tethered toxically to a person who controls you through their emotions. You always feel you have to be careful what you do and say even though they have the freedom to do and say as they wish.

You have to tip toe, acquiesce, sacrifice, be mindful, and always obsequiously attentive.

When you associate with them, you feel as though your free will has been taken from you.

Why? Because they are pulling the strings that emotionally torment. If you have been in a relationship like that, it is a relief to get away and when you look back, manipulation doesn't even begin to cover what you have experienced.

Oh God why can't I know who is playing with my innocence.

I need to set the degree of being human or it's going to cost me my life."

I saw this before I had blocked Asatya on Facebook. I was angry and just amazed that Asatya could write something like this. I thought hard, who he might be dealing with that would make him feel that way. The truth is, he always spoke his mind. The only exception to that was in his place of employment and only to keep his job. Even then, sometimes he could not hold back from speaking his mind. Asatya told me everything that happened in his life and he never seemed intimidated by anyone. He had no fear. However, he himself could be intimidating.

In fact, what he had just described in the post was my experience relating to him. I could never say everything on my mind. He could create an argument out of anything and turn it on me, so I was constantly trying to keep him calm, even pretending to agree, if that's what it took.

I am a sensitive person who is easily corrected by a gentle word, so Asatya's rage was far beyond what I had the ability to cope with. I avoided that in any way that I could. As far as I could tell, the only way to avoid his anger was through compliance. (This is known in psychology as the 'fawn' response. This is one of four possible automatic reactions to trauma, the others being fight, flight, and freeze.)

Asatya had described the experience that he was inflicting on me, and very articulately. It was so precisely accurate, that I was forced to consider that Asatya knew what he was doing to me, and perhaps he had strategized all this drama on purpose just to watch my torment.

What Asatya wrote was a perfect mirror-image projection. After that, I reflected back and was amazed to realize how much and how often Asatya had projected. It was like you could know what bad thing he had done by listening to what things he complained about the most in others.

His brother's ego seemed to be a topic of conversation at least once a month. I got tired of hearing his complaints about that. He would scold and fight Prajna, telling him to stop giving his entire paycheck to all the world, only to beg Asatya for 500 rupees because he then had no money for food.

It almost seems like he could not bear to confront his own shortcomings, so anytime he thought he saw his own flaws in someone else, he felt compelled to berate them. Unfortunately, I had seen him accuse an innocent person of doing what he himself had done. He did this to me throughout the month of May, and sporadically in the past.

We had never been brother and sister. This was a cat and mouse scenario.

I joined a support group online for victims of narcissistic abuse. Reading other people's stories helped me get even more perspective. I read about some horrifyingly hellish experiences, and some that were petty. It seemed that there were very strong patterns, though the severity had a broad range, and every form of abuse under the sun was frequently attached to this personality disorder.

Through that group I was introduced to Dr. Ramani.

Dr. Ramani is a clinical psychologist specializing in narcissistic abuse. She herself had been targeted by narcissists in the past, so she understood the topic intimately well. I followed her on YouTube, and this also was very helpful to me to validate my experience, myself as a human being, to better understand what goes on in the mind of a narcissist, and how to better keep myself safe and secure. I highly recommend looking up Dr. Ramani on YouTube.

I don't like to block or cut people out unnecessarily as that seems very unfair to me, and I know that people are not automatically guilty by association. So, I was a bit slow in blocking mine and Asatya's mutual contacts.

I think that for people who are trying hard to break away from an abuser, and who struggle to break their emotional bond, it is really necessary to block all mutual contacts if at all possible, and immediately - the second you leave. One of the reasons why is 'flying monkeys.'

The flying monkeys are the people around the narcissist who have fallen for the fake persona and become convinced that they are a good person. This makes them much more easily manipulated by the narcissist. These people are often acquaintances but they can be relatives and close friends.

The narcissist is so good at masking their evil side with the fake persona that they are also very good at creating followers, supporters, or fans. The narcissist generates sympathy in these people, and then asks them to mediate, send a message, or do anything else for them that is designed to bring them supply. (I will explain supply later.)

So essentially, flying monkeys are the narcissist's pawns.

Even after making that list of behavior patterns, even after the shocking behaviors that I was seeing, I still questioned the conclusion I had drawn that Asatya is a narcissist. It was hard to accept that he was the precise opposite of everything that I had thought that he was.

He had invested so much time and effort and relationships and more, over many years to create an elaborate but fake persona.

Even his tone of voice and the look in his eyes matched up with his fake narrative. He didn't have to rehearse; he could just react on the spot without breaking character. It looked like as if he believed his own lies and delusions, and yet it is clear that at least some of his deceptions were conscious and intentional. He was a better actor than any of the famous ones from my favorite movies.

For me, it worked out to my benefit that I was slow to block the others, because they confirmed the bad news unintentionally, as they are less skilled liars. They put more nails into the coffin of our relationship, making it easier for me to break away.

Nakali, not knowing that I had sent money to Asatya, wrote to me. I could easily recognize that Asatya told her what to write, but she wrote it in her own words to reflect her own personality and level of English.

She wrote:

"I wanted to say something to you, as you know that Asatya Bhai is making his home in his native, he has not left money and he is facing difficulty to wind up it.

Of course you must know the matter.

I wanted to say that I and Maundaata have sent him as much money as we could, at this time my school is closed due to summer vacation,so I also have facing Mony problem.i could not send him more.

I am expecting that you help him with some amount as it is our responsibility that our brother's house be built.

I know I don't have any right to say you that but I felt that you will definitely help him .

Because as his nature he never asks for money from me ,but at this time he himself is asking for it.that means he needs to much.

I hope you will understand what I meant ."

This woman had hardly ever written to me a total of two lines before this. Did they really think I would believe that she wrote this on her own? I knew it was Asatya asking for money. Did he really think that I had internalized enough of the shame that he had tried to inflict onto me, that I would send more money? Or was he just using this woman to mock me?

Asatya knew that I had already sent him $600 just a week and a half before this. Nakali did not know that. Asatya was clearly using Nakali as a money source, and as his flying monkey. I told Nakali exactly what was happening and how Asatya was using her. She acknowledged that Asatya is 'aggressive in nature,' but she continued defending him. Well, I tried to warn her, but I would not entertain this woman further, so I blocked her.

I discovered something interesting about Nakali... one day, as I was mindlessly scrolling social media, I saw a familiar face listed under 'suggested for you.' It was Nakali in the profile photo, but with the name 'Giroha.' So then, Nakali was a Giroha.

Asatya was always talking about people, and he always explained to me how various people were connected. He had introduced both Chhota and Nakali to me, but separately. He had practically given me their life stories but never gave any indication that these two people might possibly be connected to each other. I thought this seemed like a strange omission of information. I remembered the day that we had visited Nakali's school and had lunch at her house where Chhota Giroha and Asatya Bhratra had joined us for the afternoon. Supposedly Chhota had never met either Nakali or Asatya Bhratra, but they all had acted so casual and friendly with each other, like old friends reuniting after a long time. This stood out as really unexpected behavior, as in Indian culture, there is a heightened level of formality that is always given, when meeting people for the first time.

On the way back into Delhi from there, Asatya had told me not to mention to Vyapari that we had been visiting people from that region. He said that district of U.P. has a bad reputation and he didn't want Vyapari to be upset at him for not only going there, but bringing me along with him to meet some people there.

I couldn't help but wonder what Asatya was hiding from me. At this point, it is no longer relevant to me. Just another unsolved mystery to let go.

While it is true that Nakali and more people like her chose to associate with Asatya, I could not point the finger at any of them for letting him use them. All these messages that I was receiving at this time from people that I had met all over north India, had a familiar flavor.

Not long ago, my support and solidarity for Asatya were so iron-clad that I would gladly speak up on his behalf without even researching the issue. I had felt I was doing a good deed to mediate as I had been invited to, between Asatya, his sister, brother-in-law, and elder niece. When Asatya's previous boss refused to pay him his last month's salary and blocked him, I contacted his boss at Asatya's request, to talk sense into him. Asatya composed a script for me to possibly edit and then send it to his boss. This happened on many occasions, that Asatya would write a message for someone and send it to me to look over. If I agreed that it looked reasonable, I would send it to the person that Asatya intended it for, except that it came from me and was meant to look like a message from me on Asatya's behalf - NOT written by Asatya himself. I justified this in my mind because I wanted to help my brother, and I figured that if I agreed with what he wrote, it may as well have been written by me anyway. Remember, solidarity. In all those situations, Asatya was the one in the right as far as I could tell, so I thought that all was fair and right.

Now that it was summer 2024 and I was the one receiving all these messages *and* knowing both sides of the story, I could clearly see how he was using these people and I knew that meant that he had used me just the same way, as a pawn for him to try to gain leverage over somebody. I hated that I had been pulled into that ugly business. Perhaps I would have picked up on the unfairness of these scenarios sooner, if I had witnessed *all* the previous interactions prior to my involvement. In most of these cases, the previous interactions were in Hindi, which I barely know any of, so I was mainly operating on trust.

This was one more thing that I would not miss. I almost wanted to call up all those people that I had been used to get to, to apologize. The truth is that most of those people that I contacted for Asatya were just as toxic as he was or even worse, hence the problems between them that I ended up mediating. I didn't have the emotional energy to contact anyone like that. I wanted so much to evict Asatya from my head. I did try to test or warn about five or six people that I thought might be reasonable and worth holding on to.

When I had been in India visiting the two aunts and all their progeny, they had bonded with me easily and happily. Unlike so many others that I had met while traveling through India, they were not trying hard to look perfect for me or show me fake niceness. They just seemed like normal people, as you would expect to find in a small village. At first they sat quietly listening to my story, but they accepted me quickly and the horde of teenagers and children never left my side . A few of these teen cousins kept my phone number to stay in touch.

One of them had created a chat group and added the others plus myself and Asatya, insisting that he help them improve their English and I would help...That was in late April or May. We had a few sessions before the Pandora's box of Asatya's poor mental health burst open and put a stop to general life progress for a little while.

I knew that if I continued talking to those innocent kids they would come to find out that I was no more connected to their cousin Asatya, and then there would be lots of questions... I thought that if they had a good relationship with Asatya, it wasn't my business to ruin that. Asatya had been overjoyed to reconnect with some good and kind-hearted relatives, and I knew that he needed that. As weeks went by and I began to realize the true depths of Asatya's lack of real character, and his extremely manipulative nature, I felt more concern about the well-being of those kids and realized that Asatya's well-being could not come at the cost of someone else's well-being.

I didn't know if anyone would listen to me, but I warned the two brothers (the kid's fathers.)

One of them didn't respond much so I reached out to the younger one. He told me that his brother is illiterate. While I appreciated this explanation for the lack of response, I didn't like that he seemed ready to talk negatively about his brother. He seemed sympathetic to me at first, but something just didn't feel right... Then he asked me if I had had a physical relationship with their cousin. I knew that he had no good intention in asking that question. Luckily the answer to that question was no, though who knows if he really believed that.

I remembered that Asatya had told me that none of these cousins speak any English; he said that only a few of the kids knew a bit of English. Asatya spent more time with this family than with anyone else, but he didn't know that some of them spoke English? Either Asatya lied, or his cousin withheld that information from him and me, even during my visit which seems suspicious. Anyway, the net result of my talk with those two brothers was that they looked skeptical and possibly untrustworthy, so I blocked them. If they were going to still support Asatya, then I could not talk to any of them. I had to block those brothers and all of their kids. I hope those kids will be okay.

I had to block 53 out of 55 Indian contacts. In the end, only one person proved themselves to not be a flying monkey (compromised by Asatya) and a real friend to me.

Sama did not understand all that I tried to warn him about Asatya, but he knew enough to distance himself from Asatya and not trust a thing he said or did. Sama remained kindly a gentleman towards me. He is a very down-to-earth, no nonsense sort of person, very business savvy, sometimes a bit gruff or blunt, which is probably just his Haryanvi roots showing through, but actually I've seen nothing but kindness and wisdom from him, and so he has remained my friend. His wife and young son are just as nice.

I did not block Vyapari, even though he asked me one time to talk to Asatya and calm him down. Vyapari didn't quite understand the situation, but I think that is only because he is too busy in his own life to try to devote the brain cells and energy to figure out the dysfunctions of his childhood friend. He just wanted Asatya to stop harassing him about me. (Asatya was harassing many people about me.) After I told Vyapari that I can't tolerate him making any attempt to reconnect me to Asatya, he never said another word about it.

Asatya kept making new accounts on social media with variations of his name and photos without his face, undoubtedly to stalk me remotely. I kept having to block more of his accounts, and adjusting my privacy settings. I also would search all these name variations once a week to check for any new accounts to block. I got unexpected friend requests from people in India. I don't know if these were more flying monkeys, or if Asatya was hacking other's accounts now.

Asatya had reached a level of obsession and desperation that I have never seen before. I then completely understood how people end up with stalkers that sometimes end up murdering them. It is an extreme level of obsession, a total and complete absence of any respect for boundaries or laws, a level of delusion and crazy that normal people can't wrap their minds around... unless they listen to crime podcasts.

I wondered if Asatya would finally use all the 'donations' he had garnered to fly into Central America and try to sneak across the border from Mexico to come find me. I knew that he possessed the lack of ethics and the determination to attempt that.

Months later in February 2025, I was at the pool to swim laps. I saw a man at the other end of the pool who looked sort of like Asatya, but he was wearing goggles so I couldn't say for sure. I told myself that even if Asatya succeeded to reach here, he would not be at the pool. Not only does he not swim, he would not sleep until he found me. Realistically, I know he would look for easier supply, rather than come through Mexico. At least, that is what I tell myself.

By mid-July 2024, my emotions were beginning to slowly return.

The last thing that I had said to Asatya on May 18th had been that we need to not talk to each other for some time so that we can calm down and gain perspective. I didn't want to talk to Asatya at all, but I felt like I should stick to my word and allow him the chance to apologize. I wanted closure, and I wanted to see if after all these weeks, he was able to acknowledge his wrongdoings, knowing that only a sincere apology and admission of the abuse would give him even a grain of hope at reconciliation. Personally, I thought maybe there is a 1% chance that he will show remorse.

My ever even-keeled and supportive friend Cletus was at my house that day to paint the exterior. I asked if I should unblock Asatya to let him apologize. He said "Don't do it." I asked Ian. I asked my support group. Everyone said don't do it. Yet somehow, I felt compelled... If nothing else, I knew it would be closure for me as I finally said the things that I had always wanted to say but feared the response.

I knew this would be my last communication to Asatya ever, so I held nothing back. I wrote:

"Asatya-

Firstly.

Understand that I am not angry at you.

I forgave you from the moment you were doing deliberate and harmful things.

I don't want revenge; I want you to heal what made you toxic in the first place.

This is the last time I will write to you and perhaps the first and only time that you will listen to me. And you WILL listen. Memorize this message if you must, but just make sure you understand it and take it seriously.

Do you remember the dream I had while flying home on April 11th? I lost my voice because no one listened. Why do you suppose I had this dream immediately after saying goodbye to you?

You know that it was God who caused you to meet me. Did that happen so that you could help me? No.

Wasn't it that God has something for you through me? Even you called me an angel or messenger of God... So then shouldn't you have been open-minded and curious what that is, and listen carefully to all I have to tell you?

Instead, you never listened to me. Instead, you only cared that I listened to you, and you didn't mind even threatening me or trying to shame me to keep me silent.

I've been told that you are going insane and that your life is in danger.

I underestimated the peace I would enjoy after I blocked you. Believe me, I have zero interest in sacrificing the peace that I now have, but only because you are suffering and you seem to have no idea why (you think it is because you are missing me), I will give you the tools you need to heal yourself and be whole, functional, sane, and get your joy back.

Just understand that you will be doing that healing without me.

This is the last time that I will write to you.

So for the love of God, and for once in your life, stop listening to yourself talk and listen to me!

Don't you dare act like a victim instead of opening your ears to wisdom. I saw that last message that I'm certain you wrote. You're still portraying yourself as a victim to gain sympathy and support from others. Shouldn't you be prostrate apologizing??

This is your last chance to stop all the noise in your head and listen to life-giving words so you can escape from the hell that your life has become.

If you ignore what I am going to tell you, I'll assume that you actually enjoy that hell and leave you to it.

Can you listen now??

Alright.

You were right to say that I know you better than anyone. It has become apparent that I know you better than you know yourself even. I've observed many things about you that you seem to be completely unaware of.

The first step towards healing yourself is to understand what is the problem. You can't address problems if you don't know what they are or if you're not willing to admit that you have a problem. There is no shame in having a problem. The only shame is assuming that you have no problems and becoming defensive when someone raises a concern. Ego is not your friend and you know that.

I say this because I care about you: you are very much broken inside. This is why you feel dead. None of your past hurts have healed. Rather, they have become gangrenous and that gangrene is draining your life from you.

Also, it is hurting the people that you care about, mainly your siblings. I know, Maundaata and Prajna have the same problem, but right now we are not talking about them.

I think you don't actually want to hurt anyone. But you cannot avoid hurting people while you are broken inside. You will absolutely drive away from you every single person that cares about you, as long as you ignore the train wreck inside of you. Marriage will not fix you. I cannot fix you. All your good deeds will not fix your broken heart either. Unfortunately, if you have all those things in your life, your brokenness will infect them and drive them away. For example... I know why Shweta left you. Maybe her family is toxic like you said, but that is not the main reason...

Look back. You lost your mother when you were hardly more than an infant. Your father was hardly ever present, and I think you underestimate how damaging that was to you. Fathers are extremely important. Nobody guided you so you had to try to figure out life on your own. You say Prajna received no love but in fact you hardly received any love either. That void of love drove you to try to find it anywhere and by any means. As a vulnerable young person, you trusted all the wrong people. From your many experiences of exploitation, you learned to trust no one, which explains why you even didn't trust me on many occasions. Even you doubted Shweta. How could you? Because you lost your ability to trust...

You learned that good people are few and far between, and you would be afraid of losing them so you (perhaps subconsciously) learned to manipulate them into staying. You have lived in survival mode all your life. In fact, you did have times that were okay and you could have relaxed but your brain was stuck in the panic or anxiety of 'what if?' Any time something happens in which some detail of it brings back a traumatic memory, you are gripped with anxiety and your subconscious screams "Fight it!!" Or "Run!!" This is post-traumatic stress disorder or PTSD. PTSD is what is responsible for your repetitive and sad dreams.

The PTSD I feel sure is the reason why you are afraid even to trust hope, and even though you knew it would take time to work towards your immigration, you still saw time ticking by and after the incident with Shani, you panicked thinking that I am future faking and leading you nowhere, even though I was the one person on the planet who was sacrificing my time, energy, money and more... my husband was trusting you or he would not have let me invest in a business at a time when we had less money...and you knew that....You can't trust me because you have lost the ability to trust anyone.

I am not an expert but I think that you may have a dopamine addiction and you need a trauma therapist who can better help you to release the pain from your past, to unlearn some of your self-destructing habits (that you might not even realize that you are doing) and to help you create new habits to keep you mentally and emotionally healthy.

I know you are confused what I mean by dopamine... it is a hormone naturally produced by the body that gives a feeling of happiness and satisfaction. Enjoying friendships, romance, a fulfilling career, exercise, exploring nature, etc. These things promote dopamine production. Your dopamine levels become wildly out of balance which is why you have these crazy mood swings... Like one minute you're saying that I'm your cherished sister then the next minute you're threatening to abandon me. When you talk that way to someone who loves you, their dopamine gets out of balance also.

Your brain chemistry is very much out of balance. It's not just the dopamine.

If you could read your own messages to me (from the last few weeks) with someone else's eyes, you would be disturbed to see someone who is not just grieving... you are very much obsessed with me and in fact addicted. I see now why you couldn't even go a single day without a greeting. You look like someone who lost the person that they were in love with. I know that you made additional profiles so that you could stalk me through social media. This obsession is creepy and unhealthy. It is not good for you or me.

This is one of the reasons why you need to have no contact from me. You think you can't live without me, but that's the addiction talking. See, if you were mentally healthy, you would be grieving right now but still able to function and you would eventually be happy again. As it is, you are a train wreck on the inside.

Maybe you have zero desire to live and don't care about healing. But I believe that you find joy or fulfillment in caring for others. You must understand from this day forward that you must heal your broken self, or you will hurt everyone you get close to.

Ignoring this problem is an act of malice. You absolutely must address this.

If your physical appearance matched what you look like on the inside, there would be blood everywhere and bones protruding... but never ever make any excuse for abusing others. You know what it is to be abused.

You must not pass on your pain to other people.

Kind people never inflict pain onto others. Can you even imagine, after I realized what you've done to me all this time, I was worried that I could become like you and manipulate others....

About me. For the past two or three years, there have been some problems of communication with you. Often you would shut me down. It was often the case that you would not let me talk. If I tried to answer you would call it 'ego.'

In fact, I humbled myself so much when talking to you. I thought I was being humble but actually you were walking all over me and I didn't correct you because I didn't want to be verbally attacked.

I couldn't correct you about anything. You gradually became more defensive over time. Many times, you missed very important information because you didn't let me talk. Then you became more agitated because you were making poor decisions because you didn't have enough information...again, I couldn't correct you and then you would turn and blame me...

In May, when you demanded me to prove myself (after telling me not to prove myself) I only sent you that money to call your bluff. But I was so disgusted that I didn't want to even wait for a reaction.

It was absolutely impossible to talk to you. I blocked you because I knew you would continue raging and I needed you to calm down. I had to cut you off. I thought I could talk to you after some weeks.

Do you realize that I trusted you completely right up until May of 2024? Even after many toxic conflicts and many things you did this past year that made no sense and you never explained, I chose to continue trusting you. The day that I blocked you, I asked myself how can a supposedly kind person abuse their own sister so badly... I never questioned you until you became overtly cruel. For the first time, the fog lifted, the drama ceased, and I made a scientific study of what went wrong, using the search bar in the chat to identify behavior patterns that might give answers.

I can never forget that week. When I stopped trusting you blindly and I realized how frequently you silenced me, the extensive manipulation tactics, and worst of all, I saw that every conflict had a pattern: first you would find fault with me (real or imagined!) then you expressed frustration and depression, threaten to either kill yourself or abandon me, then tell me that if I would just do .... (Whatever you are wanting) then maybe everything will be ok. After I would comply, then you would revert to your nice self like nothing had ever happened...you need to understand right now that this sequence that I've just described is extremely manipulative and textbook psychological abuse. If you really believe that you are a good person, you must put a stop to this immediately and forever. It is extremely damaging. I now have PTSD/anxiety from the abuse, and after blocking you I went through about 8 weeks of dissociation. I couldn't feel any emotion at all except anxiety from you.

When I realized that you were not just never letting me talk, but also controlling me, I was sick at the time and my throat was swollen so that I could not swallow food.

This realization of what you were doing felt exactly like waking up out of a sound sleep to realize I am being suffocated and molested at the same time.

If you don't like being compared to a pervert, then don't look at people as if they are assets... yes you do that. You told me you didn't want Samaji, Nakali or Chhota in your life, among others. Not only did you keep in touch, you took my precious time (immediately after Sama said to make good use of time on this short business trip) and gave it to them.... Why?? You like to hold onto people in case they might be useful later. I know I was extremely useful to you, and not just to fuel the dopamine...

I have a question, just answer it to yourself: why did you often accuse me of things that you did?

You said that I used you. How so? You can't answer that because I didn't... it was I who was very useful to you.

You said that I am 'extremely and unnecessarily emotional.'

In fact, all my life people including my own husband, say that it looks like I hardly have any emotions.... I do have emotions. I just control them.

However, you are highly emotional. This is not a fault, just a characteristic, but you tried to make it seem like a fault of mine... ◈

That FB post that began "in a relationship like this... you find yourself walking on eggshells... manipulation doesn't even begin to cover what you have been through..."

Tell me, who was the person walking on eggshells?

If you don't even realize that you were the person doing that to me, that is all the proof I need that you have a personality disorder for which there is no cure or treatment and I am right to protect myself by staying away.

If you know that you are toxic and even have some character flaws that you are ready to admit to and change, that is your only hope for a brighter future.

I haven't even mentioned every way that you've hurt me, but my goal is not to overwhelm you, I just want that you wake up finally and realize that you are not the angelic being that you think and you are definitely not as humble as you think... but you have to abandon your ego.

If you fight this message, mark my words, you are the same as Maundaata and Prajnaparadha - Brick walls unable to see their faults and change themselves.

So

•Find a therapist who specializes in trauma, in particular childhood trauma. Talk to one and cooperate with them.

•Talk to a doctor about your depression. I feel sure that you need to take an antidepressant. (I know you don't like meds, but you need to get over it and take care of yourself.) If you don't enjoy being miserable, do it.

•Lastly, the most important thing is the spiritual component which is the foundation under everything.... Don't you dare be dismissive this time. Don't you know that your spirit is the core of your being and if your spirit is not well, no part of your life will be well.

When you will be completely healed, you will no longer be a beggar, chasing after people like me to fill the void inside of you which is larger than any human can fill.

When you will be healed, you will be overflowing with so much life that light will seem to come from your eyes and hands...

Like the gangrene in you has touched me and others... what is in you gets passed to those in your connection...don't you want to pass on more love and light?

You will be a Life-Giver.

You will have a new name.

Instead of one who starts fights, you will be a peace-maker.

When you empty yourself and invite God in, you will be full.

Instead of a victim, you will be a rescuer.

Instead of attracting evil-doers, they will be afraid of you.

You will not need people to make you happy, because you will feel the presence of the Divine Father and Lord of Eternity standing by your side as the Most Faithful Friend. You will feel overwhelmed by this blessing of familial intimacy... that you had lacked but craved all your life...searching for your mother's face in the crowd...and your search will be over as you rest in that joy.

*When you throw away your ego and you feel a voracious hunger to hear the voice of God, with no pretense, no agenda, nothing, just a ready heart and listening ears... I do believe he **will** speak to you. Because I asked him to. You* *have kept too busy and talked too much to listen. When you hear his voice, do not ignore. He wants you but only if you want him.*

You see, you think that you are already spiritual because you are generous with time and money, but you abuse your siblings and anyone else that you think is in the wrong.

The act of doing good things does not make you spiritual any more than putting on fancy clothes, paying for a wedding banquet and arriving there does not make you the groom.

What would make you the groom is that you met the bride's family and they and she accepted you. You need to know each other first.

Spirituality is nothing less than intimacy with God.

Your good acts will not save you.

Simply believing in God will not save you.

The entire human race has been estranged from God ever since the rebellion in the beginning of our history. It is only through the mediator Jesus Christ who took our punishment on himself, that we can have forgiveness from God and be reconciled to him.

The reconciliation is a personal choice. God is not interested in our rituals and superficial efforts. He wants us. He wants to be involved in our lives and that we be connected to him directly like children in their parent's home.

When you will be reconciled to God, he will put his own spirit in you and you will experience spiritual birth.

You will know when it happens because immediately you will feel different.

Where once you were stagnant and stuck, you will be growing.

Every blessing that I stated earlier will come to you, and much more that you are not even capable of imagining or understanding at this time.

Just like any good relationship, this requires trust.

I have found that the more wholeheartedly I put my trust in God, the more I witness him working in my life in every aspect.

If God is the creator and author of life, being closely connected to him will logically generate more life in you.

"For I know the plans I have for you, declares the Lord - plans to prosper you and not to harm you. Plans to give you hope and a future."

After your month-long tirade against me in May when I was forced to cut off contact, I said to God, "I know that you would not lead me astray. I know the prophecy that you showed me concerning this man (you) and you were very clear in your direction that I support this man however I could towards that future that you showed me... it looks like I wasted four years. What happened?"

Immediately I heard a voice say, "You did what I asked. He did not."

Listen.

If you could not hear God speak to you, you could at least trust me, whom he sent to you and follow what I was doing. You followed briefly but doubted me constantly, alternating between saying that I am a messenger of God, and later saying that I am ruining you. You know which it really was.

Don't you know the anxiety that you brought into my life? If I had not received that direction from God to help you, I would not have stayed with you this long, because I never tolerate anyone to shut me up and try to control everything. (Not Ian or my mother, my friends, my brothers... Get it? That behavior is not acceptable from anyone.) But this is not about me.

I talked about reconciling to God through Jesus in April, and you responded exactly as I would expect that a demon would. It was as if I had lit you on fire. I think even you surprised yourself with that extreme reaction.

Isn't it obvious now that there is a spiritual war going on? There is something very, very good in your future, but the evil forces that exist have tried to crush you at every turn of your life, even making you into a sort of monster. They didn't succeed in crushing you completely so they are recruiting you.

I know that you don't have the wisdom or strength to overcome that. This is why I told you to start by turning to Jesus.... Bro he is alive today. Alive with scars in his hands where the nails were!!! He defeated death. Can you even comprehend that power?? He is called the Servant King for a reason. Like he said that the last shall be first and the first shall be last.

It amazes me how many Indians act like karma is not real. God sees all and he is not fooled. Justice will come to those who think God is blind, and those who seek refuge in the arms of the Lord will receive healing.

Let me tell you something about me and Visounou.

Because we have the spirit of God living in us, and because we have at times chosen to run straight into spiritual battles, we have witnessed things...

I AM FAMILY

We have seen supernatural intervention, miracles, etc. We have also seen the work of the devil and imposters. We both have known immediately at times when someone was a snake, faking a spiritual rebirth.

Only the Holy Spirit is the greatest power in existence. No one can fake that influence.

When someone tries to fake the Spirit's influence, we recognize that immediately. It's as fake as an AI robot.

When the Spirit speaks through someone, that also is clear, because it will match up with that same spirit in our hearts.

There is a reason for telling you this...

I told you.

You need a therapist, antidepressants, and Jesus.

I know you will try to force or rush your way through those things in an effort to prove you are better and get me back. It won't work. I just told you why. We will know if it is real or not.

Don't do these things for me.

In fact, you need to break free from me in order to heal. Remember that dopamine addiction... your dopamine was coming from me and now you are in withdrawal.

Do these things so that you can live... not again... but for the first time. You are not old. Saying that your life is over is fatalistic and nonsense bullshit. You keep living your life until the grave forces you to stop. This is a minor thing, but start expressing gratitude to God primarily but everyone else too. Even the server in a restaurant. Being always grateful is part of being happy. Your mind is a garden and what grows there depends to some extent what you allow to stay there, what you cultivate and what you rip out.

Someday probably years from now if I hear through a friend of a friend... Asatya Bhratra is not even the same person now... he is unrecognizable. Happy, calm, balanced, not chasing people...maybe I would think of talking to you at that time.

Don't change yourself for me. Do it for yourself.

I know you want to get married but you need to heal yourself so you don't unintentionally hurt your new wife as well. Two failed marriages would end you. I know that.

I wanted to tell you this months and months ago, but I knew that you would not listen.

Again:

First step is kill the ego and humble yourself before God.

Ask for God's forgiveness, not mine. Talk to him directly and frequently, every day. You have a Bible. You are supposedly a lifelong learner. So get started.

I will unblock you long enough for you to make a real apology.

You have an hour. No need to write a book, just get to the point.

Bye." ◈

Unsurprisingly, Asatya saw my message almost immediately and pulled over on the side of the road to respond. He was already typing a response within five minutes of receiving my message, which means that he had not read it. He was a mess. He seemed to be crying and thanking God to be hearing from me. I was not interested in an emotional display; I wanted to see if he would show genuine remorse.

Asatya kept typing on and on, trying to explain himself and saying, "I'm sorry for my stupid acts, please give me another chance!" No real apology. No acknowledgment of any of his specific offenses. He reminded me that it was God who brought us together and he insisted that "Your job is not finished yet." One of the messages that he wrote was interesting because it came near to the truth although I could see that he didn't fully understand why he was the way that he was and there was still some manipulation mixed in:

"Let me try to explain this to you..

Trust me I am honest to explain this how it is...

Suppose..

Hannah was playing with her friends and someone hurt her physically or abused her..

It's possible that she would vent all her anger on you knowing that you didn't hurt /abused her..

And you would listen to her and soothe / persuade her to be normal..

Can you trust me for this that I was doing something like that except I am 45 years old man and your elder brother..

Do you why actually I did that!

I AM FAMILY

I thought I needed more attention and love..

(May be I am not able to explain this the way I should actually explain)

In 5 years..

Did you try to notice that may be I am not childish but there is a child in me and that child is never allowed by a 45 years to show /express his love and emotions..

And you have seen that my facial expressions never match with my heart and soul..

We have written to each other endless and endless past these several years and you have a good idea of me who am I as a human being...

But you may not be knowing it exactly that sometimes my love comes in form of anger and this sort of development in me is not by birth..

It's because of circumstances I have lived in..

Remember

Actually I was not looking for a sister on internet (facebook, whatsup group etc)..

Also I was not looking for any girlfriend...

I was looking for a mother..

You know..

I last saw my mother when she died in 1984 and I was a small child

And I don't remember her face even..

All my life I have tried to search her in other women' faces..

And when I found you I was finally convinced that God had different plans and He wanted to bless me with a little sister who would be equally a motherly figure too and I know that you are also like that which is true in Indian context..

And finally I claimed you as my sister ◈

If I vent my anger on you it only means I want you to know all those problem and address them even more seriously..

That's it..

But now it is understood that I will not repeat it..

Never..."

◈☺

I replied:

"There was no discussing.

245

You ripped me apart and it was done on purpose.
Yes I know you have a child's heart.
You stopped maturing because of a traumatic childhood.
Stop obsessing over me.
I was your sister only, not your world but you put that weight on me.
Heal yourself so you stop hurting other people.
READ MY MESSAGE AND STOP TYPING.
Wow.
I can care about you but also choose to protect myself from you. I will not allow you anymore.
Take care."

That was it. I blocked him for the second and last time. No apology, no real remorse. Just more explanations. He didn't even read my message first.

His message about feeling starved of a mother's love was surprisingly insightful, coming from somebody who seemed to have no self-awareness. Only a week or two before this, I had read that the current consensus in the medical community as to what causes narcissistic personality disorder, is that there is a genetic factor that increases the likelihood of its occurrence, but it is caused by extreme neglect or abuse in early childhood, especially from the mother, and also sometimes from being treated like royalty, a 'golden child,' or something like that.

According to Asatya's story, he was the center of his mother's world until she died suddenly when he was very young, resulting in a childhood marked by neglect.

Asatya had cried crocodile tears trying to appeal to my emotions and integrity to get me to reconnect. What he actually accomplished was to pound that last nail into the coffin of our relationship. If he was ever going to show any sign of changed behavior it would have been that day in late July that I briefly unblocked him. He failed at his last chance and really did a great job of making it seem like he was *incapable* of remorse or reform. I felt that my conscience was 100% clear as I had tried everything- *although* the responsibility to humbly initiate repair of the relationship was on Asatya, who had initiated our connection on false pretense, then had drained the life from me as a parasite from that time forward.

I don't know if I really was hoping that he might actually have a change of heart and humble himself, but I was angry at him, and angry at myself for letting him get under my skin to make me angry. I ran outside, jumping from the front steps and screaming just to let out the angst. Cletus was still there on the ladder, holding the paintbrush in mid swipe when I made that dramatic exit from the house. He didn't say a word but continued painting like nothing had happened. I admitted to him that I had indeed written to Asatya. No, there was no apology, just explanations. Yes, I blocked him again and forever. I somehow felt dumb for hoping for a positive outcome.

Luckily, Cletus is the most non-judgmental person that I know. No doubt he was disappointed that I disregarded his advice, but he patiently listened to my little rant.

I said, "you must be getting really tired of hearing about Asatya."

He replied, "Yeah a little... but it's okay."

Many times, I tried to remind myself out loud, "The best revenge is success," but somehow it kept coming out as, "The best success is revenge." I didn't actually want revenge, though whatever sympathy that I once had was drying up quickly. I then understood how people develop dark humor, as I was using it to cope.

I had overwhelming evidence that Asatya was not to be trusted at the very least and that he would never change. What did he try to change when his marriage was unraveling? I don't know. But I do know that he tried for two years to convince her to come back, and he only stopped trying when his brother-in-law told him that she had remarried. Even then, he held onto hope that she might come back, and he didn't let go of that hope until five years after she left, when he found out that she had a baby.

As for myself, I was married with children already, but still he was stalking me online, unable to move on, just obsessing night and day. My marriage was not a deterrent because that is not what Asatya was trying to get out of me. He knew he couldn't marry me, so he was pressuring me to set him up with someone, claiming I had a 'duty' because we were 'family.' After the hours and hours it took me to change all my privacy settings, change all my passwords, and block, block, block... I found myself grateful that I lived on the other side of the planet. If Asatya was in the U.S., I know he would be physically stalking me, no question.

Looking around on that sunny day at my house, my daughter inside, my friend on the ladder, I realized that I had very few people close to me, but the few people that I did have, had my back, even if they didn't fully understand what was going on. I knew that I was safe.

If only everyone could escape from narcissistic abuse this 'easily...'

Over the summer months and fall, I slowly untangled the chaotic mess in my mind that was giving me so much anxiety. At the same time, my emotions had not only returned, but they were at least three times more pronounced than normal, with a backdrop of extreme emotional pain most of the time, making everyday life difficult. I spent large portions of each day just trying to manage my mental and emotional well-being. I avoided people most of the time. I couldn't handle parties or going out in public if there were more than half a dozen people. At the same time, my internal pain was too much to live with and being alone was overwhelming. The resulting weird new behavior confused my poor husband who didn't understand these effects on me. I stayed home with my family but went out with my husband sometimes. I left the house to go hike or run, and to go to work. Otherwise, my lifestyle slowed way down.

One of the things that gave me anxiety at that time was worrying that I might have picked up some of Asatya's toxic habits, or that the abuse may have created dysfunctions in me that could damage my other relationships. I do believe this fear was justified.

Early on, Asatya told me how much the daily greetings meant to him, that it always made him perk up and feel fortified to face the day.

Normally I would not greet my friends twice per day every day (good morning and good evening, plus chit-chat) but I thought, what a super easy way to lift up my brother, so I never failed to do these greetings for four years and some months.

What I did not realize is that he was not just lonely or depressed; he was very much emotionally dependent on me.

He was using me to regulate his emotions though he probably didn't realize that's what he was doing. If you are a parent, you know what it takes to help a three-year-old child regulate their emotions. You must stop yourself from reacting and stay calm while removing the negative stimuli and address their underlying needs. As they age another year or two, you can begin to reason with them logically to help them feel less overwhelmed and accept things that can't be changed. If you find yourself in a close relationship with a narcissist, you will get sucked into the role of managing and regulating their emotions like this. Why? Because if you don't, you will suffer the brunt of their chaos which, coming from an adult, can mean anything from petty sabotage to murder, and anything in between. Typing this out, I'm realizing that Asatya's emotional maturity level is stuck forever somewhere between the level of a three-year-old and a four-year-old. His ability to reason is underdeveloped and coming very prominently from a self-centered perspective.

More than four years of daily conversation rewired my brain to not just accept this constant communication as normal, but also to need it - it was a steady dose of dopamine. It became my new normal. Less communication felt insufficient. I became needy or codependent very slowly over time and completely *unaware* of it. It wasn't huge, but it did change what I came to expect out of relationships overall. At least now I recognize this, and I am setting a healthier mindset and habits for myself.

I tried to be kind to my needy brother, but I didn't know that his 'neediness' could be contagious, and I 'caught' his emotional dysregulation. If I am right, I believe that is what is known as codependency.

I have been out of contact with Asatya for months but the effects last, such as this: I have been the person in my friendships that was always needy. I was afraid they would become overwhelmed by me and that I might lose them. I needed a lot of reassurance. I needed a lot of hugs. I needed people I could talk to, to help me verbally sort out my thoughts. I needed them to be flexible to accommodate my out-of-control anxiety. I felt it was a lot to ask, but these were not normal circumstances. See, I actually needed my family and friends to some degree, to help me regulate *my* emotions... for a period of time... at least I was healing, though slowly.

I found myself suddenly acutely aware of even minor red flag behaviors. Simple things like selfish or petty behavior suddenly looked highly suspect to me and I watched everyone carefully, whether they deserved that scrutiny or not. I became afraid that I would provoke anger or resentment, afraid that I would be burdensome to my loved ones. My biggest issue was a very strong hunger for deep and loving connections. I felt like I could die without this. It wasn't just because I missed daily chats. I believe it was because Asatya required so much love from me, but abused me in return, leaving me feeling totally depleted and starved. Being a mother to challenging children (who shall remain anonymous) had me already feeling drained before any of this even started. No wonder I felt dried up.

Perhaps you can see how I and other narcissistic abuse victims worry that we are the ones who are narcissists or worry that we are becoming like that. I theorize that this is a common worry because all of us in this circumstance have been repeatedly accused and shamed by a narcissist, then when we try to get away, we are very focused on taking care of ourselves- something the narcissist conditioned us to think is selfish. Narcissists do sometimes prey on other narcissists, but more often they target empathetic or compassionate people, or anyone they think will be easy to exploit.

I still feel that I can give cheerfully, but now it is more consciously measured with restraint and discernment.

I don't want to be clingy. I love my friends and want to respect their need for space, but the dysregulation of psychological and emotional abuse had left me feeling starved for *real* connection and love. I was desperate.

I am trying to love me properly, but I crave connection with others. The hypervigilance that I still have can be frustrating, but it does stop me from being too hasty, compromising my boundaries, or just being too rash in general.

Later on in my Google searches, I found that clinical psychologists speaking on the topic of healing from narcissistic abuse all agreed that the best thing to be done for healing is to seek out positive interactions. This rewires the brain and heals the damage from the abuse. This was confirmation that my instincts or intuitions could be trusted, as that is what I wanted more than anything.

I was apprehensive about putting myself out there to seek out such experiences. I guess I felt that I did not have the strength to deal with any more hurt or frustration and didn't want to risk it, though I knew that I needed to. Unfortunately, at home I was absolutely not having good experiences because my daughter's health condition was causing a lot of stress for the entire household on a daily basis. In fact, some of the things that she was doing while agitated reminded me very much of Asatya's tactics. These episodes would trigger a sort of fight/flight/panic for me every time that it happened. I think it was PTSD[2][xxxi] attacks in my case.

One day, she triggered me badly and my heart was pounding. I struggled to breathe correctly. I was afraid of hurting her or myself, so I immediately ran to the other side of the house and lay down in the grass to try to calm myself. My friend the painter was there. My daughter generally did not act like that when there were people around from outside of our household, so I stayed on the same side of the house where my friend was working, as I felt safer there. On another occasion, my daughter was very agitated and broke a window. Then she climbed into the house through the broken glass. She had almost no sense of danger. At that point, I was extremely worried about her future, and I wondered if I would have to take care of her indefinitely, and that she might continue with the volatile behavior...Those behaviors were like jet fuel poured out on the fire of my anxiety. I was terrified of the possibility of being a caregiver indefinitely of my agitated child...

So, I was supposed to be having positive interactions to heal me, but instead my daughter was repeating some of the behaviors that I had just escaped from. I wasn't improving, I was getting worse. I made a list of the symptoms I had in the weeks and months during the worst of the abuse and after (essentially all of 2024):

- Tinnitus every day
- Constant extreme anxiety
- Extreme generalized emotional pain
- Freeze or flight response to fairly small stimuli
- Hyper-vigilance
- Generalized dissociation
- Unable to talk during mental breakdown
- Low energy
- Ready to fall asleep 3-5 hours earlier than usual
- Low motivation for daily activities
- Thoughts racing and chaotic
- Randomly and frequently tuning out and forgetting things
- Difficulty with vocabulary recall and remembering scheduled events

2.   https://www.nimh.nih.gov/health/publications/post-traumatic-stress-disorder-ptsd

- Hair falling out
- Anxiety-related nausea
- Avoidance of social settings

In addition to these symptoms[3][xxxii], I discovered this winter (February 2025) another interesting effect on my health. My smartphone tracks some information like my physical activity and calories burned. Every day, it tracks calories burned during strenuous activity, and it also separately tracks calories burned during rest and minimal activity. It calls that 'resting energy.'

During a moment of boredom, I scrolled back over the past year to see if the resting energy was the same every day, or different. I found a clear-cut pattern of resting energy falling from 1,383 or so down to 1,350 between March to April. From April to September, it stayed between 1,330-1,361. From October to the end of the year, that number gradually rose up to 1,385. It is now hovering around 1,400.

That pattern directly corresponded to the time period that I had a baseline of constant anxiety, being in fight/flight mode 24/7.

Naturally, I googled this for clarification. High stress levels slow metabolism. My stats seem to verify this by the 30-70 less calories that I burned per day (in resting energy) when I was under the most stress. My eating habits did not change (except for the reduced sugar in early March 2024) and I was exercising more between June-December. Nothing else was different, just stress levels.

In August, a third source of acute stress rose to the surface. (Unrelated to the drama with Asatya). Between Asatya, my daughter, and the third thing, I felt like I was being attacked. Finally, I found myself a therapist. I had been trying to take care of my own psychological well-being, but I simply could not cope at that point, and I was afraid I might do something drastic. I started seeing her in late September. I wish I had gone to a doctor and insisted on being put on anti-anxiety medication. I was almost totally non-functional.

One day, I was leaving from work and terrified of going home. I had the strongest impulse to drive in the opposite direction and just not go home at

---

3.   https://www.choosingtherapy.com/narcissistic-abuse-syndrome/

all. Not just for one night, but indefinitely. I had three mental breakdowns in just one week.

I did go home. I didn't make dinner. I didn't do anything. I just kept to myself, trying to just stay sane.

One of the things that I often wondered about was how Asatya could be so awful, but it took more than four years for me to see it? I felt that I needed this question to be answered, so that possibly in the future, I would see the warning signs sooner, if possible, and not feel compelled to hold on-to such a person.

I do know that one of the factors was that he would use Hindi with some people and English sometimes. I realized after the fact that if he need-ed to say anything that he did not want me to hear, he could just use Hindi and tell me later, 'That person does not know English.' When we would be with people who knew only Hindi, they would not know what Asatya was saying to me in English. He mostly only translated if I asked and even then, he didn't always do it when asked.

Most of what I knew of Indian culture, I learned through Asatya. He could have misrepresented a thing to me to make me think that his behav-ior was all normal. I had lots of opportunities for speaking directly with other Indians, without Asatya, so I feel confident that most of what he told me really was accurate. However, he always insisted that he's not like every-one else as he had high moral standards, great values and rock solid integri-ty. It did happen sometimes that Asatya would speak or act aggressively and I told myself it is just that he has that very expressive Haryanvi background, but he is working on improving it.

There is another thing that numbed or blinded me to the abuse that I was unaware of. I still don't completely understand it. You may remember that I had mentioned dissociation. Any time that Asatya made me uncom-fortable or even terrorized me, like he did at his sister's house that time, pri-or to meeting Agni, I limited my responses to be very brief, monotone, and cooperative. Otherwise, I extracted my mind from the context as far as pos-sible. That is what is called a 'fawn' response. It is a reflex, or you can say, a 'knee-jerk reaction' of the nervous system to minimize pain when escape doesn't appear to be possible. Most people are familiar with the concept of 'fight or flight.' In fact, there are two other possible reactions which are 'fawn' and 'freeze[4][xxxiii].' Fawn is also sometimes referred to as 'shutdown,' or 'collapse.'

Over the extended period of time that I knew Asatya, the dissociation happened often enough that it became almost second nature. In a dissociative state, my mind was not fully present, not fully concentrating on the negative experience. Not really an out-of-body experience, but sort of withdrawn in a way. Because this instinctive and automatic numbing occurred during my negative experiences with Asatya, I was not at all fully aware of how bad the overall situation was.

You may have experienced a bit of dissociation during some harrowing experience in your life. You would have been focused on just getting through one day at a time, one hour at a time. Sometime later when life was normal again, you would look back and only then realize how bad it was.

Dissociating during abuse is a bit like that but often more severe. This is why some people have amnesia of particularly traumatic events, and most people who have been subject to narcissistic abuse, including myself, often have difficulty trying to recall individual instances of abuse, regardless of how often it occurred or for how many years. Writing can be helpful, as there is no pressure, and you can simply write something down whenever you might remember something randomly.

If you ever talk to someone who tells you that they were abused, but they don't seem to remember many details of the abuse, just understand that it is not because it 'wasn't that bad.' The precise opposite may very well be true. You know that the bottom line is be kind and don't judge.

During the four years and some months that I was connected to Asatya, there was never a dull moment. There always seemed to be some new drama or crisis for Asatya, and from my perspective at the time, it looked like most of the instances were due to Asatya being in proximity to problem people, though often he had health problems as well. He always included me in his life to the extent that was possible. For example, I expressed concern about his employment, so he suggested that I do weekly zoom calls with his English students for their language practice. In that way, I made him more valuable to his employer.

---

4.   https://www.nicabm.com/how-the-nervous-system-responds-to-trauma/

There was always a new crisis big or small, nearly every week; there was never a slow, quiet period. Also, I was texting twice daily greetings to Asatya (and occasionally to his knowns on his behalf) at Asatya's request as it was an emotional boost for him which seemed easy enough.

The movie-like ongoing drama along with the constant social interaction forced me to always live in the moment. At any given moment, there was only the time and mental capacity to address current issues.

Therefore, I rarely had a chance to take several steps back to really consider any big picture issues thoroughly to get some perspective. I was kept mentally engaged continuously, so I couldn't.

People ask how I didn't see red flags.

Most of the red flags were not events but rather overall patterns that I couldn't detect because I never had the chance to get perspective.

Sometimes I look back and wonder if I was kept busy on purpose so that I wouldn't start to question anything.

Fellow Americans and foreign friends, you will remember the dozens and dozens of scandals and questionable actions coming out of the Oval Office in the weeks following the inauguration on January 20th, 2025. Every day, there were multiple news stories to consider. Not even a discerning retiree would have had enough time to investigate the real and whole story behind each and every new earth-shaking action from this administration. Those who were sweet-talked into believing in this president enough to vote for him were still under the hypnosis and even slower to investigate any of it. Meanwhile, most of the destructive overreach of power was either swept under the rug, downplayed, twisted, or outright lied about. With so much chaos, where do we turn our attention?

I have already been through all of this. I recognize the attitudes, the strategic actions, and the psychological games. I experienced all of that at a deeply personal level, and now I can see narcissists standing out like neon signs, although the people running our country are hardly hiding their wickedness anymore. These oligarchs that are sabotaging and dismantling our country have not fooled me. Please take note of this, but for the moment let me redirect you back to my story.

My therapist helped me a bit to change the thoughts that were constantly rotating through my mind on repeat. My inner monologue had been seriously affected by trauma, keeping me in survival mode. Slowly it began to reset. At some point, I realized that when I brushed my hair, hardly a dozen hairs would fall out. I remembered that months ago, I had large amounts coming out every day, and additionally, my hair had been breaking even in spite of washing only with room temperature water and frequent conditioning. My hair stopped breaking. I hadn't changed my care routine. The only change was that my main source of stress had been removed from my life.

My daughter's health issues were causing her to be agitated every day, sometimes behaving like a scared animal. She would act impulsively with no thought of danger. Sometimes she would randomly wander off. She broke some things. She was thirteen years old, but we could not leave her alone safely. We did our best to coordinate the work schedules of the household to make sure that one of us was always with her throughout summer vacation. It seemed that she could not open her mouth to speak without being defensive. If I tried to correct her, her actions and words would be aggressive. These last behaviors were so reminiscent of Asatya's behavior towards me, it would induce a panic attack (or nearly) every time that she did it. These triggering behaviors would happen two to four times per week. It took me about two to three days to stop crying and panicking after these incidents, which meant that I was living in a constant PTSD[xxxiv] sort of state...overwhelming.[5]

One evening, I was sitting at a bar with my husband, just catching up from the week. After a couple of drinks, I realized that I didn't feel any anxiety or pain, for the first time in months. What an immense relief! I felt like I could finally rest for the first time in ages. I realized that I could easily escape this hell by using alcohol. I realized I was a perfect candidate to fall into alcoholism, and that scared me. I didn't dare get too comfortable with drinking.

I was reading that my daughter's condition is often much affected by diet. I knew that I could not flee from this situation as her mother. The only

---

5.   https://youtu.be/Gd9OhYroLN0?si=Tt-pbFe_1KfkckHb

way out of it was to help her, as I should do anyway. I learned that she was likely deficient in certain nutrients, and that she may not be absorbing them well. I googled to find which vitamin supplements are the most bio-available (easiest to absorb into the bloodstream and metabolize.) In fact, I was determined to take care of my own health for once, and in earnest. I got my whole family on a regimen of vitamin supplements. I prayed it would help and crossed my fingers.

After three months of vitamin supplementation, my daughter's very troubling agitation calmed down dramatically. It still happens sometimes but much less. The agitation and behavior problems were not so much a problem of parenting technique or poor character but was mostly a matter of health.

My daughter had always been friendly, cheerful, funny, and highly imaginative. I knew that delightful child was still in there somewhere.

I myself went from sleeping only 4-6 hours per night, to sleeping 7-9 hours per night, simply by taking magnesium glycinate every day.

I decided to listen more closely to my intuition. My intuition led me to spend a lot of time outdoors and especially in the woods. I went barefoot whenever possible. It seemed that tuning into my senses and especially in nature had a way of pulling me out of the chaos in my head and grounding me in my physical environment. It helped to calm my nerves and made coping easier. Pulling weeds out of the garden was great. I actually took a few minutes or more every day to go sit in the sun and listen to birds and other wildlife. I allowed myself to not be in a hurry... easy to do with low energy and low motivation. I even slept outside under the stars once or twice. I picked flowers, burned incense and candles, I sought out new music.

Perhaps counterintuitively, that summer I developed a great appreciation for metal music. Not the fatalistic sort of sentiments, but more of the 'We won't stand for this! We will rise up!' sort of messaging. I have always loved guitar, drums, and strong, distinct beats. This genre allowed me to release stored up emotion. Interestingly, after a few songs, something would change for me in my psyche that the metal would have a calming effect. My mind would quiet down as if on autopilot.

Sometimes I had to force myself out of bed, and to go for a mountain hike, to boost my mood. Hiking is my number one favorite hobby. Sometimes while hiking I would cry. Sometimes even hiking wasn't enough. In those moments, I reminded myself that I would eventually come through this phase of my life, but that was only possible by fighting for myself - fighting for my mental, emotional, and physical health. I had to keep doing these things.

Asatya had played me and had attempted to destroy me. He had beaten me down badly but I escaped. My strength dried up, but a fierce determination had been born in me, to be an unquenchable fire of passion for life. The legendary phoenix came to mind.

Healing like any progress, never follows a straight line. Two steps forward and one step back, as the saying goes.

That autumn, I discovered two more things that helped to validate or clarify my experience: ChatGPT and the DSM-5. (No, those are neither bands, nor sports cars.)

ChatGPT is an AI-powered personal assistant. There are numerous uses for it, but one in particular stands out to me: It can help you identify shady or questionable communications. For anyone who has been gaslit, manipulated or lied to, and who is still confused or doubting, this tool can save you a lot of guessing and misery. If you are beginning to think that someone is turning abusive or toxic, or you're just not sure if you should trust them, copy and paste your messages from those people into ChatGPT. Then, ask ChatGPT to identify the red flags. ChatGPT will give you a comprehensive breakdown, explaining things like tone, argument tactics like 'straw man' or 'ad hominem,' emotional health factors, identify gaslighting versus straightforward honesty, etc.

So, I put ChatGPT to the test by copying and pasting some old messages into it.

ChatGPT picked up on even more toxic and manipulative patterns that had flown under my radar. It even told me that if I am still in contact with that person, that I need to get away, as they are unstable and 'potentially a danger to himself or others.'

Some people would feel that I overreacted, as I was never physically beaten. However, I had witnessed Asatya engage in physical violence toward his sister, and he told me that I am not immune from the same 'correction' that she received. Regardless, violence is not the only form of abuse.

Even this unbiased 'robot' told me to stay the hell away from that guy. ChatGPT can be found in the app store.

The other thing that I discovered is the DSM-5. The DSM-5 is a diagnostic tool used for personality disorders, including narcissistic personality disorder. I am not a psychologist that I can give a diagnosis. However, since narcissists tend to stay far away from mental health professionals, an amateur opinion based on verified and analyzed facts is the closest that most of us survivors will ever get to a diagnosis.

The DSM-5 explains the diagnostic criteria of various personality disorders, as well as signs or symptoms of each. There are also brief descriptions of current treatments and therapies used for each. I found what is called a 'personality inventory for DSM-5.' On it, a clinician is instructed to answer whether a behavior applies to the patient, on a 0-3 scale. There are over 200 behavior related questions. At the end, there are instructions for how to add up the scores. It is sort of scrambled to avoid getting a biased result. You can imagine that with my life-long interest in psychology, of course I answered all those questions concerning Asatya. Looking at the final results, I was shocked to see that the score for depression was in the low to moderate range. However, manipulative tendency scored extremely high.

Please note that my action in using that personality inventory is not a recommendation for more 'armchair experts' and other unqualified people to make declarations based on this tool.

I do not have permission to link to or reproduce the DSM-5 personality inventory, but it can be found online at psychology.com and possibly elsewhere.

Naturally, I began to wonder how depressed was Asatya really? Clearly, depression was part of his game. Was he even capable of talking without a strategy, without ulterior motives, without playing a sadistic game?? It became clear from the results of this 'inventory' that my previous analysis was correct. Asatya is most definitely a narcissist: A covert, communal, cerebral narcissist who specializes in emotional manipulation, and who has a slightly psychopathic tendency.

Another great resource is a book called, *'It's All in Your Head.'*[6][xxxv], It contains an artist's depictions of personality disorders and other mental health conditions. If you need visuals to help you understand things, this could be great for you.

You may wonder why Asatya was still frequently on my mind months after cutting him out of my life. The truth is that in order to successfully break away permanently after narcissistic abuse, there is an enormous, tangled ball of emotional baggage, false internal narratives, and other after-effects to work through. That often takes months if not years, and usually a lot of therapy.

Imagine if a hoarder lived with you, and they mixed up all their things with yours. When you finally succeed to kick them out, they don't come clean up their things. Instead, you are saddled with the task of sorting out your things from theirs. One box at a time, removing their things from your house. Likewise, I have been identifying Asatya's shit that he put in my mind and heart, and consciously disposing of it, replacing these with healthy and good internal narratives and attitudes.

I remember in October that my dear friend was extremely busy wrapping up a project which meant being unavailable and failing to communicate some things that they didn't realize were important to me. They were just very focused, trying to finish things in a hurry and didn't mean to neglect me. Unfortunately, I overreacted because of my raw insecurities and emotional needs, stepping on their toes. At first, they were a bit mad at me. I hated that my unhealed heart was causing issues. Finally, when the busyness settled on their side, we talked about it. I was met with a desire to understand, and kind, reassuring words.

6.   https://anymeansnecessary.com/products/all-in-your-head-print?variant=39398424215619&country=US&currency=USD&utm_medium=product_sync&utm_source=google&utm_content=sag_organic&utm_campaign=sag_organic&tw_source=google&tw_adid=698865509880&tw_campaign=21263917380&gad_source=4&gbraid=0AAAAABZJJKkz7O0trwxsM613-_pt_K2eb&gclid=Cj0KCQjw_dbABhC5ARIsAAh2Z-QJcij74dmzKGdeyJ4CGz4P-yYqYnpEprwg07nSAN5iURhNRRfopksaAoMtEALw_wcB

The lovely thing about conflict occurring between humble, kind people is that proactive discussion occurs, leading to a deeper mutual understanding and stronger connection.

As I slowly began to accumulate positive interactions, I began to heal the most. Remember I said that tuning into my senses was helpful. Hugs became even more important to me, as they are a way to tune in to my physical environment while connecting with another person. Conflicts discussed peacefully, respect shown, reassurance given, encouragement and confidence shown in me, small crises handled calmly and without judgment, instead of berating, and other demonstrations of support had a powerful effect.

Every small but good interaction negated and silenced my fears and gave me so much peace and comfort. It felt like I was a prisoner being freed from a tyrant. The tyrant was anxiety and probably PTSD. Interactions that in years past, would have been mildly pleasant were in the context of this healing period, truly profound. I tried my best to articulate to loved ones what an enormous gift their love was at that time, but words seemed to fall short. There were times that I cried tears of happiness and relief, just because someone was considerate or respectful towards me.

Such a small thing and yet so big.

One Friday in late November, I was preparing to go to bed when I realized that I had no anxiety at all that entire day. It had been my very first day completely free of anxiety after 24/7 debilitating anxiety since April. It was an encouraging landmark moment.

Remember that in October, my anxiety and emotional dysfunction leftover from the abuse, was affecting my relationships...that led to an unusual moment of impulsivity (and clingy friend behavior) while fantasizing over airfare Google searching. I unexpectedly found very cheap tickets to visit my friends, and I pounced at the opportunity. I think my friends were irritated at my needy behavior, though they tried to be patient and understanding.

I just want to pause here and point out something that all of us need to work on. Any time someone turns to drugs or alcohol to numb their pain, or worse, they end their life, I see everyone around them sad and saying to each other, 'If only we knew that they were struggling. If only they reached out to us first.' Every time another life is lost like this, I see the entire community come together to mourn that unique soul lost to suicide.

Do you *really* wish that the suffering person had reached out to you rather than harmed themselves? What would that look like? How would you react? Be honest. A drowning person cannot yell.

Remember I said that in my nervous breakdowns, I couldn't speak? It is typically very difficult for anyone at such a low point to muster the courage to be truly honest about their suffering and to ask for support. It is much more likely that they will become very reclusive or quiet or act out of character.

If any friend or relative or coworker of yours is acting strangely, it wouldn't be a bad idea to check in on them, and not just with a text message. Make some excuse to see them face to face if possible. Ask how are they really. Let them know that you have their back and reassure them that you're happy to be there for them and that it is no burden at all. (But if you do say things like this, be sure to follow through!)

People who are in a very low place mentally or emotionally are under such an immense weight themselves, that they generally worry about being a burden to others and do not speak up or complain enough at a time when they really should. Remember, they might never tell you how much they are really suffering, but their behavior might tip you off that they need you to step up and be a real friend.

For example, if your normally well-adjusted friend becomes antisocial or reclusive, or they go the opposite direction and become needy or clingy, or if they seem to be getting drunk more often, something might be up. See if they are willing to talk about it, at least enough to know whether or not they are in serious trouble. Don't push the issue but be a willing listener. You could save someone's life.

It is not just suicide that could be a threat. Depending on circumstances, there may be other risks such as human trafficking or domestic abuse. These things can happen anywhere to both males and females, young or old. It does not always look like what you might think. Learn to recognize the signs of abuse and exploitation to help keep yourself, your loved ones, and your community safe.

All these months I would greet Sama from time to time. I was not sure how close I wanted to be, but he had proven himself to be a friend in hard times. I wondered if that dress that Asatya had withheld from me with such pettiness was still at Sama's house. Sama found it and mailed it to me. I put it on and sent a photo to Sama, thanking him. After everything that I had endured, it felt like one tiny piece of justice or vindication, that Asatya did not succeed in that petty act.

In mid-December, I found myself on the curb outside Key West airport, climbing into a familiar vehicle. I was there to spend some time with my buddy Cletus Beauregard and his girlfriend and take a much-needed mental break from life in general. Some days later, Cletus seemed disappointed or concerned that I had not planned lots of activities for myself during my stay. I explained that I was taking a mental break. One day, my feet were tired and blistered from walking several miles. I wanted to lie down, but both the house and the beach were far. I walked to where my friend was working nearby and lay down in the back of the car.

For months, a question had lingered in my mind that I was a bit afraid to answer. I googled it again to be sure. Yup. The incident that took place in my life at age three was indeed rape. I had suspected that, so it wasn't a surprise, but it was still upsetting to know. I just felt a personal need to have that clarified. At least now I know the truth.

I realized in that moment that at a very young age, I had experienced what many people consider to be the very worst form of abuse. It is true that it is not an easy thing to talk about it, and yes, I developed a... I don't know what to call it, it's more than an aversion... It was something similar to a PTSD panic type reaction, to the thing that 'inspired' that rape. Maybe some of my weaknesses could be traced back to it, I don't know. I just know that the sexual abuse did not cause any direct inner pain or turmoil for me. I grew up undisturbed except for some shame that I was eventually able to throw off by reminding myself over and over for some years that I was just an innocent little baby.

By contrast, the psychological and emotional abuse from Asatya had made me extremely dysregulated and caused immense pain, such that I have undergone very significant changes and going back to who I was before Asatya is not possible.

In my experience, the psychological and emotional abuse did far more damage than the sexual abuse. *That is not necessarily the case for all survivors of both types of abuse,* but it is important to recognize the extremely destructive power of psychological abuse and emotional abuse, which includes coercive control. In the U.K., these are punishable offenses. In coming years, I hope that the law across the globe will also recognize it and offer more justice and protection to victims...

Around lunch time, Cletus came out to his car and saw me lying there. He looked disappointed that I was not out and about enjoying myself. I explained about my feet but said nothing about my Google search. I had ranted and confided so much bad news to this friend that I didn't want to bring up more bad news. It wasn't relevant at the time, anyway. I didn't tell him that lying down in the back of his car on that quiet street was a bit comforting. I didn't want to be out in public just then. Anyway, he gave me a ride to Fort Zachary Taylor State Park where I just hung out on the beach for some time. From there, I walked a few blocks to receive my first tattoo. When it was finished, I asked Cletus where to find him, and realized he was on the other side of town.

"Take the bus!" he said. Just as he said that, a bus pulled up to the curb. So, I joined Cletus at a local's hangout for a game of ping-pong. We had some dinner at home and then Cletus went into town for a social commitment. I enjoyed the serenity alone by the water and taught myself to play the tongue drum. I was determined to learn to play a song. When Cletus returned, I joyfully demonstrated the song I had learned and then he also learned it.

Most days on that trip went something like this. It was totally carefree, aside from a bit of book writing and that disturbing google search. I felt lucky to have a sincere friend who lived in such a beautiful place.

One night, we went to a small punk rock concert. We were all psyched to enjoy that, but when it came time to go in, the crowd was so thick that claustrophobia overwhelmed me. At once I turned on my heels and went to listen near the door. As much as Cletus wanted to be in there, he stayed with me until I was ready to go back in. I was surprised to realize that I was more important than the music, in my friend's eyes... that kind consideration was a healing experience to me. Cletus' girlfriend and another friend joined us there. In fact, it was a wonderful evening.

Another time, I went with Cletus to his game of ultimate frisbee. I knew the others would ask me to play. I tried to explain to them that the team sports segment of my brain is actually completely missing, but they completely ignored that statement. I told them that my throw is terrible (it was.) I absolutely assured them that if I joined them, I truly would just be a warm body and would probably cost them points. Well, I joined... I felt very lost and could not mentally keep up with the team dynamics and fast plays which was pretty stressful. However, everyone gently guided me without making me feel like an idiot. What precious few helpful plays I made, they praised. They wanted to know if I would come back.

I had gone to ultimate frisbee that evening determined to break out of my comfort zone and interact with other people. I fully expected it to go poorly, and that they would be annoyed at me for screwing up their game. I was surprised by how kind and supportive those people were. This incident was one more healing experience for me.

Shortly after I arrived, my wallet went missing. I know that if I had lost my wallet in India, that Asatya would never stop berating me for being careless. He would have made me feel traumatized and stupidly irresponsible. I mentioned the wallet to Cletus, cringing. I thought he would be super annoyed. He spent half of his day off from work helping me search all over town for it. He seemed totally unbothered, though relieved when I eventually found it. That experience definitely made me feel safer in general, as it was a reminder that Asatya was crazy, and most people are reasonable.

These experiences did more for me than my therapist ever did.

All my responsibilities, all stressors, everything was left behind for a few days. In this environment, and staying in the home of the most chill person I know, it was easy to tune everything out and shut my brain down to some degree. I had had tinnitus for the better part of a year, almost constantly, due to stress. The tinnitus just went away. I didn't even make a lot of conversation; I had become so quiet inside. It was such a sharp contrast to the constant screaming of my mind and heart back in the summer and autumn.

I learned that attitudes and internal narratives create new connections between neurons[7], actually changing brain structure. To me, that is just amazing. It shows that psychology is not simply abstract or theoretical; it is also physical.[xxxvi] Every time that the lies in my mind were disarmed and removed by positive experiences, my neurons were rearranging themselves into a healthier configuration.

Still, for the most part I felt disconnected, easily triggered into anxiety, doubting myself, and questioning whether anyone loved me as much as I loved them.

I knew that 2024 was somehow a pivotal year for me. I knew that after all that had happened, that I could not be the old me.

At the time this goes to print, it has been almost one year since going no-contact. Recently, I had two panic attacks. Around the same time, my tinnitus that I've had 24/7 for a year is now gone. I only get it occasionally now, which is normal. I have mostly separated in my mind which things are insecurities or lies from what is true and healthy. That is a huge win. Healing is a long road of two steps forward and one step back.

Recently I dug through old photos for this book. Seeing Asatya's photos from before he met me, (please don't judge. I haven't deleted them because I am hoping someone will weed him out of my India photos for me, so I won't have to see him) I was reminded why I had felt compassion. Asatya has an expressionless face, but his eyes held tremendous pain. It was true. He is a tortured soul. At the time, I did not know why, but I came to learn of his hardships. It was not until last year that I learned the cause of most of those hardships, which is his unsalvageable mental condition.

---

7.   https://www.google.com/search?sca_esv=fc2dc54ee7eb1be7&q=neurons+forming+new+con-
nections&udm=39&fbs=ABzOT_CWdhQLP1FcmU5B0fn3xuWp6IcynR-
Brzjy_vjxR0KoDMp_4ut2Z3jppK72fzdIpWsBpYmR8fwcVczrRGmP-Hf4k8TNdw0hYkrFPY-
GyfZnlaQTXsgCV5v5F-ZEusHyPYUmAQeWqC_LtreH7GhcDZp9D06xYETyjVh58jNJ-
tyf5ReNOIhRUDCjWrlGddDxW5Z7A77ej9bDtsBthGA1KdMsuf-
VO4LhoA&sa=X&ved=2ahUKEwjIuqSmobeMAxWXFFkFHRhZG-
TUQs6gLegQIFxAB&biw=1920&bih=953&dpr=1#fpstate_43ec3e5dee6e706af7766ff-
fea512721_ive_6cff047854f19ac2aa52aac51bf3af4a_vld_43ec3e5dee6e706af7766ff-
fea512721_cid_853ae90f0351324bd73ea615e6487517_4fab28af_c0cb5f0fcf239ab3d9c1fcd31fff1ef
c_vid_853ae90f0351324bd73ea615e6487517_9ebifjoFtJs_c0cb5f0fcf239ab3d9c1fcd31fff1efc_st_85
3ae90f0351324bd73ea615e6487517_0

Now that I have quite a lot of perspective and I am armed with a good general understanding of NPD, I can more accurately interpret many things that he said. In Asatya's case at least, I can figure out that most of his experience that he told me about was true, in terms of *what* happened. I strongly suspect that he switched offender-victim roles, as he did with me. Also, it is easy to figure out that his faults were minimized and virtues inflated or even invented. About his description of others, I can figure out that he praised those who elevated or helped him, but villainized those who did not, or who were no longer of use. (His insult of choice was to call someone 'useless'). The only parts of his stories that were consistently true were the what, where, and when. I have a theory that Asatya switched roles once or twice to avoid extremely painful memories. Like his mother might actually have been the opposite of how he described her. Maybe Asatya was the one who was sent to be exploited and neglected by the uncle, not his brother. That, we will never know. I hope these reflections help you make sense of Asatya's memoirs. You may wish to reread some parts...

Asatya had claimed that I was the most important person in his life. So many times, he would express his love with great emotion like I was his world (not that I wanted such pressure on me), so he had said many times. After months of no contact, he surely realized that he had lost me forever. He had said in the spring that he could not take losing me, that he would be dead.

The last I heard of him (unwillingly) was in late March 2025. I had just set up a new social media account under my pen name. There is nothing on that page that can identify me. Two days later, Vyapari called me. I had not heard from him since the summer before, so I panicked thinking that someone figured out my real identity attached to my pen name, told Asatya, and now Vyapari is calling me because it is only he and Sama who are not blocked... I ignored the call. He called again. Again, I ignored. Finally, Sama called, and I answered.

Asatya had been in a terrible traffic accident and was in ICU. Apparently, he had talked to Vyapari and Sama, harassing them and demanding that they tell me his news and ask me to call him. In fact, Vyapari said to me, "Please do not call him. He is out of his mind, and he will never calm down or stop bothering us if you talk to him. Do not encourage him."

Well, I had not been 100% sure if I could trust Vyapari to not be manipulated by Asatya or tell any of my news to him. It became clear that Vyapari understood and supported me breaking away from Asatya completely. That was reassuring. What was also reassuring was realizing that I had no emotional reaction whatsoever to finding out that Asatya was in critical condition. I'm pretty sure I would have more compassion on a stranger. However, that initial panic over my concealed identity was so bad that I had nausea and a headache the rest of the day. Remember that he had been stalking me online and maybe still was trying to.

As for myself, I had crossed over a great gulf and the path behind me was closed. I had dedicated much of myself to a lie for four years. My reality shattered. How *could* I be the same? It was as though I was in a wandering valley that had no paths. With the added unknowns of other family relationships, and health problems in my household, I had no idea what lay before me in the next five to ten years. I knew I would not try to bushwhack my own trail to force any path forward. I felt that trying to force anything could land me in more trouble. God would show me the right way forward when the time was right. I was in a time of rest and reflection, and I knew I should not rush that. I kept telling myself, "What will be, will be."

Normally, I am a person that feels an innate need to know what to expect. I had no idea what was next and yet surprisingly, I felt such great peace about that, the sort of peace that only God gives. I felt perfectly content in that limbo state of not knowing. It was time for simply living in the moment. Time to appreciate small things, time to appreciate sincerely kind people. My people.

In this time of focused healing and introspection and growth, I thought, I know who I was. But who am I now? I had always believed that people can change their interests and character, but their core personality is always the same. This great shake-up caused me to re-evaluate that belief... Some things can affect a person so very strongly that they are changed at a deep level and long-term.

As for me, the proverbial dust had not settled. No new norm was established. If ever there was a time to reinvent myself or reach for something even higher, now was the time, while I had that inner drive from survival mode. I trusted that God would show me in time what comes next.

I AM FAMILY

I was not exactly angry, but I was very deeply dissatisfied with the appalling lack of love and justice in the world. I thought about the fact that one of my life-long friends got divorced after twenty-five years of marriage and we were disappointed, but nobody seemed really shook up, and no one really talked about it. This totally life-altering and excruciatingly painful event didn't get much shock and grief from others, because divorce is so commonplace. When someone is abused, the same thing happens. There is a brief moment of sympathy and then people move on. Meanwhile the person who suffered the abuse feels like they have been cut open and left to rot, and they are mostly alone to try to heal that gaping wound.

Humanity is so accustomed to seeing such inhumane actions that we are desensitized.

We all very much and desperately need each other to slow down our busyness and not focus on our individual lives to the exclusion of others. We need to look at each other and truly see. Look long enough to understand and feel for that person.

In Key West, I saw a bumper sticker everywhere which said, 'One Human Family.' Oh, but are we really? Do we really believe this? We think that beggars are scammers (and a few of them are). We think that billionaires are not real people. We mock cult members instead of viewing them as prisoners and victims of a scam. We tend to associate with people in the same general income bracket, same political or social values, maybe even same skin color. We segregate ourselves.

We see another war or disaster on the news and breathe a sigh of relief that the destruction is not near our own homes. But if we really see everyone as family, it doesn't matter who is suffering or why; we would have compassion without judgment. We would break out of our cliques to check out the new place on the other side of town where we don't know anyone and give our support to that new business owner. We would give people a chance instead of dismissing them based on nothing more than prejudice, emotion, and knee-jerk reactions. We would throw away our pettiness and our prejudices and our disrespect.

We could initiate an authentic conversation with a brain-damaged drug addict, a soccer mom with four baby-daddies, the yacht owner who just tied up in the wrong spot, the dude in drag who just got glitter in your drink, the annoyingly chatty gynecologist, the teen neighbor who doesn't know about boundaries, the super weird hippie, or the local pastor or priest. Use your imagination. I mean talk to anyone and then let them talk. Tell them, "Good talk, bro," and mean those words.

I have this crazy dream of seeing love and justice being the prevailing traits of culture, from the international level down to the interpersonal level.

It *always* starts not by marching brazenly forward as a revolutionary, but by listening. Listen to the person or people in front of you as they tell their stories. If you are feeling brave, seek out those people that you used to avoid or ignore. Not to form a clever reply. Not to make a judgment. Set aside your biases and agendas and listen purely to better understand people, simply so that you can do a better job of loving them. When you hear them, and begin to understand, they will be more inclined to listen to you too, and that person will cease to be 'one of them,' and you will realize that they are 'one of us.' They always have been, it's just your perception that has changed.

Treat everyone like they are your favorite cousin and eventually maybe you will begin to see everyone as the 'one human family' that people mostly just talk about.

Truly seeing and hearing other people changes the one who sees and hears. It *also* changes the person who has been seen and heard. This is the most underrated and effective tactic for real peace that has been conveniently ignored throughout history, as it requires throwing away ego, ulterior motives, and pretense.

What are you willing to change or give up in your personal life to gain personal peace and contribute to world peace?

Well, I was talking about reinventing myself. I thought, instead of letting my angst stagnate and become bitterness, perhaps I can channel or alchemize my disgust and angst of my abuser into a passion to uplift those who have been robbed of their autonomy, personal agency, and dignity through various forms of abuse.

I have never been a super chatty person, (verbally) but I will never forget that in spite of being a healthy, happy, confident, and stubbornly independent person, I had unknowingly let a villain in close to me who then controlled and silenced me. I was a puppet who was silenced by the fear of retaliation... or at minimum, the fear of being yelled at. I want to speak up for those who have been robbed of their voice. I want to help victims feel dignified once more as they find their voice.

Asatya had tried to crush me and indeed I felt all that crushing. But I was not crushed. Asatya had unwittingly woken a sleeping dragon. He tried to hunt the bird, but the bird was a phoenix. The crushing was not a death, but a rebirth. 'Under great pressure, diamonds are formed.'

A will to thrive, and a passion for love, for authenticity, for justice, sprang up in me greater than before, like flames lifting me out of the dirt.

When I was a small child, I assumed that the reason why my mouth was small was because I spoke so little.

Now I will speak.

My flaming wings will guard my voice. My armor will keep me secure.

During my time of rest in Key West, my first tattoo was cut into the base of my neck:

The invincible bird, the phoenix.

Ephesians 6:13-17 and 2 Corinthians 4:8-9 (Bible):

'Therefore put on the full armor of God, so that when the day of evil comes, you may be able to stand your ground, and after you have done everything, to stand. Stand firm then, with the belt of truth buckled around your waist, with the breastplate of righteousness in place, and with your feet fitted with the readiness that comes from the gospel of peace. In addition to all this, take up the shield of faith, with which you can extinguish all the flaming arrows of the evil one. Take the helmet of salvation and the sword of the Spirit, which is the word of God.'

'We are hard pressed on every side, but not crushed, perplexed, but not in despair; persecuted, but not abandoned; struck down, but not destroyed.'

The Spiritual Journey

I hope you remember what I had written that I saw after meeting Asatya - the vision that I had. The fierce determination that I had to support Asatya towards that future. I knew that Asatya would have to follow my lead for this to work.

It is my nature to be a follower. I also tend not to initiate unless I feel very strongly about something. I prefer to have someone else take the lead. I'm not entirely sure why. I suspect that a big piece of it is that I don't want to seem pretentious or egocentric. Humility is easier. Confidence or lack thereof could be part of it also. Leading is work, and it is easy to do it incorrectly. It's an extra responsibility. Well, regardless, God put me on a quest that involved the spiritual destiny of somebody who doesn't know Jesus. I thought, 'this should be interesting.' Obviously, it was.

I knew that it was essential that Asatya trust me and trust God. I prayed for him constantly and encouraged him to reach out to God in prayer directly, himself. (I don't think he ever did, though I don't know.) I had tremendous respect for Asatya, so I didn't pressure him. Imagine your grandfather whom you love, wants to learn a skill and you want to support him in that. It was that kind of leadership that I was going for. I prayed, asking for specific direction but only received a little of that. Maybe God wanted that we learn some things as we went along...

In the beginning, Asatya showed trust in me. Later on, he would trust then doubt, trust then doubt. Sometimes he asserted his ideas. I thought, it's his life, I can't really stop him, but some of his ideas I knew would be counter-productive. Like when he suggested starting up a dairy operation with the woman who had exploited him for months.

With Asatya's trust issues, it was hard at times for him to believe me and cooperate because if I countered what he said, or tried to defend my position, he would accuse me of showing my 'ego.' As it turns out, *all* authority and leadership look like ego to a person who is rebellious, or who himself has a monstrous ego...

I say this as a warning to those who have a humble spirit: Narcissists know that you are humble, that you will admit when you are wrong, that you will introspect. When they accuse you of having a big ego, (or almost any accusation), they know that their accusation is baseless, but they also know that you will take what they said to heart and question yourself. We have been taught to listen when someone tells us that we hurt them, which is the right thing to do, but a narcissist will use that against you. The narcissist will tear you down like this over time. If you know they are wrong and try to stand up to them, WW111 will break out and they will just find another way to destroy you.

If anyone accuses you, I suggest getting a second opinion from a trusted friend (who is in no way connected to the accuser) to be honest with you if there is anything you need to change in yourself. Then you will have a better idea whether you should apologize and change, or if you should question that the accuser may be trying to make you doubt yourself. There were a few times that I had wanted an outside opinion about some interaction that I had with Asatya, but I hesitated to say anything because there was usually a lot of backstory and cultural context that I would have to explain, which would be tedious, and the listener might feel lost. It made me feel alone. I didn't know anyone else in my shoes who could relate.

Asatya would seem to become depressed any time that somebody screwed him over or gave him a lot of stress, and these events would resurrect all his doubts, which he would then project onto me. At least, that is how I understood his behavior. Or maybe (probably) that was just more manipulation. He wanted me to doubt myself. Sometimes I thought that I was wrong, and he was right, and it would make me inclined to lean on him for direction, but that meant that he would have more control. Whichever the case, the result was that Asatya would not cooperate with me, or else he would say that he was with me, but he didn't put in any of his own effort, which was basically the same as not cooperating.

In the first couple of years, Asatya seemed like such a saint, a human being operating on a higher plane, so when he would correct me on something that I had not noticed in myself, or that I thought was really a small issue, I just thought that he has very high standards and he believes in me to also operate on a higher level. Asatya expected perfection out of me. It

273

wasn't until much later that I noticed his double standards. His expectation of me did not match up with what he allowed in himself. For example, Asatya said that our relationship was baseless if I did not completely trust him, while his trust in me was on and off. Or like when he scolded me up one side and down the other for leaving my water bottle behind at Music Man's house and refused to go collect it, but when he realized that his jacket was also left there, he didn't say anything but simply went back to get the things. Music Man lived just 100 meters from the main route.

That is when I realized that I had literally crossed (more than one) ocean for someone who would not even cross the street for me.

It seemed like Asatya was always the one who was super busy with work or whatever, so I would do as much as I could without him. It was confusing when Asatya would talk like he was excited for the launch of the business, but after leaving the teaching position in Chamba, he didn't do a single thing other than chat with one or two local tailors. It was confusing, because I have seen many times that Asatya is the sort of person who, when he had set his mind to do something, he launched straight into it that same hour. I was communicating daily about developments and what I needed him to do next. He insisted that the house building projects must be done first. It made no sense.

I coaxed Asatya to make himself very busy with our business project immediately, to minimize his gap in paychecks. Instead, he was using up his savings by building... Finally, when I told him that I urgently needed him in Jaipur, he turned on me.

Did he really think that God would lift him up while he was actively abusing and sabotaging?

We had talked about Jesus before and we even studied the gospel of John together, but I had never told him point blank, 'You need a spiritual rebirth,' or You need Jesus.'

Asatya claimed that he believed in the vision, but his actions indicated that he only wanted to do it his way. His way involved making zero inward changes, which I did not fully see until the end.

I had wanted to respect him by not being pushy. But I knew that the only way that Asatya could really fulfill that prophetic vision was that he himself be full of the Holy Spirit. Only then would he have the power, life, and direct guidance within him for that sort of destiny. I knew that to welcome God in like that, would mark day #1 of real healing and life for this guy.

As it was, every day was a painful struggle for him. Well, I wrote to him about his need for Jesus, as you may recall. I put so much thought and prayer and gentleness and encouragement into those messages.

His reaction was so vile that I had to question whether he might actually be possessed...the reaction was truly abnormal and explosive.

It makes perfect sense now why he said, "I can't look to God for help anymore. I must rely on me. I can't give my everything to everyone else anymore, I must take care of me."

Self-love is valid, but Asatya was actually doing self-worship with no care for others.

I think at some point he realized that the blessings of God come when we relinquish our ego, our self-centeredness, pettiness, grudges, etc. He didn't want to let those things go. Asatya didn't worship The Almighty Creator, the Christ, Allah, Ram, Krishna, Vishnu or any other god... He claimed to be innocent, never doing any intentional wrong, all while using everyone around him as far as it was possible and maintaining his fake saintly persona to garner praise and admiration far and wide. He was his own god. The idea of humbling himself to any other was repulsive to him. And so, he dooms himself to an existence void of life.

It is true that it has happened many times that God chose a really horrible or hopeless person to be a hero or protagonist in an amazing story, and the story started with God totally transforming that person, sometimes through miracles. I thought to myself, that if God is going to use this wretched creature, it will indeed take a supernatural intervention, more than just the loving support of a sister. It would require something dramatically miraculous.

That man is more impervious than Fort Knox. He is as dark as a black hole, for that is what he is. He speaks seven languages and yet just one: manipulation.

I brought my best dynamite to break through that iron exterior, to reach his heart, and I just about blew myself to bits.

I asked God "What happened?? I did what you asked for four years and now I am forced to abandon the person that you sent me to." Every once in a while, I hear the voice of God in my head as if by telepathy. It happened when God told me to help Asatya, and it happened again at this moment. The response was immediate: "You did what I asked; he did not."

This was tremendously helpful to me as it would have been easy to wonder where I went wrong. This empowered me to move forward without looking back in regret or guilt. All the shame and doubts that Asatya had tried to sink into me, did not work. Also, this response seemed to imply that Asatya could have listened to God and obeyed if he really wanted to. He was not a totally depraved slave of his personality disorder or sinful nature to the point that he was incapable of admitting a wrong-doing, even just a small wrong-doing... change starts somewhere. I know that if he had asked God for the strength to come to terms with his toxic patterns, he would have been granted that. I do believe that the spiritual is stronger than the physical. The One that gave us life surely has strength to heal those that sincerely ask and believe in his benevolence and power.

If there is anything inside of you holding you back from reaching out to God, realize that Jesus forgave the criminal who was executed beside him. God also forgave a man named Paul who was hunting down Jesus-followers to kill them, but God turned his life around to be a great leader, and he even sent me to offer a chance of new life to a pretending scoundrel. It was never about deserving, as God can transform anyone that is willing. It was always that God loves and wants all of us -and I do mean all.

My faith was still intact, but this experience was a gut punch. Obviously, God knew that Asatya would not cooperate and that he would try to pervert the true goal of our efforts, manipulating me and ultimately turning on me. I wondered what was the point of my pain and suffering?

I was reminded of two things:

God is about mercy. He gives everyone second chances that they don't deserve. I know I am included in that. As a mom, I know that I have given my kids second chances when their patterns indicated that they would very likely just do the same thing again. Sometimes they have surprised me, and they actually did conquer whatever thing that they had stumbled over a thousand times before. I gave my kids another chance, not because they deserved it, but because I loved them. I have to do the right thing as a parent regardless of how my kids respond.

It should stun us that we as the collective human race have basically rebelled against our creator and instead of just wiping out our planet, he came here to sacrifice himself to satisfy both love and justice simultaneously. It doesn't stun us though. Because it is so incredible that we hesitate to believe. We don't want to give up our egos. We don't want to confess anything to God. Guess what? God knew that most of us would ignore or even mock what he's done for us. He did it anyway for the few who are interested to reconcile and have new life. It was an immeasurable sacrifice, but he still felt it was worth it for those few.

God sent me to reach out to Asatya not because Asatya deserved it.

God did this act of love for him because God stays true to his own character, and he *is* love. God put the ball in Asatya's court and Asatya fumbled it. As the ancient saying goes, "Let his blood be on his own head."

The lesson I learned from that is to not only never sink to someone else's lower level; do not preemptively base your decisions and morality on how others will respond. Always act according to your values. This is integrity. This is the difference between a person of character and a petty strategist with wishy-washy morals. In the end, we are each responsible and accountable for ourselves only. If we react to pettiness with more pettiness, we all sink lower and lower, because invariably some people overcompensate. Instead of rising up together, we work together to bring each other down. Not good. We must choose to speak up and act rightly. How others react is on them. Let us stay true to ourselves and our values and keep a clear conscience.

The second thing I was reminded of, is that God absolutely does not need anyone. Whatever it is that God wanted to do through Asatya, he could simply find someone else for that role. Or possibly that supernatural lightning bolt moment could come and Asatya will turn around 180 degrees like a sanctified, elevated soul - a new person. It's possible. This has happened before. I'm not holding my breath though. I played my part in that man's life and that chapter is now closed for me.

Asatya tried to guilt me into staying in touch by claiming that "Your job is not finished, sister."

Yes. Yes it is. Does it make sense for me to hurl my body into a land mine?

If the audience has an open mind and heart, something can happen. But it is not wise to offer a gentle hand towards a raging person who has no conscience. Now that I know Asatya has utterly rejected every good thing that I presented to him, the time has come to pivot and move away.

Jesus once said, "Do not throw your pearls to swine, or they may trample them underfoot, then turn and tear you to pieces."

In years past I could only vaguely sense the meaning of those words.

I now understand it to mean this: that pigs are not able to understand the value of pearls. They value just food. If you throw pearls, they will be both hungry and angry that the pearls are not food, and they will come after you. Pigs are dangerous when they go hungry.

What is also dangerous is trying to give pearls of wisdom to people that are deeply invested in their own greed, immorality, or folly.

So naturally, if you talk to someone who values ego, selfish gain, and their excuses for terrible behavior, they will become angry at you if you talk of humility, repentance, salvation, new life and that sort of thing. You don't even have to mention their wrong-doings to illicit a vile response. Simply implying that we all are in a position that necessitates asking God for forgiveness is enough, sometimes. In fact, I have even seen it happen many times where good people simply existed near evil people, and the good peoples' presence alone was enough to incite rude and abusive behavior towards them.

The thing is, when we find something truly invaluable, we want to share it with the people that we care about. That is natural. But it is essential to read the room and use discernment to understand who is absorbing what you have to share, and who wants to attack you for it. We can't judge superficially. This requires discernment and discretion.

Unfortunately, in my case I was dealing with a wolf in sheep's clothing. Life sure is complicated, isn't it?

For some months, I continued to feel hurt by God and I hesitated to trust again. One Sunday, I was at church, and I could not bring myself to sing any worship songs. I did not feel the praise or thanks. I was still grumbling inside. I was frustrated with God and frustrated with myself for grumbling against God. I cried. I left.

But I kept going back. I remembered what I had signed up for: A life of following Jesus with no hesitation and going all in. Of course it's a wild ride. It is a revolution of love, as well as a ministry of reconciliation and a dedication to spiritual growth.

Committing to this revolution means being willing to do the things that look crazy.

I took a young man on a different continent, whom I had not yet met in person, as my honorary son. Some people still think I am crazy for that. I don't care. That young man is full of sunshine and encouragement and never stops praying for me and my family. He now has multiple degrees and many useful skills. Sometimes I think he is wiser than me. But I never heard him talk about these things; I simply came to discover them over time by observation.

It has happened countless times that I felt prompted by the Spirit to say something specific to somebody and I thought, "Ridiculous. I can't say that, that's crazy." But again, I was told to go say it. Finally with heart pounding and feeling a bit like a lunatic, I spoke to that person whatever I had been prompted to say. Surprise, surprise... every time I have done this (except in Asatya's case) the listener seemed almost stunned by the timeliness and relevance of what I said, and the words had great impact. So, I have learned to trust these 'crazy' prompts.

They only seem crazy because we can't see the entire picture, but the Holy Spirit in us sees all and knows all.

'...Even Satan disguises himself as an angel of light. Therefore it is not surprising if his servants also disguise themselves as servants of righteousness, whose end will be according to their deeds.' ~ *2nd Corinthians 11:14+15*

Even in following the guidance of the Holy Spirit, I have learned a hard lesson to never take off the 'armor of God' as I mentioned earlier.

Along with that, I have learned the importance of identifying where my personal boundaries should be (for example, I will immediately disengage from anyone using shaming tactics) and unapologetically keeping those boundaries very firmly in place. This rule applies across the board:

with one's spouse, friends, relatives, anyone. **There are no 'extenuating circumstances' to excuse disrespect or abuse; that is a slippery slope.**

See, I had made the mistake of allowing exceptions to my boundaries because someone I loved was under a lot of stress, and so I accepted such excuses for poor behavior. I will no longer accept any excuse for abusive speech or actions. If you can't be civil, go take some time to chill out before re-engaging. You can't connect positively with someone whom you allow to use you as a punching bag.

On the other hand, Jesus had said, "take up your cross and follow me." He knew that if he could be mocked, falsely accused and condemned by rebels, that for sure his followers would encounter the same. Why? Truth is uncomfortable. Truth came down to us in the form of love, who is Jesus Christ, and look at the hate that has come at him over the years...but still he loves.

Even without saying anything, just following Jesus quietly, some people will resent you. In some parts of the world, they will try to end you. Some will reject and even attack, but others will be drawn to that aroma, that light of Christ. Some will claim that for themselves.

'For the word of the cross is foolishness to those who are perishing, but to those who are being saved, it is the power of God.'

I consider the risk of being wrongly attacked to be worth it for the sake of the few who are given new life, and for the sake of remaining humane in an inhumane world.

Elsewhere, it is written:

'If anyone will not welcome you or listen to your words, leave that home or town and shake the dust off your feet.'

There, Jesus was explaining that if someone rejects the word of God, to simply move on; don't fight them. There may be risks of being targeted as a follower of Jesus, but it doesn't make sense to stay and press the issue after a rejection. In fact, continuing can sometimes cause more harm than good. The 'gospel of peace' is a matter of choice, not force, and this advice is applicable to any good news or teaching. Anything forced doesn't really work anyway.

These are my thoughts and experiences to date. It is totally possible that in the future I will gain additional perspective and change my assessment of my experiences, or my attitude a bit.

It is true that in this journey of faith, that I am fully equipped, and I have the support and comfort of a God who came down and lived among us and can actually empathize with me.

To be really honest with myself and everyone, if I had not distanced myself from God in resentment last year, I might have had more peace and healed faster. I know that even though I prayed less and ignored my Bible for too long, God still helped me find tools and people that aided my healing. He was there, even though I was giving him the cold shoulder.

In the spring of 2024, I discovered a song called 'Egypt[1],' that is now a favorite of mine. The lyrics talk about being rescued out of oppression, and the joy of freedom. I had used this song to pray for Asatya. When Asatya wrote to me rejecting my benevolence and the promises of God, it was a rejection of that rescue, freedom, and joy. Later when I broke free, I found those things to be mine. The story in the song is historical and yet feels allegorical of this recent experience of breaking free, and the journey that followed.[xxxvii]

In the end, I felt like I needed to unlearn some things and relearn some other things concerning best guidance for how to navigate relationships, as the emotional abuse had disoriented me. That familiar voice in my mind reminded me that the Bible is stuffed full of excellent advice on the topic. This is how I began to crave the Word of God again. It started in Florida when I was searching for my wallet and found a Bible instead. I started reading again, this time with fresh appreciation for the precious words contained therein.

I particularly like the random snippets found in the ancient book of Proverbs. Here are a few such random snippets from Proverbs and a few other scriptures, (in addition to those I've quoted elsewhere) that I've found to be particularly relevant and helpful at this time:

"Humble yourselves, therefore, under God's mighty hand, that he may lift you up in due time. Cast all your anxiety on him because he cares for you. Be self-

---

1. https://youtu.be/6BBYtt1tkwU?si=D4JR7BXZRiJdU-EF

controlled and alert. Your enemy the devil prowls around like a roaring lion looking for someone to devour."

"But mark this: There will be terrible times in the last days. People will be lovers of themselves, lovers of money, boastful, proud, abusive, disobedient to their parents, ungrateful, unholy, without love, unforgiving, slanderous, without self-control, brutal, not lovers of the good, treacherous, rash, conceited, lovers of pleasure rather than lovers of God - having a form of godliness but denying its power. Have nothing to do with them."

"Plans fail for lack of counsel, but with many advisors they succeed."

"To do what is right and just is more acceptable to the LORD than sacrifice."

"A righteous man is cautious in friendship, but the way of the wicked leads them astray."

"A kindhearted woman gains respect, but ruthless men gain only wealth."

"Rescue those being led away to death; hold back those staggering towards slaughter."

"Like one who seizes a dog by the ears is a passer-by who meddles in a quarrel not his own."

"Speak up for those who cannot speak for themselves, for the rights of all who are destitute. Speak up and judge fairly; defend the rights of the poor and needy."

"So when you give to the needy, do not announce it with trumpets, as the hypocrites do in the synagogues and on the streets, to be honored by men. I tell you the truth, they have received their reward in full. But when you give to the needy, do not let your left hand know what your right hand is doing, so that your giving may be in secret. Then your Father, who sees what is done in secret, will reward you."

"Look at the birds of the air; they do not sow or reap or store away in barns, and yet your heavenly Father feeds them. Are you not much more valuable than they? Who of you by worrying can add a single hour to his life?"

"A bruised reed he will not break, and a smoldering wick he will not snuff out."

"Dear children, let us not love with words or tongue but with actions and in truth. This then is how we know that we belong to the truth, and how we set

our hearts at rest in his presence whenever our hearts condemn us. For God is greater than our hearts, and he knows everything."

"For we do not have a high priest (Jesus) who is unable to sympathize with our weaknesses, but we have one who has been tempted in every way, just as we are - yet was without sin.

Let us then approach the throne of grace with confidence, so that we may receive mercy and find grace to help us in our time of need."

"Even youths grow tired and weary, and young men stumble and fall; but those who hope in the LORD *will renew their strength. They will soar on wings like eagles; they will run and not grow weary, they will walk and not be faint."*

"So do not throw away your confidence; it will be richly rewarded. You need to persevere."

"Now faith is being sure of what we hope for and certain of what we do not see."

A Summary of This Condition, and the Abuse Often Associated with It

I believe it is important to clarify the definition or diagnostic criteria of narcissistic personality disorder, (NPD) as there is a lot of misinformation out there and general confusion on the topic. (Oh, the irony!)

It will be super helpful to everyone if people would stop calling others 'narcissists,' who are just self-centered, egocentric, or rude. None of those traits by themselves constitute narcissism. It is actually very important to understand the difference between a narcissist and someone who is just not good, because their brains operate quite differently. If we try to apply normal, standard logic, reasoning, or therapy to a real narcissist, it absolutely will not work.

I believe it is important to know what it looks like, both for the sake of assisting a loved one to escape if they become enmeshed with such a person, as well as to better protect one's own peace and autonomy from becoming compromised, by hopefully detecting the warning signs earlier rather than later.

It is also important to have some knowledge and understanding of this topic, because the more society as a whole breaks down under a lack of moral integrity, slippery ethics, and self-centered dysfunctions, the more we will see various mental health conditions becoming prevalent, especially those conditions that are caused or exacerbated by childhood trauma, such as Narcissistic Personality Disorder (NPD.) The good news is that the patterns of this disorder are very strong, so once you have become very familiar with it, it will be much easier to spot the second time around. That said, there are a few variations that will be explained later.

The definitive traits below can be found in the DSM-5 and published by many other medical authorities:

1. Grandiose sense of self-importance.

  • *Overestimating their capabilities or holding themselves to unreasonably high standards.*

- *Bragging or exaggerating their achievements.*

2. Frequent fantasies about having or deserving:

- *Success.*
- *Power.*
- *Intelligence.*
- *Beauty.*
- *Love.*
- *Self-fulfillment.*

3. Belief in superiority.

- *Thinking they're special or unique.*
- *Believing they should associate only with those they see as worthy.*

4. Need for admiration.

- *Fragile self-esteem.*
- *Frequent self-doubt, self-criticism or emptiness.*
- *Fixation on knowing what others think of them.*
- *Seeking out compliments.*

5. Entitlement.

- *Inflated sense of self-worth.*
- *Expecting favorable treatment (to an unreasonable degree).*
- *Anger when people don't cater to or appease them.*

6. Willingness to exploit others.

- *Consciously or unconsciously using others.*

- *Forming friendships or relationships with people who boost their self-esteem or status.*

- *Deliberately taking advantage of others for selfish reasons.*

- *Mental or emotional manipulation.*

7. Lack of empathy.

- *Saying hurtful things.*

- *Seeing the feelings, needs or desires of others as a sign of weakness.*

- *Not returning kindness or interest that others show or offering empty promises and fake interest.*

8. Frequent envy.

- *Feeling envious of others, especially when others are successful.*

- *Expecting envy from others.*

- *Belittling or diminishing the achievements of others, possibly sabotaging them.*

9. Arrogance.

- *Patronizing behavior.*
- *Behaving in a way that's snobby or disdainful.*
- *Talking down or acting condescendingly.*

People with NPD may also show other behaviors related to these nine traits, but still different, such as:

- *Fear of or avoiding vulnerability.*

- *Withdrawing from others to hide feeling vulnerable.*

- *Perfectionism (with or without a fear of failure).*

- *Hypersensitivity to criticism, rejection or failure.*

- *Experiencing severe <u>depression</u> related to rejection or failure.*

- *Reacting with anger (or even rage) when they feel criticized or rejected.*

- *Faking humility to hide their feelings or protect their sense of self-importance.*

- *Avoiding situations where failure is possible or likely, which can limit achievements.*

- *Lives by a personal victim narrative.*

- *Sabotage, attack, or shame others when they feel threatened, or to manipulate.*

A person must exhibit at least five of these nine traits to qualify for a diagnosis of narcissistic personality disorder.

Just as having a clear-cut definition is important, having real-life examples is also important. It may be hard to imagine what this condition looks like in the real world. This is one of the reasons that I have shared my story. Many of the things that I witnessed or experienced from Asatya are universal in NPD, and some of them are simply common.

Any one of the traits mentioned above can be destructive. Consider that a person with NPD by definition, has five or more of these traits all working together. These combinations of narcissistic traits all together can cause truly devastating and unbelievable scenarios. The first three traits mentioned can and often do lead to delusions, so if some of the actions of a narcissist seem unbelievable or nonsensical, this is why. They often do crazy things.

I've heard a few people say to survivors things like, "Nobody cares that much that they would plot that far in advance, in that much detail, and make personal sacrifices, just to hurt you. You're being paranoid." It is true that normal people are not that obsessive to go to that much trouble. Unfortunately, delusional, self-centered sadists exist. Sometimes narcissists are petty and irritating, and sometimes multiple people end up dead. There is a broad range of severity.

Narcissists are fully developed physically and cognitively, but their emotional maturation stopped in early childhood. Imagine a hangry, over-tired 3-year-old that has access to a car, weapons, your bank account, house keys, etc. but they have adult level intelligence and experience.

A true narcissist (or psychopath) can be incredibly diabolical and will have their games strategized ten moves in advance. You only *think* you know what cunning means - until you fall prey to one of these people. At first, you will be totally convinced that they are James Bond, only to realize too late that they are Spectre.

In the context of very close relationships such as marriage or between a parent/child, toxic patterns may be there. How do you know if it is just a matter of some toxic rubbish that you can work to improve, possibly with therapy, or if you are dealing with a narcissist, in which case they *will not ever* improve?

The answer to that question may determine whether you completely cut them off, or if you try harder to improve the relationship. You can see how it becomes important to know the difference between random toxic behaviors versus a personality disorder that can potentially destroy your life.

If at this point, you realize that you are in a relationship with a narcissist, but you feel it's not that bad and you don't want to leave, there is one more thing that you should know:

The mistreatment always worsens as the relationship progresses. It will become dangerous if it has not yet already. Also, narcissists tend to become worse with age. I am sorry to be the one to tell you that Santa Claus does not exist, but please cut your losses and get out now.

I want to take a moment to say that not all people who have a personality disorder are life-ruiners. For example, borderline personality disorder (BPD) is a personality disorder that can be treated, and many people with this condition lead fairly normal lives. However, successful treatment of NPD is so exceptionally rare that unfortunately, you are better off keeping your distance from any person who has it.

I sincerely hope that in coming years, the medical community will find effective ways of helping NPD sufferers consent to treatment, and create more effective treatments.

Much of the ailment comes down to brain chemistry and neural pathways, which are plastic (malleable) in nature, if I understand it correctly.

Considering what NPD looks like in the context of relationships and also understanding that many narcissists go to great lengths to try to mask or hide their negative traits (such as grandiosity) let's look at typical relational behaviors of NPD. Click here[1][xxxviii] to find a link to a few very informative and helpful videos[2].[xxxix] Here is how it all plays out:

•Love-bomb

Love-bombing is the first step, and it means to lavish an unusual amount of kindness or romance, possibly lots of sex, lots of praise and words of admiration, an unusual amount of consideration, and in every case, making efforts to move the progress of the relationship ahead at a precocious speed. For example: claiming boyfriend/girlfriend title on the second date, proposing marriage after just a few weeks, wanting a baby right away, asking to move out of the country to be together without even meeting in person first, etc.

Future-faking and mirroring may be included in this phase. Future faking is essentially making empty promises. Mirroring simply means to copy you like a parrot, your good traits and good ideas, to try to gain your approval and make you feel like you have a lot in common.

During this stage, the narcissist studies you to understand what is important to you, so that they can create an act and a narrative that is custom designed for you, so that you will be inclined to bond with them and give them all your trust. They will likely point out how much you (supposedly) have in common and throw around words like 'soul-mate.'

Even after the love-bombing ends, they will reinforce their 'good guy' narrative often and toss you just enough 'breadcrumbs' to keep you believing that the nice version of them is the real them. 'Breadcrumbing' is an emotional abuse tactic that involves giving attention, affection, gifts, help, and other signs of love only just often enough to retain you in the relationship. It is a starvation slow enough that the victim doesn't leave, thinking that things will improve. At some point, the victim begins to feel the dis-

1. https://youtu.be/POq_YcMB9CU?si=yANZqdHvbBNNZqCj
2. https://youtu.be/f6Kat36uN0w?si=FGmLZ9FLuBNYAxM1

tance or coldness, so they give more love and attention to the narcissist, thinking that will help. The narcissist basks in the attention, but is slow to reciprocate, giving the same or less next time. This scenario repeats with the victim trying harder each time, and the narcissist giving less, and less frequently... but always just barely enough that their victim (supply) does not give up. The victim becomes thoroughly exhausted in their efforts to love the narcissist, while they themselves are simultaneously starved of love. By then, they are enmeshed.

In my case, Asatya only did a little love-bombing. Because our relationship was founded on the narrative of 'Asatya is an exceptionally kindhearted person of character that is in depression and has no one close,' so the relational dynamic from day one was that I was there to be his sister so that he would not be alone. It was about me helping him. Because Asatya knew that I wanted to help him, he didn't invest much in love-bombing.

I theorize that the lack of significant love-bombing had the long-term effect of a weaker trauma-bond, (more on trauma-bond later) which made it easier for me to disconnect from him in the end. I was there to extend charity, not because he did anything for me. After I cut him out of my life, I missed having someone greeting me every single day, but I absolutely did not miss him. Additionally, from my side it was a real human relationship; I sincerely thought of Asatya as my brother.

The lack of genuine emotional intimacy, and the disrespect and abuse that became infused as time went on, left me feeling starved of love and anxious, even while I was pouring myself out in personal sacrifice.

One last thought about love-bombing:

An empathic person will likely get a general sense of who you are before other people do, naturally, without studying you first. This means that they might decide very early on whether they are interested in you or not. Autistics, expressive people, and people without well-defined boundaries all have the capacity to become very devoted very quickly. In those cases, the intention behind the sweetness may be completely innocent, but they would still be wise to slow themselves down a bit in their new relationships.

It's totally possible that these innocent types of quick bonds might be confused with love-bombing or vice versa, but if the fast pace feels forced or the 'love' you're receiving is on an extreme obsessive level, this is not healthy in any case, no matter how they may try to excuse it or market it to you. Under those circumstances I would recommend politely declining the next invite or suggestion, or make them wait longer than they want to. Tell them directly that you need a slower pace. Watch carefully how they react.

The bottom line is that lots of affection and kindness early on is not automatic proof of shady intentions, but it is always best in such situations to institute healthy boundaries and slow the pace a bit, while keeping your eyes open for any other possible red flags. It might also be a good idea to pause sometimes and ask yourself, 'Who is controlling my emotions right now?'

•Devalue

Just as in the love-bombing phase, there is a vast library of tactics at a narcissist's disposal in this phase as well. Some examples of devaluation include:

Shaming, backhanded compliments, questioning the victim's competencies, knowledge, or sanity, silent treatment, cold responses, excessive pettiness, putting the victim at the bottom of the priority list, becoming increasingly critical, frequently 'correcting' the victim, sabotage, etc. It is both sad and amazing the vast array of creative strategies employed to make the victim feel inferior. It may be as subtle as asking you, 'Are you sure?' to make you doubt yourself. Even more amazing is how some of these people can do these things while still looking innocent. For example, locking your car keys inside your car and then accusing you of doing it, shaming you for making 'Such a dumb mistake.' I remember that Asatya love-bombed and exploited me at the same time through weaponized incompetence, claiming that I was so much better at google research than he was, telling me that I should continue doing that myself. However, that research project was the number one thing consuming copious amounts of my time. He knew that. Still, from time to time he would come back around to this topic to heap shame on me for not having serious results yet.

One obvious example of the training into self-doubt was that Asatya would express doubts about the business project and ask me to do a lot of market research, after I already showed him my market research. He dismissed all of the other stats that I had presented to him, saying that we need to see what Sama and Vyapari think. I agreed to seek their advice, but the problem was that he didn't take me seriously as an entrepreneur.

See, in my case he failed in making me doubt myself as a businessperson, because I tend to be analytical and make business decisions based on available information and logic. It was Asatya's baseless doubts against objective numbers which don't lie and don't care about anyone's feelings.

Another time, I told him about plans that I had suggested to Visounou. My approach to those plans was according to my own American understanding of family dynamics. Asatya scolded me up one side and down the other, insisting that I didn't really see Visounou as a true family member. He said this because I was not doing things according to Indian family dynamics. I tried to explain that, but he told me to stop defending myself and admit that my thinking was wrong. He succeeded in getting me to believe him and apologize even though there was no real problem.

From time to time, he told me that soon, he would be too old to think of starting a family, and I should have worked harder to find him a wife sooner. I did say that I would help look, so some of that shame did stick, even though I did look, and I had put a few people in touch with him. He said that marrying after 45 or 50 years of age is not acceptable in India, but two of his acquaintances said that he is not too old and can do what he wants. That confused me. In retrospect, all that talk of me helping find a wife was only ever spoken of through gaslighting and shaming. Interestingly, at least six Indian women met with him during the time that I knew him, but he didn't accept any of them. It seemed clear that he only wanted an American or other foreigner. He said an Indian woman wouldn't dream of leaving her relatives behind to live in a different country... He tried to inflict so much shame on this topic.

He succeeded in making me question the *way* that I handled relationships. He made me question my motivations, my timing, and my ability to communicate clearly. It has taken me a long time to dismantle the lies that he implanted in my mind concerning those things.

You have probably heard of the concept of grooming. As I understand it, love-bombing and devaluing are a two-part strategy of grooming. First, you're conditioned to love and trust the narcissist, then you are conditioned to question yourself and your value. The narcissist will trick you into shifting value away from yourself and place it on them. Their fragile but highly prized sense of superiority can't let you look better than them. It is preparing you to accept abuse and exploitation. That is the definition of grooming.

As soon as the narcissist senses that their supply (victim) is really beginning to question themselves, but also still trusting the narcissist, (remember the good guy narrative is still there) the next phase is employed:

●**Manipulate, Gaslight, and Control**

I think there may be some narcissists who don't do these things much, as it is not necessarily a required trait of NPD, but I am not aware of any narcissists that do *not* seek control. In the context of narcissist/supply relationships, seeking control is a very typical pattern.

Here are a few tactics that are typically employed by a narcissist:

Boundary Violation - Every narcissist has their own patterns or preferences for how they control their supply. Grooming continues through this stage. It often looks like pushing you out of your comfort zone a little bit at a time, in unhealthy ways. Consistently stepping just one step beyond your personal boundaries until you just accept it, then they take another step beyond. They may try to make this look cute or funny, which is easy to accept if you're in love or think the world of them. They may create a sort of crisis or hype that they use to justify making exceptions to your boundaries, except that these crises may become more frequent or chronic, and before you know it, your boundaries are gone, and your life has become simply an extension of theirs. Your autonomy slowly dissolves, and you don't realize it for a while, because you buy into their 'us' and 'we' narrative. Except it is not 'us.' It is only about them, and you enmeshed with them. You may no longer even know who you are.

Triangulation - The narcissist manipulates and deputizes other people to reinforce their narrative and do their dirty work, so that essentially, they gang up on you. Sometimes the third party is not actually involved in this conversation. Remember that Asatya had said to me, "Mauna is proving to be more useful than you..." He was trying to manipulate me through shame – the shame of appearing to be a worse person than Mauna, whom he always complained about to me.

Isolation - The narcissist may separate you from your friends and family, by controlling your social media or forcing you to delete it, or they may put on their charm for your loved ones while badmouthing you to the point where your people are all on the side of the narcissist (this really does happen, they are very good at this) and they start to believe that you are crazy or an abuser. Alternately, becoming so enmeshed in the narcissist's life may very well mean that you don't have time or energy left for the other people in your life, so they see you less and they may begin to resent you or pull away. Or, they may see the narcissist for what they are (not understanding the depths of the mind games) and they become disgusted with you for staying with the narcissist. The narcissist may accuse you of cheating to justify keeping you under surveillance and not letting you go out with your friends, not letting you have access to the car keys, accompanying you everywhere you go so you can never have a private conversation with anyone else. After I got free of Asatya, I realized that all my friendships had grown more distant, even though I thought that I was balancing my time enough while connected to Asatya. I was so distracted that my friendships suffered, and I realized after the fact that my support network had grown smaller and weaker.

Isolation often comes as an after-effect as well, because when you finally break away from the narcissist, you may discover that some or all of your support network has been compromised by the narcissist, so that you can only be safe if you break ties with all of them, which could leave you with no support network.

Intermittent reinforcement- This is perhaps the most dangerous form of manipulation. The narcissist will go through cycles with you between love-bombing and devaluing. They will love-bomb just barely enough for just barely long enough to make you believe that the nice them is the real them, or that they have turned a corner, or whatever maintains your trust and loyalty in them.

With your love and faith in them reinforced, they slip back into henpecking you, exploiting your money, time, resources, and possibly sexually abusing you or becoming violent towards you. The love-bombing phase may include fake apologies and empty promises. These cycles slowly worsen over time. In the context of an intimate relationship, the victim not only becomes enmeshed, but also addicted. It often happens that the worse the abuse is, the more intense the love-bombing is. It is a roller-coaster ride. If the narcissist was consistently horrible, their supply would just leave. If they were always kind and unselfish, they wouldn't be abusers. An abuser retains their victim by pretending to improve.

See, it's called love-bombing because it is intensive affection and dramatic display of love. It feels really good. A narcissist can be incredibly tender, romantic, and sweet. Then the narcissist deprives you of any love and even turns mean on you. The niceness might slowly fade, or they might blow up in your face suddenly like a land mine. The extremes between love-bombing and devaluing can become really wild. They might threaten you with violence, suicide, or abandonment, then go silent, leaving you terrified, and then they swing back to sweeping you off on an epic vacation with a marriage proposal or something like that. Up, down, back and forth. With this extreme yo-yo action happening on repeat, a chemical imbalance is created in the victim's brain. They begin to live for the love-bombing, telling themselves that the abusive, mean narcissist is not the 'real them' and they will come out of it. They believe so strongly in the narcissist, not just because of the narrative, but because the love-bombing always comes back. Even after the victim finally realizes that they are in an abusive relationship, they still find it difficult to stay away, thinking that they still love the narcissist. They know at that point that they need to stay away, and they usually don't understand why it's so hard to stay away from the abuser, until they realize that the relationship itself is an addiction. If they stay with the narcissist long enough, the love-bombing/abuse cycles are what feels normal to them, and they can become codependent and accepting of abuse in future relationships. Friends or boyfriend/girlfriend that only talk to them once or twice per week feel boring. They become accustomed to the intensity. A relationship with a narcissist is full of tension.

Back to the narcissist-victim bond. Eventually the victim realizes that they are in a bad relationship, and they attempt to break up. We all know a woman who keeps going back to a douchebag, and we all wonder what was wrong with her for taking him back. Well, now you know. It takes an average of seven break-up attempts for a victim to leave a narcissist. Partly because the narcissist will manipulate or sometimes even force (hold captive) their victim, but mainly because of the trauma-bond[3][xl]. The trauma-bond refers to the addiction that is formed by the intermittent reinforcement.

To sum up, a trauma bond is an addiction formed in the victim through intermittent reinforcement, showering lots of (fake) love, withdrawing it, abusing, then repeating the cycle.

I have not heard this said directly by any expert, but I would like to theorize that the narcissist is also addicted, and probably more so. They employ all means imaginable (except for love and respect) to keep their supply. I can never forget how Asatya acted exactly like a drug addict experiencing withdrawal, after I cut off contact. Just imagine if you take an addict's drugs away from them, that they will fight you one way or another. This was distinctly different from the death of a normal relationship leading to grieving.

Joking and Sarcasm-

Obviously, joking and sarcasm can be a good and healthy addition to life. In the context of grooming and abuse, sarcasm can be used to gaslight you into believing that the verbal abuse was not really malicious, but just light-hearted banter. You can know if the intention was good or bad by the overall context of the relationship. Does this person gossip and slander others as well? Do they sabotage you or engage in other red flag behaviors? Or, are they a humble, kind, friendly jokester in general? Regardless of their intention, they should not do it if you tell them that it makes you feel disrespected.

All the same applies to jokes. There should never be endless practical jokes played on you that bring down your spirit or humiliate you. No one should ever wield a knife over your head, 'pretending to act out a scene,' or to laugh at you because they got you to react to the knife. No one should ever disrespect you or behave toxically towards you and later claim that they were 'only joking.'

Any joke or sarcasm that disrespects you, humiliates you, intimidates you or causes needless anxiety is not okay. Some people are not malicious but simply have a bad sense of humor, so if you're not sure, just tell them why you do not want them to do it anymore. Watch how they react and see

---

3.   https://youtu.be/xBOXuTdL1tM?si=MsAA-cLGE9xgHg36

how their behavior changes. Anyone who loves you will feel terrible that they hurt you and will make changes.

The sort of sarcasm and joking described above may simply be poor humor, grooming, or abuse depending on the details of the situation.

'Rebranding'-

I have not seen this addressed in psychology or relationships literature, (it's possible that it might just be called something else) but I certainly encountered this in my 'familial' relationship with Asatya. Imagine if the creators of almond milk tried to sell it as 'nut juice,' nobody would buy that (except for a few weirdos.)

Remember Asatya's idea for me to falsely accuse his enemy. He knew and intended that I do it on my own without his involvement. I think he knew that it would be a very weak case, and that I could be charged with false litigation, or defamation of character. What if I got a court summons and had to go there? I could be fined or put in jail in India. It's possible. At minimum, I would be under a mountain of additional stress.

The result of such an accusation against Shani would most likely land either Shani or I in jail. Either way would be a win in Asatya's mind. See, it was revenge against me, rebranded as a chance for me to prove my solidarity to Asatya.

Two more examples of rebranding:

Verbally abusing me or his siblings but referring to that as 'correction.'

Forcing me into situations that he knew would be extremely uncomfortable to me but calling it an 'honor.' Like getting roped into Nakali's awards ceremony or being a peacemaker in Agni's case.

If you think about it, a narcissist is a person who has a tremendous burden of trauma and toxic traits, who rebrands themselves as an amazing person. It is all clever, deceitful marketing.

Confusion-

You can imagine there are myriad ways that an abuser might cause confusion, but I'll just list a few examples.

Turn off alarms, throw away sticky note reminders, put away household items in a completely unexpected place, and otherwise act like a secret gremlin to cause disorganization and chaos.

Speak or write in a nonsensical or vague manner, such as with 'word salad.' (Asatya would do that more often when he was agitated. It would compound the tension, because I would not be understanding when he was already tense, and he can't stand not being understood.)

Gaslighting is a type of confusion and is a form of abuse in itself.

'Explain' a situation by getting the chronology of events totally out of order and use only pronouns and not names so that you have no idea who did what, or when.

Leave fake evidence to throw people off their trail.

Do or say any of these things confidently and seriously, so that the victim feels crazy for not understanding what is going on. (This is almost always done with gaslighting.)

Express totally fabricated emotions, which will keep the victim riding a roller coaster of stress because the abuser appears to have unpredictable reactions. What made the abuser 'happy' one day makes them 'sad' the next. Actually, that is a form of shifting goalposts, which I will explain later, although the abuser's emotions might actually be just that volatile.

Distraction-

In some cases, the narcissist continually has some new crisis or drama going on, and even if there is a brief period of smooth sailing, they make their supply busy with various responsibilities or petty arguments. The supply/victim is inundated by the never-ending goings-on of the narcissist's life, so that the victim can only ever focus on the current matter at hand. In this way, they never get a chance to get any distance to think over their general situation and get some broader perspective. While they are constantly distracted, they are less likely to question the narcissist. They might send you out to do errands so that they will be free to hook up with their secret other partner. They may change the subject or twist the conversation to avoid accountability. They might go on and on about some scandal, so you won't notice what they are doing right under your nose.

Perhaps a narcissist's 'favorite' distraction is projection. They cannot bear to look at their own shortcomings, so they accuse others of what they themselves have done. The lack of self-awareness coupled with a propensity to whine about other people's actions is just about universal among narcissists.

Intimidation and coercive control-

Asatya's personal attacks most often came from out of nowhere. Because I was not at all mentally or emotionally prepared, it was very intimidating. The way that his eyes grew wide and black as he seemed to almost shoot lasers through me with them while yelling at me, was also terrifying.

Coercive control can look like rendering their victim dependent. One who is dependent can be much more easily controlled. You may have your access to bank accounts restricted. You may be told that you are the problem for not trusting (even if you do trust them), just as I was told. "Without trust a relationship dies,' is a true statement, but a narcissist wants your *absolute* trust. They may promise to take care of you, telling you not to concern yourself with whatever, that they will handle it. A narcissist might withhold basic necessities from you until you comply. I've met a couple of women who knew they had to leave, but they couldn't because they had no support network, and they were extremely weak from being starved by their narcissistic abusers.

Children are very frequently used to control their other parent. Imagine that your kids are with their mom for a week, according to the custody arrangement. She might threaten to leave the kids overnight with a relative who is a suspected (but not proven) pedophile, if you don't agree to all her demands. The narcissist very often slanders the other parent to the kids, perhaps giving the kids whatever they want to make the kids think they are so nice, but they are undermining and attacking their other parent behind the scenes. The kids might grow up preferring the narcissist parent even though they are receiving no guidance, no discipline, and may be neglected in some ways. Those children are also under coercive control.

Coercive control can be sabotaging your means of independence. It can also be fabricating a burden of guilt on you or otherwise making you feel like you owe them somehow. In fact, coercive control can take many forms. The point is to force or pressure you into doing what they want. It is tyranny.

Remember how Asatya would accuse and shame me. I knew that he was wrong. I knew I could not correct him or question his lack of reciprocation, because he would attack me further and launch into a lengthy monologue declaring, 'I am the victim here.' He wanted me to prove his accusations wrong by being a 'great human being,' which just meant me doing more for him. He always put the focus on me, that I must prove my words by backing them up with action (while he ignored everything I had already done for him). You can see how he used a false narrative with verbal abuse and distraction to get his desired results out of me. Gross.

Gaslighting-

A common tactic used by narcissists and abusers alike is gaslighting. Sometimes this is employed simply because they sadistically enjoy watching you lose your mind. Sometimes it is to groom you to not recognize red flags. Sometimes it's about maintaining their fake persona. There are plenty of reasons why a narcissist might gaslight you, but regardless of the reason, gaslighting can break your barriers and boundaries down to be more susceptible to abuse, and will also cause neurological damage.

Imagine that you are responsible for navigating a naval vessel, but one of your crew mates is secretly employed by the enemy. When you are not near the instruments, they purposefully ruin the calibration of the instruments so that they give false readings. As far as you know, your gadgets are telling the truth, but they are not. You might keep feeling like something doesn't seem right, but you can't put your finger on it. You look in the binoculars, seeing a small island further to one side than you think it should be, but the instruments say that you're in the right place, so you assume that it must be a different island. Eventually, you have a near miss, nearly running aground or following the wrong channel.

Gaslighting will 'uncalibrate' you, altering your perception of reality without your knowledge. You question the reality of what you are seeing with your own eyes.

In general in this day and age, I think most people understand the concept of gaslighting but just in case this is new to you, I'll provide the definition of the words 'to gaslight' as found in the Merriam-Webster dictionary, and I quote:

'Psychological manipulation of a person usually over an extended period of time that causes the victim to question the validity of their own thoughts, perception of reality, or memories and typically leads to confusion, loss of confidence and self-esteem, uncertainty of one's emotional or mental stability, and a dependency on the perpetrator.'

Another way of saying this is that a person's perception of reality becomes warped through doubts, half-truths, invalidating remarks, etc. inflicted by the gaslighter.

The most classic and simple form of gaslighting is to simply deny that something happened, or you may be told that you're not remembering it correctly.

Use of a straw man argument is very similar to gaslighting and is another way that a victim is kept disoriented, confused, and easier to manipulate.

A narcissist or other perpetrator of abuse might retell what happened but make slight changes to the story that seem insignificant (if you even notice them) but that have the result of you seeing the matter more from their perspective, or leaving you with doubts about what actually happened.

Gaslighting is not always about perceptions of the past. It can come in the form of invalidating your feelings and reactions, making you think that your natural, true feelings or intuition are off. All that invalidation can make you think, "What's wrong with me? Why do I feel this way?" When in fact your original feelings and perceptions were accurate, and nothing was wrong with you at all.

Gaslighting can also look like you making a completely valid statement, and the narcissist responds by giving you the side eye and raising an eyebrow. (Not because they are skeptical, but because they want you to doubt what you said or to feel stupid.) They may say, "What were you thinking?" They may play with you by pretending to be happy or angry or any other mood, then later claim to have a totally different attitude, and tell you that you don't know how to read them. Asatya was very good at faking his facial expressions.

All the 'correction' and dismissal of your feelings over time can make you think that you are the problem, or at least part of the problem, even if you are completely innocent. You may look inward to evaluate yourself, but you might not find any huge problem in yourself and then you will think, 'How can I not find the problem? Or how did I not detect this problem? Am I blind to my own faults? Am I a narcissist??' You may feel very confused and unsure of yourself as your confidence falters.

The more gaslit you are over time, the more confused you will be as you question reality, and you start to feel like you are going crazy. The person who gaslit you might even claim that you are crazy, and you may nearly believe it. I know of a few narcissists who succeeded in having their perfectly sane partner put away in a psych ward- a locked facility. In that case, there may have been some gaslighting of the victim, but mostly it was that they were extremely good at playing 'the system.' Those stories remind me of the movie 'I Care a Lot,' which is about a con-woman who makes a lot of money from getting sane, rich people locked up in mental hospitals. Diabolical.

With gaslighting, you start to question the reality or truth behind everything, and you don't know who to believe, or if you can even trust your own thoughts. It is sickening and incredibly anxiety-producing.

This cognitive damage caused by gaslighting continues long after the victim breaks free from the narcissist. It generally takes a lot of therapy and time to identify and separate fallacy from fact, to believe in oneself again, and to develop the ability to trust others again without fear and doubts.

It is important to note that many people coming out of a bad relationship will be advised to move ahead and don't look back. However, if you do not identify the lies that a narcissist imprinted into your mind, and cancel them with the truth, if you do not identify your own specific dysfunctions and broken parts, and then heal them, these things *will* come back to haunt you later. In order to heal, you will have to identify the lies and other destructive narratives that your abuser imprinted into your psyche, so that you can purposefully refute, disarm, and heal every specific hurt and lie. *Then* you will have the direction, the strength, and the confidence to move forward and truly leave the abuser in the past along with their baggage. Remember the hoarder analogy.

In my case, Asatya would often say things like, "No, no, you're not getting it. That's not what they are doing. Let me guide you how to deal with these people..."

It is true that in his context, I was dealing with a lot of people in a culture that was totally unfamiliar to me, and I had to rely on his guidance a lot. However, it was extremely easy in that circumstance for him to tell me that things were not as they appeared, and he could interpret the situation to me in whatever way he chose. He made me feel that I could not trust my own discretion and that I needed to just follow his lead, which I did. This scenario in particular happened routinely between Asatya and I. Remember that he had introduced me to dozens of his friends and acquaintances and had asked me to keep in touch with some of them for various goals that were meant to help him. All that had to be according to his guidance. He would get angry if I made any moves without letting him know. Later after the anger, I would reach out to him first for direction before contacting one of these people.

Then he got angry again saying, "You're not a child, use common sense!" In those moments I felt really unsure if the problem was my sort of autistic tendency to miss a few social cues here and there, or if Asatya was overreacting. It almost seemed like he flipped the script. Asatya insisted on instructing my every social move (in his sphere,) but making me feel dumb for relying on him, knocked down my confidence. I had become dependent, not trusting my own discretion to simply talk to people. Asatya knew that I've always been an introvert and that there is autism in my family, possibly even affecting me at some level. It had never occurred to me that he may have been exploiting what he viewed as my weaknesses, for his own sadistic entertainment.

A year later, I still question my judgment on many things and ask for other's opinions more than I really need to, because I don't trust mine. I am retraining myself to listen more to my intuition, and I am going back to studying the scriptures because that is where I find the best, most accurate, and well-rounded perspective of life.

Gaslighting is indeed used almost universally among narcissists, intentionally or unintentionally. It makes sense. Their entire life is built on a false persona, a web of lies. They gaslight themselves.

Silent Treatment- This is sometimes done as a form of punishment as well as manipulation. When there is no communication being received, especially after any tense exchange, the victim is left to fill in the blanks and try to read the narcissist's mind. They worry why the narcissist has gone silent, trying to anticipate what might be next, to try to mentally prepare for it, but they have no idea what 'it' is, so they have multiple scenarios running in their minds. They can't sleep, they might be nauseous, and they definitely have lots of anxiety.

Verbal, Physical, or Sexual Abuse- I include these things under forms of manipulation because these traumatizing experiences absolutely do change the way that a victim interacts not just with their abuser, but with the world. When a person's dignity and autonomy is stolen from them, it is a traumatic event. Such experiences invariably trigger a nervous system reaction. There are several possible reactions: fight, flight, freeze, or fawn. Unfortunately, most of these responses work out in favor of being further controlled by the narcissist. For example, when Asatya would yell at me for hours or days and ultimately threaten me, I would freeze. If a response was required from me (which was generally the case) I would have a fawn response. The reason is that the only way for me to avoid worse abuse was to be quiet and comply. That is why I had the dream about losing my voice. In that relationship, my voice was stolen from me.

Essentially, overt abuse is used to terrorize and intimidate the victim into submission. It is less about sneaky mind tricks and more about coercion by brute force. The narcissist's perceived superiority leads them to aim for domination. Overt abuse is very often about domination, although sometimes it is just an inability to control emotions such as anger.

There are a number of other recognized manipulation tactics commonly employed by narcissists, but these are among the most common. I know that the time that I saw Asatya slap his sister, he said it was to 'correct' her. He struck her to get a different result out of her next time. That is coercive control in the form of physical abuse.

Weaponized Incompetence/Weaponized Idiocy-

Pretending to not have a skill to avoid responsibility.

Pretending to not know something to avoid culpability.

Pretending to have never done something before, and therefore don't know how to do it, so that you have to do it for them.

Being aware of important dates and other important info, but hiding it, then after you have missed the important thing, claiming to be totally unaware of the important thing. Just imagine how a narcissist might pair this with isolation... as an example, you're invited to a bachelor party for one of your close friends. The narcissist hides the invitation. The date goes by. The narcissist calls up your friend that is about to get married and explains that 'You were still angry at them about the thing from two years ago, and you refuse to go to their wedding, also.' Now your friend thinks that you are unfairly holding a grudge, and he is upset at you, but befriending the narcissist who is offering them sympathy. Meanwhile, you have no idea about all this drama behind the scenes. Later, the narcissist claims to know nothing about the bachelor party, saying that maybe the invitation got lost in the mail. The narcissist will play both sides, while pretending to be 'out of the loop' and unaware.

A few more examples:

Using a health problem as an excuse to make zero effort, rather than do as much as they can, within the scope of their ability.

Saying that they are afraid of doing it wrong, but that you are good at it so you should do it.

Knowing that someone you need to avoid will be around, but pretending to know nothing about it, because they want to see you have an unfortunate encounter or at least be flustered. An absentee father often starts with these behavior patterns in regard to care of their children. A lazy person may use these tactics often. Weaponized incompetence/idiocy is definitely not limited to narcissists. My daughter used to pretend to be asleep in the car so that I would carry her into the house. It was a sort of manipulation, and yet I was aware that it was only a game and there was no harm done.

Speaking on my own experience with manipulation... on numerous occasions Asatya would be going through something very frustrating such as having a disruptive student that he wasn't allowed to discipline and neither school administration nor parents would discipline, either. A maddening interaction with one of his siblings would be another example.

He would express his frustrations to me and appeared to fall back into his recurring or underlying depression, saying things like 'my life will amount to nothing,' or 'my life is going nowhere.'

I would try to encourage him and remind him of the good things. I would remind him that he had goals and plans, and I was helping him with that.

At that point he would turn it on me and accuse me of doing nothing 'all this time.'

I had always thought that when he said that, it was the depression talking, like he couldn't see the progress from my efforts because he was depressed.

In fact, Asatya knew how much I had done for him. He was like a black hole, never full, never satisfied.

It wasn't until months after I cut Asatya out of my life that I realized that it was not that depression had made him think I had 'done nothing.'

The thing is that he never cared about my efforts, he only cared about results, for which he had no patience.

He even said one time that only results matter.

To Asatya, I was a means to an end.

Remember that in September I found a diagnostic tool (a type of behavior rating scale in the DSM-5) for personality disorders and a few other conditions, along with instructions at the end for how to add up and interpret the numbers.

I did it thoughtfully and honestly. I guess I still was in a bit of disbelief that Asatya was so night-and-day opposite of the persona that I had known. I wanted to see what the totally unbiased numbers would say, if it would be any different from what I had concluded earlier.

I was very surprised to discover that Asatya's markers for depression were in the low to middle range but the markers for manipulation were extremely high.

All the suicidal and depressive talk had been fake or over-inflated.

He knew that he could tap into and use my compassion by talking like that.

What else had he been faking??

Threatening suicide or to discard me as he had done on several occasions, was not 'his depression talking.'

It had always been to control me.

He knew I would cling tight as a loyal person and a sort of rescuer; he just wanted me to do even more for him.

The whole relationship was built on my desire to lift up a broken but good person to have a second shot at life in an unfair world, so I never felt like I was being used except that I felt that Asatya had poor relational skills on the intimate level of family matters.

When I allowed myself to accept the possibility that everything Asatya did was to control and exploit others, and that he knew exactly what he was doing, most of his behavior patterns suddenly made much more sense. It was a super disturbing thought, and an icky, creepy feeling.

I know that one of the hallmark traits of a narcissist is grandiosity, which just sounds like a fancy way of saying 'big ego.' Asatya would tell me about his achievements but then downplay them. I thought that seemed normal enough. Asatya did not publicly talk about any of his qualities or achievements, but he *did* tell me and other friends of his in a 1-on-1 setting. However, anytime he did any of his heroic or self-sacrificing acts, there were always witnesses. One time he appeared in a news article. He was being highlighted as an exemplary and productive teacher. When he brought the money to his sister from the sale of his property, there were plenty of people around to witness that. Remember in Shani's village, he had been there just four months, but already local women were calling him 'master ji.' Or were they? I have no idea if that detail of the story was completely fabricated, or if Asatya really had developed a following there.

It is true that Asatya, like many other narcissists, is highly charismatic. He is friendly and very proactive and has a personality that just pulls people in. So naturally people notice and are intrigued and then amazed when they see him doing unheard-of acts of kindness... they start to talk, because it is so unusual...Asatya always seemed happiest when everyone would appreciate him, when he would be receiving all that positive attention. He would say things like, "It's not really a big deal," trying to look humble. But he loved that attention. Asatya had told me that he had never done anything wrong deliberately. For a long time, that appeared to be the case. He looked like a man of unusual integrity.

Unfortunately, I now know that he misrepresented stories to me. Like he would say that he had to 'correct' his brother or sister. Like my daughter and I had witnessed him slap his sister in the street, right in front of their relatives and passersby. Last year he inadvertently confessed to breaking his brother's rib during a dispute. That's abuse, not just correcting. That came almost a year after he said that he needed to work on his anger. Obviously, that problem only grew, if anything.

In July when I gave Asatya permission to apologize, he called his abusive speech from May 'correction,' or 'motivating me to be more serious.'

It took time for the truth to manifest itself, but it became clear that Asatya thought of himself as a person who always did what was right. No, it is not that he is a pure soul or a saint... it is that he cannot see any of his faults. He thinks he is unusual, a real human being in a sea of filth. While he would be emphasizing to me his goodness while being blind to his faults, I noticed that he was quick to identify all the faults of others.

Actually, whenever he met a new person, he would idealize them, only noticing their qualities, but later he would invariably find all their faults and would even mention to me any faults that he imagined them to have. Like he would say, "what is he doing out late at night far from home? A man of his background is most likely searching out prostitutes."

I thought at first that Asatya really has very high standards and ideals and that's why he becomes dissatisfied with most people. I witnessed him call out others on their bullshit when no one else had the courage to do so. I appreciated that in him. As time went on, I saw him scold or give up on people too easily, though I didn't have the full story, so I wasn't quite sure. I realize now that he was devaluing them and me, to make himself feel bigger and better. You can see his mentality in the messages that he wrote to me. The claim to spiritual superiority, and the claim to impeccable character, became very loud towards the end.

It is clear that he had not an ounce of real humility by the way that he became enraged when he believed that I was implying that he needed to do any introspection or growth... even though it is common knowledge that every single one of us must never stop maturing, and he used to talk at length about how important growth is, claiming that he always seeks to improve himself.

Asatya was always talking about the 'deplorable human condition' of India: the lazy parenting, the common prejudices, the nepotism and social climbing, the fake religious devotion, etc. He spent so much time denouncing these things that of course I thought that meant that he himself was innocent of such things. It was a distraction. In the past, he never claimed to be on par with Acharya ji or any of the well-known gurus, but in our late April chats, he had implied that he didn't need to make any personal improvements. Asatya always took it as his job to teach, guide and correct others but he did not feel that he himself needed correction. In fact, he would become angry if I implied that he needed to adjust something. He did let me correct him in the very beginning, but that facade slipped pretty quickly. Actually, he had set such a great example of accepting correction gracefully, that I was able to change my attitude and do the same. That was one of few positive lessons that I have chosen to retain.

It is true that during the years that he knew me, Asatya had a steady supply of admiration and encouragement and attention from me.

I want to talk about this word 'supply.'

Because a narcissist is by nature completely self-centered, everything they do is in one way or another, for their own benefit. Even if they attempt to be loving, it will always be just an attempt to imitate the love that they have seen in others, and their 'love' ends up being self-serving because they are trapped in that mindset. Like Asatya had called me 'sister' and had claimed to love me even more than himself, that he would do anything for me. Even when he was angry at me, he would say that I am more precious to him than anything. When I looked back on the last four years, I tried to remember anything that Asatya may have done for me that was just for me and not for him. I realized that he made big promises but those were set to be fulfilled eventually at an unknown date. What things he actually did for me: he shielded me as far as he could, from perverts or other exploiters. He made travel arrangements for me. He would answer messages promptly. He would encourage me and praise me to others (when he wasn't mad at me.) He often let me borrow his phone as I didn't have cellular data while in India. He let me memorize his passcode.

All these small acts of 'love' I can identify as things that had a net positive result for himself also. The main positive result is that he made me feel safe and I trusted him, remaining connected to him so that he could use me. Remember the breadcrumbs. If you are wondering about the issue of travel safety, just think first of all, how he would look if something bad happened to me while he was entrusted with my travel arrangements. Not good for him. Also, if anyone else started exploiting me, then there would be less of me and my resources available for his use. I remember one dude in India who shamelessly approached me, asking if I could advise or help him to immigrate. Asatya looked more insulted than I did. He laughed sort of nervously at that guy's audacity.

There was such a very strong narrative that in his life, Asatya was an honorable, innocent, kind, and trusting man who didn't have any good people around him, who deserved a better life. The result of that was that I became a solid believer in the goodness and potential of Asatya, so I attempted to move heaven and earth to lift him up. Right from the very beginning, the whole dynamic of our relationship was about me helping Asatya.

Coming to the U.S. was his idea. He made it seem like my idea so well that I believed it until after I cut him off. It wasn't until May when I searched old chats, that I discovered that he was the first one to suggest that he immigrate to the U.S., and that after we had only been getting to know each other ten days. He would simply talk openly to me about his life, the good and the bad. He had figured out that I am a compassionate person. He would make small requests seemingly without pressure. Later he would add more to those requests and turn up the pressure. He knew that he could just talk about a sad circumstance of his and that I would want to help somehow, because that is what compassionate people do.

I think I mentioned elsewhere the story of the frog who was put into a pot of cold water. The frog was perfectly content and detected no danger, so he didn't jump out of the pot. Then someone turned the heat to the lowest setting. The frog being cold-blooded, could not feel the slight change in temperature. He stayed. The temperature under the pot was turned up very, very slowly over time, so slowly that the frog didn't even notice when it was becoming hot. By the time that steam was coming up from the water, the frog was already quite disoriented because it's internal body temperature was very high and affecting cognitive function, so the frog still did not sense danger even though its body was already very much affected. Eventually the frog boiled to death, having never understood what was happening to it.

Narcissistic abuse happens just the same way. In my case, the subtle disclosure of personal needs later becomes 'innocent' little requests or implications that you should do something about it, then later down the road there were larger requests, then demands and manipulation mixed in, including shaming for 'not doing enough,' threats, triangulation, and more.

In the same way, the heat gets slowly turned up on other forms of abuse. It starts out seemingly innocent, but it becomes grooming under clever disguises and myriad excuses. Later the excuses and cover-ups become thinner and weaker as the abuse becomes more overt. Phrases heard at this stage might include, "We could have had a great weekend, but you provoked me." "You had to be taught a lesson." "Yes well, I have sexual needs, and you were depriving me." "You're going to eat the whole thing? Really?" "You went over by $10.56. Obviously, you have no idea what a budget is, so I took your name off the account." "You brought this on yourself." On it goes, worsening over time. By the time that the victim of this abuse realizes *why* their friend or partner is acting this way, they are often already in serious danger of losing their sanity, their home, their kids, possibly their life. At that point the narcissist has become highly volatile, dangerous, and truly delusional in their justification of their extremely damaging actions.

Sorry for the brief but relevant rabbit trail. Back to supply.

Essentially a narcissist identifies people who can bring selfish benefit to their lives. Because they have only selfishness and no love in themselves, they do not feel love (or barely feel it) and are not able to give it. In the absence of love, they see people only as potential assets to use. They know that other people tend to give what you want if they feel loved, so they study kind people and try to copy their actions to get what they want. They mirror the behavior of those nice people, trying to seem nice themselves, to win over the trust and benevolence of those people. The narcissist is just going through the motions; they become very good actors this way. Some narcissists even practice facial expressions in a mirror.

Typically, there is one main person that they attach themselves to. That person is most often their spouse or significant other, but sometimes that person is their child, parent, or closest friend. That person becomes the main source of supply. Supply can be money, sex, material possessions, status or reputation, fame or other access to lots of attention, praise and admiration, etc. Unfortunately, supply can also be anything that makes people around them look bad, making them look good by comparison. Sometimes it's as simple as a reaction to something they said. They may provoke you to

get a reaction, and they may even get a sadistic high from their main supply becoming upset at them, because it gives them justification for shaming
that person and making themself seem superior.

Remember last May when Asatya was provoking me badly and creating
an argument out of thin air while saying, "I don't want to start a war." I
couldn't understand why he became angrier when I was giving short, calm,
submissive replies. He wanted me to become angry and defensive, but I
didn't take the bait. He was trying hard to build a case against me, but it
wasn't working and that made him even more furious. It was a rigged game,
with no possible winning scenario. I have even heard of some who have
been extremely provocative, and when their supply could not take it anymore and they finally became angry or broke down in tears, the narcissist
began filming them to try to prove to others that their supply is abusive,
crazy, or unhinged. They often will attend every fight that they are invited
to, because it is attention, and they feel a deep need to prove to everyone
that they are superior or the one in the right. They want any and all attention. Having a spouse is a great source of supply because it ensures daily dos-
es of attention at the very least, and usually sex and many other things.

One can say that supply is anything that makes a narcissist feel good
about themselves or feel more superior and in control of others.

There are many differences between a healthy relationship and a narcissist with their supply. Once you have a solid understanding of what each of
these looks like, it will be easier to know in the future when any connection
has no hope and to cut it off, or to strengthen a connection that has only
minor issues.

I had mentioned that one form of supply can be status or gains in reputation.

I knew that Asatya had never officially finished high school (called +2
in India), that he didn't hold any high position, owned no home and wasn't
married. According to Indian society he was a nobody. All he had was a reputation as a skilled teacher and a good man, and the love of his sister (me.)

I always encouraged Asatya to stop being so extremely generous and to
save some money so he could enroll in a program to earn some certifica-
tion or do anything that would improve his overall quality of life. In India,
shmoozing and networking are well-accepted ways to get things done. It's

important to know the right people. Asatya having no prestige, no family support, and no wealth, had very little leverage to move himself forward in life. I became very conscientious of every opportunity to talk him up and show my support to bolster his reputation and I did it however I could. Any time that Asatya did or said anything that I knew would not help his reputation, I just never mentioned it to anyone. If it became necessary to talk about such things (as in talking to his boss about his paycheck after he was fired) I would paint the incident in the best possible light. My husband knew that Asatya had a bad temper, but he did not know that Asatya was fired for slapping a student. I thought that eventually, Asatya will immigrate to the U.S., and it was up to me to help him develop good relations in advance of coming. Proclaiming to others all of Asatya's worst moments didn't seem like a good idea at the time.

I wanted to encourage Asatya's brother and sister to reconcile with him. I didn't tell them that sometimes Asatya and I had our own disputes. I didn't tell anyone that whenever we had a disagreement, that I pretty much had to concede that Asatya was at least mostly right if not 100% right, in order to settle the conflict. As far as I could tell, Asatya *was* right most of the time, it is just that he was too dogmatic, too harsh, and too black and white in his thinking. As time went on, he found fault with me more and more which didn't make sense. The narrative started with, "I am so elated to have such a kind, understanding sister," to "You're not doing enough" to "Ok, but it's the results that matter and this is taking too long" to "You've been playing me." I had not changed all that time, other than gradually doing more and more for Asatya, by request (or coercion). What had changed is that Asatya ran out of patience for something that he knew from the beginning would take time. These were childish reactions...

Because I never spoke ill of Asatya to my friends and relatives, it came as shock when I worked up the courage to explain to Evan that I had to completely cut Asatya out of my life and forever.

Any time over those four years that Asatya asked far too much of me, or caused me great anxiety, or caused confusion, or said or did things that I could not support, I didn't tell anyone. Instead, I thought that he is only acting like this because he is under a lot of stress (which was in fact always true; he is a high-strung person who attracts drama) and that when he gets settled into a better life, his nerves will calm down and he will finally stop reacting to everything like he has PTSD or something. I felt sure of this.

I recognize that in one or two of those points, I was gaslighting myself

Because I almost never told anyone anything negative about Asatya, I was alone and had no support for the stress and conundrums that I often found myself in with him. I was chronically stressed, and no one knew. I thought I was doing a good deed, so I powered through it.

In relationships between a narcissist and their main supply, isolation of the victim is very common. I feel lucky that the isolation was much less in my case, compared to that of other narcissistic abuse victims. Although I had no support, as I mentioned. Also, all the daily time and attention that Asatya took from me made me less available and less mentally present in my friendships, so those connections weakened. I generally keep very few but very close friends, so this development left me with almost no friend support.

It happens often that when a victim of narcissistic abuse tries to confide in a friend or seek help, they are met with disbelief. This may be due to the narcissist's false positive persona, a smear campaign that is circulating against the victim, or because the story itself seems unbelievable. It may seem unbelievable because it is extreme and sounds crazy. When people are met with extreme, crazy-sounding stories, they tend to assume that it is exaggerated by the speaker's emotions and that the real story is more moderate. They think, 'Well, this is just one side of the story.' Remember, a narcissist will **never** give you the true and balanced story of what they did. The victim's story sounds extreme and crazy, because what was done to them was indeed in most cases, extreme; it was perpetrated by a crazy person.

I was asked by my therapist what I might have done to contribute to the mess. (I realized around that time that she is not trained to address narcissistic abuse.)

While it is always the responsible and right thing to try to understand how your roles have added to or taken away from your relationship dynamics, it is very important to recognize that in a relationship with someone who is diabolical, subliminally manipulative, and exploitative or malicious by nature, it might not make any difference how the other person responds to them; they will be played regardless. In such cases, it is possible that 100% of the innocence is on one side, and 100% of the blame is on the other side. A relationship of any kind with a narcissist is by nature, very atypical, and standard reasoning and relational advice do not apply.

Standard advice generally assumes that both parties possess empathy and an ability to recognize and correct personal faults. A narcissist has neither.

Most narcissists seek control wherever they can gain it.

I have met women in my support group who were told, "Let's start a family! You don't need to work. I want to provide for you."

What then happened is that the woman had shared children with that person, the narcissist then used the children as pawns to torture their wife/victim, and took complete control over her life as she had none of her own income and had become dependent on the narcissist and especially because of having babies to support. Their phones would be monitored, their car sold, or the keys would be hidden from them. Absolutely every detail of their life was controlled by the narcissist, sometimes even having food withheld from them. These stay-at-home moms would very often be falsely accused of cheating as an excuse to control them and supervise their every move. These women found it extremely difficult to escape this, having been robbed of their support network. How so? The narcissist would turn their victim's friends and family against them one way or another. For example, in some cases the narcissist would act like a saint around other people, having all their support, while crying about their 'horrible, abusive' spouse (who is in fact the real victim.) Sometimes the victim would be forced to block people or delete social media, or use a joint account, with threat of harm if they did not comply.

I know of many people who have fled their own homes with literally nothing, not knowing if they would find space in a domestic violence shelter or church. They would rather be homeless than risk one more hour with their abuser, who cunningly turned all their victim's family against them...

Another lady from the same group told us that her husband removed her name from their assets somehow (I don't know which country or state this is) and secretly put them into a trust before he died. After his passing, she found herself destitute, as her jointly shared assets were then in a trust that she could not legally touch.

I've lost count of the number of times that somebody had the balls to speak up about their abuse, and every time someone would say, "Just leave!" It is true that in situations of abuse, the bottom-line solution always boils down to removing access of the abuser to their victim. To just get away. That is the number one most important thing.

However, that is not the only necessary thing to do, nor is it that simple. In my case, I was 'lucky' that I had no shared assets *yet* at the time that I stopped contact with Asatya. Nor did we have any children together. Also, he lived on the other side of the globe, and he had no legal means of coming here, which is an immense relief to me. Judging by his delusional online activity, there is no doubt in my mind that he would be physically stalking me if he were here in this country.

Where there are children involved, one parent cannot simply take their kids and leave indefinitely without either making a very strong court case that the children are not safe with their other parent, or else obtain consent from their other parent for custody, (which a narcissist will almost never do; remember that the children are their pawns). The other alternative is to flee alone, leaving the kids with the narcissist parent, where they will most certainly be raised to have serious dysfunction, if not neglect and abuse, and be brain-washed against the parent who left. Raising children requires selfless action from time to time, if not daily. Narcissists are not capable of true selflessness. It is true that fleeing without the kids runs the risk of being accused by the court of abandonment. Narcissists like to have children involved because of the power dynamic.

Asatya had specifically wanted an American wife who is a simple, kind, home-body type, who would agree to having at least one child together. That seems innocent enough, until you consider everything that I've been writing about over these last several pages. Think about that for a minute.

Even without any children involved, there are always other complicating factors making it difficult to escape. Many narcissists are keenly aware of laws regarding domestic disputes, and some have succeeded in manipulating the courts. Imagine that you own your own home outright, but your abusive narcissist ex-spouse is still in your home due to 'squatter's rights.' You may lack the substantial evidence that the police have asked for in order to give you the restraining order that you need. Imagine that the narcissist is friends with the entire police department. It is possible and perhaps probable that leaving the abuser means having peace and safety, but no one to be there for you as you choose possible destitution in exchange for peace. Narcissists *want* to become enmeshed with their supply. They make sure that a clean and easy break up will not be possible.

If you are one of the people who is tired of hearing about abuse and drama, and you have told someone to 'just leave,' please be prepared to be an active support to that person. It will not be quick and easy. It will probably get messy. The narcissist does not want their supply to get away - except in some cases where they already have other supply lined up, in which case they may still try to keep their talons sunk into their current prey.

If the narcissist finds out that their supply intends to leave them, this is the most dangerous time of all. This is when things like sabotage, rape, arson, theft, vandalism and even murder are more likely to occur. 'Just leaving' is not a reality. A carefully laid-out plan must be made in advance, which may require some help. The escape plan must be made and implemented very quietly without the abuser's knowledge. Now, imagine trying to pull that off without the support of any family or friends, which would be the case if the narcissist succeeded to isolate you.

As I said before, be prepared to help, and without judgment.

I guarantee that whatever bullshit you have seen or heard about in that relationship, that it was just the tip of the iceberg and the whole situation is more complex and unbelievable than you ever imagined.

Not all narcissists are masterminds. Their level of intelligence is not affected by the condition, so there is a broad range of intelligence levels among narcissists. However, while a healthy person matures over time, a narcissist does not but rather hones their skills of manipulation to a level many normal people do not even realize exists.

Narcissistic personality disorder comes in different 'flavors' and varying degrees of severity.

Based on my analysis of what I saw in Asatya, he is a covert, communal, cerebral narcissist whose most prominent characteristic of the condition is manipulation, in all its forms, but especially emotional manipulation.

Other types include malignant/overt, somatic, and comorbid types like NPD/ASPD (narc/psychopath), NPD/BPD (narc/borderline), NPD/BPD (narc/bipolar).

I could go into detail to really explain these different types, but we are already at page 202, so instead, to understand these types or narcissistic life stages better, please visit Sam Vaknin's YouTube channel. He can be long-winded, but he explains these very well, tying it all together, helping to make sense of it all.

Here I'd like to write about the rest of the narcissistic abuse cycle. As of the time of this writing, the topic of mental health has been trending in on-line discussions which is good in a way, but unfortunately misinformation travels fast. This is a problem because well-meaning but misinformed people can sometimes do more harm than good. I'd like to write about a few things and provide references for more in-depth information on this topic from truly qualified sources.

I myself am just one person writing about my own personal experience, and what I learned about this condition from my research on the web, using sources like Dr. Ramani, Professor Sam Vaknin, various medical journals, well-known hospital websites like Mayo Clinic, and anecdotes from hundreds of other narcissistic abuse survivors.

●**Exploitation**

Since a narcissist is by nature self-centered, they are takers or consumers. They have only a hint of empathy in some cases, and in other cases, no empathy at all. They are blind to their own character deficits. These three traits together mean that narcissists are able to use others without feeling bad about it, and the depths they go to, to suck you dry can be extreme.

Each has their own preferred forms of supply. They may seek out sex, admiration, attention, acts of service, money, control or power, sense of superiority, etc.

They may gently ask for your help with something, only to later make it a demand or requirement.

They often ask you about your values and your life goals, which coming from a normal person is a good basis for a deep, mature conversation, but a narcissist will use this information about you later to weaponize these against you.

They may knock you down by claiming that you don't live up to your own standards. They will frame their requests to you in terms of your values. For example, Asatya knew that I wanted to make a difference in the world. Therefore, he would say things like, "your involvement in this matter could really make a difference!" They will make service to them seem bright and shiny to you.

Obviously, other's experiences of exploitation may look a bit different than mine, but the stories from other victims of narcissistic abuse tend to have strong similarities. This is not a complete list. Some or all of these may be present, in addition to other forms of exploitation not listed here which could also be present.

To recap some of the ways that my compassion and kindness were exploited, as well as other forms of exploitation that are commonly reported by narcissistic abuse survivors:

Time-

Hundreds of hours spent researching immigration. (He didn't lift a finger. I did it all.)

Hundreds of hours spent researching and building the foundation of our business project.

3-10 hours per week spent on chats and occasional calls (he talked a lot.)

1-2 additional hours per week spent on other forms of support.

Emotional Energy and Regulation-

As NPD forms in early childhood, their normal emotional maturation comes to a halt. They seem like very emotional people because they are. Every time that they overreact to something and start talking out of depression, anxiety, or whatever, you will find yourself using all your energy to keep yourself as calm as possible to try to calm them down or at least prevent further agitation from them. Their lack of emotional maturity will often have them hyped up about something or other. You will become their chronic emotional regulator. You will get very tired and stressed from this role, but you don't want to stop because if you do not coddle them, their blow-ups will be worse and often directed at you, so you donate your own emotional strength to avoid being hurt by them even more. You may not even realize that you are doing this as you are distracted by the narcissist's crisis-du-jour and you yourself may be in survival mode.

In contrast, some narcissists gain a sense of superiority by *appearing* to be calm and in control, while provoking reactions out of you to further make them look superior. They may call you crazy, moody, bitchy, or unhinged. They may mock or discredit your feelings by claiming 'It must be that time of month,' or 'You always get your panties in a wad over nothing.'

The dismissing of your feelings is a form of gaslighting.

Brain Space-

The narcissist may use weaponized incompetence/idiocy by telling you that you are so much better at something than they are. (Asatya told me this about the online research.) Whatever narrative will keep you doing all their brain work for them. They might ask you to plan an event or create a budget (which they will later walk all over by their reckless spending).

Your Social Network-

Narcissists are the ultimate schmoozers and nepotists.

They will find out who is connected to whom, and what all their resources are.

They may put you in group texts with them and those others, against your will, expecting you to help build useful alliances for them.

They might even use you to line up their next main supply, directly or indirectly.

Your Material Resources-

Remember that a narcissist has the emotional maturity level of a child. In their mind, what's yours is actually theirs.

They may borrow without asking.

They may or may not return items.

They may claim 'squatter's rights' in your home.

They may eat your food and not even care if no food is left, letting you go hungry.

Your Body as Their Sex Toy-

Narcissists have very little, or no ability to feel love. All they can do is try to copy other people's actions to try to *simulate* love. Therefore, they do not truly fall in love, (they fall into infatuations), nor do they make love.

Sex for them is a self-centered act that is simply for sexual release, for the oxytocin boost, possibly as another arena in which they can assert their control and dominance, to ward of depression or boredom, possibly to enact sadistic fantasies, or to attempt to feel love which results in frustration for them as they cannot feel it, leading them to make greater demands on their partner.

Unfortunately, the narcissist's sense of grandiosity, coupled with their belief that they do no wrong, in many cases makes them feel strongly that they are above rules and boundaries. They think they know what is best, when in fact they are very selfish. This creates the perfect setup for rape and other forms of sexual abuse to occur.

Unfortunately, this is not just theoretical, but I am writing this based on the thousands of individual stories that I've encountered of victims telling their stories via YouTube, and victim's support groups. Sexual abuse in a relationship with a narcissist appears to be extremely common, and a narcissistic relationship involving healthy sex appears to be non-existent, as what looks or feels healthy generally turns out to be love-bombing.

They feel entitled to your body, (though cerebral narcissists are not interested in sex, generally) as they think that everything that is yours is actually theirs. They might claim that you 'owe' them sex, or they may threaten you with infidelity if you don't give them sex whenever they want it, in whatever form they want it.

They may sabotage your birth control on purpose.

They may be addicted to sex or porn and put unrealistic expectations and demands on you.

They may withhold sex as a form of punishment or manipulation.

Non-consensual sexual contact may be initiated in a variety of forms.

Remember, they think the world revolves around them and that you owe them.

Your Body as Their Human Punching Bag-

Not all narcissists are violent, but it is very common, especially in later stages of the relationship.

It is important to remember that verbal abuse is an indicator that physical abuse could be next. Not all verbal abuse leads to physical abuse, but there is consensus among behavioral experts that verbal, emotional, or psychological abuse increases the likelihood of physical abuse occurring simultaneously or eventually. It is possible that physical abuse may occur without warning, but typically there are red flags that precede it, which may include:

- Jealousy
- Intimidation
- Domination
- Excessively critical, baseless accusations
- Possessive of a person
- Sexist, racist, or otherwise disrespectful
- Controlling
- Entitled
- Hypocrite
- Isolates a person from their support network
- Rage, explosive temper
- Vandalism or destruction of property, punching walls or wielding objects in a menacing manner, threatening harm to pets.

Many therapy groups and domestic violence support organizations publish helpful blogs and articles that can further clarify domestic abuse.

Also very important to know, is that a person who strangles someone is much more likely to actually kill them in the future. If you have been choked or strangled, and the person who did that to you still has access to you, please understand that your life is in danger. You must leave at once even if you have nowhere to go. You are better off homeless than dead, and chances are that you will find some help. Do not stay, and do not let the abuser know that you are leaving.

As the narcissistic supply, the victim is typically the one person who is the kindest and most forgiving to the narcissist. The narcissist will feel safe taking all their ugliest and unpresentable emotions to their victim, in contrast to the public where their fake image is their paramount concern. Narcissists often see their supply as a sort of doting, understanding mother figure.

All their anger and frustration at the world is released onto the victim and it often does turn into physical violence.

One of the reasons why other forms of abuse can lead to physical abuse is when the other forms of abuse are not having the effect that the abuser wants. For example, when they begin to sense that their victim has figured them out or calls them out on their terrible behavior. The abuser's other forms of abuse aren't working anymore, so they fall into a rage or use brute force, or both.

Money-

Writing from my own experience, Asatya always claimed not to care about money or wealth. That turned out to be a half truth. I never, ever saw him spending a large amount of money on himself (until his house project). In fact, he was too frugal, neglecting his health or other needs at times.

At some point, I had offered to help him with his living expenses while he went back to school to increase his value in the workforce, but he refused, saying he didn't want to take my money.

Around that time, I went to India to visit. He kept insisting that I am a guest, and I should not bear my own expenses. He insisted that I would be a guest to himself, his sister, and a few friends. No hotels. I wanted to do a little shopping but still everyone rushed to pay for my things, no matter how much I insisted that I pay for them. That was more love-bombing.

As I was leaving India, I gave Asatya a significant chunk of money - to pay back the cost of bus and train fares, food while traveling, and to float him for a couple months as he had lost his job while I was there. He did not count it.

Later, he was angry that I gave him so much... while simultaneously blaming me for not having a job (I had *nothing* to do with that) and blaming me saying that he now had obligations to reciprocate his friend's hospitality somehow, which he had no means of doing.

In fact, he was finding fault with me for coming to India at all, in stark contrast to his tears of joy when I had told him that I would be coming, and he said how happy he and everyone would be to meet me...

Since that visit, Asatya has requested my monetary help many times for various things. He would say, "Family will do anything for each other," and "there is no distinction between me and you; we are family," which was in contrast to a year or two before when he insisted that it is for brothers to help their sisters, and brothers should never ask sisters for money except in case of a real emergency.

During my second visit, I paid for absolutely everything, by transferring money to Asatya's account and using his cash from that account. It made sense, as many small shops and public transport only took cash. It *looked* like Asatya paid for everything.

In May during the great 'missile strike' of verbal abuse, Asatya was complaining that he was jobless but needed to finish the construction of his and his brother's house. Actually, he should have paused that until he got a job.

Instead, he said that my sympathy was fake and compared me to his sister who wouldn't say a word to him but supposedly sent him a chunk of money. She is a widow on a kindergarten teacher's minimum salary.

He then screamed at me to 'prove myself' (which seemed purposefully vague as to what was wanted) or else lose him.

I sent him a few hundred dollars with my *credit* card as I actually didn't have money on hand (he couldn't believe that an American would ever be short of money) really just to call his bluff. I wanted to see his reaction.

Actually, I was so disgusted by him that I ended up blocking him right then and there.

A week later, a mutual acquaintance (Nakali from UP) tried to appeal to me, calling me 'sister,' attempting to get sympathy from me to send Asatya money.

It is clear that Asatya put her up to that. In fact, she knows little English, so Asatya likely instructed her what to write in the note for her to send to me, as I've mentioned before. She didn't know that I had sent money already, but Asatya knew and did not tell her that.

Asatya tried to tell me through someone else that he didn't know that I had transferred money as he's been very busy and hadn't looked at his account.

That's bullshit. He was spending tons of money on building supplies, and he had always monitored all his accounts and other personal things almost obsessively.

Meanwhile, Asatya was finishing up building the house for his brother funded on donations he had garnered from sympathetic people. People who had no idea that he had abandoned the position that I had given him in my business.

At this point, the pattern began to crystallize for me: Asatya would be broke and use the victim narrative to gain support from others.

Once he had money in hand, he would publicly give it in an act of charity (in a different sphere than that of the donors), gaining more support and bolstering his reputation. In this way he used money to play with people, while playing on people's emotions to get money.

I am now realizing as I type this, that what I have just described in the above sentence, would have made it much easier for Asatya to relocate from one area to another. Remember that Asatya tended not to live in one location for more than a year or two at a time. The donors may have started to resent his money requests, so they would not miss him or bother him further after he left. Meanwhile, people in his new place would look at him like he is a messenger of heaven on account of his 'philanthropy.' He did say that he wanted to shift away from his friends in U.P. At the same time, it looked like he was getting himself settled back into his hometown in Haryana.

Chess player indeed.

Asatya would often get into fights with his brother because he tried to tell his brother to stop giving away all of his meager wages, which would force him to beg from family and friends.

It's really incredible how anyone can look in the mirror like that and not realize that they are doing exactly the same. Actually, Prajna seems a bit less guilty as it appears that he did not strategize, he just simply gave too much.

●Discard

This is the part where the narcissist pretends to break up with you. The thing is, even if they become disgusted with you and have even gone so far as to marry someone else, they always want you to be available on the back burner. We will get to that back burner in a bit. For now, let's talk about what a discard looks like. The truth is that there are many varieties of discards that are all wildly different. Sometimes it is dropped on you like a bomb with the simple words, "Get out!" Sometimes they just fade out slowly and act totally indifferent towards you. Sometimes they attempt to murder their victim. Sometimes they amp up the abuse to hit you where it hurts the most, provoking you to the best of their ability to make you want to leave them (that one is called a reverse discard, and is what Asatya did in my case.)

During the discard phase is when the very worst behaviors come to the surface, and you may start to question whether they might actually be possessed. Common behaviors seen at this time:

Betrayal and sabotage- This is exactly what it sounds like. They make a huge scene at your important event. They call up your boss to talk shit about you and try to get you fired. They set fire to your house. They dump your father's ashes in the toilet. They lure you into a trap. You get the idea.

Smear Campaign- Really this is a form of sabotage. The narcissist says shit about you to everyone. The most common story is that you are crazy. (Honestly, you might be a tad bit crazy from the gaslighting and PTSD that you may have, but that is not a character flaw, and you can overcome these.)

They might make a drama on social media. They will very likely talk about how you have ruined them, and you were 'such a monster' to them... That leads me to another discard move...

Increased abuse in general-
This is self-explanatory.
Silent treatment or ghosting-
Changing phone settings so that you don't know whether they have seen your messages. Taking a very long time to respond or not responding at all. Ignoring phone calls. Pretending to not be home. Avoiding you in general.
Flaunting new supply-
Making beautiful, flowery, sickeningly sweet posts on social media to show the world how 'happy' and in love they are with their new supply. Hiding the new supply from you but 'accidentally' leaking info or setting you up to 'stumble across' evidence of their new supply. Sending the victim/supply photos and videos of themselves with the new supply. Some narcissists have even brazenly walked right past their partner with the new supply to go defile the bedroom in a cruel and sadistic act of infidelity.

Projection- In fact, projection might be done often throughout the relationship, but it may become more prominent and distinct in the end. They may accuse you of every single thing that they themselves have done, while claiming to be every good thing that you have been to them. You might even see them doing this same sort of projection on other people. They switch their attributes with yours. They will claim to be all the opposite things of what they actually are. It can be so total, it is surreal to witness. It is like living in the 'upside down' depicted in the Netflix series, 'Stranger Things.'

To give one example of projection, Asatya saw people around him preferring to associate with Americans, feeling like they might gain something by that association. He wrongly accused Africans in general (and Visounou specifically) of feeling the same way about Americans. My experience in Africa proved that to be false. I was not flaunted, I did not appear in their social media posts, and I was introduced to less than five people. The only people who stared at me were small children and one old man. A while ago, Visounou told me that he would make his own way, and he told me not to help him pay tuition, or for anything else.

Projection can take the form of D.A.R.V.O., as mentioned earlier in a link. (D.A.R.V.O. stands for deny, attack, reverse role of victim and offender.)

•Hoover

If you thought that the discard was the end of the story, you are wrong. Narcissistic abuse is the 'gift' that keeps on giving. Remember that you have been reserved on the back burner. It does not matter how much they may have claimed to hate you, it doesn't matter if they are married with babies on the way, it doesn't matter if they moved to a different country. I have heard of cases where some actually did move on permanently, but it appears to be the exception to the rule. I think this is why Asatya did not make a smear campaign against me (as far as I know.) He has been manipulating most of his people to be able to use each of them eventually, so he needs them to continue thinking highly of him. They will not think highly of him if they see him reconnecting with me after he tells them that I am vile.

We use the word 'hoover' because it is the phase in which a victim might get sucked back in (as with a vacuum cleaner.)

Typically, there is a fake apology and a resurgence of love-bombing. If the victim has blocked the narcissist, these attempts might come through

one of the flying monkeys (the people who have been deputized to manipulate or harass the victim.)

This phase is when many narcissists (and psychopaths) resort to stalking. In fact, stalking is quite common at this stage. In many if not most
cases, there is already a history of physical abuse and control between the
narcissist and their victim, so the stalking is particularly unnerving. I very
much hope to see stalking made illegal in the future. At the very least, it is a
form of intimidation. In some cases, the stalking was later shown to be evidence of scoping out and pre-planning harm to the victim.

Whether it was you who left them, or they who left you, they will always want access to you.

It doesn't matter how final or clear you have been that you have moved
on, they will feel that you always belong to them and that they can cash
in and pull you back whenever. Maybe they can't imagine actually letting
someone go as you have, because they are very emotionally dependent in
relationships and almost never let go.

The hoover phase can continue off and on for years, even decades. The
hoover phase will only be cut short if the tactics work and the victim gets
sucked back into relationship with the narcissist, although sometimes the
narcissist does truly move on if they find plenty of supply elsewhere.

There is one particular component of narcissistic abuse that makes it
very difficult to get away and stay away: The **trauma bond.**

Remember that this type of relationship begins with love-bombing followed by devaluation. This two-part cycle continues throughout the relationship, repeating over and over and over. The love-bombing phase can
feel sincere and intensely good, so much that when the devalue comes, the
victim feels that this ugly side is not truly them; they believe that the loving
actions represent their real partner or friend.

By the time that the abuse reaches such an advanced level that the victim finally wakes up and acknowledges that a truly loving person could never do those things, they have generally experienced many cycles of love-
bombing and devaluation. This is a problem because the very high highs of
love-bombing followed by the very low lows of devaluation start to cause a
chemical imbalance in their brain. The first time that they break up from
the narcissist, they feel disgusted and heart-broken but then they remember

the love-bombing and even though they know it's wrong, it is very hard for them to stay away. That intense yo-yo action of their brain chemicals created an actual addiction. After the break-up, they experience withdrawal.

Remember I said earlier that it takes on average, seven break-up attempts.

You can imagine that after six break-up attempts, the victim's friends and family might be super annoyed with them for always going back to the narcissist. They may have made a lot of personal efforts to help their victim friend to get away, and when the victim is later in serious danger, they might have no one left that is willing to help them or even listen to them cry. At the same time, the narcissist has now experienced rejection several times (which is a lot for even a sane person to take in) and they can become very volatile, vindictive, and dangerous.

I just want to make it clear that **a close relationship with a narcissist is by nature, almost always addictive. Most people don't know this.**

Most people closely connected to a narcissist also have no idea that the person they love is a narcissist, until they are already trauma-bonded (addicted.)

Listen. No matter how much the person you love just makes you melt like butter, if they start doing the yo-yo love/hate thing, get out immediately. It feels amazing and then there's heart break, anxiety, addiction, and isolation.

Never, ever tolerate that shit. Insist on a reasonable amount of consistency, or else cut ties.

Additional Behaviors or Attitudes that Often Coincide with Abuse:
Sabotage can play out in a thousand different ways.

It's very common for narcissists to self-sabotage quietly and then loudly draw attention to their suffering in order to gain sympathy, manipulate the scenario to gain money or resources, or at least for attention. This is often referred to as a 'victim complex,' or 'victim mindset.'

It is also very common for them to sabotage others. There are myriad motivations for this, because each one has their own personality, goals, etc.

Truly, there are times that a narcissist does things for which we can't even form a hypothesis for why they did that, it looks so nonsensical. Such actions only make sense in the warped corners of their minds that only they know.

Jealousy is a common trait among narcissists. It deeply bothers them to see others lifted up higher than them. Revenge can be another motivator. Unfortunately, some narcissists are sadistic and simply enjoy watching others suffer.

Perhaps because I am not competitive by nature and feel no need to compare myself to others, I don't always notice the subtle indications of another person's jealousy. I had never noticed Asatya to be jealous towards me until sometime while I was in India for the business trip.

He said, "*You* can travel anywhere you want, when you want." He said it in such an annoyed tone. I had never heard him talk to me like that before.

Looking back, I thought of the times when Asatya had expressed doubts in the business project. I thought it was simply his depression making hope difficult for him. I had explained to him all the evidence I had that our plan should work, so I thought he was just having his own inner difficulty. I didn't realize that he himself lacked true confidence (he had hidden that insecurity expertly,) and he was jealous of mine. All that last year, he was expressing doubt in me 90% of the time. He was trying to knock me down.

He took me straight away to Sama and Vyapari thinking that these businessmen would shoot down my idea, but instead they supported it.

Asatya, as my travel coordinator, filled my precious two-week business trip with his own errands and visits to friends in spite of my enthusiasm and emphasis that we absolutely must visit Jaipur. We only got to Jaipur on the second to last day. We had only one day there, but we had great success in those few hours in Jaipur.

Asatya knew that more than one day would be required there.

The truth is that my business trip was successful *in spite of* Asatya.

I wanted to make that man my local coordinator or manager. His view of reality was warped to the point of being backwards. Instead of seeing what I was doing for him, I became the villain in his eyes.

I can't help but wonder if that extreme disorientation confuses narcissists, which scares them, putting them in stealth attack mode. I would love to hear a psychoanalyst weigh in.

Reactive abuse comes not from the abuser, but from the victim. This does not happen in all cases. I myself never did this as I felt unsafe to stand up for myself. Some victims of abuse, however, reach a point where they have been so provoked that they can no longer contain themselves and they lash out in anger. Sometimes reactive abuse is revenge. Sometimes it is self-defense. Sometimes it is just bottled-up anger finally let loose, nothing more. I personally feel that laws that apply to self-defense might also be appropriately applied to reactive abuse (but not in cases of revenge). That would mean that those who engage in reactive abuse would have the same or similar leniency in court as someone acting in self-defense. Just an idea.

Actually, I think this really should be considered. I know of many people who were badly provoked, because the abuser wanted to film their angry reaction in order to incriminate their victim or at least discredit their victim's testimony. Some abusers are incredibly cunning and strategic like this.

Shifting goal-posts is a tactic often employed by narcissists in their relationships to keep the victim on their toes. Essentially, the abuser makes a particular demand, but when the victim follows through and delivers on that demand, the abuser becomes upset, claiming that the victim has misunderstood the original demand and that more is required, or that something else entirely is required.

This behavior may be partly due to the narcissist having volatile moods and frequently changing wants. Sometimes it is just for the 'supply' of watching the victim jump through all these hoops for them. The victim becomes like a hamster running on a wheel, spending all their energy but never getting closer to making the narcissist happy.

A Letter to Those Seeking Freedom, and Their Friends

Increasing various security measures is strongly advised for anyone who has escaped any abusive relationship, but especially if the abuser lacks empathy or remorse, as is generally the case with NPD or psychopathy (ASPD.)

It is universally agreed among knowledgeable psychotherapists that the single best thing that any victim or survivor of narcissistic abuse can do, is to cut off *all* possible contact with the narcissist. That means blocking their phone number and blocking them from all other accounts, blocking their flying monkeys and unfortunately mutual friends also. Cut off all contact except where mandated by the court, in the case of sharing children. Remember that many of the problems that the victim has, came about because the narcissist systematically and intentionally demolished their boundaries. 'Give them an inch and they will take a mile,' applies in this case, because a hoovering narcissist will put all their effort into any tiny crack in your wall of defense.

Cutting off all contact will help the victim to heal more quickly internally and dramatically decrease the chance that they will be further victimized.

I know that in most cases, one cannot simply end a relationship all in one day with a clean break. Sometimes people are forced to wait for available housing, for example. So how to cope and stay safe while the narcissist has access to you? I learned something sort of by trial and error that helped minimize agitation in Asatya and therefore minimize stress and threats to some degree. Obviously, it was not fail proof, and I didn't do it consistently...

I am talking about the 'grey rock' method of communication. 'Grey rock' means to only initiate communication when necessary, and to give very boring, unemotional, brief responses. For example, 'Okay.' 'Yup, I hear you.' 'Mhmm.' Talk like it's a business relationship with someone that you have zero emotional attachment to. Psychotherapists could explain the psychology behind why this method usually works best, but all experts and survivors agree that this is the wisest approach, until you can remove your-self from that person's life.

It is worth repeating that in the case of victims who live with an abusive narcissist (even if they have only experienced verbal abuse so far), that they do need to plan ahead to ensure a safe departure. When a narcissist knows that their supply is about to leave them, that is the most dangerous time for the victim. They will have to either leave with a police escort, or else leave when the narcissist is not at home. They could leave without help, and when the narcissist is at home, but not without significant risk of being at-tacked, escape efforts sabotaged or even held captive.

I would encourage anyone that sincerely loves a person who has suf-fered from narcissistic abuse to be ready to listen without interrupting and without judgment. Be ready to be patient with the many rants, and the failed escape attempts. They might defend the narcissist and go back, and they might even block you, if you warn them while they are still under the mind control.

That looks like the behavior of an addict because in most cases they are trauma-bonded which means they *are* addicts.

Be ready to facilitate an escape and possibly let them crash on your couch for a few nights if you are able.

They might be stand-offish, or clingy at first. They might still talk like they have hope for the narcissist. If they do, it just means that they are still partially under the mind control. Staying away from the narcissist and spending time around sane, healthy people like you will give your friend some of the perspective they need to make the separation total and final.

Be gentle, kind, and tell them that you believe in them. Verbally offer hugs. Ask how you can be the most supportive. They will be going through withdrawal and would benefit from some low-key, low-pressure distrac-tions. I would suggest outdoor exercise, naps, and venturing out in public somewhere calm, like a library.

Walking away from abuse is ugly and beautiful at the same time. It is a walk towards survival and there may be bruises, hair falling out, dead look-ing eyes and low motivation, *but* there is a determination to live. The per-son you love is still in there. They want to thrive.

A little love can go a really long way at this point in the life of an abused friend or relative, and whatever kindness you show them during their escape and recovery, they are not likely to ever forget. You may have saved their life without even realizing it. As they heal, you will see them become an even sweeter but more balanced friend than before.

Being a real friend to a survivor is a truly noble act and a worthy human investment.

Do not be so cocky as to think that it could never happen to you. Who would be there for you, if the person you loved most sucked all the life out of you? It is very easy to think, "I would never do that," or "I would never fall for that." All of us survivors once had those exact same thoughts.

People often make the false assumption that an abuser was always awful from the very first day, or that they are nasty all the time. If that were the case, all their victims would have run for the hills ages ago. It is a sinister and effective game that abusers play.

I myself used to hear women talk about their 'fixer-upper' boyfriends, and I thought, "Why? Find someone better." Then along came a fixer-upper into my life, pretending to be a mature, elevated soul. Ironically, such so-called fixer-uppers never do get fixed up...

It is possible that you too could fall into the trap of narcissistic abuse, but I hope that now you will be able to recognize it in the very early stages and save yourself from the misery.

If you are not able to be there for your abused friend in the way that they need, please do not feel guilty. You cannot be everything for everyone, and you are not under any obligation. You are allowed to feel tired or annoyed by the neediness of your traumatized friend.

However, if you do have a friend that has reached out to you for support while coming out of abuse, it means that they believe in you as a good person and they trust you. They chose to trust in you as a genuine human being in spite of their abuse-induced fear of people, and instead of turning to drugs, alcohol, or self-harm, which they very likely have thought about. No doubt you do not want your friend getting into drugs or hurting themselves.

So, please take the need very seriously, but respect your own limitations. You need to take care of yourself, too.

If the only way you can show your support is simply to tell your abused friend, "I believe you," rest assured that you have made a difference. The survivor community thanks you.

After immense and deep trauma is the number one time in a person's life when they need real friends more than ever. They won't always be needy. This is a good time to gently remind your friend what healthy boundaries look like, for their sake, but also for your sake. Not that they might hurt you, but that they may still be disoriented from their unhealthy encounter with the narcissist.

There is an excellent chance that you will find abuse survivors to have very low tolerance for bullshit, whether from you or from anyone, and also that they may be acutely tuned in to your needs and be very considerate, though every case is a bit different.

All that to say, let us be there for each other, while never allowing disrespect or dismissal of our own needs.

We do not connect with each other to see how we can use each other. We connect because we were made for unity, for symbiosis. Never forget brothers and sisters, that we are family.

Autonomy or Connection?

I was a confident, happy, healthy person, and not any more naive than an average person, and yet an evil mastermind gained control over my mind and exploited me. What was supposed to be a brother-sister relationship became a tyrant-slave relationship. My autonomy and dignity were taken from me slowly.

I had always been strong-willed, independent, having zero tolerance for mistreatment (I once quit a job on the spot when I realized that the boss had sort of black-mailed me), and I always cared a lot more about staying true to myself and my values rather than fall into people-pleasing or worrying what people think of me. All my life, any time anyone tried to pressure me, I would reflexively dig in my heels stubbornly and do the opposite. Bossy, pushy people repel me. So then, understand now, how my name came to be Petra, which means 'rock.'

I found myself on a quest to understand how I could have fallen into the trap of coercive control, and how can I prevent this in the future?

Among other related topics, I found myself exploring the very relevant concepts of autonomy and connection. It is true that I can have a very big heart towards the right people, but it's more than that...

From the beginning of time, the human race has existed in community.

Is it just something that we have done because all of our ancestors have done it, or because it was always more practical? Or to cure loneliness?

As an American, I'm witnessing something different happening in my home country.

I'm not an anthropologist, so I can't say for sure what exactly led to the current state of affairs (I am talking about the average American understanding of community or family), but I do know that history has often shown what happens with the very best societal innovation and progress: it starts out like a revolution, sweeping through the land bringing life-changing reforms and inspiration for even more progress.

Unfortunately, because humanity is flawed by things like ego, greed, corruption, and a spineless desire to evade accountability, over the years these noble values adopted by culture eventually become slowly perverted and atrophied.

The particular value I'm thinking of is freedom- liberty, particularly personal liberty and autonomy. In our constitution, our rights to life, liberty and the pursuit of happiness are assured. Our constitution was written to limit the government so that it could not steal our freedoms.

Freedom in the modern American sense means that we are not forced to all be and do the same. Everyone can follow their own religion, or none, if they choose. Anyone can start a business, seek employment, or purchase land for whatever purpose (so long as it honors zoning laws). Your family size, sexuality, whom you associate with, what you say in public, and a hundred other choices are 100% according to your own personal discretion and you don't have to explain such actions to anyone. In this way, the American experience is highly individualized. If you have met one American, you have met just one American; you still don't know the 300+ million others. This liberty to use personal discretion exists not only because the law says so; personal freedom is a very highly prized value in the hearts of Americans across our country, perhaps above all others. While our freedoms have been whittled away in recent times, our collective love and value of our own personal freedom, and the collective freedom, has never, ever died from our hearts and minds.

Truly freedom is so very important and must be protected for the sake of all. There can be no individual freedom without collective freedom.

However, having come of age at the dawning of the internet, I often see freedom abused, and pursued to the neglect of other important values.

I am witnessing my fellow Americans (and many in some other 'western' countries) to be so caught up in their own individual lives that as a whole, we are losing our sense of community.

We have freedom to have whatever worldviews and values that we wish. Many of us feel very strongly about these and become embroiled in verbal wars with those of opposing views. Many people not wanting to fight, refuse to talk about spiritual or political matters at all, saying 'that should be kept private.'

So instead of having mature discussions to seek mutual understanding, we either fight or avoid deep conversations completely.

We are not pioneers anymore. There are over 300 million of us, and we have become far too comfortable with burning bridges or 'ghosting' the people who have made us uncomfortable, rather than repair a broken relationship. After all, we can always find like-minded friends elsewhere. This approach leaves a person with zero accountability, or anyone present to criticize them, leaving the person's ego and misconceptions intact. The age of internet could have made us more connected, but weirdly it's done the opposite. It has given us the opportunity to be socially lazy, favoring a homebody lifestyle rather than immersing in the community. We can just send off a text message rather than approach someone at a social gathering. If someone makes us uncomfortable (whether in a good way or bad way) in a digital communication, we can simply block them or turn off read receipts. We are raising an entire generation of young people who have no experience and no training for how to handle conflict, so social anxiety has become epidemic.

Because of the advancement of communication technology, we are hyperconnected but not making true connections. With the world at our fingertips, we gravitate toward like-minded people who do not challenge us to expand our minds and hearts, setting the stage for cultish groups to form, as we can now see. Our pioneering forefathers built tiny settlements and relied heavily on each other to survive in those early years. We lost something.

We avoid each other when there is a kerfuffle and lazily hide behind keyboards.

Notice some of the words I used above: lack of accountability, ego, burning bridges, lack of healthy conflict resolution, etc. In that sort of environment, it shouldn't be a surprise that we have a lot of depression, anxiety, narcissism, and other mental health problems. We were meant to live alongside each other and for each other, but we hardly do that. We act like 'survival of the fittest' is something to aspire to.

Busyness plays another role. Our fast-paced lifestyle of 40+ hour work weeks, sports, yard work or house projects, Netflix addictions and other time-consuming activities get crammed into every hour of the week, leaving us with no margins, no time buffer. It doesn't help that our country has so much suburban sprawl but so little public transportation, forcing us to spend a ridiculous amount of time behind a steering wheel. We can't afford to get caught up in an unexpected conversation because we will be late to the next thing on the agenda.

If a friend is in a crisis and needs our help, we struggle to squeeze out an afternoon to go be there for them, because it means we have to say 'no' to something else in our life.

Right now, there is a multitude of young women who do not want to have children. (This is sort of a tangent or rabbit trail, but it is relevant, so please bear with me.) Biologically, this is an unnatural development which warrants a deeper understanding of why this is the case.

I strongly suspect that a significant number of these women (though certainly not all) are secretly in love with the fantasy of becoming a mother, but they are afraid of becoming pregnant because what if their boyfriend or spouse leaves them later or turns nasty, forcing them to leave? There is no paid maternity leave. They know they will have to rely on someone for support for the first few weeks or months at minimum, if that other person's income is even enough to support them. Everyone is so busy that it is very unusual that a relative moves in to help care for the baby. Usually, the new mom is still working at least part-time while caring for the baby, the home, and generally neglecting herself because she has no time or energy left over.

Young women know that it does 'take a village to raise a child,' but they can see that the village has nearly disappeared, as the village is busy in their own cubicle or bubble life.

Have you ever thought about who your grandmother was? Who was she really, aside from being a wife and mother? Sure, being a wife or a mother is a good and noble thing, but that is just a part of a person's life and is not meant to be their entire existence, though it seems that historically, it was just assumed that 'mother' is a person's entire identity somehow. Young women see how much work it is to raise a child, and without a real support network, they fear that they will lose themselves in the exhaustion of it all.

Did you know that breastfeeding in the first year takes about 1,800 hours? That is roughly equivalent to a full-time job. While also working a regular full-time job, how can she have any time or energy left for anything?

I know a few supermoms will pipe up and say that they do that, it can be done! Please understand that because a few of you have incredibly managed to pull that off, that does not mean that it is fair or practical to make such an exhausting, high-pressure life the expectation for all. It is impractical at best, and impossible in many cases.

Raising children absolutely does take a village, but that village has become a bit hostile or indifferent towards children in their community. That 'village' will not materialize until we see this as a collective and joyful effort. This is just one piece of looking out for each other as a society. I bring up the point about raising children because in spite of some people's general disdain for children, our existence as a species does require that some of us procreate. Parenthood is critical to our survival. But yes, it is hard. You don't have to have children yourself but at least look out for the well-being of your young neighbors if you notice that anything is amiss. Children are human beings deserving of basic rights and respect no less than you. In fact, as vulnerable members of society, they need more communal support, not less. You who are reading this are grown adults who are capable of showing tolerance towards the tiny human beings around you whose brains are not fully developed yet.

It is also true that nobody wants to be helpful to lazy parents, and those who say, "Mind your own business!" later wonder where everyone is when they are facing hard times. There are two sides to every coin.

I bring up the matter of raising children because it demonstrates some of the pitfalls of weak or non-existent community.

We are so caught up in the freedom of running our own lives as we see fit, that we have forgotten each other. That may sound like an exaggeration, but when was the last time that your next door neighbor asked to 'borrow' some flour? We are living in bubbles.

We have 300 million 'I's' and no 'us.'

As a nation, we look like a couple ready to divorce. We are so fixated on finding ourselves that we are out of touch with each other.

However, it is true that we need to know ourselves in order to develop healthier connections with those around us. (Think about it, you cannot mature without first having self-awareness.) We need to know each other to develop a well-rounded perspective to better understand ourselves.

Remember that bumper sticker that I saw with the phrase: 'One Human Family.'

The sentiment is right, but I think we forgot what family even is.

I AM FAMILY

As a human race,

We tried community without autonomy and started wars from the lack of freedom.

We tried autonomy without community and neglected each other, while idolizing ourselves.

It would appear that one without the other will not work, but we are not very good at balancing these things, in general.

I grew up in the rural northeastern state of Maine. The small-town culture of having each other's backs while also talking behind them is still present here to some degree. Some of these towns were among the first in this country to be founded. The current residents of this region are mainly descendants of the founders and they're not much different from their pioneering predecessors: stoic, humble and yet somehow proud, very hard-working and not complaining, independent, practical, unpretentious and self-sufficient.

I myself am much like the rest of my family, who are locals.

From birth I was an introvert. I always found small talk to be an annoying waste of time. From a young age I was raised to study the Bible, which has a number of admonitions to make our speech of benefit to the listener. Our words should be truthful, useful, and uplifting in some way. So, right from my early years, I adopted that mentality, which was perhaps a bit easier for me, being a person of few words. Training aside, I had always felt innately and strongly that truth and authenticity are of paramount importance, and they are among my top values.

So, you can easily imagine that I valued quality over quantity in my personal interactions. I often felt a bit lonely (people wrongly assumed that my introversion meant that I hardly needed any human connection.) I was shy but being a hugger in a stoic environment, I often felt a bit deprived of physical affection. I will speak for myself, though perhaps other quiet folks might relate, that my main reasons for speaking so little was that I had a modest view of myself, and I used to think that others would find my thoughts to be boring. Also, I typically find it difficult to organize my thoughts and articulate them verbally. Thirdly, I have enough self-respect to not fight for my place in a conversation. If people want to talk over me, they do not deserve to hear what I have to say. I do not want the ears of someone who does not care what I have to say.

In my early childhood I was content in my own little world, but as I grew older, I realized that my introversion was holding me back from enjoying a lot of things, socially. I was intent to live my life to the fullest, so I decided to continually step out of my comfort zone to interact more.

Through my early years, I was also finding that much of God's work involved people. Sure, I could go live in a cabin alone at the edge of the wilderness and live off the land, and I would have been happy to do so, but I knew that personally, that's not what God had for me. I could see that the work God had for me meant getting involved with people which I wasn't excited about, but I knew it absolutely would cause me to grow as a person, so I could accept that. I often felt that I could really understand and relate to Moses, who for a while lived an avoidant lifestyle as a shepherd on the edge of the desert until God told him to go speak to the Pharoah. To paraphrase his response, he replied something like, "But God! I'm not articulate! Pharoah will just laugh at me. My brother is a public speaker, send him."

God was like, "Nope. Take your brother if you wish, but I'm sending *you*."

Oh, how very relatable for me...Growth is outside of the comfort zone.

As years went by and I made the uncomfortable efforts of being more interactive, I found a few real and good friends, but just as many others never understood me, or worse, left me traumatized. In between those extremes was a sea of people who seemed content with gossip and superficial interactions, which I never wanted to get involved with.

So, I began my life favoring autonomy, then seeking connection, then wishing for autonomy again. I suspect that many of you can understand an inner monologue that from time to time shifts between the opposing attitudes of, "People suck!" and, "I'm lonely."

Jesus set the example and told us, "Take up your cross and follow me," meaning to be ready to make sacrifices and face pain inflicted by a world that hates God. He also said, "Don't throw your pearls before swine," and "Shake the dust from your feet when leaving a place where the people refuse to listen to my message," meaning don't throw yourself at people who choose to remain hostile, instead redirect your efforts to more receptive people.

The life lesson for me in that, is to be ready for anything, but to develop discernment to see when the path is closed off and it is time to adjust or redirect.

I find myself at a place in life where I know that running into the arms of either extreme (of independence or codependency) will not help me or anyone. I need to find the balance between autonomy and connection. I must seek homeostasis and symbiosis.

In case you forgot these two scientific terms, homeostasis is a physical state in which everything is at a healthy and sustainable level, and stable.

Symbiosis is essentially harmony in ecology; it is the state in which multiple organisms are in a mutually beneficial relationship, creating a sustainable and healthy biome.

In this case, I am using these words figuratively.

Peace in me.

Peace among us.

This is the essence of the Jewish greeting, 'shalom.'

I'm saying that I want to change my behavior to help ensure harmony, sustainability and balance in my personal relationships, as far as it depends on me.

What does that balance look like?

I can tell you how it should not be...

Over the first couple of years that I knew Asatya, he would often talk passionately on the topic of family. He would say things that resonated deeply in my conscience, with such wisdom and insight that was truly on a higher level.

For example, he would put a very strong emphasis on the 'us' mentality.

He would rightly say that within a family, there is a bit less individuality and more inclusiveness or unity. If one hurts, the others lift them up. If one has reason to celebrate, the others celebrate with them. In a family, there is no room for self-centeredness, but each one should think of the needs of the others. Knowing Christ's intention for the church being like one body made up of many parts, all working together for a common purpose and for mutual benefit, this thinking made perfect sense to me. Seeing Asatya think that way was refreshing to me, as American families tend to not be very close, and generally living their lives individually.

Asatya would talk about brother's and sister's roles. In the beginning, he was adamant that no self-respecting brother could accept money from a sister, as men are supposed to be self-sufficient and women (in that culture at least) generally are not.

Very slowly over time, the narrative began to change imperceptibly, subliminally.

In fact, what happened was that I'd ask Asatya, "how are you?" and he would give me the rundown of his day.

Oftentimes things would be going very poorly for him as this was during Covid and maintaining good employment was not easy. Sometimes I felt helpless being half a world away, wishing I could help somehow.

The narrative shift began with things like, "Well, I suppose you could put in a good word for me with so-and-so," or something like that. I insisted that I wanted to help. Asatya pointed out that for sure, some Indians would listen more intently to me being a white American (yes, I know that is wrong, but unfortunately many Indians still think like this) than to him who just looks like a 'Joe Schmoe.'

This is how I came to be slowly over time, shmoozing more and more Indians on Asatya's behalf. All of those were ongoing communications that I had to maintain. I began to feel like public relations staff. I never enjoyed it as shmoozing is a transactional connection and not authentic. Remember that truth and authenticity are extremely important to me. So, there I was sacrificing my values in a way, to try to lift up my brother in the way that he said he needed.

At some point, a significant financial need arose with Asatya's older sister. Asatya was trying to make amends with his sister though he had no money.

The whole reason that Asatya had originally claimed me as a sister was that he had no strong ties to his family and felt alone in the world, so naturally I wanted to support his desire to restore his broken relationship with his sister. Some months later, it was his niece that he asked me to help. Later he needed money and asked for it...

Aside from talking about family, Asatya would often talk about the virtue of generosity and kindness; of not keeping track of who gave more. What's mine is yours, what's yours is mine. Asatya himself could be unusually generous with others, so it was very easy for me to be generous towards him. He would say that he would pay me back, but I would say, "We are family though. We're not keeping track."

Indeed, I was not. It was not until after I had cut ties that I looked at my transaction history and was shocked to see how many times that I had sent money that I don't even remember doing. It baffles me that I have no memory of many of those funds transfers, but it is clear now that Asatya created the 'we are family' narrative between us in order to exploit my time, my emotions, and to financially abuse me.

At some point, I realized that we both were always talking like, 'us, we, our,' but our whole relationship was centered around me helping Asatya in whatever way that I could. In reality, it wasn't about us, it was about him. Asatya would talk about his dreams and ideas of things he wanted to do for me and my family. All that he wanted to do for me (supposedly) was in the future. I never saw him reciprocate, though he faked reciprocation a few times.

So then, where does the delicate balance lie, between the roles and relationships within a family - family by biology or by choice? We don't want our relationships to be transactional, but we do want them to be reasonably fair.

Anyone can easily say that the correct balance with an abuser, whether they are family or not, is to completely cut them out, but what if you don't even see the abuse for what it is? What if you think they are a good person, and all the good things you did for them were your idea? What if you are unaware that they gaslighted you into believing the generosity towards them was your idea, but actually they manipulated you the whole time, undetected? An abuser can be anyone, and some of them are shockingly good at camouflaging their motives.

Can we protect ourselves without knowing a person's true intentions? I think so, but it requires a bit of self-discipline.

In light of what I have learned through unfortunate experience, I now know that there should never be any exception to maintaining personal boundaries. This is where that self-discipline comes in.

Also, it is imperative to take note that just because someone's toxic behavior can be explained, does not mean that it should be excused.

There were plenty of reasons why Asatya was toxic towards me. He still should not have been. Anyone who has experienced any abuse on any level can either internalize that garbage and then regurgitate it to the next person they become close to (as he did to me) *or* one can make a conscious decision to pursue healing of the internal wound and break the cycle of toxicity, which includes being correctable and accountable, but also not a doormat.

This is why personal awareness and emotional intelligence are important. You do not want to transmit dysfunction as if it were the flu.

Hurt people hurt people, but they do not have to.

It is unfortunately true that the people who have the most potential to really hurt us are the people who are the closest to us, and yet, trust is essential in close relationships...

It is just true that one's personal boundaries are much more likely to get bulldozed if one has not even identified what their boundaries should be...

Unfortunately, there are some people who will agree to talk with you about boundaries and terms of a relationship and they may seem to be wholeheartedly on the same page, but later they just do whatever the hell they want, boundaries and agreements be damned.

I believe that the real solution is to have the discretion to recognize when a gentle confrontation solves the problem, or when the disrespect is intentional or habitual, necessitating a separation.

I would like to point out that boundaries are not just for what we will allow from others. We should also have boundaries of what is acceptable in ourselves. For example, an alcoholic might refuse to attend a friend's party if they know that alcohol will be served. You need to be aware of your own weaknesses and limitations and proactively avoid situations that will bring out the worst in you.

Because we need autonomy *and* connection, what do these two things look like in combination?

The Bible has a few lines saying, 'Submit to one another.' It does *not* say to demand submission from others.

There is a very clear pattern in the Bible showing us that good things in the context of a loving relationship are always given willingly and joyfully, never demanded.

For example, you trust someone because it feels right and you want to, not because the other person tells you that you should trust them.

You might help pay an unforeseen expense because you are concerned about the person, not because they pressured you for money.

You listen to someone because you want to understand them, not because their ego demands your attention and silence.

Love in all its many forms, including respect, should always be given willingly and cheerfully, never demanded. There is no room for coercion in love. I am *not* saying that loving acts can never be requested. I am saying that love cannot be demanded like a tyrannical edict, as that is conditional love, and even if love is given under that circumstance, it is not genuine, because it is laced with fear. Perfect love casts out fear.

We connect with each other without placing a world of expectations on each other, and yet ready to receive goodness.

We do not hold each other so tightly as to rob each other of freedom, so tightly as to lose our personal identity. We hold each other just close enough to establish the identity of brotherhood, of a couple, of a community, a nation, or a family. We develop shared values, shared goals, shared love.

There can be no personal freedom without collective freedom.

Unfortunately, at some point our relationships break down because we are imperfect human beings which means sometimes there is pushing of other's buttons, pettiness, disregard for other's needs, poor decisions followed by 'white lies' and broken trust, to name a few hurtful behaviors. Also unfortunate, it is quite normal to do some of these things unknowingly from time to time or at least be unaware of the extent of the impact of such behaviors.

Considering our love for the person that we hurt, we must be honest with ourselves: how willing are we to be confronted about our poor behavior?

Is it really fair to expect them to suffer in silence so that our egos remain intact?

If we truly love that person, we need to be willing to listen to them when they say that we have hurt them in some way.

Correction is a gift if it comes from someone who sincerely cares about your well-being, and not just their own. How much correction you are willing to receive is yet one more way in which you must decide how to balance connection and autonomy.

What if a loved one wishes to advise or correct you regarding something that does not involve them? It may be worth listening to... but again, it is your choice whether to listen to that or not.

The matter of correction was one more way in which Asatya had me like the proverbial frog in a pot of cold water where the temperature is slowly raised, boiling it to death.

In the very beginning Asatya would accept little corrections from me seemingly with such grace and ease, he never seemed embarrassed or annoyed. He set such a good example like this, and the way that he talked showed so much wisdom that finally in my late thirties, I came to a place where I myself felt totally comfortable to be corrected. Asatya's tone was at first gentle but serious. As time went on, that tone became a bit harsh, then a bit of shame got mixed in. Later he sprinkled in other ingredients such as triangulation and threats. The first few times that this happened, I tried to gently give some perspective as his words were not fair. He would tell me "Don't try to defend yourself, you're showing your ego."

I know that people typically do indeed become defensive out of ego, so I really did question myself. I knew it was possible that I might make a mistake and not recognize it, so I was always willing to consider what Asatya said. Sometimes I knew that he was right, and I was wrong, but I still felt that he drove down the hammer too hard. I told myself it is just because he is Haryanvi. Haryanvis are very expressive and can appear aggressive in their speech. Other times he would find fault with me, but no matter which angle I examined the issue from, it seemed like he was making a mountain out of a molehill, if there even was a molehill.

I knew that Asatya had impossibly high standards for himself as well. I thought he just wanted me to be performing at his level. I did not want to disappoint my role model of integrity.

It was not until winter and spring of 2024 that the cognitive dissonance of all this gaslighting and personal attacks (let's face it, that's what it was this whole time, just cunningly dressed up to appear innocent) finally caught up with me and I was very confused. Asatya was making less and less sense at that time. By May, his abuse was no longer carefully wrapped up in disguise. It was blatant, custom-crafted, undeniable abuse.

In July when I unblocked him to give him the opportunity to apologize, he referred back to the abuse in May as him "Trying to get you to take the things seriously, forcing you to listen."

That right there was an unintentional confession of his manipulation attempts.

I had heard him use that phrase before.

Many times, he told me that he had to talk seriously with someone, trying to get them to take something more seriously.... Knowing this, I realize now that the screaming and personal attacks and manipulation that he had done to me, he was also doing to other people. In particular, his vulnerable, but stone-willed brother Prajna. I had personally witnessed his very harsh tone towards his siblings, but I didn't know what he had said to them, as it was generally in Hindi.

It is important to be able to accept occasional corrections from a few key people who truly care about your well-being.

Unfortunately, the 'correction' is one of the conduits through which narcissists and other abusers can gaslight you into questioning your intentions, your efforts, your successes, your qualities, your everything, totally gutting your confidence. It absolutely can reach a point where you no longer know what is true or false, leaving you in a sort of psychosis, and it can do serious neurological damage. Successful gaslighting rewires the brain.

Narcissistic abuse is a hijacking of another's mind and heart, and sometimes body.

Just imagine that if you are under someone else's mind control, your autonomy has not just been violated, it is gone.

So how to be open to correction but not susceptible to gaslighting?

You may not be able to stay 100% foolproof, but having a clear vision of who you are, and your strengths and weaknesses, can help a lot. Asking a trusted friend for a second opinion about questionable criticism or statements can also keep you grounded in reality.

Narcissists very often try to isolate their victims. Do not allow yourself to become isolated. That is the proverbial lion separating an impala from the herd. You need that herd. Being able to talk about personal things with another friend (preferably somebody that does not know the one who is correcting you) might help catch something before it gets out of hand.

Earlier, I was writing about my own experience beginning in introversion, attempting to reach out, getting hurt, and then recalibrating.

This experience with Asatya changed my approach to relationships by giving me some dysfunction from the abuse:

The traumatic days and the fear of more traumatic days put me into a subtle or not-so-subtle freeze response and sometimes a fawn response, which became sustained, and I believe I developed PTSD in the end. The freeze response was mainly in the form of dissociation, which very likely was a contributing factor to my inability to see the abuse sooner. The dissociation had a numbing effect. Remember that in May through July, I could not feel any emotions. I think it is that the dissociation simply became more extreme.

A brief side note about the neurobiological effects of abuse: Extreme or on-going trauma (emotional stress) shrinks the hippocampus and enlarges the amygdala[1].[xli] The hippocampus houses our memories and recall ability. I believe that dissociation contributes to mental fog. The amygdala processes emotions and survival instincts. This can explain why many of us who have undergone psychological abuse feel depressed or unusually anxious (my nausea during Asatya's heightened abuse) but can't understand

---

1. https://www.google.com/search?q=enlarged+amygdala+effects&oq=enlarged+amygdala+effects&gs_lcrp=EgZjaHJvbWUyCQgAEEUYORiABDIICAEQABg-WGB4yCAgCEAAYFhgeMg0IAxAAGIYDGIAEGIoFMg0IBBAAGIYDGIAEGIoFMgoIBRAA-GIAEGKIEMgoIBhAAGIAEGKIE0gEJMTUzMjRqMGo3qAIAsAIA&sour-ceid=chrome&ie=UTF-8

why. We could not connect the dots or the abusive patterns, because our shrunken hippocampi left gaps in our memory, and the dissociation and fog made us less clearheaded. The gaslighting made us question what little we could remember and further damaged our minds.

Interestingly, an enlarged amygdala is associated with epilepsy (remember Shweta.) She did not have epilepsy when she met Asatya, and she is very likely one of many people who now have neurological dysfunction as a result of narcissistic abuse.

When the dissociation finally began to wear off, I entered a phase of extreme emotional pain, 24/7 anxiety, and a million questions.

Remember I had always been an introvert.

I had always been content with just two or three good friends and not much interaction. It is not that I did not care about people. It just meant that rather than spreading my love out thinly to many friends, I funneled all my care into a few people that meant everything to me. Within a span of five years, one person whom I loved like my own son, abandoned me and my family without giving any reason, a lifelong friend also abandoned all of us suddenly, another lifelong friend died tragically, and the man I had adopted as brother turned out to be my enemy and abuser.

I was gripped by a fear of abandonment, and I found I had become very clingy.

At the same time, the rug of reality had been ripped out from under me, and I found myself questioning myself, those I loved, everything. The idea of trusting anyone felt unsafe but I knew I had to if I was going to survive this.

I was so afraid of losing more people that I tried my best to hold myself back and not seem clingy. I could not live with myself if I scared off my precious few supportive people. This led me to the questions, How close do my friends actually want to be to me? What is the preferred amount of space? What IS the proper balance between autonomy and connection? I would have been delighted at that time to have endless hugs and daily conversations.

After four years of being silenced, exploited, traumatized, and fed sweet venom, all in a void of any real affection or care, followed by a month-long rage-fest from a black hole in the shape of a man... I felt totally drained dry of all I had to give and deprived of love.

From that point onward, even the smallest show of respect or appreciation to me felt like a sudden gasp of fresh oxygen bringing a little life back into me. The psychological expertise that I sought out all agreed that to heal from this type of damage, the most helpful thing to do to expedite healing is to accumulate positive social experiences. These experiences silence the negative spiraling garbage in the mind and rewire the brain the way it should be.

I had so much anxiety, and the idea of putting myself out there almost made me panic, but I knew that I had to do it - and somehow without seeming too needy.

I've found that most people really are not familiar with narcissistic abuse, though they *think* they know what a narcissist is, thanks to internet trends. It is true that the level of severity varies from case to case, and how it manifests itself also varies, though there are patterns or subtypes. Like some narcissists are sex-obsessed and will get it from absolutely anywhere.

Some others are more cerebral and try to gain their supply through mind games and appearing intellectually superior. Cerebral narcissists are often asexual and ignore or neglect their bodies. In addition to flaunting his teaching ability, I noticed that Asatya neglected his health and even seemed almost unaware of his body until he had nausea or migraines.

Some narcissists have failed at the cerebral and the somatic (mainly sex) strategies for gaining supply, so they carefully craft a public persona, and they disguise all their abuses, as Asatya did. This last one is called a covert narcissist. They are extremely stealthy, cunning, and subliminal in their strategies to gain supply. But all these have the same underlying traits and general tactics. Back to the topic of connection...

Last summer, I told just four people all the main details of what had happened and how it was affecting my current mental and emotional state at that time. They had trouble understanding the abuse, but they saw the rough shape I was in and believed me when I told them what I needed. One friend in particular was such a healing presence at that time. I think that seeing me in that state stressed him out a little, but he listened kindly. He took everything to heart but always remained chill. I believe everyone needs a friend like this who always has an even keel. That friend was one of the main things that held my head above water at that time. (The water being my brain and heart screaming in chaos 24/7.)

All he did was answer his text messages faithfully and provide reassurance. Nothing scandalized him. He did not judge me or get annoyed at my rants. He simply practiced active listening and expressed his belief in me.

He also did *not* contact me every day, and would always respond, but never right away, in contrast to Asatya who did not honor my time. I appreciated that this friend maintained reasonable personal boundaries concerning time and availability. It sets a good example.

He and a few others did so many little things that they didn't even realize healed me profoundly, one little peace at a time.

My pastor and his wife were also hugely supportive, once they became aware of my struggles. We were not really close friends, so I wasn't expecting much, but they rose to the challenge. My experiences with these and other people gave me perspective to combat the effects of the gaslighting.

For example, the lost wallet incident in Florida. It just seemed amazing to me that my friend did not freak out or even grumble that I was irresponsible. He just calmly helped sort out the problem, and that taught me that I was *safe*, which had a profoundly good impact on my internal well-being.

You alone are responsible for yourself in the end.

However, in the context of loving relationships, your loved ones will want to know what your needs are. Not so you can sit back and demand for them to do everything for you, but because if they love you, they will *want* to initiate kindness. Likewise, you should want to do the same for them.

As a Christian, it is my understanding that I should be ready to make personal sacrifices.

However, there are scriptures in which God would say something like, "I hate your burnt offerings and festivals! You go through the motions, but your hearts are far from me."

God is not interested in the superficial rituals of religion.

If you only give when you feel forced to, God does not want your gift. He wants your heart. As it is said, "God loves a cheerful giver."

Remember the New York fire fighters who ran into the world trade center to try to rescue more people. That was not required of them. They laid down their lives purely out of love for the random human beings who were trapped in the building.

That is what I meant by sacrifice: to prioritize others not out of oblig-ation but out of a genuine desire for the well-being of others. Remember that the next time you witness someone remind a relative of their 'family obligation.' That may be something worth questioning. Maybe. That is an-other area that needs discretion.

Love is responsible. Love is secure. Love does not control or coerce. In that context, freedom is promoted.

Let the love you give, be given eagerly with joy and sincerely, and put the brakes on takers.

In human society, in the context of sex, we have this concept that we call consent. I think consent is the bare minimum, and we can do better than this. Consent implies that something is being requested from you.

Love (in general, not just in the context of sex) in its purest form, should be *offered*, not requested. Yes of course, requests have their legiti-mate place, but I will repeat this again:

Let the love you give, be born out of your own desire to give with joy, and do not allow exploitation in any form.

Closing Thoughts Before One Last Story

Every single detail of Asatya's story I have written unchanged from what he told me and wrote for me. Every detail of my part in this story is exactly as I experienced it; I have changed nothing. The only details that are different in this book from our real, lived experience, is that I have changed the names of people, especially Asatya's and my own.

I do not write this book for revenge, though if anyone recognizes themself in any character in this story, I say if the shoe fits, wear it.

Names have been changed to protect the innocent and to avoid provoking retaliation or further drama from those who did wrong in this story. The aliases that I chose for the people in this memoir, I chose with intention. For each person, I chose a name from either their native language, or the language of their ancestors, that is a word to describe their role or most dominant trait in this story. You will find name translations in the back of this book.

You may wonder why I bothered to include all of Asatya's back story if he is such a horrible person.

I wanted you to see the world through the eyes of a narcissist without first knowing that he is a narcissist. I want you to see how he craved the care of a mother, his deep need to feel loved though he was never able to absorb it, leaving him ever grasping for more... I want you to see his deep distrust of the world, that his true self was dead, that his growth and maturity had aborted, that he habitually sabotaged himself and capitalized on his own victimhood, and that he would defend his web of lies unto his dying breath. In his fake alternate reality, Asatya believed that "Good people are born to suffer," and that he was such a person.

I wanted you to see who I was going into that 'family by choice,' and what the end result was of four years connected to a narcissist- my crippling anxiety, the confusion, the chaos, the nauseating mixture of raw emotion, the numbness that followed, the complex damage of gaslighting, and other narcissistic abuse. I wanted you to feel my joy and relief with every milestone of healing that I reached.

I wanted you to see the context of society and family, and how these things played their roles, both good and bad. I hope that now you have a much broader and deeper understanding of many things, but most importantly, you have been warned of the tragic evil that is narcissistic personality disorder.

It is important to be aware for a few reasons. I will mention two.

#1. Narcissists and predatory people of all kinds do not just stumble randomly across their future victims (supply). They actively seek them out and can be very strategic to groom and ensnare. They spend their lives honing this 'skill.' They care more about narcissistic supply than they care about food, water, or shelter. I am a witness of this, and I am not the only witness.

Estimates for the number of narcissists in the general population (just narcissists, not including other personality disorders or exploiters) are around 6.2% in the U.S.[1][xlii]That means that for every 17 people, one of them is a narcissist. Because they are by nature opportunists, it is very likely that a narcissist will at some point in your life, analyze you for their potential use. You can see how important it is to learn how to be kind while simultaneously making yourself less appealing to predators by displaying zero tolerance for shady behavior and calling out any that you observe. Narcissists like to have their deeds exposed about as much as a vampire likes to sunbathe. Oh, the symbolic irony there...

#2. Just as physical diseases can be contagious, so one person's mental illness can so deeply impact the people closest to them that they also develop some mental health problem such as depression or PTSD. It's not exactly contagious, and yet some kind of illness or suffering is often passed on.

In the same way, spiritual things can be contagious. If you are loving and peaceful, you are promoting the same in those around you. If you are selfish and petty, you are encouraging others to respond the same way, or to become self-protective.

We as individuals, as families, as nations, as the race of humanity have a responsibility to keep ourselves healthy - by mind, body, and spirit. What affects you affects everyone around you. Seek your own health and do not neglect your spirit in particular. Public health includes mental health.

---

1.   https://pmc.ncbi.nlm.nih.gov/articles/PMC2669224/

Galatians 5:22+23 tells us: *'But the fruit of the Spirit is love, joy, peace, patience, kindness, goodness, faithfulness, gentleness, and self-control...'* These things are the natural result of allowing the Spirit of God to work in you, so logically, becoming closer to God will heal much and help all this. If indeed God is the origin of life, of love, and every good thing, then it should not be surprising that closer connection with God gives us more life. However, the acknowledgment of sin in one's life and the need for forgiveness and new life is requisite and this is where many people get turned off and refuse to go that way... though usually not as dramatically as Asatya did. Most of us know we are not perfect, but we let ourselves off the hook too easily.

We say 'Be the change you want to see.' Well, peace in the world begins with peace in us. In fact, every good or bad thing begins at the most intimate level.

The truth is that every narcissist and every psychopath is in fact also a human being, as much as we may wish to demonize them. They are often sadists without conscience. They themselves are tortured souls. They desperately need love although they don't deserve it, and they don't feel it. The need of love and inability to feel it creates desperation which leads them to do many unacceptable things.

I do wonder if narcissists were raised in a loving and healthy manner, if their outcomes would be different. Maybe they would only have narcissistic tendencies and not full-blown NPD. I don't know. I do know a mother whose eight-year-old son is showing signs of narcissism, and his mom is being very intentional to train that out of him, hoping that he will not grow up to be like his narcissist father (who does not live with them.) I'm very interested to see if her efforts will be successful in time.

It is very easy to dehumanize a narcissist. Yes, it is true that they have no self-worth, so they dehumanize others to feel superior, but it is more than that.

We don't want to associate ourselves with abusers. We call them monsters because if we call them human, we recognize that it's possible that the monster could have been us if all our conditions were the same as theirs. Every single one of us is capable of great evil and great goodness; the main difference is our varied life experiences and how we choose to react to them. In early childhood, external factors play an even stronger role.

357

Narcissists are extremely and deeply damaged people with a destroyed self-worth that never heals. They cope with that by creating a dream world for themselves in which they are exceptionally amazing people deserving of all love and admiration. Their profound insecurity can't be totally imagined away however, so the insecurity and grandiosity inside them are always at war. I personally believe that this is where most of their anger comes from. The unhealed damage over the years often snowballs into more dysfunctions or comorbidities.

Narcissists often do have comorbidities, such as borderline personality disorder, anti-social personality disorder (psychopathy), obsessive-compulsive disorder, depression, etc. Their desperation for attention and love gives rise to the development of manipulation, which they become the great masters of, over time.

Narcissists almost never improve. Do not talk yourself into believing that the narcissist that you know is the exception to the rule and that surely they will get better if loved and supported enough. Some of the most loved and supported people on earth are narcissists. You could die for one and they will hardly notice. Really.

Normally, being loving towards another person has some good effect on them to a greater or lesser degree (remember my healing experience), and we always encourage loving behavior. However, loving a narcissist generally backfires and in every case, will not have the positive effect that you hope for.

It pains me to tell you to give up on anyone, but if you stay in proximity to a narcissist, the net result will be that you become collateral damage in their chaos. Imagine that the narcissist has a terminal illness, and coming in contact with them can make you very sick.

You can't help them, but they will likely hurt you. Until modern medicine finds a solution to effectively treat NPD, it is wisest to keep your distance.

There are several narcissist subtypes. I'll mention two before explaining more about three other well-recognized subtypes.

A malignant narcissist is what I think comes to most people's minds when they think of a narcissist. A malignant type makes much less effort to hide their unpleasant traits. They tend to be arrogant, entitled, overtly malicious and sometimes sadistic.

A spiritual or religious type is generally covert, because a fake spiritual persona helps to win people's trust. They say all the right things. If you have ever been in a church that felt toxic, and the pastor was very outspoken and charismatic, but also was very controlling, and perhaps avoided scriptures that didn't serve their purpose, or even that it all felt sort of cultish... the pastor or leader in question could have been a narcissist. A male religious narcissist will twist scripture to mean what he wants, which is usually a patriarch-dominant set-up. They will weaponize your values against you with double-standards. For example, you must be humble and generous, but narcissists exempt themselves from such standards.

I want to write a bit more about the other three most common subtypes. According to twice-diagnosed narcissist and Professor of psychology Sam Vaknin[2],[xliii] (one of the few self-aware narcissists) this is what happens to an individual after NPD has developed in them in their young adult years: A narcissist begins as either a cerebral type or a somatic type.

A cerebral type builds their persona on academics and intelligence. Remember Asatya's story of teaching German after only one week of studying, and how many teaching positions he filled only on merit of his reputation. He also told me last July that he was originally online in language learner's chat groups because he secretly hoped to find a 'mother.' (It is very common for narcissists to 'parentify' the person that they are closest to.) Side note: the fact that he sort-of viewed me secretly as a mother would explain why he couldn't stand to see even a tiny bit of neck or ankle and insisted on me dressing in a very conservative, matronly fashion while in India, even where it wasn't necessary. Speaking of cerebral narcissism, I remember that Asatya never seemed bothered by environmental factors of physical discomfort such as twisted backpack straps and collars, rough surfaces, extreme weather, etc. He seemed totally oblivious to all of that all the time, but remained hyper-focused on communications, preparing speeches, lessons, etc. Asatya also made facial expressions so infrequently that at 46 years old, he did not even have any fine lines or wrinkles in his face.

---

2. https://en.wikipedia.org/wiki/Sam_Vaknin

The somatic type searches out supply not with their mind but with their body. They might have multiple social media profiles full of their self-ies, showing off their muscles and smiles. This type is generally very sex oriented. They might even feel that they must procreate to perpetuate their 'superior' genes.

What happens eventually in the case of both these types is that eventually their fake persona and tactics fail to bring supply, as people become wise to their tricks and might even confront or expose them. This results in narcissistic collapse and mortification. (You may remember that last summer I was hearing reports that Asatya was deeply depressed and even deranged after losing me. I suspect that he was in a collapse.)

After the collapse, narcissists switch from cerebral to somatic or vice versa and attempt to gain supply that way instead. Eventually, that also ends in collapse.

At that point, they become more desperate and cunning, taking great care to hide what they are and what their intentions are.

They become covert narcissists. Asatya was an excellent example of this. He did such an excellent job of disguising his abuse and exploitation that even the few people closest to him, the same people that he abused and exploited privately, if pressed for an opinion, would tell you that his only faults were his bad temper, depression, and poor money management. He hid himself in plain sight. From the anecdotes that I have heard, it seems that covert narcissism tends to last longer before collapse. Not surprising... it is under cover.

What happens after a covert experiences collapse? According to Professor Vaknin, they cross over the line from narcissism into psychopathy.

It makes logical sense. At that point, the narcissist is older, they have exhausted every strategy they can think of to keep the supply coming and keep their fake persona inflated, and all have failed. They can no longer attract praise and approval or any positive attention, so they turn antisocial, no longer caring if they are accepted or not. This type of psychopathy is formed later in life. There is psychopathy that is genetic and emerges in early adulthood, but that is different.

I am not writing a book about psychopathy. If you want to learn more about that, by all means look into Vaknin's YouTube channel[3][xliv]or his other published work or consult the myriad other resources available online or in your library.

I share Asatya's story because he is a real person. His stories about himself were skewed and possibly some of them were fabricated, but he himself is real. His traumatic childhood and life journey shaped him. His choices ensured that he continued on the same path of positive public image and private sabotage. No one chooses to be a narcissist, though some people choose to not seek healing.

NPD is perhaps partly genetic, partly influenced by culture, but perhaps the largest factor for developing this condition is extreme neglect, abuse, or extreme preferential treatment. This is the current consensus from the medical community, as I understand it. Notice that all three of those factors are outside of the child's control. The parents are the ones who can have the most influence over ensuring the best outcomes for their children. They can't prevent every bad thing, but they can minimize them. There is a responsibility of society to encourage good values. There is a responsibility of parents to care for and love their children while reinforcing good values. If you don't want to live under tyranny in your elder years, I advise investing your love and energy in children, particularly your own, if you have any. They are called the 'formative' years for a reason.

What happens in the home collectively adds up to what happens overall in society. Just like when that one family whom we all know, refused to vaccinate or keep their distance, and so Covid did not die out, but continued to spread. In those times, we began to understand that our individual decisions directly impact public health. The same is true with our psychological and spiritual health.

There is a responsibility of neglect and abuse victims to seek healing so that they minimize the chance of becoming dysfunctional, depressed, or worse - abusers, themselves. That is my opinion and recommendation.

Even if we as survivors don't become abusers, we continue our own misery if we do not address the mess. Time does not heal *all* things. Some

---

3.   https://www.youtube.com/@samvaknin

things might quiet down a bit on the back burner, but unresolved traumas come back to haunt you later, in some form or another, whether through poor relationship dynamics, substance abuse, inexplicable anxiety, or a host of other possible 'symptoms.'

People tend to forget that their personal choices have a ripple effect that can be contagious, even being handed down to future generations. Part of narcissistic abuse is pathology, meaning they can't help but be toxic to some degree, but in many cases, the abuse is consciously chosen. Some people truly choose to be horrible and don't deserve good things. Nobody starts out like that. If we are ever going to slow down the growth of epidemic personality disorders and cold-blooded self-centeredness, we need to take the time to look into all the typical circumstances that allowed or encouraged these bad traits and disorders to develop in the first place.

Asatya was not the only narcissist that I encountered. I met probably more than one hundred Indians face to face in their own homes. I routinely kept in touch with at least one quarter of those. I can say that out of thirty or so people, at least four of them had very strong narcissistic traits. Four out of thirty makes 12%. There were many more that were self-centered, manipulative, or who had high opinions of themselves but who were probably not actual narcissists. I know that I experienced just one corner of India, though the people that I met represented a broad demographical range. If you are Indian, ask yourself if this has been true in your own experience, if you have encountered such people quite often. Think back on Asatya's life story. Think how his life experiences shaped him. Ask yourself how many times you have seen those scenarios play out. I challenge you to consider what parts of your modern culture (culture in this case meaning patterns of social behavior across the subcontinent in general, or your region in particular) are not serving the greater good and need to be re-evaluated?

The United States of America has its own toxic patterns in our culture. We also need to be honest with ourselves about what effects our culture has and why. What needs to change? If we ask these questions under the assumption that we have an ego problem, I believe we will hit near to the truth. Whoever and wherever you are, consider how the culture impacts the individual, and how the individual impacts culture. Be honest. Each of us impacts the whole. The whole impacts each of us.

Case in point: Millions of Americans were swept up in one man's false public persona enough that they each voted for him, and now our entire country is getting a point-by-point object lesson in narcissistic abuse on a massive scale. Go ahead and compare the typical narcissistic abuse patterns to what is happening to the U.S.A. in 2025. I am not saying that the two men in the Oval Office are narcissists, but the patterns are striking.

Disclaimers

It must be acknowledged that a person who only has one or two narcissistic traits is **not** a narcissist. To qualify as a narcissist, they have to possess at least five of the most common traits as listed earlier in this book. Please understand the difference between NPD and simply being a jerk.

This book is not meant to incite a witch-hunt.

It is true that it is possible for a narcissist to have a small amount of empathy, and it is possible for them to have some self-awareness. Therefore, I conclude that it is possible that some narcissists are not abusers. However, self-awareness is rare in narcissists, and empathy is either low or even non-existent in every case. Therefore, it is not logical or wise to expect healthy interactions with a narcissist.

I would like to clarify what I mean by abuse, when I use that word throughout this book.

Abuse is any act towards another person (or animal) that is done with intent to harm.

It is neglect of a person or animal that a person has responsibility towards (as indicated in marriage vows or by default of parental status, work contract, etc. as examples), including withholding basic necessities for living.

It is any act towards another person or animal that is found to have a negative effect, but no change is made to prevent further negative impacts (continued harmful behavior).

It is using a person as an asset (exploitation).

It is blatant disregard of expressed boundaries or moral boundaries, such as in the case of sexual contact without consent, or use of mind games to confuse and control.

This is not a complete list. This is just my feeble attempt as a layperson to try to summarily define this complex topic.

I am describing these things to help you exercise your mind and encourage you to re-evaluate your understanding of abuse in case something may have slid under your radar.

I am not looking for everyone to think exactly the same as me. I just want to encourage critical thinking that results in all of us taking better care of ourselves and each other.

There are legal definitions which you can simply google, as well as consensus of field experts that you can also google.

Please also note that every time I use the word 'narcissist,' I am referring to someone who has the required markers for a diagnosis of NPD. When I use the word 'narcissistic,' I am referring to the traits associated with the condition, which may be greater or lesser than the number of traits required for a diagnosis of NPD.

I have stated elsewhere that I have done my best here to present factual information to the best of my knowledge, and to tell you when the things I am writing are my own opinion. I have always been a curious and analytical person by nature and perhaps you can imagine the hours that I have put into trying to eliminate bias and misinformation.

Please note that this book, whether in part or whole, is not written with the purpose of slandering or endorsing any nationality, ethnicity, family, organization, or person, but only to bear testimony to personal experiences, and to make a good-faith effort to bring to light some difficult topics that should be considered, discussed, and addressed.

I have linked a few informational resources in the text and in endnotes, making a good faith effort to honor copyrights and intellectual property rights.

I have made efforts to protect the privacy and anonymous identity of the real people in this story.

I do not endorse or support in any way, anyone who may quote this book for the purpose of slandering any person,

nor do I support or condone the use of any quote from this book for the purpose of taking legal action against any person or entity.

I do not support the promotion of this book under my real/legal name.

I have written about many deeply personal things, and I deserve to at least have the privacy of my pen name.

I was ready to mentally move on and put Asatya out of my mind before the completion of this book, but I chose to do the uncomfortable work of focusing on this topic which caused me a lot of pain, so that perhaps I might empower a few people to develop better empathy, or have better outcomes than I did. This writing is an act of service to the public. Please honor my privacy.

I hope to inspire soberminded consideration and truth-seeking open dialogue among readers, informed individuals and others who wish to better understand these issues for the purpose of being more conscientious humans who seek to better society and themselves.

This book is not a cry for help or an invitation for advice or judgment. I have my parents and a few others for that. (One exception to that... if you are a therapist trained to address narcissistic abuse, and you want to offer me services at a reduced rate, the offer is appreciated.)

I am not any kind of expert on psychology or narcissistic personality disorder. This book is a composition of my own real memoirs, and that of Asatya Bhratra (not his real name) according to how he told them to me, along with what information I have been able to learn on the topic of narcissistic personality disorder through Google, analysis of personal experience, anecdotes of others, and feedback from therapists.

It is true that even in the field of psychology, there is still so much of our understanding that remains fluid. Star Trek used to say that space is the final frontier, but it appears that it is our own minds that hold that distinction. What is shouted as fact today might be disproven after a couple years. The important thing is to remain curious and flexible to consider new information.

There. There are my disclaimers. I would appreciate that you leave your torches and pitchforks at home.

Purpose

I have written this book for solidarity for victims, and to arm the general population with information to help protect them from grooming and abuse. It is also a wake-up call to parents to break generational trauma and abuse. By providing an intimate, first-person account, I seek to help people understand this topic through a personal, human lens to equip them with hopefully much greater understanding and empathy.

I also hope that along the way, you learned something new and interesting about another culture, and perhaps gained a new perspective of your own.

Shortly after publishing, I will put on my YouTube channel one or more musical playlists of songs that spoke to me or helped me during my dark days as well as the days of healing. If you find that music helpful as a survivor of narcissistic abuse, well then, that was for you. Be blessed.

What follows on these next pages is a story in metaphor. It is the story of every survivor of narcissistic abuse. If you have been paying attention to details so far throughout this book, you will be able to understand the symbolism and meaning in the following story, which is meant to express the shared experience of encountering NPD through dramatic, artistic imagery. Of course, like any word picture, one cannot tell the full story in a few images, but I hope you find this helpful. Sometimes mental images are more helpful than bullet point explanations. I will get to that story shortly after a few more words.

I share this story to honor all survivors as well as those who did not survive the narcissistic abuse.

Some of you do not share your story because you think no one will believe you.

Many more of you do not expose the narcissist for fear of swift and devastating revenge.

In many cases it is not safe to speak up.

Some of you don't want to excavate the painful past.

I do not claim to speak for all of us, but I write this to give more credibility to those of us who never received justice or support.

Most of us keep a low profile trying to stay safe.

As a result, this epidemic of NPD and its related abuse is under-represented in global conversations and not well understood, where it is even known.

Far too many people are suffering in silence because it is not safe for them to speak up.

It is not completely without personal risk that I write this book, but I am safer than most survivors, so I *will* speak up for the others who deserve to have a voice but do not.

I am a private person, and I was ready to put this whole experience behind me long before this book was finished, but I chose to write and publish my painful story to warn the unsuspecting innocent, and to empower those who have been crushed.

For my fellow survivors,

I hope in time that we all find safety,

that stigmas lose their grip,

that real justice comes,

that our respective societies and cultures develop understanding, empathy, and a culture of mutual support without judgment or condescension.

I hope that more people will raise their children with love and proactive intention so that the next generation has less mental illness, not more.

Together, we are stronger.

It would be exciting to see activism result in positive changes being made to our respective justice systems concerning the topics of mental health and overlooked forms of abuse.

If no one else sees you or cares, just know that I do.

I believe in you. I believe in us.

You are a silent army.

We were submitted by the narcissists because they were intimidated by us.

Claim your freedom and your strength.

We rise up from ashes with fire in our wings.

If no one else will have our back, let us at least have each other's.

This is for you.

I AM FAMILY

If you are Asatya (you know your real name) or anyone else who might feel threatened (though I have made no threats) by what I have written in this book, and if you feel motivated to attack, undermine, or sabotage me, just understand this:

I am now immune to the terror tactics, and I am no longer naive.

We know your schemes now, you have been exposed.

The global collective of survivors are my brethren, and they outnumber you.

Pain means nothing to me when I am on a mission.

I had my back stabbed full of ink repeatedly for 90 minutes; I chose pain just for the symbol of new life.

You now know from reading my story, the great lengths that I was willing to go to,

to support that one person that I believed in.

Just imagine how much I am ready to do, to protect myself and others like me.

I believe much more in us, for we all are of this same mind.

I pledge to always call out manipulation and exploitation.

I will not be shut up.

You tried to crush us into the earth, but we rose up in flames.

The flames did not consume us, they came from inside of us.

Before you think of touching me again, remember that I am fire.

The flames of truth would consume you.

Suburban Vampire

I once had a friend who was so kind-hearted and understanding that it felt like the most natural thing in the world to think out loud, telling her anything on my mind. I was grateful to know her, as I lived alone and didn't know many people, having just moved to the area.

I met her at the dog park. Our dogs bonded easily and instantly. We discovered that they had been litter mates. We agreed to meet up often so our dogs could be together.

We ourselves bonded very quickly and naturally.

One day, I was whining at her about my bad disc. It wasn't terrible, but it did limit my mobility somewhat.

My friend (let's call her Lindsey) perked up suddenly. I asked why she looked happy about my hurting back. She looked slightly offended and assured me that she wasn't happy about my pain. She explained that she is a neurosurgeon and started asking me more questions about my back. The more I told her, the more a look of satisfaction and confidence came over her face.

Finally, she told me, "I actually specialize in the surgical procedure that corrects this disc problem!" She looked so happy, feeling totally confident that she could fix me.

I could hardly believe that my sweet friend just happened to be a neurosurgeon. Amazing.

I told her I would be grateful for her advice, but I didn't have money for an operation now. Maybe eventually. At the time, my back wasn't too bad, and I could get by just fine. She said it's fine, she would talk to the receptionist about scheduling and that she would forfeit the surgeon's fee and even help pay for the remainder...I insisted that I really couldn't take advantage of her kindness like that.

The next day she texted me to let me know that I had been scheduled for pre-op the next week. I didn't like that she did that without my consent, but I thought, she has her heart set on helping me, I should go to the appointment.

I thanked Lindsey but reminded her one more time, "You know, you really don't have to do this..." She did not hear me.

I kept the appointment. It went as smoothly as butter. I had gone in nervous, but I left thinking how quick and painless that was. They said that the operation will only work if I have a certain blood type. They told me this was a cutting-edge new method and that's why. Apparently, I had the correct blood type.

Incredibly, they were able to schedule me for the surgery just two weeks out. It was on a Saturday which I thought was weird, but I didn't think too deeply on it. Wow! I could really be pain free in the near future. I had not hoped for this. It seemed like an immense blessing just fell out of the sky. I was beginning to get excited.

The morning of surgery came. I hardly slept the night before, I was so excited to think that soon, my broken body would be mended, and I could even enjoy some favorite activities that I had to give up years ago because of the bad disc.

In the surgical suite, I lay face down and counted with the anesthesiologist down from ten... nine... eight... seven... sicks... fine... floor...

After the surgery, while I was still groggy and disoriented, I was told to schedule my physical therapy sessions. Lindsey hadn't mentioned these earlier. I had not factored in the cost of those sessions. I was instructed to keep my arms in front of my body to avoid disturbing my back muscles.

Later at home, I tried to make sense of the post-op meds that I had been prescribed. I followed the instructions on the labels. I had never had an operation before, so I wasn't quite sure what was the normal experience. I didn't receive any papers from the medical office to explain my post-op self-care. I didn't realize that they should have given those to me. Trying to call the office was a hassle, as I always got put on hold, or else they were on lunch break.

I just did not feel quite right, but I could not put my finger on it. I thought that maybe this is how I was supposed to feel in the early stages of healing. I wanted to ask Lindsey to come visit, and I could address my question to her then. It turned out, she was out of the country on vacation - not reachable.

As the weeks went by, I dutifully went to physical therapy, which oddly enough was also on Saturdays, in the same medical building. The physical therapy was not comfortable. I was told that the discomfort meant that it was working. Well, what did I know? Nothing. I just had to trust them.

As time went on, my back did feel better, and I was so glad. Lindsey was happy for me. I thanked her profusely and asked how could I repay her? She said that she really didn't want to be repaid, but if I insisted, well... She was buying a house and needed some help for moving day. I said sure, why not? That seemed like a small thing after what she had done for me, so it was a plan. Moving day was two months away.

As moving day approached, I was still going to physical therapy every Saturday although I was starting to feel like I didn't need it. At the same time, I wasn't sure how I felt about helping Lindsey move. My energy level was unusually low, and I often felt light-headed. I thought I should rally myself to get through moving day, to show my gratitude to my friend. I showed up, and I tried.

By lunch time, my heart was pounding, and I was super light-headed.

I wanted to tell Lindsey that I really needed to go home and rest, but just as I was about to say this, she said, "One more load and then we are done!" Ok. Ok. I can muster through, I thought.

Halfway through that last load, I passed out and fell from the back of the truck.

When I woke up, there was a blurry but concerned face bending over me. I was in an ambulance. I felt too delirious to ask what had happened...I couldn't remember.

Later at the hospital, I felt more coherent. Outside my room I saw a man from the forensics department of our local police force. I recognized him, as I worked in the same building. I was curious why he was lingering outside my room.

A woman that I didn't know was sitting next to me. I asked her name. She introduced herself as Laura. She explained that she lived across the street from 'the new neighbor moving in.' I explained to her that the new neighbor is named Lindsey.

She told me, "I saw you collapse and fall from the truck. I ran to see your condition and call 911. Lindsey had come out and expressed some concern but tried to assure me that you would be fine, that she would take you to the hospital herself. I wouldn't have it. Lindsey said that she would take care of you, but... something didn't feel right, and I had already called 911 anyway.

You had blood in your hair. You had blood on the back of your shirt also. You were facing Lindsey's house. She did not see the blood at first. When she saw the blood, she freaked out, saying you would sue her and that I can't take you to the hospital. But why? It was obviously an accident. Well, I don't know what Lindsey's issue is, but it made me feel more determined to have you seen by the ER staff. What is your relationship to Lindsey? Should we be concerned?"

I lay there stunned and confused. Didn't I simply fall out of the truck onto the asphalt? Why would my back bleed so much just from falling on the ground? I did notice that it was a stranger rather than Lindsey that took care of me. I asked to see my phone. Had she even called to check on me? Oh wow. Twelve missed messages. She must be worried about me.

I opened my chat with Lindsey. What's this? Lindsey is mad that my car is blocking in the moving truck. She is blaming me for having to pay to keep the truck longer. Yes, my keys were in my pocket, that's true...

I had a raging headache. I felt a bit nauseous. A nurse came in to check on me. She said that I had a concussion. She said that the doctor would be in to see me shortly. The friendly neighbor excused herself and wished me well.

When the doctor came in, she looked very serious, which worried me. I thought maybe the head injury was worse than I thought. I asked about the concussion. She said that I would be fine after a few days, but she was more concerned about my back.

I said, "Yeah, I don't understand why my back was bleeding so much from falling on the ground." The doctor looked baffled.

She explained, "When you were brought in here, we found a port on your back, but the port was partially ripped out, possibly from the fall. The bleeding was mostly from the site of the port."

I sat there looking at her stupefied and for several seconds, all I could do was blink. "The *what?*" I asked. That couldn't be what she actually said.

The doctor went on to explain further. "The port... I can't imagine why you would have that there in the first place, as your records don't indicate anything that would require a port. Maybe it snagged on something when you fell, and that's why you have blood all over your back and your shirt. Also, we've been monitoring your vital signs. Your blood pressure is low.

Ma'am, I know you just woke up not long ago and you need to recuperate, but there is a man from forensics that would like to speak with you. You're not in any kind of trouble, he's just trying to understand how that port came to be on your back. It is not according to any approved procedure or treatment... I am saying that you should perhaps do more research on whatever doctor installed that for you... this should not have been done."

My head was swimming. If anybody needed a blood sample from me, wouldn't they just take it while I was there, instead of sending me home with a port attached? What was it doing there at all?? Is this why I felt so tired and weak and light-headed? And why on earth had I never felt it against my back?

I told the doctor that I never felt anything on my back, and I had no idea that it was there. Now it was the doctor who looked bewildered and speechless. She opened her mouth to say something but then shut her mouth again. She paused and then asked me to carefully roll onto my belly so she could look at my back.

"Can you feel this?" she asked.

"Feel what?" I answered.

"What about this?" She asked again.

"I can't feel anything. Are you poking my back? I don't know. Is my back numb? I don't understand!" I replied in horror. I was feeling more nauseated now and super confused.

"Ok," she said. "Can you feel any of this?" Now I could feel fingers moving in a circular motion around my lower back. I told her that yes, I could. I felt only slightly relieved.

She told me that she would like to run a test to check nerve functionality. It turned out that one entire six-inch segment of my back had no feeling at all, but there was no evidence of any injury to my back in that area, other than the disturbed port.

By now, it was getting late. The nurse told me to try to sleep. I tried but I couldn't. I just had a bad gut feeling about that port, and the part of my back that had no feeling. Did Lindsey put that there? If she did, why? It didn't seem to serve any purpose, and my blood pressure was low.

In the morning, the forensics guy came to talk to me. He asked me a lot of questions and photographed my back, including the port. He asked if it would be ok to talk with my doctor about his findings. I said, "sure." So, they both sat with me. Forensics Guy talked to my doctor in medical jargon and the doctor replied in a similar fashion. They both looked somber. Finally, they turned to me and asked about any recent surgical procedures that I may have had.

I told them everything. That my friend was a neurosurgeon, and she got me a deal to save me money so I could afford the operation for the disc, and I told them about the Saturday physical therapy sessions. I told them that I've been weak and light-headed.

They asked the names of my surgeon and anesthesiologist, as well as the physical therapist. I suddenly realized that I did not know the anesthesiologist's name. I didn't remember noticing a name badge. I gave them the surgeon's and therapist's names.

They looked at each other and I saw them both nod ever so slightly.

They explained to me that during my operation, my 'friend' had installed a port on my back, but they couldn't say for what purpose. Forensics Guy thanked me for talking with him and told me that he would be in touch as soon as possible, hopefully with answers for me, and that whatever cooperation I could give would be most appreciated.

Later that day, I was discharged and given instructions to be mindful of my concussion. I wanted to talk to Lindsey. I didn't want to believe that she had done anything shady. She was such a sweet, understanding, caring person... wasn't she?

I didn't go back for physical therapy. I began to regain my energy, inexplicably. Forensics Guy called. He asked if I could come in to the police station as they had some important information for me. I felt so apprehensive, but I wanted answers so desperately. They called me in. I sat down, shaking a bit. Forensics Guy was there with the police chief and another investigator.

The chief explained to me, "Ma'am, I regret to inform you that you have been used in part of a black-market operation."

Oof. Here it comes, I thought. I knew deep down that something was very wrong. My stomach knotted up.

"We had strong evidence that these 'physical therapy sessions' that you went for, were just a cover so you wouldn't suspect their real reason that they wanted you to come in every week. While you lay down, trusting them to help your back heal, they were attaching a blood collection sack, which filled while you were there for this so-called therapy.

We went there on a Saturday with a few FBI agents. They were collecting blood from another individual in the manner that I've just described. The therapist was arrested on the spot, and the surgeon and the anesthesiologist were both arrested in their homes. We found full blood sacks in storage in the back, packed for transport. There is no record in their system anywhere of this blood collection, nor is there any record of where that blood might be going.

Well, we sent a small sample from one of these sacks to the lab. As it turns out, it is a very rare blood type that facilitates the production of far more stem cells than usual. Stem cells that can be assimilated into any type of human tissue. This blood type is highly sought after among trafficking groups and can be sold for thousands per filled sack. Ma'am, if you are willing to disclose to us, do you know what your blood type is?"

I knew it. I couldn't believe it, but I knew it. I opened my mouth, but nothing came out. "Ma'am?" Forensics Guy asked.

"Uh..." I stammered. I almost felt mute and paralyzed as I felt the blood draining from my face. I picked up a pen and wrote my blood type. I saw the three men look at the paper, look at each other, shake their heads, and then looked at me.

"It's you," I was told. "They have been taking a little of your blood every week. They are selling[1][xlv] it. Your friend made you think that she was doing you a very great kindness by foregoing the surgeon's fee, but really you were her cash cow (no offense, ma'am.) She bled as much out of you as she

---

1.   https://youtu.be/IU2wBKoDOzg?si=a6-7xWhfKf6upZm0

could without causing a cardiac event, and without you realizing what was happening.

She severed a few key nerves on one side of your spine so that you would not be able to feel the port or the blood sack. She made you believe that she was helping you, so you kept going to the physical therapist of her choosing, who is also a part of this trafficking business. Outwardly, she looks like a philanthropist, but you can say that she is like a real-life vampire, taking your blood for her own illegal gain.

After going through Lindsey's phone, we discovered that she was using social media and support groups to discover more people who needed back surgery. We have followed up with some of the others that she found this way, and their stories match yours. There may be a lawsuit in the future. I can give you the name of the law firm that is interested to take the case."

I told them I would think about it...

That was all months ago. The port was removed. I have a scar there and that area is still mostly numb. It's hard to express how violated I felt from that whole experience. My trust was thoroughly exploited to the greatest degree.

Lindsey had discovered me through a chronic pain support group and knew what town I lived in, and that I had a dog. Absolutely no part of her friendship had ever been real. I want to have normal and meaningful friendships, but I am afraid to trust.

I had so much faith in Lindsey's character that I didn't even think to question why was the surgical theatre accepting patients on a Saturday, and why was I the only patient in physical therapy? I didn't cross paths with other patients. So many things I can now see clearly as red flags that I didn't notice or think about in the moment, and I never even knew that blood was draining from my back.

I became hyper-aware and very anxious. I was traumatized.

I have relaxed a bit now. I am enjoying my friendships. But my carefree nature is gone. While I smile sincerely and enjoy my life, I sleep with one eye open.

Take care, friends, that no vampire may lay hold of you.

Pseudonyms (aliases) for the people in this story, listed name first, then meaning of name, then origin language:

Petra Cineálta/rock, kind/Greek and Irish Gaelic
   Asatya Bhratra/false, brother/Sanskrit
   Chhota Giroha/youngest, mafia or gang/Hindi
   Nakali Madhur/imitation sweetness/Hindi
   Prajnaparadha/crime against wisdom/Sanskrit
   Maundaata/silent giver/Sanskrit
   Sama/balanced/Sanskrit
   Agni/fire/Sanskrit
   Vidushi/wise woman/Sanskrit
   Priya/dear/Sanskrit
   Visounou/son/Fongbe
   Pareshani/troublesome/Sanskrit
   Vyapari/businessman/Sanskrit
   Pāśana/a trap/Sanskrit
   Samaji/socialite or networker/Hindi
   Sakhi/friend/Hindi
   Tamo/darkness, ignorance/Sanskrit
   Ausmeronne/name of one of my daughter's original characters/?
   Ian/God is gracious/Scottish Gaelic
   Cletus J. Beauregard, III/A combination of character names from his
favorite TV show/American

Web Addresses to All Links Mentioned in This Book

[i] Map of Haryana https://surveyofindia.gov.in/webroot/UserFiles/files/STATE%20MAP%20OF%20HARYANA%20ENGLISH.jpg

[ii] Raksha Bandhan additional info
https://en.wikipedia.org/wiki/Raksha_Bandhan

[iii] Map of Andhra Pradesh
https://surveyofindia.gov.in/files/ap_final_1.pdf

[iv] What is honor killing?
https://en.wikipedia.org/wiki/Honor_killing

[v] The Yamuna River
https://www.google.com/search?sca_esv=96ee89d9f9e65c74&q=the+Yamu-na+River&udm=2&fbs=ABzOT_CWdhQLP1FcmU5B0fn3xuWpA-dk4wpBWOG-soR7DG5zJBjLjqIC1CYKD9D-DQAQS3Z7dSS-bel2zwklne_sXTpFS99c8bT3cM5e7v7nsjDwtyFkp6fOOQaHSEu-jn6ess_LVB3T6P_okf_uFVZ-Fsvon9afDB6AurmV-jHG-7HLMGISQW9-_9ZMHlw97kRg5fY4I78tOGsHkhxSbq8fPNfqxSFR-rGemQ&sa=X&ved=2ahUKEwjF1IGTyNCLAxVFGVkFHb1nOzwQtKgLegQI-GRAB&biw=1461&bih=881&dpr=1

[vi] Map of Himachal Pradesh
https://stategisportal.nic.in/stategisportal/Home/Map/2

[vii] Video of Himachal landscape
https://www.youtube.com/shorts/AjRvozEnJ6I

[viii] Video of Maine landscape
https://www.youtube.com/shorts/sL9XlSypd-E

[ix] Cotonou, Benin
https://www.youtube.com/shorts/sVcX8pOJYj0

[x] Gurukul in Wikipedia
https://en.wikipedia.org/wiki/Gurukula

[xi] Video showing new road construction in Himachal Pradesh.
https://www.youtube.com/shorts/AMtg0gkkF34

[xii] Scenic backroads of Himachal
https://www.youtube.com/shorts/dQAEVxeKR-Q

[xiii] 'Jiye To Jiye Kaise Bin Aapke' video with lyrics
https://www.youtube.com/watch?v=b0LpFrr85_Y

[xiv] Sunset train ride from Solan
https://www.youtube.com/shorts/zoupeE1hFRI

[xv] The Purdah system
https://en.wikipedia.org/wiki/Purdah

[xvi] Map of Punjab
https://surveyofindia.gov.in/webroot/UserFiles/files/State%20Map%20Punjab_english_2022.jpg

[xvii] Visa bulletin
https://travel.state.gov/content/travel/en/legal/visa-law0/visa-bulletin/2025/visa-bulletin-for-march-2025.html

[xviii] EB-1 green card
https://travel.state.gov/content/travel/en/us-visas/immigrate/employment-based-immigrant-visas.html

[xix] L1 transfer visa
https://travel.state.gov/content/travel/en/us-visas/employment/temporary-worker-visas.html#overview

[xx] Map of Benin
https://www.worldatlas.com/maps/benin

[xxi] 'The Woman King'
https://www.google.com/search?q=the+woman+king&oq=The+Woman+King&gs_lcrp=EgZjaHJvbWUqDQgAEAAY4wIYsQMYgAQyDQgAEAAY4wIYsQMYgAQyCggBEC4YsQMYgAQyB-wgCEAAYgAQyBwgDEAAYgAQyBwgEAAYgAQyBwgFEAAYgAQyBwgGEAAYgAQyBwgHEAAYgAQyBwgIEAAYgAQyBwgJEAAYgATSAQg5MDU5ajBqN6gC-CLACAfEFRawQWqwmgy_xBUWsEFqsJoMv&sourceid=chrome&ie=UTF-8

[xxii] Sanganeri block prints
https://www.youtube.com/watch?v=pw3qs-DdKYo

[xxiii] About Sikhism
https://en.wikipedia.org/wiki/Sikhism

[xxiv] Preparing the evening meal at the Golden Temple.
https://www.youtube.com/shorts/UVg8eOBZssc

[xxv] Also, at the Golden Temple
https://www.youtube.com/shorts/effxEYUjuug

[xxvi] Countryside of Rajasthan as seen from the train
https://www.youtube.com/shorts/mL7n2o23AW8

[xxvii] Searchable online Bible

https://www.biblegateway.com/versions/New-American-Standard-Bible-NASB/#booklist

[xxviii] Rape and consent definitions
https://www.un.org/sexualviolenceinconflict/wp-content/uploads/2019/06/report/rape-and-sexual-violence-human-rights-law-and-standards-in-the-international-criminal-court/ior530012011en.pdf

[xxix] The Truman Show
https://www.rottentomatoes.com/m/truman_show

[xxx] 'Numb' with lyrics
https://www.youtube.com/watch?v=UFfSicxjmIY

[xxxi] PTSD info
https://www.nimh.nih.gov/health/publications/post-traumatic-stress-disorder-ptsd

[xxxii] Common indicators of narcissistic abuse
https://www.choosingtherapy.com/wp-content/uploads/2021/07/4-6.png

[xxxiii] Trauma response graphic (note copyright in images)
https://www.nicabm.com/how-the-nervous-system-responds-to-trauma/

[xxxiv] Yet another song that explains perfectly how I was feeling in August-October 2024
https://www.youtube.com/watch?v=jYlyylkO2hE

[xxxv] 'It's All in Your Head' sales page
https://anymeansnecessary.com/products/all-in-your-head-print?variant=39398424215619&country=US&currency=USD&utm_medium=product_sync&utm_source=google&utm_content=sag_organic&utm_campaign=sag_organic&tw_source=google&tw_adid=&tw_campaign=22151992467&gad_source=4&gclid=CjwKCAiAiaC-BhBEEiwAjY99qMGXxmzfxEyBTr3M7bVSHOyYpVdD6TNfe-b8deBwRp4jPITs_8eVqho-CLK4QAvD_BwE

[xxxvi] Neurons forming new connections
https://www.google.com/search?sca_esv=fc2dc54ee7eb1be7&q=neurons+forming+new+connections&udm=39&fbs=ABzOT_CWdhQLP1FcmU5B0fn3xuWp6IcynRBrzjy_vjxR0KoDMp_4ut2Z3jppK72fzdIpWsBpYmR8fwcVczrRGmP-Hf4k8TNdw0hYkrFPYGyfZnlaQTXsgCV5v5F-ZEusHyPYU-mAQeWqC_LtreH7GhcDZp9D06xYETyjVh58jNJtyf5ReNOIhRUDCjWrlGddDxW5Z7A77ej9bDtsBthGA1KdMsufVO4LhoA&sa=X&ved=2ahUKEwjIuqS-mobeMAxWXFFkFHRhZGTUQs6gLegQIFxAB&biw=1920&bih=953&dpr=1#fpstate=ive&ip=1&vld=cid:4fab28af,vid:9ebifjoFtJs,st:0[1]

---

1.   https://www.google.com/search?sca_esv=fc2dc54ee7eb1be7&q=neurons+forming+new+connections&udm=39&fbs=ABzOT_CWdhQLP1FcmU5B0fn3xuWp6IcynRBrzjy_vjxR0KoDMp_4ut2Z3jppK72fzdIpWsBpYmR8fwcVczrRGmP-Hf4k8TNdw0hYkrFPYGyfZnlaQTXsgCV5v5F-ZEusHyPYU-

[xxxvii] 'Egypt' with lyrics
https://www.youtube.com/watch?v=6BBYtt1tkwU

[xxxviii] Brief video explaining narcissistic abuse
https://www.youtube.com/watch?v=POq_YcMB9CU

[xxxix] D.A.R.V.O. explained
https://www.youtube.com/watch?v=POq_YcMB9CU

[xl] Trauma bond
https://www.youtube.com/watch?v=xBOXuTdL1tM

[xli] Effects of enlarged amygdala
https://www.google.com/search?q=enlarged+amygdala+effects&oq=en-
larged+amygdala+effects&gs_lcrp=EgZjaHJvbWUyCQgAEEUYORiABDIICAE-
QABgWGB4yCAgCEAAYFhgeMg0IAxAAGIYDGIAEGIoFMg0IBBAAGIYD-
GIAEGIoFMgoIBRAAGIAEGKIEMgoIBhAAGIAEGKIE0gEJMTUzMjRqMM-
Go3qAIAsAIA&sourceid=chrome&ie=UTF-8

[xlii] Prevalence of NPD in the U.S.
https://pmc.ncbi.nlm.nih.gov/articles/PMC2669224/

[xliii] Sam Vaknin
https://en.wikipedia.org/wiki/Sam_Vaknin

[xliv] Vaknin's YouTube channel
https://www.youtube.com/@samvaknin

[xlv] 'The Man Who Sold the World,' sung by Midge Ure
https://www.youtube.com/watch?v=IU2wBKoDOzg

mAQeWqC_LtreH7GhcDZp9D06xYETyjVh58jNJtyf5ReNOIhRUDCjWrlGddDxW5Z7A77ej9bDtsBthGA1KdMsuf-
VO4LhoA&sa=X&ved=2ahUKEwjIuqSmobeMAxWXFFkFHRhZG-
TUQs6gLegQIFxAB&biw=1920&bih=953&dpr=1#fpstate_43ec3e5dee6e706af7766ff-
fea512721_ive_6cff047854f19ac2aa52aac51bf3af4a_ip_43ec3e5dee6e706af7766ff-
fea512721_1_6cff047854f19ac2aa52aac51bf3af4a_vld_43ec3e5dee6e706af7766ff-
fea512721_cid_853ae90f0351324bd73ea615e6487517_4fab28af_c0cb5f0fcf239ab3d9c1fcd31fff1efc_vid_853ae90f035
1324bd73ea615e6487517_9ebifjoFtJs_c0cb5f0fcf239ab3d9c1fcd31fff1efc_st_853ae90f0351324bd73ea615e6487517_0

Don't miss out!

Visit the website below and you can sign up to receive emails whenever Petra Cineálta publishes a new book. There's no charge and no obligation.

https://books2read.com/r/B-A-LMOSD-HEOGG

BOOKS 2 READ

Connecting independent readers to independent writers.

About the Author

Petra Cineálta is a native of beautifully wild Maine, U.S.A. where she lives with her husband Ian and three teenage children.

Petra enjoys spending time in nature, and in particular, loves mountain climbing and anything that takes her out on the water.

Having been raised by parents who devoted themselves to her education, she loves all the sciences and has a special interest in anthropology, geography, and travel.

Petra's interests and desire to learn led her to meet and become connected with the other person whose memoirs appear prominently in this book.

Petra's personal connections have developed in her a lasting love and appreciation for the places and cultures from which she made such connections, for example: Nicaragua, France, Benin (West Africa), India, and various regions of the U.S.